How to Be Intimate with 15,000,000 Strangers

How to Be Intimate with 15,000,000 Strangers is an investigation into how the fields of mental health and media can work together more collaboratively.

Drawing upon his extensive experience in media psychoanalysis, Brett Kahr explores how a rich collaboration with radio, television, film, and other forms of public outreach can be accomplished while also embracing the weight and gravitas of depth psychology. In addition to describing his work as Resident Psychotherapist at the B.B.C., Kahr also examines the ways in which references to the media enter the consulting room and provide clinicians with important insights about hidden aspects of the minds of their patients. Moreover, he investigates the historical hesitancy of psychoanalysts – experts in confidentiality – to engage with such a public arena as the media, thus providing important insights about how one can collaborate broadly and loudly while also maintaining one's ethical commitment to silence and privacy.

This book will be of interest to psychoanalysts, psychotherapists, and anyone intrigued by the intersection between media and psychoanalysis.

Professor Brett Kahr has worked in the mental health field for over forty years. He is Senior Fellow at the Tavistock Institute of Medical Psychology in London and Visiting Professor of Psychoanalysis and Mental Health at Regent's University London. A trained historian, Kahr is also both an Honorary Fellow as well as the Honorary Director of Research at the Freud Museum London. He is the author of seventeen books and series editor of over seventy-five additional titles. A Visiting Professor in the Faculty of Media and Communication at Bournemouth University, he is also Consultant Psychotherapist at The Balint Consultancy. He works with individuals and couples in Central London.

Psychoanalysis and Popular Culture Series
Series Editors: Caroline Bainbridge and Candida Yates

Consulting Editor: Brett Kahr

This series builds on the work done since 2009 by the Media and the Inner World research network. It aims to consider the relationship between psychoanalysis and popular culture as a lived experience that is ever more emotionalised in the contemporary age. In contrast to many scholarly applications of psychoanalysis, works in this series set out to explore the creative tensions of thinking about cultural experience and its processes whilst also paying attention to observations from both the clinical and scholarly fields. The series provides space for a dialogue between these different groups with a view to evoking new perspectives on the values and pitfalls of a psychoanalytic approach to ideas of selfhood, society, politics, and popular culture. In particular, the series strives to develop a psycho-cultural approach by foregrounding the usefulness of a post-Freudian, object relations perspective for examining the importance of emotional relationships and experience. We nevertheless welcome proposals from all fields of psychoanalytic enquiry. The series is edited by Caroline Bainbridge and Candida Yates, with Brett Kahr as the Consulting Editor.

Other titles in the Psychoanalysis and Popular Culture Series:

Toy Story and the Inner World of the Child
Animation, Play, and Creative Life
Karen Cross

How to Be Intimate with 15,000,000 Strangers
Musings on Media Psychoanalysis
Brett Kahr

For more information about this series, please visit: https://www.routledge.com/The-Psychoanalysis-and-Popular-Culture-Series/book-series/KARNPSYPOP

'This is a rare and special treat ... a gem of a read. Professor Brett Kahr combines his scintillating Freudian intellect with his forty years of experience, in radio and television, to put media itself on the couch, revealing a whole gamut of captivating insights. An absolute delight!'

Dan Chambers, *Creative Director and Co-Founder of Blink Films (one of Real Screen 100's Top 5 Non-Scripted U.K. Indies) and former Director of Programmes, Channel Five Television, UK*

'Brett Kahr invites us on his extraordinary journey of popularising psychoanalysis through the media. Writing with clarity, humour, empathy, and great warmth about his long experience as the United Kingdom's foremost media psychoanalyst, he details his adventures on television and radio as well as sharing wide-ranging reflections about celebrity culture and the history of mediated psychoanalysis. Kahr thereby contributes enormously to dissolving the secretive aura of psychoanalysis while being deeply respectful to the boundaries of a private profession. At a time where psychoanalysis through popular culture is more needed than ever, this book is essential reading for clinicians, academics, and anyone concerned about the shared future of humanity and psychoanalysis.'

Professor Jacob Johanssen, *Associate Professor in Communications, St. Mary's University, and author of* Fantasy, Online Misogyny and the Manosphere *and co-author of* Media and Psychoanalysis: A Critical Introduction

'No one has done more to lead psychoanalysis out of the closet and into the hearts and minds of 15,000,000 – and counting – than the brilliant Professor Brett Kahr. Readers are in for a treat, because he does so in beautiful, accessible language, never compromising theoretical or ethical rigor; a rare, impressive feat.'

Dr. Steven Kuchuck, *Immediate Past President of the International Association for Relational Psychoanalysis and Psychotherapy, and Faculty, New York University Postdoctoral Program in Psychotherapy and Psychoanalysis and the National Institute for the Psychotherapies*

'*How to Be Intimate with 15,000,000 Strangers: Musings on Media Psychoanalysis* makes a unique contribution to clinical media psychology. Professor Brett Kahr has devoted his career to the dissemination of complex psychoanalytical concepts among the general public. In this book, he uses creative and courageous means to demystify, destigmatise, and demarginalize psychoanalysis through his collaborations with the media. Entertaining and educational, this work inspires psychotherapists and psychoanalysts to venture beyond the consulting room and to provide public outreach.'

Professor Caroline Sehon, *Director of the International Psychotherapy Institute, and Clinical Professor of Psychiatry at Georgetown University Medical School, as well as Executive Committee Board Member and Chair of the Committee on Community Psychoanalysis of the American Psychoanalytic Association*

'As Radio 2's Resident Psychotherapist, Professor Brett Kahr was one of the first brave pioneers who championed mental health on the B.B.C.'s airways, thus fulfilling the B.B.C.'s remit to "inform, educate and entertain". His insights have paved the way to destigmatising mental illness and have forever changed the landscape of media psychoanalysis.'

Jenny Slater, *Music Project Manager, European Broadcasting Union, BBC Radio, UK*

How to Be Intimate with 15,000,000 Strangers

Musings on Media Psychoanalysis

Brett Kahr

LONDON AND NEW YORK

Designed cover image: Maxiphoto / Getty Images

First published 2023
by Routledge
4 Park Square, Milton Park, Abingdon, Oxon OX14 4RN

and by Routledge
605 Third Avenue, New York, NY 10158

Routledge is an imprint of the Taylor & Francis Group, an informa business

© 2023 Brett Kahr

The right of Brett Kahr to be identified as author of this work has been asserted in accordance with sections 77 and 78 of the Copyright, Designs and Patents Act 1988.

All rights reserved. No part of this book may be reprinted or reproduced or utilised in any form or by any electronic, mechanical, or other means, now known or hereafter invented, including photocopying and recording, or in any information storage or retrieval system, without permission in writing from the publishers.

Trademark notice: Product or corporate names may be trademarks or registered trademarks, and are used only for identification and explanation without intent to infringe.

British Library Cataloguing-in-Publication Data
A catalogue record for this book is available from the British Library

Library of Congress Cataloging-in-Publication Data
Names: Kahr, Brett, author.
Title: How to be intimate with 15,000,000 strangers : musings on media psychoanalysis / Brett Kahr.
Other titles: How to be intimate with fifteen million strangers
Description: Abingdon, Oxon ; New York : Routledge, 2023. | Series: The psychoanalysis and popular culture series | Includes bibliographical references and index. |
Identifiers: LCCN 2022050668 (print) | LCCN 2022050669 (ebook) | ISBN 9781032355177 (paperback) | ISBN 9781032355191 (hardback) | ISBN 9781003327240 (ebook)
Subjects: LCSH: Psychoanalysis in mass media. | Psychoanalysis—Social aspects.
Classification: LCC P96.P74 K34 2023 (print) | LCC P96.P74 (ebook) | DDC 150.19/5—dc23/eng/20230124
LC record available at https://lccn.loc.gov/2022050668
LC ebook record available at https://lccn.loc.gov/2022050669

ISBN: 978-1-032-35519-1 (hbk)
ISBN: 978-1-032-35517-7 (pbk)
ISBN: 978-1-003-32724-0 (ebk)

DOI: 10.4324/9781003327240

Typeset in Times New Roman
by codeMantra

For Adie, whose impending contributions to media and culture will, I know, blaze a trail with sensitivity, compassion, and bravery.

Contents

Books by Professor Brett Kahr   xi
Series Preface by Professor Caroline Bainbridge and Professor Candida Yates   xiii

Prologue: How to Publicise Psychoanalysis   1

SECTION I
Introduction to Media Psychoanalysis   7

1 The Bulimic Lorry Driver: Championing the Media in Spite of Hesitancy and Envy   9

SECTION II
Media Psychoanalysis in Action   19

2 "You have five minutes to cure the nation": My Years at the B.B.C.   21

3 How to Dramatise 13,553 Sexual Fantasies in Only Forty-Seven Minutes   30

4 *Making Slough Happy*: A Television Experiment   44

5 On Stage at the Royal Opera House   67

SECTION III
Television in the Consulting Room   77

6 Television as Rorschach: The Unconscious Use of the Cathode Nipple   79

7 Dr. Paul Weston and the Bloodstained Couch: Some Critical Comments on *In Treatment*   92

SECTION IV
Celebrity and the Psyche   103

8 Fame and the Unconscious: Toxic and Inspiring Aspects of Celebrity Culture   105

9 On Not Being Shakespeare, Mozart, or Picasso: Creativity, Bereavement, and the Wish to Be Famous   128

SECTION V
Uneasy Bedfellows: Freud and His Progeny Confront the Media   143

10 Media Monasticism and Media Whoredom: The Uncomfortable Marriage Between Psychoanalysis and Popular Exposure   145

11 "I think analysts are not very good as broadcasters": Donald Winnicott's Contribution to Media Psychology   163

Conclusion: The Future of Media Psychoanalysis   198

Notes   203
Original Sources of Chapters   211
Acknowledgements   219
References   223
Index   263

Books by Professor Brett Kahr

D.W. Winnicott: A Biographical Portrait (1996).
Forensic Psychotherapy and Psychopathology: Winnicottian Perspectives, Editor (2001).
Exhibitionism (2001).
The Legacy of Winnicott: Essays on Infant and Child Mental Health, Editor (2002).
Sex and the Psyche (2007).
Who's Been Sleeping in Your Head?: The Secret World of Sexual Fantasies (2008).
Life Lessons from Freud (2013).
Tea with Winnicott (2016).
Coffee with Freud (2017).
New Horizons in Forensic Psychotherapy: Exploring the Work of Estela V. Welldon, Editor (2018).
How to Flourish as a Psychotherapist (2019).
Bombs in the Consulting Room: Surviving Psychological Shrapnel (2020).
Celebrity Mad: Why Otherwise Intelligent People Worship Fame (2020).
On Practising Therapy at 1.45 A.M.: Adventures of a Clinician (2020).
Dangerous Lunatics: Trauma, Criminality, and Forensic Psychotherapy (2020).
Freud's Pandemics: Surviving Global War, Spanish Flu, and the Nazis (2021).
Hidden Histories of British Psychoanalysis: From Freud's Death Bed to Laing's Missing Tooth (2023).

Series Preface

The application of psychoanalytic ideas and theories to culture has a long tradition and this is especially the case with cultural artefacts that might be considered "classical" in some way. For Sigmund Freud, the works of William Shakespeare and Johann Wolfgang von Goethe were as instrumental as those of culturally renowned poets and philosophers of classical civilisation in helping to formulate the key ideas underpinning psychoanalysis as a psychological method. In the academic fields of the humanities and social sciences, the application of psychoanalysis as a means of illuminating the complexities of identity and subjectivity is now well established. However, despite these developments, there is relatively little work that attempts to grapple with popular culture in its manifold forms, some of which, nevertheless, reveal important insights into the vicissitudes of the human condition.

The "Psychoanalysis and Popular Culture Series" of books builds on the work done since 2009 by the Media and the Inner World research network, which was generously funded by the United Kingdom's Arts and Humanities Research Council. It aims to offer spaces to consider the relationship between psychoanalysis in all its forms and popular culture, which has become ever more emotionalised in the contemporary age.

In contrast to many scholarly applications of psychoanalysis, which often focus solely on "textual analysis", this series sets out to explore the creative tension of thinking about cultural experience and its processes with attention to observations from the clinical and scholarly fields of observation. What can academic studies drawing on psychoanalysis learn from the clinical perspective and how might the critical insights afforded by scholarly work cast new light on clinical experience? The series provides space for a dialogue between these different groups with a view to creating fresh perspectives on the values and pitfalls of a psychoanalytic approach to ideas of selfhood, society, and popular culture. In particular, the series strives to develop a psycho-cultural approach to such questions by drawing attention to the usefulness of post-Freudian and object relations perspectives, examining the importance of emotional relationships and experience.

In *How to Be Intimate with 15,000,000 Strangers: Musings on Media Psychoanalysis,* Brett Kahr provides a compelling narrative that combines rich clinical experience and meticulous historical scholarship with fascinating personal accounts of media psychoanalytical work and psycho-cultural commentary. He observes that since the inception of psychoanalysis, very few mental health practitioners have collaborated with the media. Many have no skills in that area, and spend their days, instead, in much silence in the consulting room, rarely speaking publicly. Moreover, no psychological trainings encourage practitioners to engage with the media.

Fortunately, as we see in this book, Kahr has made a considerable contribution to the development of what he calls "media psychoanalysis", by having collaborated with the media across many decades. During his long career, Kahr has appeared on over 1,000 radio and television programmes as a mental health commentator. He has embraced the media while working as a full-time clinician and scholar. His contributions have included his former role as "Resident Psychotherapist" on B.B.C. Radio 2 and as Spokesperson for the B.B.C.'s "Life 2 Live" mental health campaign. Through his work as a media psychoanalytical practitioner, Kahr has managed to reach those members of the public who, under ordinary circumstances, would have little access to depth psychological therapy.

This book provides a detailed written set of accounts of his various projects, from radio and television programmes to an event at the Royal Opera House, demonstrating the numerous ways in which he has endeavoured to share his knowledge with as many members of the public as possible. He describes the processes of working in the media industry, of turning a private idea in the company of friends into a cultural contribution, and he provides a frank account of what one experiences on a moment-by-moment basis while shooting a television documentary.

Kahr underscores the importance of a greater collaboration between mental health practitioners and media professionals and, also, of a more targeted strategy to improve the impact of psychological workers within the realms of popular culture. He writes about how media psychology practitioners can actually intervene directly and make an immediate impact on mental health. Kahr discusses the importance of educating the general public about mental health matters; indeed, he emphasises the *necessity* of doing so. As Kahr writes in his chapter about a bulimic lorry driver: "Our profession needs to embrace media psychoanalysis in a much more unashamed manner. It should be possible to preserve the sanctity of the consulting room and yet still reveal some basic truths about psychological work, namely: Mental illness ravages lives." At a time when mental illness is on the rise, Kahr's message of democratising psychotherapy through the practice of media psychoanalysis takes on an added significance.

Crucially, Kahr explores not only how outward-facing mental health workers can collaborate with broadcasters and other media professionals, but, also, the ways in which media can penetrate the consulting room and the different styles in which that setting is portrayed. In addition, he discusses how fame and celebrity (as by-products of the media) both impact upon mental health and serve as representations of our cultural state of mind. Kahr's important and pioneering book makes a new and timely contribution to the art and practice of media psychoanalysis, and we are delighted to have it published in our series.

Professor Caroline Bainbridge and Professor Candida Yates

Prologue
How to Publicise Psychoanalysis

Tragically, psychoanalysis has long suffered from a very profound image problem.

Our founder, Professor Sigmund Freud, had to endure a great deal of suspicion and hostility from his many adversaries who lambasted him as a "Casanova" (Weiss, 1970, p. 2) ... and much worse besides. For instance, the British physician Dr. David G. Thomson (1917, p. 32), then President of the Medico-Psychological Association of Great Britain and Ireland – the forerunner of the Royal College of Psychiatrists – excoriated Freud for his "dirty doctrines", dismissing them as little more than "pornographic abominations" (Thomson, 1917, p. 32).

The hatred of Freud persevered long after his death.

When Jean MacGibbon (1997, p. 2), an educated, literate woman, first met the Freudian psychoanalyst Dr. Adrian Stephen, brother of Virginia Woolf, back in 1942, she came to regard his work with great suspicion, explaining that she considered psychoanalysis to be, "a profession I then associated with witchcraft". And Noël Coward (1941, p. 83), arguably the most eminent figure in British popular culture during the World War II era, denounced psychoanalysis in his play *Blithe Spirit* as "months of expensive humiliation".

During my own lifetime, Professor Hans Eysenck, for many decades the leading figure in British clinical psychology, attacked Freudian psychoanalysis at every opportunity. Contemporary psychologists may not quite appreciate the influence of Eysenck throughout the 1950s, 1960s, 1970s, and beyond. His clarion call for a more empirically focused, evidence-based psychology helped to shape the field greatly, but so, too, did his passionate hatred of psychoanalysis and his consequent promotion of behaviour therapy (Eysenck, 1990; cf. Gibson, 1981).

Back in 1984, in the spirit of fostering dialogue among the bitter factions then regnant in British psychology, I invited Professor Eysenck to deliver a talk at the Oxford Psycho-Analytical Forum, an interdisciplinary organisation, which I had founded the previous year, based at the University of Oxford. Eysenck (1984) spoke to a packed audience in the lecture theatre

DOI: 10.4324/9781003327240-1

of the Department of Experimental Psychology on South Parks Road, addressing the subject, "How Wrong Was Freud?" Although I had earnestly hoped to have a serious discussion with this man, it soon became clear that he enjoyed rhetoric and pontification far more than dialogue, in spite of the fact that he possessed an extremely limited knowledge of psychoanalysis. For instance, Eysenck had sloppily assumed that Sigmund Freud had treated the hysterical woman known as "Anna O" when, in fact, virtually every first-year undergraduate could confirm that Freud's mentor, Dr. Josef Breuer (1895), had done so.

The following year, Eysenck (1985, p. 71) produced a scandalous book entitled *Decline and Fall of the Freudian Empire* in which he reviled psychoanalysts as little more than "prostitutes" who sell affection and emotional intimacy just as hookers peddle sex. Although few psychoanalytical sympathisers treated Eysenck's work with any seriousness, the literary establishment certainly did; indeed, Great Britain's leading psychologist had convinced none other than Viking, a subsidiary of Penguin Books, arguably the country's most influential publisher at the time, to release this vicious tract under their imprimatur.

After Eysenck delivered his talk in Oxford, I treated him to supper and we embarked upon a most convivial conversation about his life, his research, his future plans, and so forth; but I realised that it would be futile to engage him in any discussion about psychoanalysis. He had already made up his mind in a most grandiose and narcissistic way, and he never once asked me about my own commitment to, and enthusiasm for, Freud's ideas. I suspect that he had little interest in anyone else.

Although I found Eysenck's lecture at the Oxford Psycho-Analytical Forum extremely shoddy and rather disappointing, so much so that it made me wonder how carefully he undertook his other projects, I do owe Hans Eysenck an everlasting debt of gratitude for having unwittingly launched me upon a career in the media.

Eysenck's talk on "How Wrong Was Freud?" had generated something of a buzz in the local community, and, not long thereafter, I received a very unexpected telephone call from a member of staff at B.B.C. Radio Oxford, asking me to speak on the *David Freeman Programme*, one of the station's most popular shows, in order to examine Eysenck's critique of Freud. Although only a young man at the time, I had already begun to teach Freud and it seems that the British Broadcasting Corporation thought that I might well have something useful to say.

I agreed to the interview with a considerable amount of trepidation, in part, due to the enormity of Eysenck's reputation, and, in part, due to the fact that I had never appeared on the radio before. Nevertheless, I took a deep breath and cycled into the local B.B.C. radio studio and perched myself behind a microphone and a headset.

Fortunately, David Freeman, the presenter, welcomed me in a very pleasant manner and immediately put me at ease. We then began to record our interview.

I explained to Mr. Freeman that although the anti-Freudian supremo Hans Eysenck had courted a large following of British clinicians, many others regarded Freud as a serious thinker whose work still provided the basis of much of contemporary psychology and, indeed, mental health practice. Apparently, I acquitted myself sufficiently well on David Freeman's programme and, in consequence, the British Broadcasting Corporation began to ring me on an increasingly frequent basis, inviting me to participate on other radio shows.

Over the next thirty-five years and more, I appeared on well over one thousand radio and television programmes, as a mental health commentator or "media psychologist", and I have since written articles for newspapers, magazines, and other popular publications. For three years, I even served as "Resident Psychotherapist" on B.B.C. Radio 2, broadcasting to some fifteen million people weekly on psychological matters while also spearheading the B.B.C.'s mental health awareness campaign, "Life 2 Live".

I must confess that I had never set out to devote so much time and attention to the media. As a young eighteen-year-old psychology student, I simply assumed that I might become a practising mental health professional and that I would work all day in a little office, treating one patient after another. In fact, I have become a practising mental health professional who does work all day in a little office … but, in addition to my clinical activities, which have become the bread and butter of my professional life, I have always enjoyed the privilege of possessing an extra string to my bow by collaborating with the media in order to help disseminate psychological knowledge to the general public. And I owe this work in great measure to Professor Eysenck for having quite unwittingly prompted my very first invitation.

When I started to broadcast in 1984, very few members of the mental health profession did so, at least in Great Britain. Quite prominent men such as Dr. Donald Winnicott had often delivered talks on the radio during the 1940s and beyond (e.g., Winnicott, 1945a, 1949a, 1957a, 1957b, 1987, 1993; cf. Kahr, 2013, 2018a), but he had proved to be rather a rarity among his colleagues. During the 1960s and 1970s, psychiatrists such as Dr. Anthony Storr then took up Winnicott's mantle (e.g., Kahr, 2020b), followed not long thereafter by the pioneering feminist psychotherapist Susie Orbach (subsequently, Dr. Orbach (2016, 2018)). But, by and large, most psychoanalytically orientated clinicians regarded media work with considerable suspicion. Nowadays, the landscape has changed dramatically, and hundreds, if not thousands, of colleagues have since appeared on radio and television, and even the most conservative clinical training organisations now boast websites, podcasts, Twitter feeds, and, even, full-time public relations officers, in an effort promote psychological knowledge in a world overcrowded with communication.

In spite of the growth of media psychology, media psychiatry, media psychotherapy, and even media psychoanalysis, very few practitioners of the craft have written about the process of collaborating with radio producers, television executives, public conference organisers, film writers, and the like. Hence, I have prepared this collection of essays in the hope of exploring some of the diverse aspects of this burgeoning field of endeavour.

This book consists of a range of chapters, some of which have already appeared in print, mostly in journals and, in one instance, in an edited book. But I have revised them all substantially and updated them with new material. Many of these essays appear here in print for the very first time.

I have divided this book into five sections.

In the first section, "Introduction to Media Psychoanalysis", I endeavour to describe the work of the media psychology practitioner, emphasising the ways in which public interventions into popular culture can help to reach those individuals in need of mental health assistance who might not be able to access psychological understanding in any other way.

In the second section, "Media Psychoanalysis in Action", I provide autobiographical accounts of four different pieces of work, in which I spoke to members of the general public about psychoanalytically orientated concepts and ideas through radio programmes, television documentaries, and, in one instance, through the staging of a night of music and psychoanalytical discussion at London's Royal Opera House.

In the third section, "Television in the Consulting Room", I explore some of the psychodynamics of this powerful medium of entertainment which consumes, on average, eleven years of every human being's life (cf. Anonymous, 2020a, 2020b). I offer, first, a clinical essay, based on my psychotherapeutic work, investigating the ways in which references to television programmes have become an increasingly significant portion of the free-associative process in the typical clinical psychoanalytical session; and then I provide some comments, expressing deep concern about the ways in which the television industry has often scathingly portrayed the members of our profession.

In the fourth section, "Celebrity and the Psyche", I offer some consideration of the meaning of fame, an inextricable component, if not underpinning, of popular culture, examining some of the unconscious roots of the need for recognition and its perversions. I also provide some further clinical observations on my work with patients who have sought fame in a compulsive manner.

In the fifth and final section, "Uneasy Bedfellows: Freud and His Progeny Confront the Media", I explore the interface between media psychology and the history of psychoanalysis, considering, in particular, the impact of

Sigmund Freud's suspicion of the media and how this helped to inhibit the growth of communication with the general public. I then conclude with an historical essay on Donald Winnicott's much more comfortable embrace of the general public, and with an explication of the ways in which these pioneering efforts have facilitated a dissemination of mental health knowledge in a more impactful, more responsible, and, I trust, more inspiring manner.

I very much hope that these essays may provide some helpful thoughts, particularly for younger colleagues, who, having grown up in a post-internet era, will find far more interesting ways to develop this important field of endeavour and who will facilitate the flourishing of media psychoanalysis in an even more bold and creative manner.

Section I

Introduction to Media Psychoanalysis

1

The Bulimic Lorry Driver

Championing the Media in Spite of Hesitancy and Envy

It is very late at night, at least it is for me ... round about 12.40 a.m. ... and on a Tuesday no less. Having begun work with the first of my patients earlier this morning at 7.00 a.m., I must confess that I am somewhat sleepy, and thus I have had to drink an extra cup of coffee.

I am seated in the radio studio of the British Broadcasting Corporation Birmingham, in the West Midlands, in conversation with Janice Long, the host of one of B.B.C. Radio 2's most popular late-night caller programmes. Ms. Long has always attracted a very wide listenership – literally millions upon millions of Britons – having previously served as the presenter of the iconic television series *Top of the Pops* during the 1980s. A Liverpudlian with a very salt-of-the-earth accent, she sounds invariably friendly, chatty, and approachable. One would never have guessed that this humble and straightforward woman enjoyed a long-term friendship with such superstars as Sir Paul McCartney of the Beatles!

The B.B.C. thought it might be helpful for me to appear on her show on a regular, monthly basis, in the hope of introducing psychological ideas to members of the general public.

As a very no-nonsense woman, Janice Long has created a solid audience base of people from every walk of life. And because of the late-night timing of her programme – generally from midnight until 3.00 a.m. – she has proved to be very popular with lorry drivers, who listen to her with rapt attention while chuntering down the British motorways at ungodly hours.

Although slightly tired, I do not feel at all nervous, having appeared on air with Ms. Long on quite a number of previous occasions.

The programme always begins promptly at the stroke of midnight, and, after greeting the audience, Ms. Long then introduces me and asks me a series of questions about mental health matters. Tonight, she wishes to know something about eating disorders: anorexia nervosa, and bulimia nervosa and, also, obesity. We begin to chat, and I endeavour to provide Ms. Long and her millions of regulars with a crash course in the psychodynamics of eating disorders, attempting to situate our complex relationship to food within the context of the parent-infant relationship. Ms. Long, a

DOI: 10.4324/9781003327240-3

consummate radio disc jockey and presenter, invariably listens to me with serious consideration and does, from time to time, interrupt our psychologically orientated conversation in order to play a piece of pop music.

Throughout the course of this hour-long interview, Janice Long often encourages her loyal listeners to "phone in" with any questions, comments, and thoughts about our difficulties with eating.

"Shirley", a young teenage girl, awake way past her bedtime, rings in to tell me and Ms. Long that she has struggled with anorexia for many years but that, quite fortunately, she has recently begun to work with a trained mental health professional and that she now finds food far less frightening. Ms. Long becomes very excited and congratulates this young person on her achievement, and then turns to me, "So, Brett, can people with anorexia ... people like Shirley ... really be helped by therapy?" I reply that psychotherapists, counsellors, psychologists, psychiatrists, and psychoanalysts have worked very successfully with anorexia for more than a century, often with great success. I then encourage those who may be suffering in private with food-related issues to speak to their general medical practitioner for a referral to a local community psychology service. I also remind listeners that the B.B.C. boasts a webpage devoted to our special new campaign, "Life 2 Live", which contains many helpful resources. From time to time, I go "online" to this web page and answer questions from members of the public about psychological issues.

Helpfully, Janice Long then reiterates the details of our webpage address: "That's right, just go to www.bbc.co.uk and then click on 'Life 2 Live'."

Thereafter, Janice and I chat some more about anorexia and bulimia, and then we listen to yet another track of music, after which we proceed to take several more calls from members of the public.

Many of our listeners on this late-night, early-morning programme happen to be young women battling with food and body image, and some have even admitted, live and on-air, that they had become either anorexic or bulimic in the wake of early experiences of sexual abuse.

Having spoken with so many female anorexic and bulimic callers over the course of this particular programme, neither Janice nor I quite expected that our very last "phone-in" caller of the evening would be a burly, gravel-voiced, middle-aged man.

"Good evening, caller, you're on with Janice Long. And we're here with our Resident Psychotherapist, Brett Kahr. Tell us, how can Brett help you?"

"Well, Janice, you and Brett keep talking to *young girls* about bulimia. But I'm forty-five, and as you can hear, I'm a *man* ... and guess what? ... *I'm* bulimic."

Without missing a beat, Janice invites this gentleman to tell us his story, and he promptly does so. To our great surprise we discover that not only does he work as a lorry driver, spending hour after hour on the road, but, also, he devotes quite a lot of time to vomiting up his food after each and every meal.

Having facilitated quite a number of "call-in" programmes over the years, I had come to develop a way of speaking live, on-air, with members of the public about their psychological issues. I would like to believe that I have cultivated the capacity to communicate with a calm and compassionate voice which evokes a sense of comfort and safety so that callers will feel more able to share the substance of their stories without exposing private details which would in any way compromise their identities. And so, rather than interrogate this lorry driver about his early breast-feeding experiences, I congratulate him, instead, on his boldness in being able to talk to us about his situation in such a frank manner. I then challenge the stereotype that only teenage girls will succumb to bulimia; men can also display signs of eating disorders. I ask this gentleman whether he has received any professional help and whether he might wish to do so, and we arrange that I will speak to him privately on the telephone after the programme has ended and point him in the direction of some trusted local psychological services.

Janice and I speak a little bit more about food and its vicissitudes, and then, after listening to one more track of music, she and I bid our loyal audience goodnight.

The vast majority of my mental health colleagues – many of whom have impressive academic backgrounds and intellectual interests – do not listen to B.B.C. Radio 2; most, by contrast, prefer B.B.C. Radio 4, the more "high culture" branch of the British Broadcasting Corporation. But Radio 2 boasts the widest listenership of any B.B.C. service, even more than its television stations. Hence, a late-night conversation on Radio 2 has the capacity to reach millions and millions of people – the very men and women (and, possibly, even children) who constitute the backbone of our country and who would, under ordinary circumstances, have little access to psychoanalytically orientated conversations.

Although some of my colleagues might have sneered at my efforts to introduce a few psychological ideas to the wider general public, I did derive some small satisfaction from knowing that I may have steered at least one bulimic male lorry driver towards proper psychotherapeutic support. Certainly, with the aid of the chipper Janice Long, we had worked hard throughout the conversation to destigmatise mental health among those many individuals who do not live in Hampstead, North London – at that point the veritable epicentre of British psychoanalysis. Instead, we hoped to spread a little bit of psychological information to the fishermen from Cornwall and the farmers from Ayrshire, as well as the occasional middle-aged eating disordered male driving up and down our motorways.

And one really *does* need to reach out to men with eating disorders, because this lorry-driving gentleman who rang the B.B.C. to speak with me and Janice Long may not be the only one.

***

Several years later, I found myself reading a most interesting book entitled *Doing Psychoanalysis in Tehran*, written by the Iranian clinician, Dr. Gohar Homayounpour. To my great surprise, this pioneer of psychoanalysis in the post-Ayatollah Khomeini era, reported the following case: "A very big, macho truck-driver comes in, saying: 'I heard there is a psychoanalyst in this clinic, and I want to understand myself better.' I am ashamed of how I feel, because I have to face what by now, it has become painfully clear, are my own value judgments, since I expected any response from him except a desire for self-knowledge. But why should this be so? Can't big, macho truck-drivers desire to know themselves? Later on, I learn that he is afraid of the dark, and has made his wife leave the lights in their bedroom on every night for the last twelve years" (Homayounpour, 2012, p. 118).

It seems, therefore, that the demography of potential psychoanalytical clients may be shifting from the socialites of the Upper East Side and the intellectuals of Hampstead to the bulimic lorry drivers of rural England and the frightened truck drivers of modern-day Iran.

Needless to say, psychoanalysis, psychotherapy, and other varieties of psychological treatment have huge applicability to most, if not all, human beings. But many members of the public still do not know the difference between psychologists and psychiatrists, between counsellors and psychotherapists, between talking therapy and behavioural therapy, or between open-ended, long-term work and time-limited, short-term work. Therefore, those of us who practise in the mental health field should be obliged to make some contribution to the education of the population at large, without whom, we would have no clients.

In this respect, the still burgeoning arenas of media psychology and media psychoanalysis play a vital role in both the dissemination of mental health awareness and in the stimulation of an even greater interest in our emotional lives.

When Dr. Sándor Radó, one of Professor Sigmund Freud's very first disciples in Hungary and, later, a leader of Freudian psychology in the United States of America, exclaimed that, "psychoanalysis has a still undreamt-of-future" (quoted in Roazen, 1995b, p. 147), I suspect that he might not have had media psychology in mind as part of his blueprint for a more potent, invigorated discipline. But, nowadays, psychoanalysis and all related branches of mental health care will simply not survive without a more targeted media strategy and without more forward-thinking colleagues who can devise creative ways to introduce members of the public to the very best of what our field might have to offer.

Throughout the history of our discipline, various practitioners – both clinicians and those sympathetic to our work – have endeavoured to promote the legacy of Sigmund Freud across a wider audience, often with considerable success. Throughout recent decades, a small band of media psychologists (or media psychoanalysts, media psychiatrists and, even, media psychotherapists) have laboured intensively to educate the public in a number of different ways.

Sometimes, we write books for the general readership about mental health issues, rather than for our professional colleagues, and sometimes, we contribute articles to newspapers, magazines and, also, nowadays, to websites. Sometimes, we appear on radio programmes, television programmes, or on podcasts and, more recently, on webinars. Sometimes, we deliver lectures to local, national, and international audiences about mental health matters. Sometimes, we devise creative community-based mental health projects which might offer wider outreach than our more traditional, isolated private practices. Sometimes, we consult to businesses, whether government agencies or private industries, in an effort to provide enlightenment about organisational issues. Sometimes, we work with advertising agencies in a consultative capacity. Sometimes, we stage cultural events. And, sometimes, we function as media psychologists by helping our individual patients become more compassionate, more mentally robust, and more efficacious as personalities, and, in consequence, *they* can ultimately become honorary media psychologists on our behalf, promoting the benefits of their psychotherapeutic experience through conversations at dinner parties or even by becoming potent agents of psychological change within their own personal and professional communities. (For instance, in the wake of the coronavirus pandemic of 2020 and beyond, one of my patients – a generous and forward-thinking businessman – paid for each member of his staff team to receive psychotherapy free of cost).

Psychoanalytical and psychotherapeutic training organisations have long harboured a suspicion towards media work, while nursing at the same time a tremendous longing to become more involved.

Many years ago, a prominent national psychoanalytical registration body invited me to meet with its chairman and with its chief executive officer to brainstorm about how this organisation could promote the very worthy mental health work undertaken by its many highly trained, highly skilled members more effectively. I held both of these officers in great esteem, and I deeply appreciated their creative thinking capacities as well as their wish to make this organisation a more impactful and penetrative one. Over the course of the calendar year, the three of us met on many occasions and we agreed that, in the first instance, it would be ideal if the organisation could sponsor a series of podcasts in which eminent clinicians would have the opportunity to speak about their work to members of the general public. Dr. A., for instance, could talk about his research programme devoted to the cure of seemingly treatment-resistant depressive patients. Dr. B. could speak about her pioneering endeavours as a parent-infant psychotherapist, helping chronically anxious babies to sleep peacefully through the night. And Dr. C. could pontificate about his clinical experiments on the use of psychoanalytically informed group therapy in the prevention of paedophilia. Together, we developed a shortlist of the best and the brightest members of this professional organisation whose work deserved a far wider audience.

When we discussed how this podcast project could be operationalised, I offered what I thought might be a helpful suggestion. Needless to say, we all agreed that these broadcasts would succeed *only* if we could produce them in the most high-class, sophisticated manner, with excellent casting, recording, and editing, and with highly focused scripts. I explained to the chair and the chief executive of this large and well-funded organisation that I had enjoyed a long collegial friendship with one of the United Kingdom's most outstanding radio and television producers, a man whom I had come to know through my work at the B.B.C. This gentleman had produced, *inter alia*, the famous intellectually rigorous radio series *In Our Time*, presented by Melvyn Bragg – *Lord* Bragg, in fact – one of the most venerated broadcasters in the world. I knew that this producer harboured a great sympathy for psychology, because he and I had talked about Freud on many occasions, and I had, indeed, appeared twice on Lord Bragg's programme, discussing the life and work of the esteemed founder of psychoanalysis. I thought that this person might well be willing to help us produce these podcasts about mental health.

The eyes of both the chair and the chief executive lit up immediately with tremendous interest and excitement, and they encouraged me to speak with my producer friend about whether he might be able to assist us with this incipient project. I then met with my B.B.C. colleague, treated him to a lovely lunch in Central London, and, together, he and I spent a considerable amount of time talking about the potentiality of this idea and, moreover, about the desirability, if not the necessity, of such an undertaking, in order to help destigmatise psychotherapy. My media colleague immediately saw the value in mounting a mental health-related podcast series, and he offered to consult with us and to help us produce these short interviews for no fee at all – a most generous, indeed unparalleled, offer. I then spoke to the chair and to the chief executive officer of the psychoanalytical organisation, explaining that this gentleman – one of the nation's most experienced media producers – had graciously agreed to advise us on this project and that he would do so *gratis*, out of the kindness of his heart. The chair and the chief executive shouted "Hoorah", thrilled by this extraordinary good fortune.

Sadly, however, this tale does *not* have a happy ending.

Even though the two most senior and influential leaders within our large mental health organisation supported the proposed project with great enthusiasm, they knew that they would have to make a presentation to their board of trustees in order to ratify the plan to proceed with a series of podcasts under the aegis of one of the most highly regarded professionals at the B.B.C. Posting straightforward podcasts on a website hardly seems the most shocking of ideas in this digital era, and none of us could ever have imagined that any of the board members would possibly have objected.

But all of us failed to remember the ubiquity of human *envy*.

In due course, the chair and the chief executive convened a board meeting and explained to their colleagues that if we could sponsor a series of podcasts, featuring some of our most cutting-edge, impressive clinical members, and if we could appoint this venerable B.B.C. producer as project manager, for no fee at all, this project would be of unparalleled help in promoting not only the organisation but, also, solid mental health knowledge for the general public. Most of the board members beamed with delight at the prospect of such a unique opportunity, but, alas, one very senior and outspoken board member objected vigorously. Although I did not attend this meeting, as I did not serve on the board, I later learned that this particular individual objected fiercely because no one had invited *him* to participate in the planning stages of the podcast series. In fact, as this man had no media experience whatsoever, the chair and chief executive thought it both unnecessary and unhelpful to have consulted this person. But, at the board meeting, he felt so narcissistically injured that no one had sought his special approval that he instantly created such a brouhaha, ranting about the importance of keeping psychoanalytical work private and confidential, thereby attacking what most of us regarded as an obviously meritorious and, also, noncontroversial opportunity. The Chair should have put the matter to a vote, but, as he had once worked as a junior to this disputatious psychoanalyst some years earlier in the National Health Service, and as he feared an angry attack from this grandiose and, often, destructive man, the Chair folded and decided to defer the project indefinitely, eviscerating all of our creative work thus far.

Psychoanalysts and psychotherapists – though often brilliant at helping individuals in distress – can be remarkably sabotaging to colleagues, as demonstrated by the way in which an organisation in need of better public relations literally shot itself in the foot and foolishly destroyed a unique opportunity to work with one of the leading producers at the British Broadcasting Corporation.

The media provokes great anxiety among psychoanalytical practitioners and prompts us all to ask a number of uncomfortable questions: Will we compromise our integrity if we bring our theories and practices to the attention of the general public? Will we expose ourselves in an unflattering way if we collaborate with the media? Will we be misquoted? Will we embarrass ourselves? Will we turn the world's most private profession into the most public one? And, most worryingly of all, why did the television company invite *that* person to appear on their programme rather than *me*?

One year later, I attended the annual general meeting of another mental health organisation at which several colleagues complained about a decline in referrals of patients to members' private practices. A very bitter and naïve psychotherapist stood up and expostulated, "I think we really need to find ways of working more closely with the media. We need to get *out there*. We need to become better known. Let's think about how we can do that." Suddenly, everyone in the room nodded their heads passively, agreeing that a media strategy would be helpful, although no one had any idea how best to proceed. At this point, another colleague, who noticed me across the lecture hall, called out, "Maybe Brett Kahr has some ideas. He's done a lot of media work." My heart simply sank, and I gritted my teeth, careful not to verbalise too many of my frustrations with my professional colleagues who had, over the years, scuppered themselves and our profession on far too many occasions by having refused a plethora of perfectly reasonable requests and invitations from journalists and broadcasters. Instead, I smiled and replied that I would be happy to provide consultation about this matter to the organisation. Not a single person from this grouping ever pursued any clear plan in a serious way and, five years later, this particular institution actually folded and became absorbed by another organisation. I did offer my assistance, but this psychotherapeutic society suffered from too much ambivalence about being seen and heard.

Our profession needs to embrace media psychoanalysis in a much more serious and much more unashamed manner. It should be possible to preserve the utter sanctity of the consulting room and yet still reveal some basic truths about psychological work, namely:

1. Mental illness ravages lives.
2. It costs the country billions of hours in lost earnings.
3. Mental illness can be cured, and psychotherapy has proved itself to be one of the most effective forms of treatment.
4. Psychotherapy *does* work, and we now have the research evidence to prove it.
5. In the wake of the coronavirus pandemic of 2020 and 2021, and beyond, mental health has become increasingly more challenged than ever before, resulting in immense suffering worldwide. Hence, the professions of psychotherapy and psychoanalysis need to be made infinitely more available.

Simply by promoting these very basic messages, mental health professionals could potentially transform the psychological landscape of the country without compromising our integrity, our ethics, or our much-cherished professional values. Indeed, we could certainly create a strategy for collaborating with the media without violating privacy or confidentiality in any way. And if we should agree to consider working more fully with broadcasters, I know from my many decades of experience that these men and women would welcome us warmly, now more so than ever before.

Media psychology should not, however, be the preserve of only a tiny handful of media psychologists. The entire mental health community must reorientate itself to become much more media savvy and much more media friendly. We must all find a way to contribute to make psychological knowledge very widely available.

By doing so, we might well be able to help a great many lorry drivers and their brethren.

Section II

Media Psychoanalysis in Action

2
"You have five minutes to cure the nation"
My Years at the B.B.C.

In July 2004, I became the Resident Psychotherapist for B.B.C. Radio 2, the most popular radio station in the United Kingdom, which attracts approximately 15,000,000 listeners weekly from all parts of the British Isles. Some four months earlier, Lesley Douglas, the forward-thinking and visionary Controller of Radio 2, had invited me for a breakfast meeting atop Saint George's Hotel on Langham Place, near her offices at Broadcasting House in Central London, to discuss the possibility of presenting solid psychological and psychotherapeutic ideas on the radio. As we munched our delicious croissants, Lesley told me that, as the Controller, she hoped not only to maintain and, indeed, to expand upon the high quality of Radio 2's current music and arts programmes, but, also, that she wished to find a way for her station to help foster a greater sense of wellbeing and "citizenship" in the United Kingdom, and she wondered whether a mental health professional might be able to make a contribution to the network.

Having first appeared on radio some twenty years earlier, back in 1984, on the *David Freeman Programme* on B.B.C. Radio Oxford, defending psychoanalysis against heated attacks from the vituperative behavioural psychologist Professor Hans Eysenck, and having subsequently participated in many such programmes thereafter, I had, by this point, accumulated a goodly amount of media experience. I applauded Lesley Douglas on her very exciting proposal, and I thanked her for this kind invitation. Lesley revealed that she not only wished to champion mental health through the B.B.C. but, also, that she had an ulterior motive, explaining that the British Broadcasting Corporation would soon be required to renew its Royal Charter – a complex process in which this distinguished organisation would have to demonstrate its ongoing worthiness. Certainly, Lesley believed, and rightly so, that by championing mental health, this might make the B.B.C. even more valuable to the public in the eyes of Her Majesty The Queen.

Just at that very moment, as Lesley and I continued to sip our coffee, the famous, indeed, iconic television presenter Terry Wogan, who also happened to have popped into Saint George's Hotel for his own snack, prior to recording a programme, passed by and he waved at Lesley very warmly indeed. She acknowledged her esteemed colleague and chirped, "I hope the broadcast goes well, Terry." Having had the pleasure of watching Mr. Wogan on television across the decades, and having admired his very delightful interviewing style, I smiled and thought to myself, "If Terry Wogan should take the time to wave to Lesley Douglas – the woman who will soon be my new media boss – she must be the 'real deal'."

In order to progress this plan, Lesley told me that she would arrange a meeting as soon as possible with her staff at B.B.C. Radio 2 in order to sort out the practicalities. This impressive woman did not waste a moment. Within a week, she had organised a planning session with her senior colleague Dave Barber, the Editor of Specialist Programmes, and with the members of his "Social Action" team, consisting of the Senior Producer, Mark Hill, and the young Broadcast Assistant, Nicky Davidson. After several months of regular team meetings, we had successfully crafted the infrastructure for a nationwide radio initiative, "Life 2 Live", designed to provide coverage of psychological themes and topics in the most basic language, for members of the general public. We launched this new campaign on 23rd July, 2004, on *Jeremy Vine*, the flagship lunchtime news programme, which attracted a regular audience of several million people, and we devoted our roll-out programme to a discussion of the psychology of intimate relationships. The charming and intelligent Jeremy Vine, the host of the eponymous programme, interviewed me about the challenges of long-term romantic partnerships, and I then responded to callers who wished to speak about the causes of marital breakdown and related topics.

Lesley Douglas and I had agreed that, in order to promote psychological knowledge as widely as possible, it would be best for me *not* to have my own slot on Radio 2 but, rather, that I should visit as many of the already existent radio programmes as possible as a regular guest, thereby helping to disseminate a psychotherapeutic presence across the radio station more broadly. During my tenure at Radio 2, I made frequent appearances on such staple shows as *Jeremy Vine* and, also, *Johnnie Walker*, the early evening Drivetime programme, as well as the highly popular and hugely durable *Steve Wright* afternoon programme.

We soon developed a special "Life 2 Live" section on the B.B.C. website, for which I would write regular short pieces (fact sheets, responses to Frequently Asked Questions about the nature of therapy, book reviews, and so forth), and through which I would conduct web chats with members of the public who wished to speak to a psychotherapist more directly about particular mental health matters. The website, diligently maintained by my colleague Terri Sweeney, a woman who had extensive experience of working for B.B.C. Interactive, helped the "Life 2 Live" campaign to reach an even wider audience, and we soon received literally tens of thousands of page impressions (i.e., website "hits") on a weekly basis. We also maintained a B.B.C. Message Board, through which members of the public could write to me with queries and concerns about their personal problems – often about quite heart-breaking difficulties and traumas – to which I would respond with bespoke referrals to particular trusted mental health practitioners or well-known mental health organisations throughout the United Kingdom. In doing this work, we made, I trust, a contribution to raising the level of public awareness about psychotherapy and mental health issues, especially in the less well populated parts of the country where we, as psychological professionals, had not yet made much of an impact.

Initially, when we discussed how the radio announcers should refer to me on air, colleagues at the B.B.C. recommended that I should be called a "life coach". I told them that this would not suit me, as I have neither trained as a "life coach" nor would I describe myself as one. I explained that I would prefer to be known quite straightforwardly as a "psychotherapist", my formal professional title. The Social Action team seemed somewhat concerned that this very clinical-sounding term (at least to their ears) might be too off-putting or indeed too scary for some listeners, but I held my ground with insistence; and soon thereafter the announcers began to describe me as "Radio 2 Resident Psychotherapist Brett Kahr". So, if nothing else, I succeeded in having the word "psychotherapist" broadcast regularly on Radio 2 – hundreds of times, I suspect, over the course of my tenure at the B.B.C. – thus turning a hitherto "taboo" title into a more user-friendly one.

After I had begun to find my sea legs, talking to the hosts of the daytime radio shows, speaking with callers, and web-chatting with internet users about mental health matters, Dave Barber rang me to enquire whether I would be willing to make a regular appearance on Radio 2's late-night music programme, hosted by the delightful and talented presenter Helen Mayhew, who had only recently joined the network. Essentially, I would go on air with Helen from 1.30 a.m. until 2.30 a.m. in the Saturday night/Sunday morning slot and chat with her about psychological matters and then take calls from listeners, "*Frasier*-style". Although somewhat concerned about my ability to function therapeutically at such an unusually antisocial hour, I nevertheless accepted the challenge with alacrity, prepared to plunge in at the deep end.

On 17th October, 2004, I braced myself for my first late-night appearance, napping uncharacteristically during the afternoon so that I would be sufficiently alert to engage in on-air psychotherapeutics in the small hours of the morning. A car fetched me round about 11.15 p.m. and delivered me to Broadcasting House just before midnight. Helen Mayhew and the team greeted me warmly and I then settled down to drink several cups of boiled water, which kept my throat well lubricated. The staff and I reviewed the structure of the evening and I enjoyed chatting with Helen Mayhew, whom I had only recently met for the first time some days previously. And then, at approximately 1.20 a.m., Helen and I perched ourselves in the studio, surrounded by our microphones and headphones and control desks, and then braced ourselves for the red light to flash at precisely 1.30 a.m., thus signalling the start of the programme: live, unedited, with no turning back! Fortunately, due to the considerable preparation of Mark Hill, my Senior Producer, Helen and I had already made a pilot programme together, complete with real callers, so that we could begin to acquaint ourselves with the process, and so that we could test the technology, as Helen would be working from a completely new studio and would have to operate many of the panels herself, bringing callers on air, and then signing them off again. So, in spite of the unusual nature of our task, both Helen and I felt reasonably ready.

When I began my job as "Resident Psychotherapist" for Radio 2, my colleagues at the B.B.C. asked me whether I might be keen to know the identity of the callers in advance and whether I might also wish to be given a synopsis of their problems and concerns beforehand. After thinking carefully about this matter, I explained that I would prefer to be surprised. I reasoned that if I knew the nature of the calls in advance, I might find myself researching their "issues" or, indeed, pre-scripting answers in my mind in ways that might not be particularly helpful. Instead, if I could respond spontaneously, exactly as I would do in the consulting room, this would give the audience a clearer and more authentic sense of how psychotherapy unfolds and how the process proceeds. So, after some preliminary chat with Helen about the "Life 2 Live" initiative, the producer signalled to us that we had our first caller on the line – and neither Helen nor I had any idea what we might expect. I knew only that I would have approximately three, or four or, at most, five minutes with the caller. (This may seem a ridiculously short period of time in which to engage with crucial matters, but radio producers consider five minutes an eternity – a luxury, in fact – and I felt privileged to have even this tiny space in which I might try to say something psychotherapeutically edifying).

Indeed, one of the members of the production team once quipped, "You have five minutes to cure the nation, Brett. Good luck mate."

Although I certainly could not cure the nation, I endeavoured to do my very best in as professional a manner as possible. Because several million people would be listening to each of my broadcasts, this raised important questions regarding confidentiality, as callers would be speaking about intimate matters before a large audience. Those ringing in could, of course, opt to use a pseudonym, if they chose to do so, but most, it seems, decided to introduce themselves by their real names. The expert broadcast assistants who screened the telephone calls in advance would, at my insistence, discuss questions of informed consent with each member of the public, asking these callers if they had really thought carefully about whether they wished to discuss their private concerns on national radio.

Not long after my coffee with Lesley Douglas, I did of course spend a great deal of time mulling over whether I should undertake this unique and unusual appointment at the British Broadcasting Corporation. In thinking about whether to accept this post at Radio 2, I spoke, of course, with several of my mental health colleagues, all of whom encouraged me to avail myself of this opportunity. In fact, my former boss at the Tavistock Clinic told me, "Brett, I know that you'll speak to the callers with compassion. By doing that in front of millions of people, you have a real opportunity to destigmatise therapy. Of course, the callers will be sharing their real problems, but they are entitled to do that. They are entitled to talk about their own lives. And you'll respond respectfully. The callers won't be shamed. So, go ahead. Do it!" Fortified by much encouragement from senior colleagues, I persevered.

I now braced myself for my very first late-night caller. I had absolutely no idea whatsoever about the sort of matters that might emerge.

After I grappled with a crackling headphone, which had to be repaired rapidly by the sound technician, my first caller appeared on the line. In her calm and soothing voice, Helen Mayhew entreated this member of the public to speak to me: "Hello, 'James', you're on the line with our psychotherapist, Brett." "James", a middle-aged man, said "Hullo", in a deeply flattened tone of voice, and after I greeted him with a "Good morning, 'James'", I asked how I might be of help. With a teary tone, he told me that his wife, only forty years of age, had died just a few weeks previously from an undiagnosed brain tumour. Tragically, she had experienced a rapid onset of headaches, and shortly after entering hospital she lapsed into a coma from which she never emerged. So, horrifyingly, James had no opportunity to say goodbye to his much-loved spouse, and now he had to care for their three tiny children all by himself. My heart sank as I listened to this aching tale of pain and loss.

Quite unsurprisingly, James had already used up *three* minutes of our anticipated five-minute time slot by telling me his story. Needless to say, I knew that I simply could not provide sufficient comfort in a mere matter of two minutes. Through the glass partition of the studio, I could see my producer looking extremely anxious. I contorted my shoulders, clenched my teeth, and made a desperate face to the producer, trying to communicate with gestures: "Look, this is a serious trauma. We will need more time. Please, *please* give us some more time."

I began my response by extending deepest condolences to James in my most heartfelt voice. Any reasonable human being – clinician or otherwise – would have done exactly the same. I then asked a few pointed questions as to whether James had any support network available (family, friends, work colleagues) to help him through this absolutely ghastly, traumatic loss. Unfortunately, James seemed to have devoted most of his time to his wife and children, and therefore he had no real friends and no work colleagues with whom he felt particularly close. His office mates did, of course, know of his wife's death, but James explained that they would avoid talking to him about his bereavement, as they found the subject too painful, too awkward.

I then commented on the importance of connectedness and the dangers of isolation, and I tried to think with this widower about how he might access better sources of psychosocial support. James then confessed that he and his children had not managed to shed a tear since the unexpected death of his beloved spouse.

At this point, Helen intervened, most helpfully, and asked me whether James *should* be crying and whether I might be able to speak in more detail about the various stages of the grief and bereavement process, as this would be of great value to our listeners. I could have hugged Helen for asking this question at this time because earlier she and I had both discussed the fact that in three or four minutes we would not manage to "solve" anyone's problems, but we could, at least, try to transmit some basic mental health advice not only to the caller but to our millions of listeners as well. I then did my very best to provide a brief, clear, potted summary of the some of the highlights of basic research on the psychology of grief and mourning. I explained to James that he might still be entrapped in the first phase of the grieving process, namely, palpable shock and numbness. As James realised that he might improve and move on to further, more manageable stages of grief, he then began to cry more fully for the very first time. I praised him on national radio for his ability to begin risking tears, explaining that, ultimately, this would bring relief.

By now, I had used up *nine* minutes of highly precious, highly expensive broadcast time, nearly twice the length originally allocated, but we continued to soldier on. James spoke further about the lovely qualities of his late wife and of his young children. I then explained that, of course, we would not be able to talk about all the important aspects of his circumstances on this occasion, but that, if he stayed online, one of my colleagues would communicate with him at greater length afterwards and would be only too pleased to recommend the name of a counselling agency in James's local area, far from London. I asked James whether he thought that some bereavement counselling might be of assistance, and he agreed that he would think about this as a possibility.

Helen and I each extended further condolences and warm wishes to him, and we said our goodbyes – again, all on national radio – finishing this part of the programme just a few minutes before the 2.00 a.m. news bulletin.

After James rang off, Helen and I remained on air, and we had a chance to speak about his challenging and painful situation. We praised James for his courage and for having taken the risk to telephone us and to talk about his almost unbearable personal and family tragedy. Helen then suggested to our listeners that if anyone at home wished to convey a message to James, they would be most welcome to do so, by telephone, by text, or by e-mail. We then switched to the news bulletin, having spent fully ten minutes on James's call. My producer certainly understood that we could not have offered this man any less, and undoubtedly, we could have provided a great deal more. I sipped some of my hot water, which had now gone cold, and after the news bulletin I read out some e-mails to James from various listeners, very much of the "Well-done-James-keep-your-chin-up-mate" variety, but highly appreciated, nonetheless. Each person, in his or her own emotional vocabulary, wished to reach out and make at least some contact with this likeable, bereaved gentleman. We all hoped that James, having struggled heretofore with loneliness, will have found some of these simple, gentle expressions of kindness and camaraderie to be helpful and touching.

One of my young colleagues at the B.B.C., with whom I had worked in preparation for such calls, spoke to James at greater length later that morning, and she provided him with details of several local professional organisations. Apparently, James seemed to be much calmer, and our assistant told him that he would be welcome to make further contact with us at any point in future, and that he could certainly avail himself of our "Life 2 Live" Message Board at any time, as well as our "Life 2 Live" telephone helpline.

Helen and I then took several more callers on air, including a woman who had suffered sexual abuse at the hands of a close family member many decades earlier, and who had now begun to experience panic attacks, having recently encountered her abuser once again, after many, many years, at a family funeral. Needless to say, this call required more than three or four or five minutes as well. By this point, Helen and I felt confident that we would not have to plead for a few additional minutes of conversation. The mental health of this woman certainly took priority ... and rightly so.

After the programme ended, at 2.30 a.m., Helen and I had a "de-briefing" meeting with the producer, the sound engineer, and the broadcasting assistant. The producer – somewhat vexed that we had devoted more than five minutes to several of the calls – told me that, in future, we would have to think twice before putting "depressed people" on the line, as these individuals, in his estimation, simply do not make for "good radio". Helen, to my relief, upbraided the producer and told him that she thought that James had proved to be a wonderful guest, and that by daring to speak of his bereavement and by crying on national radio, he would have helped many men (and women) in comparable circumstances to know that one *can* reach out, and that talking to a psychotherapist need not be a scary experience. I could not have agreed more.

At that moment, the telephone rang in our studio. James had called on our private number, which the assistant had shared with him, and he asked whether he might speak with me directly. The producer escorted me to a quiet cubicle next door to the large and noisy studio, and I took the call. James and I talked privately, off-air, as he wanted to thank me for helping him. We spoke for over one hour. He knew that he had to cry. He knew that he had to have help. And now, the grieving process could begin. Earlier that morning, our broadcasting assistant had already referred James to a counselling organisation. I reviewed this recommendation with James and also discussed the possibility of a direct referral to a particular psychotherapist as a further possibility. He seemed very grateful indeed.

After a long and late and somewhat exhausting but, also, invigorating evening in Broadcasting House, a chauffeured B.B.C. car collected me and returned me home at approximately 4.00 a.m. I must confess that it took me more than two hours before I could wind down from the experience, and I did not fall asleep until nearly 6.00 a.m. In the months which followed, I appeared many more times on the *Helen Mayhew* show, and somehow, I found a way to drift off rather more quickly upon my return home, and to incorporate these extremely late-night and early-morning radio psychotherapy forays into my weekend timetable. Rather than regarding them as a disruption, I soon came to consider them a real pleasure and a true privilege – a unique opportunity to reach out, in some small way, to those people round the country who had never before encountered a mental health professional of any shape or form.

In view of the fact that the "Social Action" team at the B.B.C. had originally expressed a great concern about using the term "psychotherapist" on national radio, we had now managed to deploy this title hundreds and hundreds of times in the most straightforward and non-scary manner. I hope that, in doing so, I will have contributed in some small way to the destigmatisation of our profession.

Of course, these little on-air conversations – only several minutes in length – in no way represent the ordinary psychoanalytical work that I undertake during my typical clinical day, which always consists of carefully timed, supremely confidential fifty-minute sessions, in which I endeavour to offer deep unconscious interpretations of, and engagements with, private free-associative material, often over a period of many, many years. But in the absence of being able to provide intensive psychotherapy or psychoanalysis to everyone, I regard this media psychological experiment as an important means of allowing people to experience something of the seriousness and the compassion that only the mental health professional can provide in this way. Although I never embarked upon a full course of psychotherapeutic treatment with anyone who approached me through the B.B.C., I do know that by having dipped a toe into these larger waters I did have the opportunity to reach many millions of people whom I would not have encountered otherwise.

I really do take my hat off to the British Broadcasting Corporation for having established the "Life 2 Live" project with such seriousness and such professionalism, and I feel honoured to have taken part in a campaign of this nature. When I first began working at the B.B.C., I wondered whether a few minutes of therapy here and a few minutes of therapy there would really make much difference at all but, having immersed myself in the process for the three years of the campaign, I came to know from letters and e-mails and postings on our Message Board that people really did listen; and, moreover, that they really did derive considerable benefit. Indeed, during my tenure as Resident Psychotherapist, I referred an untold number of individuals to colleagues for psychological therapeutic work – people who, under ordinary circumstances, would have steered clear of mental health practitioners entirely.

Perhaps I had some small success in helping to popularise psychotherapy among my fellow Britons.

Four minutes on air may seem a drop in the ocean, but when 15,000,000 people listen to those four minutes …

3

How to Dramatise 13,553 Sexual Fantasies in Only Forty-Seven Minutes

In the spring of 2002, I enjoyed a very pleasant lunch with my friend and colleague Oliver Rathbone, then Managing Director of Karnac Books, the leading psychoanalytical publishing house in London. Oliver had just released my edited book, *The Legacy of Winnicott: Essays on Infant and Child Mental Health* (Kahr, 2002a) – my third title for Karnac Books – and he wished to discuss plans for my next project. As we sipped our soup in a restaurant near the Aldwych, not far from the London School of Economics and Political Science, Oliver asked me what I had in mind for the future. To be frank, I cannot, at this point, remember exactly what idea I had suggested, possibly a selection of the very charming letters from Sir Frederick Winnicott, former Mayor of Plymouth, to his son, the psychoanalyst Dr. Donald Winnicott, which I had located in the Archives of the British Psychoanalytical Society, and which now reside in the Archives and Manuscripts collection at the Wellcome Library in London. Oliver looked bemused and, with utter tact, managed to convey, through subtle movements of his eyebrows, that such a volume would be of little interest to anyone other than myself, and that its publication, however historically worthy, would earn very little money for the coffers of Karnac Books.

Desperately, I began to search for another topic, ranging from an introductory guide to the writings of Melanie Klein, to a book on the management of a private psychotherapy practice. I knew that I wanted to produce a big book on the traumatic origins of schizophrenia, based on my clinical work, but at that point I had not yet digested the material sufficiently to begin writing. I then offered a few more ideas. Again, my esteemed publisher tolerated my suggestions with a benign smile.

Seizing the moment, Oliver leaned over the table in conspiratorial fashion and intoned: "Brett, *I* know what your next book should be." I sat with bated breath, delighted that Oliver had a clearer insight into the development of my writing trajectory than I did. With a cheeky grin on his face, he announced: "You must write a book on the psychoanalysis of sexual fantasies!" Choking on my risotto, I became extremely disconcerted and told Oliver that I could not think of a more unpalatable or unnecessary subject for my next project. I explained that I had no special knowledge of the field of sexual fantasies, and that I had not studied the literature in a comprehensive manner, underscoring that the American author Nancy Friday (1973, 1975, 1980, 1991) had already cornered the market in this field with a quartet of extremely well-written and highly popular compendia of male and female sexual fantasies, all still in print, and penned from a psychoanalytical vantage point as well. What more could one possibly contribute to this topic? I quickly dashed Oliver's hopes of commissioning a bestseller on the erotic fantasy, and, in spite of his excellent lunchtime companionship, I returned to my consulting room in North West London, somewhat despondent at Oliver's lack of interest in the wartime letters of Sir Frederick Winnicott.

But, unbeknownst to Oliver, he had certainly planted an idea in my mind, which, to my surprise and, indeed, consternation began to take root. As I re-immersed myself in my clinical work with patients that very afternoon, I suddenly became increasingly aware of the role of sexual fantasies in the private lives of these individuals. One male patient began to report masturbatory fantasies about an attractive female colleague in his office; another male patient sheepishly confessed that he often thought about a sadomasochistic scenario with an ex-girlfriend while having sex with his wife; and a few of the couples who consulted with me for marital psychotherapy painted very compelling portraits of their divergent fantasies, which often resulted in a veritable sexual anaesthesia in the bedroom. Sexual fantasies seemed to abound, but I quickly realised that I had not really thought about the subject in a considered or systematic fashion until now.

I must confess that when I trained in couple psychotherapy and couple psychoanalysis at the Tavistock Marital Studies Institute, some of my teachers – mostly older women from the pre-war generation – often discouraged me and my fellow trainees from speaking to couples about sexuality in a direct manner, as many considered this to be potentially intrusive (Kahr, 2009). It may well be the case that I had silently internalised some of this sexual sheepishness and, therefore, it took me some time before I could begin to facilitate more frank and more straightforward conversations about sexuality with my patients.

Intrigued by Oliver Rathbone's encouragement, I returned to Nancy Friday's books, which my undergraduate tutor in psychopathology had first recommended to me many years before, back in 1980. I have such great admiration for Nancy Friday that, in spite of her lack of any formal clinical credentials, I would position her in the pantheon of pioneering sexologists such as Professor Sigmund Freud, Dr. Havelock Ellis, Dr. Magnus Hirschfeld, and Professor Alfred Kinsey, among others; indeed, Friday's books had stirred a revolution in the 1970s, especially among women, by helping people recognise that women *also* possess the ability to enjoy vibrant masturbatory and coital fantasies, and that they have the capacity to become every bit as sexualised as their male counterparts.

As I dipped back into Ms. Friday's books, I could very much appreciate their historical importance in helping to inaugurate a public discourse around the much-neglected subject of fantasy. But I soon realised that, having read her publications as a green undergraduate, I had, in fact, idealised her psychological analysis. Upon re-examining her texts, I found them unabashedly blunt and often shockingly revealing about the content of individual fantasies, but rather skimpy on their explication of the unconscious meanings of sexual fantasies. I deeply admired the tremendous compassion and non-judgemental attitude that Friday displayed towards her correspondents – those who generously shared their private masturbatory thoughts. Throughout her writings, she espoused a "whatever-turns-you-on-as-long-as-no-one-gets-hurt" attitude. Nevertheless, in spite of my huge respect for her approach, I did wonder whether many of her research subjects would have benefited from psychotherapy or whether someone could have helped them to achieve a different set of less persecutory or less violent sexual fantasies.

Gradually, I began to scour both the clinical and the empirical literature on this subject, which, I discovered, to my great surprise, to be quite sparse. I soon came to realise that although we, as psychoanalytical investigators, claim to be obsessed with sexuality, we do, in fact, know much more about actual sexual *behaviour* than we do about sexual *fantasy*. It became increasingly clear that the arena of sexual fantasies posed many rich questions, for instance: (1) What might be the difference between masturbatory fantasies and coital fantasies? (2) Should people ever share their fantasies in the context of an intimate partnership? (3) Should couples ever enact their sexual fantasies? (4) To what extent might fantasies be autonomous creations of our minds, and to what extent do they derive, fatalistically, from early child-rearing experiences, or from subsequent trauma? (5) Do fantasies cause us harm in our daily lives? (6) Can the content of our fantasies be altered as a result of life experiences or as a result of intensive psychotherapeutic treatment? It seems that neither psychoanalysis nor sexology offered a clear or well-researched answer to any of these aforementioned concerns.

I realised that the topic of sexual fantasy – that most private part of our conscious mind, which Donald Winnicott (1963a, p. 187) might have dubbed the "incommunicado" – had received little or no emphasis in our training programmes as mental health professionals. It soon became evident that a study on sexual fantasy would be of some interest and, I hoped, of some value as well; and by mid-summer of 2002, I had told Oliver Rathbone, perhaps rather rashly, that I would soon embark upon the preparation of a fresh, modern, psychoanalytically orientated book-length study of the secret world of sexual fantasies.

My ongoing academic and clinical study of erotic thoughts took a rather unexpected turn in the final days of 2002, when I attended a dinner party at the home of Dan Chambers, one of the whiz kids of British television, who had worked as a commissioner of science programmes at Channel 4 Television, and who became, subsequently, Director of Programmes at Channel Five Television. All the guests (many of whom produced or commissioned films and documentaries in their own right) enjoyed a most convivial supper, and midway through our pudding, Dan – son of the esteemed child psychiatrist, Dr. Florence Chambers – asked me whether I had yet chosen a subject for my next book. Until now, I had kept my plans very much private, unsure that I would be able to conjure enough relevant material about sexual fantasies and quite uncertain about the structure or methodology for this germinal project. But, disinhibited by jet lag, having recently returned from a trip to Manhattan earlier that morning, I blurted out: "The psychology of sexual fantasies." Within a matter of seconds, six television producers leapt for their wallets or purses, and each produced a business card, tripping over one another as they frantically enquired, "Who's making the television programme?" Georgina Chignell, a charming woman, seated on my right, who worked at that time as a member of the Development Team at Tiger Aspect Productions, a venerable London-based independent television company renowned for its comedy programmes, but, also, for its history and science documentaries, won the commission, and within a matter of days, she hauled me into her offices in Soho Square, just off of Oxford Street, to meet with Paul Sommers, the Head of Factual programmes at Tiger.

Paul Sommers listened with analytical attentiveness as Georgina Chignell and I talked about the subject of sexual fantasies. A distinguished television producer with a sterling track record, Sommers had developed a reputation for being somewhat facially inscrutable – he would have made an excellent poker player, or, indeed, an old-school "blank screen" psychoanalyst – and throughout our meeting, I had no idea whether he found the material of interest at all. Several months passed by before I heard another word regarding the possibility of making a television documentary about sexual fantasies but, eventually, Georgina called me into the office to meet Dunja Noack, a German-born historian who had worked at Tiger Aspect Productions for several years as the Head of Factual Development, a crucial role as the person who helps to transform germinal ideas into viable television programmes. Dunja told me that Paul Sommers had approved the project and had authorised us to collaborate in order to transform a body of psychological observations into an irresistibly compelling programme. In stolen time, I began to brainstorm with Dunja during breaks between sessions with my patients, and I soon began to elaborate on the psychoanalytical understanding of sexual fantasy, explaining, in particular, Professor Robert Stoller's (1975, 1979a, 1979b, 1985) ground-breaking work on the importance of the sexual fantasy as a means of eroticising traumatic experiences. A clever academic in her own right, Dunja understood the theory straightaway, and we began to outline what a documentary about sexual fantasies might look like.

We spent ages pondering whether I might have enough data for a three-part series, or indeed, even for a landmark six-part series on sexual fantasy; but the very thought of committing myself to such a gargantuan project at this early stage simply terrified me, and I plumped instead for a one-hour film (in television terms, forty-seven minutes, with a discretionary forty-eighth minute, as required, interspersed with twelve or thirteen minutes of advertisements to pay for the production costs). This seemed an altogether more manageable proposition, especially in view of my full-time private clinical practice.

As we explored the feasibility of making a documentary about sexual fantasies, it became palpably clear to me that I could not in any way use material from my psychotherapeutic sessions with patients, as that would constitute an unthinkable breach of confidentiality; and a simple review of the skimpy literature would not give us enough meat for the programme. It would be absolutely essential for me to undertake some *new*, primary research on the topic, and I told Dunja Noack that we would need to have a substantial development period so that we could obtain fresh data. In my experience, most television producers wish to keep the commissions rolling in, so that they can generate revenues with lightning speed, but fortunately, the scholarly Dunja appreciated the potential value of undertaking original, cutting-edge research, and I thus outlined my wish list.

I told Dunja that, in an ideal world, I would be very keen to conduct approximately 100 clinical psychodiagnostic interviews with randomly selected members of the public (aged eighteen years and above), each of five hours' duration, in order to obtain a detailed life history, as well as a sexual history, with a view to establishing any causal relationship between early biographical experiences and subsequent adult sexual fantasy content. I would also need to undertake a more extensive national survey of approximately 50,000 British men and women who could respond anonymously to a lengthy, comprehensive questionnaire and provide more details about their sexual fantasies. Dunja gulped at the prospect of authorising such a large piece of research, but she quickly appreciated the potential merit of such primary data, especially when I told her that, in my clinical experience, many individuals suffered great embarrassment and shame about their sexual fantasies, and that a proper study could help to shed light on such a private yet pervasive source of human misery.

As Head of Factual Development at Tiger Aspect Productions, Dunja had cultivated close relationships with all the relevant commissioning editors for science at the major broadcasters in the United Kingdom and, also, with many of those stationed abroad. For those unfamiliar with the vicissitudes of television commissioning, I should clarify that only a small percentage of programmes will be made in-house by the broadcast channels themselves, and many of the programmes will, in fact, be solicited from independent production companies such as Tiger; thus, anyone wishing to create a television programme must first court an "indie", which will then romance one of the commissioning editors at a major broadcaster, in the hope of receiving the requisite funding and authorisation. In due time, Dunja ferried me to Covent Garden in the heart of London to meet the delightful Justine Kershaw, commissioner for science at Channel Five, a long-standing colleague of Dan Chambers, at whose late-night supper party this television idea first took shape. Justine had already heard quite a lot about both me and the sexual fantasy project from Dan, and she swiftly provided us with development money so that I could undertake ten preliminary clinical interviews as "pilot data" to see whether we could generate enough interesting and useful stories. Shortly thereafter, we developed a relationship with the political pollsters YouGov, with whom I had worked on a previous project, and they promptly arranged for ten men and women, randomly chosen from their database, to meet with me for lengthy, confidential clinical interviews to discuss sexual fantasies.

Dunja arranged the timetable with military precision, and in the early months of 2004, nearly two years after my initial lunch with Oliver Rathbone, I began to interview complete strangers about the details of their sexual fantasies, sacrificing many Saturdays and Sundays in the process. The psychodiagnostic assessment interviews lasted for five hours, and each conversation proceeded with such intensity of concentration that most participants did not even stand up to stretch their legs or pop to the bathroom for a comfort break. The frankness of the interviewees, none of whom had ever before spoken about their sexual fantasies to another living soul, amazed me. They wanted, nevertheless, to talk to a psychotherapist, partly to aid research, partly for confessional purposes, and partly as a means of trying to understand more about their often baffling and bewildering fantasy lives. As the interviews unfolded, I became increasingly impressed by the courageous capacity of these women and men to speak with such candour and with such seriousness. Needless to say, the data which derived from these preliminary psychoanalytically orientated psychological interviews, and from those which followed, proved to be both riveting and shocking in many instances, and these in-depth conversations ultimately came to form the backbone of the books which followed, namely, *Sex and the Psyche* (Kahr, 2007a, 2008b), and *Who's Been Sleeping in Your Head?: The Secret World of Sexual Fantasies* (Kahr, 2008a), which addressed, respectively, both British fantasies and, subsequently, their American counterparts.

By mid-2004, we had sent a development report to Justine Kershaw at Five, updating her on our progress, and, after a few further meetings, including one key conversation with Dan Chambers himself, the broadcaster Five agreed to fund a special one-hour television documentary, entitled *Britain's Sexual Fantasies*, with yours truly as the presenter. With the encouragement of two research-minded colleagues – one of whom worked as a psychologist and the other as a sexual health epidemiologist – I devised a lengthy multi-item questionnaire which we sent to some 15,000 men and women on the YouGov database of randomly selected individuals, representative of each cell of the British adult population (e.g., age group, geographical location, religious affiliation, political affiliation, etc.). Combining these new findings with some earlier pilot data, I soon came to possess an archive of more than 20,000 British adult sexual fantasies, which I then supplemented with nearly 4,000 American adult sexual fantasies. We based our television programme, however, solely on the first 13,553 participants in the study – all British adults aged eighteen years or older.

After months and months of data analysis, we finally went into production in January of 2005, and we began to make the film. This required seemingly endless rounds of scripting and re-scripting, supplemented by further interviews with men and women up and down the country who had kindly agreed to speak on camera about the role of fantasies in their lives. Dunja Noack became the Executive Producer, and, in time, she hired a production manager, a team of researchers, a publicist, and many other personnel; and the hard work began in earnest. Justine Kershaw from Five went on maternity leave, replaced by Peter Grimsdale, a kindly and incisive television stalwart with whom I had worked some years previously on a Channel 4 Television project. He came to supervise the programme with benignity and concern, creating the right sort of facilitating environment in which our little project could begin to flourish.

The final piece of the jigsaw fell happily into place after Dunja and I interviewed a brace of potential Producer-Directors. None of the many people whom we met initially quite fitted the bill but, eventually, we encountered the enthusiastic Fred Casella, a sharp and witty alumnus of both the University of Oxford and the science department of the British Broadcasting Corporation. Dunja appointed him immediately and, not long thereafter, Fred engaged his favourite lighting cameraman and his best sound editor, and by February of 2005 the filming began at last.

Needless to say, the shooting of a television documentary consumed a great deal of time. Fortunately, the cameramen and sound technicians and editors undertook most of the nuts-and-bolts practical work. I merely had to stand still in a well-pressed suit and recite my lines.

I shall never forget one particularly long and exhausting day of filming. At a certain point, I stood in the centre of London's Millennium Bridge, amid the blistering cold, on a Tuesday morning in April, with St. Paul's Cathedral looming behind me and a veritable flotilla of noisy tugboats tooting below. Overhead, a bevy of jets continued to whoosh by, whipping up the wind; and with no overcoat to protect me, I began to freeze. (I had, of course, brought an overcoat with me to the shoot, but Fred insisted that I must not wear it on camera, as he wished to create a more summer-like atmosphere). Hundreds of mid-morning commuters rushed past in both directions, wondering why I remained so absolutely stationery in the centre of the bridge, sporting merely a thin cashmere jacket, with makeup smeared all over my face. While waiting for the camera to roll, I stood virtually motionless, for approximately two hours, by which point I had very little sensation remaining in any of my extremities.

With microphone wires concealed beneath my shirt, and a battery-operated microphone pack in my back trouser pocket, I waited patiently for the cue from our makeup artist who, as it happened, doubled as a technical assistant. She carried a large walkie-talkie in her hand, awaiting instructions from the director, Fred, who stood some forty feet away, at the end of the bridge, with an executive producer, a cameraman, a sound engineer, a production coordinator, and a "runner" (the ambitious, eager young "gofer" who would fetch our tea and coffee) poised nearby. Fred spoke to the Irish makeup artist through this walkie-talkie, and, at long last, he called out "Action". The young woman then relayed Fred's instructions to me, because I could not hear his voice at a distance of forty feet, especially amid the buzz of London noise; and then, like a well-trained puppet, I began to speak my carefully scripted line: "But what *exactly* does it tell us about *ourselves* if we have a masturbatory fantasy about someone *other* than our regular sexual partner?" Unfortunately, just at that moment, another tugboat motored past beneath the Millennium Bridge, and Simon Dyer, our perfectionist soundman, indicated to Fred that we would have to re-shoot the entire sequence yet again.

Undaunted, I managed to contain my mounting frustration, reminding myself that I had enjoyed the privilege of undergoing quite a lot of personal psychoanalysis over the years and, thus, I resumed my position, ready for another "take", only to be told through the walkie-talkie that we must wait for the next two approaching airplanes to fly past. At last, we stumbled upon a moment of relative quiet and, consequently, I began to recite my line once again: "But what *exactly* does it tell us about *ourselves* if we have a masturbatory fantasy about someone *other* than our regular sexual partner?" I delivered my words with, I trust, full vocal resonance, breathing from my diaphragm. Upon having done so, I felt tremendously relieved, and, also, eager to move to the next sequence; but, sadly, Fred then came running up the length of the bridge to join me, wrapped warmly in his puffa jacket, and apologised: "Sorry, Brett, we shall have to do this line yet again. You were absolutely brilliant ... absolutely brilliant ... but there was a young hooligan jumping up and down behind you, purposely ruining the shot." Because Fred had insisted that I must not wear my comfortable floor-length overcoat in this sequence "for aesthetic reasons", icicles had, by this point, begun to form on my eyelashes. Fred took pity on my frozen state, and he started to pat my back and shoulders in a vigorous manner, in the hope of restoring my blood circulation. Unfortunately, in doing so, he dislodged the microphone wire taped carefully to my pectoral region and, as a result, Simon, the sound engineer, had to sprint up the bridge, looking mortified, and then tried desperately to rectify the situation.

After another top-up of powder from the eternally patient makeup artist, and further fiddlings with the microphone, we braced ourselves for yet another "take".

When I had told various psychotherapeutic colleagues that Channel Five had commissioned me to make a documentary, many of them responded with unmitigated envy or jealousy: "God, how glamorous. I wish I were doing that. How much are they paying you?" As I braced myself to recite my line in the freezing cold for the umpteenth time, I fully appreciated that making a film offers absolutely no glamour at all. Indeed, I had to wake up at 5.00 a.m. that very morning, knowing that, in all likelihood, we would not finish filming until near-on midnight. Certainly, I would have much preferred to spend the day seated in the comfy leather chair of my centrally heated consulting room. After all, on my ordinary clinical days, I do not have to arrive at work until the luxuriously late hour of 6.45 a.m., in time for my first patient at 7.00 a.m.

Finally, the tugboats and the airplanes and the obstreperous commuters decided to take pity on my near-glacial circulatory condition, and they all managed to remain quiet for fifteen seconds, just long enough for me to speak my carefully chosen words yet again, and this time without interruption. After I had done so, Fred cried with ecstasy through the walkie-talkie, "Excellent! Into the van everyone!" As we had to adhere to a tightly timed schedule, we then headed for the Piazza in Covent Garden where we would film the next shot. Fortunately, our young runner kindly produced my greatcoat and draped it over my shoulders, and then, this generous soul asked me whether I would like anything to drink. "Hot water, please", I murmured feebly, and off she dashed to the local Starbucks coffee house in search of my medicine.

Retrospectively, I feel rather sheepish to have complained in any way; after all, I had just completed a large-scale research project, fully funded by the broadcasters themselves, which eventually formed the basis of a popular psychology book for the publishers Allen Lane (Kahr, 2007a), the hardback imprint of Penguin Books. I also enjoyed the wonderful opportunity to work with a carefully selected team of creative and vivacious television professionals; and, most of all, several million people eventually came to watch this film, which, I trust, might have helped to alleviate the widespread shame and guilt that many men and women experience in relation to their private masturbatory and coital sexual fantasies. All in all, I would describe myself as pleased with the final result. But, nevertheless, no one should *ever* envy the television presenter, because those ostensibly glamorous moments really do not exist.

After my morning of filming in Southwark, not far from the newly restored Globe Theatre of Shakespearean fame, the team and I journeyed to Central London in a convoy of vans. The production coordinator, the makeup artist, and the runner had all bundled into one vehicle, and I took a seat in the camera van with Fred, the Producer-Director, with Will, our clever cameraman who had recently won an award from the British Academy of Film and Television Arts (the British version of the Oscars), and with Simon, the sound engineer. And, with a plastic cup of hot water in hand, we drove into the heart of town for our next shots.

Following an interminably long period of scouting out locations and setting up camera angles, I then embarked upon four or five hours of walking through various streets of Covent Garden: The Piazza, Neal Street, and many others besides. This time, Will's camera remained in full view, no longer positioned at the end of a bridge; and I soon began to master the fine art of walking and talking simultaneously, in preparation for a series of travelling shots. Fred barked out quite a number of relatively challenging directorial instructions: "Now, Brett, start here at this traffic cone, then walk forward about twenty paces, and as you pass by the green-painted door on the left, turn your head sharply to the right, then look over your shoulder and walk out of the shot, while you are saying your lines." I smiled to myself internally, realising that I understood very little of what Fred had just requested, but, after a little practice run, I discovered that I had absorbed more of the directions than I had thought, and Fred patted me on the head, flattering me, "Ah, Brett, you're quite the old pro." So far, so good ...

For this scene I recited an historically orientated line: "In the nineteenth century, psychiatrists believed that anybody who had a sexual fantasy must be either a degenerate or a pervert; indeed, Sigmund Freud believed that if you fantasise, then you must be very sexually unfulfilled." Apparently, the combination of a film crew clogging up a narrow street in Covent Garden, with a balding, bespectacled presenter talking about degeneration and perversion, had proved too irresistible for a group of teenage lads who took every opportunity to insert themselves into the shot, pull their trousers down, and "moon" us. With impeccable charm, Fred tried to reason with them and, eventually, they acceded and disappeared from view. Needless to say, we had to re-shoot this particular sequence six or seven more times.

Although no one in the streets recognised me at all, crowds of people kept gathering round to watch the filming process. Goodness only knows what people found so intriguing – perhaps, at some unconscious level, the sight of a camera pointed so exclusively at one man's face activated a yearning to be looked at attentively by the preoedipal mother. Whatever the explanation, various onlookers became quite absorbed by our outdoor shooting, and as I began to walk through the streets of London, a bevy of strangers started to follow in my footsteps, maintaining only a slightly respectful distance from the cameras. Japanese tourists kept stopping us for a photograph and, of course, numerous people constantly asked us, "What are you filming?"

Will and Simon, an inveterate double-act who had worked together before, knew only too well that, if we told the truth, we would soon become lost in conversation for hours, with bystanders desperate to learn more about sexual fantasies; thus, without missing a beat, whenever anyone enquired which channel we worked for, these camera and sound supremos would reply in unison, "We're from the Christian Channel." Generally, this proved to be a sufficiently sober rejoinder, and inquisitive members of the public would then walk away at a fast pace, unimpressed by the ostensible sexlessness of the Christian Channel. If we had told them the actual title of our programme – *Britain's Sexual Fantasies* – we would have had to endure an unending interrogation. At one point, a devout practising Christian accosted us, and, after Will and Simon had informed him of our supposed Christian credentials, he asked me the name of the church to which I belong. Caught off guard, I muttered something both unconvincing and incomprehensible, and I felt very guilty to be masquerading as a roving Christian Channel reporter.

By 7.00 p.m., we wended our way towards Oxford Street, as Fred had insisted on filming one of my lines set against a huge crowd. Unfortunately, the large red buses and the omnipresent street sweepers on Oxford Street made much more noise than the airplanes or tugboats at the Millennium Bridge location, and it took us one hour or more in freezing conditions for me to pontificate about the meaning of heterosexual people who have homosexual fantasies, and vice versa. As I walked down Oxford Street, with the camera practically stuck up against my face for a tight close-up, revealing every wrinkle on my skin, Fred continued shouting, "Running up ... speed ... and action!", whereupon I expounded, "Our survey has indicated that many self-identified heterosexual people have homosexual fantasies, and many gay men and lesbians have heterosexual fantasies." Because of the noises from the streets, we had to shoot and re-shoot and then re-shoot this little sequence yet again, with Fred constantly shouting, "Louder, Brett, louder." At this point, I found myself not only frozen, but, also, exhausted as my otherwise sturdy voice had become extremely ragged from an entire day of exterior filming. Furthermore, I felt rather silly talking about heterosexual and homosexual fantasies on Oxford Street at the top of my lungs. The crowds continued to walk by, fascinated and perplexed by my rantings. I know that had it not been for the very visible presence of the camera and the sound boom, the passers-by might have thought that I had just escaped from a nearby psychiatric institution, as I seemed to be talking to myself!

Because the noise problem had proved so relentless, we had to film this one small sequence literally fifty or sixty times. Some documentary makers might regard this as excessive, but the intrepid and highly professional Fred Casella prided himself on his absolute perfectionism, and I trusted him implicitly, having chosen him out of a large number of potential short-listed candidates for the job of Producer-Director.

As my tired feet began to bleed in my tight, newly purchased leather shoes – a result of having to stand the entire day – the well-known popular actor Ross Kemp, a former star of the British soap opera *EastEnders*, suddenly ambled past me on my left side as I began to speak my little line for the forty-third time. Infinitely more experienced before a camera than I will ever be, the generous Mr. Kemp flashed a deeply supportive and sympathetic smile as he walked up Oxford Street, as if to say, "Good on you, mate, I really do know how exhausting filming can be!" This one simple gesture of kindness from a veteran performer certainly helped to fortify me for the remaining scenes in the gardens of Soho Square.

At nearly 10.00 p.m., we finally finished filming the last sequence of the day, about the potential dangerousness of certain sexual fantasies and about the role of early sexual abuse in the genesis of adult sexual fantasies. Fred took mercy on me, and he allowed me to shoot this last segment seated comfortably on a park bench. Needless to say, a fire from a nearby building caused further delays but, thankfully, no one perished, and the crowd cheered the valiant fire brigade who, rightfully, had begun to attract far more attention than our tiny film crew.

After reciting the final line, "If you have been at all disturbed by anything that you have heard in this programme, then you might want to consider contacting a registered mental health professional", Fred announced, "Well done, guys ... that's a wrap." Fred's words brought me unparalleled joy, and, with great relief, I collapsed on the park bench. My very maternal Executive Producer, Dunja Noack, then trundled me into a waiting taxicab to escort me back home. After an hour in a near-boiling bath, my body temperature finally returned to normal, and I slept soundly, braced for yet another day of filming.

I hope that I have sketched out the often unexpected, fortuitous twists and turns by which an innocent lunch in the spring of 2002 became transmogrified into a national television programme, ultimately broadcast in the autumn of 2005. When Oliver Rathbone and I sat down for soup in the bistro near the London School of Economics and Political Science, neither of us had ever imagined that the proposed book idea on sexual fantasies would eventually develop in this way. As I have indicated, this adventure proved to be rather lacking in glamour. It consisted, rather, of much waiting, much uncertainty, and an immense amount of hard work, composed of many long weekends of physically exhausting interviewing and data analysis, crammed into windows of opportunity amid the regular, uncancellable sessions of my full-time clinical practice and my domestic commitments. And yet, it certainly proved to be the most extraordinary of journeys and taught me so much about the hidden contours and caverns of the human mind. I remain quite humbled by what I learned and by what I hope to have shared not only in the documentary but, also, in various books (e.g., Kahr, 2007a, 2008a, 2008b).

But sometimes, late at night, I wonder why it had taken me three years to make a forty-seven-minute film.

After recuperating from the draining process of filming, the production team then set about editing this television documentary, ensuring that they had pieced the different segments together in a coherent fashion and that they had managed to adjust the colour and sound quality to exactly the right levels. Of course, having no expertise whatsoever in these technical areas, I deferred to the skills and talents of the production team, but I did pop into the editing suite from time to time to watch the show develop and unfold and to ensure that the narrative made psychological sense. I also had to return to the studio for some additional indoor filming, for some further close-ups, and for the reciting of the voice-over narration which would accompany some of the frames of footage.

Eventually, the film appeared on the United Kingdom's television network, Five, late in the evening, on 5th September, 2005. Regrettably, I could not watch the live transmission of the film with family and friends as I had had to travel out of London to Birmingham that very afternoon in my role as Resident Psychotherapist on B.B.C. Radio 2 in order to go on air at midnight. Consequently, I caught only the first few minutes of the programme in my Birmingham hotel room before proceeding to the B.B.C. recording studio for my broadcast. Having already trawled through the film several times during the editing process, I had become rather tired of seeing my face and hearing my voice by this point, and, in many ways, I felt pleased that I did not have to sit through it all again. Fortunately, a number of kindly people rang me afterwards to offer congratulations. The next day, I learned that the film had attracted approximately one million viewers – a very respectable ratings figure for a late-night British television programme unsuitable for young audiences.

As one might imagine, reviews appeared in quite a number of the main British broadsheet newspapers – most rather complimentary, but some less so. One of the papers waxed very snide; in fact, a certain critic became rather upset by my conclusion that many sexual fantasies derive from early childhood trauma, and this man then accused me in print of knowing far less about psychology than a first-year undergraduate. I must confess that this remark rather stung me, but I took it in my stride.

Two responses, in particular, pleased me greatly. Several days after the transmission of the film, while walking through the car park at the Tavistock Clinic where I then worked at the Tavistock Marital Studies Institute, a very senior member of staff, known for his conservatism, approached me and, quite unexpectedly, wrapped his arms around me with great enthusiasm and hugged me tightly. Although I had known this man for many years, I do not think that we had ever so much as shaken hands previously. But apparently, he enjoyed the film greatly and he waxed rhapsodic about how I had made an important contribution to the field of psychoanalysis. This unexpected and generous comment from a noted tribal elder certainly helped to alleviate the sting of the newspaper reporter who proclaimed in print that I knew much less about psychology than a newbie undergraduate.

And, some days after this, I received yet another truly welcome acknowledgement. A woman whom I did not know at all rang me out of the blue. She had found my telephone number, presumably through directory enquiries. She thanked me for having made the film and then proceeded to explain that for the whole of her adult life she had experienced immense shame and sleeplessness over what she regarded as her apparently unusual sexual fantasies. She told me that she had no idea *why* she had these particular fantasies, and this troubled her greatly. But now that she had watched *Britain's Sexual Fantasies* on television, she finally understood the origin and the meaning of her fantasies for the first time. This lady did not share the content of her fantasies with me, and I certainly did not ask her to do so. Instead, I told her that I deeply appreciated her telephone call, and that it pleased me to know that this forty-seven-minute film had proved to be of some value.

4

Making Slough Happy
A Television Experiment

I am seated on a swish leather banquette, discreetly tucked away in the alcove of a bustling, sun-streaked restaurant in Waterloo, South London, just a stone's throw from the Old Vic theatre, lunching with a very attractive, dynamic Welshwoman called Patricia Llewellyn – "Pat" to her friends – one of the United Kingdom's most enterprising independent television producers. I have known Pat for some time, having met her through her boyfriend, Ben Adler, also a television executive, with whom I had worked on a project one year previously. Pat owns a thriving company, Optomen Television, which supplies programmes to our nation's major terrestrial networks, such as the British Broadcasting Corporation and Channel Four Television. And, recently she has begun to conquer the world as well. Hugely creative, energetic, and successful – as well as charmingly self-effacing – Pat has specialised in making cookery programmes and, in her time, she has discovered quite a number of extremely popular chefs, most particularly Jamie Oliver – "The Naked Chef" – now a superstar here in the United Kingdom, and also culinary experts Clarissa Dickson Wright and Jennifer Paterson, better known as the "Two Fat Ladies". More recently, Pat has served as the brains behind several series of "restaurant transformation" programmes featuring the increasingly popular entrepreneur, ex-footballer Gordon Ramsay, the twenty-first-century equivalent of Julia Child or Delia Smith … with bite.

As I have never mastered the culinary arts, I remain very uncertain as to why this high priestess of grand cuisine has not only invited me to lunch but seems intent on paying for it as well.

Over roast suckling pig, an admittedly unusual, though tasty, choice, as well as a bottle of Retro 55, Pat explains that although cookery programmes and gardening programmes will never go out of fashion, all of her senior chums at the B.B.C. have told her that *psychology* will soon become a growth area, and some of the executives in the commissioning department – those benighted individuals who decide which programmes will eventually be transmitted into our homes – have even begun to speak of psychology as "the new gardening". Never one to miss an opportunity, Pat decides to pick my brains, knowing me to be a media-friendly mental health professional who has already worked in radio and television for quite some time.

Chewing on our delicious food, Pat and I engage in conversation about what sort of psychology programme I might wish to make. I respond instantly that I would love to write and present a multi-part documentary on the history of psychology, covering all of the great heroes and pioneers in the field, and surveying their major contributions. I try to sound as engaged as possible, but, as a trained clinician, I can tell quite quickly that, in spite of her sympathetic head nods, Pat really has little interest in bringing Sigmund Freud, Carl Gustav Jung, and Alfred Adler to the big screen. After all, none of them had bequeathed any memorable Austrian or Swiss recipes to us. I can see that Pat's interest has begun to wane, and in a kittenish way, she desperately attempts to stifle her yawns. A little voice inside my head tells me that this might be a good moment to mention the one-time bestseller, *Freud's Own Cookbook*, co-written by the popular Jungian analyst Dr. James Hillman (Hillman and Boer, 1985), which contains recipes for such delectable delicacies as "Banana O." and "Little Hansburgers", but decorum triumphs, and I swallow my thoughts with another sip of my costly drink.

Pat then explains that *she* has an idea that might be of interest. Clearly, she asked me about my own dream plans merely to humour me. This "free" lunch has had a secret agenda all along. It seems that some wag has proclaimed Swindon – a dour industrial town in the backwaters of England – as the most depressed location in the country. Would it not be wonderful, Pat beams, if she could send a team of psychotherapists into Swindon to cheer up the entire population? Would that be possible? Ethical? Crazy? According to Pat, this could be not only a socially responsible piece of television, but compulsive viewing as well – a sort of modern-day Freud meets *Beat the Clock*. Can the shrinks cure Swindon's melancholia in a mere matter of weeks?

Needless to say, Pat's idea has an instant appeal, and proves to be a great challenge. Even after an excruciatingly long day, having worked with ten private patients, back-to-back, in fifty-minute chunks, I often leave my consulting room feeling that I have made only the tiniest of impacts on the amelioration of psychological suffering in the United Kingdom. Pat's proposed project speaks instantly to my broader social and political desire to use psychotherapeutic and psychoanalytical ideas to reach the widest possible audience. But how could I ever treat the tens of thousands of neurotic individuals in Swindon, a place whose grimness has not escaped me, having visited there on a multitude of occasions, en route to many pleasant journeys to the bucolic Gloucestershire countryside?

I assure Pat that the idea intrigues me and that it would be a great treat to brainstorm with her and the Development Team at Optomen Television to see how we might cure Swindon of its misery without needing to bring the entire membership of the British Psychological Society, the Royal College of Psychiatrists, the United Kingdom Council for Psychotherapy, as well as the British Association for Counselling and Psychotherapy and, also, the British Confederation of Psychotherapists (since renamed as the British Psychoanalytic Council) into town as reinforcements. Pat seems deeply relieved by my encouraging response. As a cookery expert, she clearly wanted to meet with a workaday clinician to discover, first of all, whether anyone had ever "treated" an entire town before, and, second of all, whether such a seemingly mad idea might even be possible. If Pat could conjure up a plan for curing Swindon, this might well be her greatest recipe to date.

After a series of meetings with Ms. Llewellyn and her staff at Optomen Television, she and I crafted a blueprint for a sure-fire series: a team of five experts will be shipped into Swindon, consisting of a mental health professional (possibly me), a town planner, a workplace consultant, a physical trainer, and perhaps a social entrepreneur skilled in helping large groups of people to work together more effectively. Collectively, this expert group would offer its skills aplenty in an effort to improve the psychological state of the Swindonians. But Pat also wished to ensure that this proposed television series would be amusing and entertaining; hence, the members of her Development Team generated literally hundreds of ideas as to how we might improve everyone's mental health by importing a fleet of dancing policemen who would make people laugh by doing jigs in the town square and, also, by baking the world's largest-ever cake, hundreds of feet long, hundreds of feet wide, and hundreds of feet high, which could then be consumed by every one of the local residents, bringing a new meaning to community activity.

Although I have no objection to dancing police officers and delicious gargantuan cakes, I do feel obliged to underscore the importance of providing good, solid mental health interventions as a veritable bedrock for this project; and, in my own rather predictable way, I suggest to Pat and her colleagues that we might endeavour to identify those members of the town most in need of psychotherapy and then set up a series of analytically orientated groups that my professional colleagues and I could facilitate. The television executives look somewhat misty-eyed in response to my very traditional suggestion for promoting happiness (i.e., the "talking cure"), and one of them sneers, "Yes, of course we *could* offer them therapy, but it's not very visual." I explain that Sigmund Freud did not design psychoanalysis as a spectator sport. This cheeky television buck then replied, "Yes, that may be, but what will we *see* on screen? Just some chap looking sympathetic? Viewers will turn off in droves."

In any event, I did *not* recommend that we should offer psychotherapy on camera. Rather, I had thought that we might provide some short-term interventions *off-screen*, in the hope that this would make an impact, and that the participants could then speak about this experience afterwards, if they so wished.

Clearly, the needs of the television producer and the needs of the psychotherapist could not be more divergent, but I have always espoused the idea that, although we come from different traditions, we should strive to find ways to collaborate with one another nevertheless, because, at the end of the day, those of us who work in the mental health field can each reach only ten patients a day, at the very most, whereas the television supremos can make contact with literally hundreds of millions of people worldwide. Perhaps we have something to learn from them.

After many intense, creative discussions, we all agree that this emerging television programme should offer serious psychological interventions along with more playful, visual, fun-loving activities as well. I certainly could not object to that suggestion.

Eventually, a title emerges for our proposed four-part series: *Making Swindon Happy*. Cheers erupt throughout the Optomen Television offices, and everyone waltzes around the converted chocolate factory with inane grins, predicting that *Making Swindon Happy* will become "cult" television and will win all of the awards: Emmys, B.A.F.T.A.s, and the like. Further, we predict that this programme will become so successful that we shall have to repeat it in every downtrodden city in the land and, that, in due course, we could certainly create a franchise: *Making Basildon Happy*, *Making Scunthorpe Happy*, and *Making Puddleby-on-the Marsh Happy*, to boot. Now all we need is a commission from the B.B.C. for many millions of pounds!

I wait, and wait, and wait.

Indeed, I wait for quite a long time.

Three years later, Patricia Llewellyn invites me out for a dinner with Ben Adler, once her boyfriend, now her husband. In the intervening years, I had the privilege of attending their glamorous wedding, an event so star-studded that the "best man" began his toast with the following salutation: "Ladies and Gentlemen ... and Television Presenters ..." As we settle down to a Japanese meal round the corner from my consulting room in North West London's Hampstead, not far from the onetime home of Freud himself, Pat and Ben tell me gleefully that, after years of prevaricating, the B.B.C. has finally agreed to fund the project, and they thank me for having waited so patiently for so many years. Unfortunately, Swindon has fallen by the wayside because the B.B.C. has decided that Slough, an equally downtrodden town of 120,000 residents, in the county of Berkshire, would better suit their purposes. Thanks to its investment of a lot of money in promoting a sitcom starring Ricky Gervais called *The Office* – set in Slough – the B.B.C. could now count on viewers having already formed an affectionate relationship with that town, so, therefore, the pundits have decided that the programme must be called *Making Slough Happy*. Alas, the poor residents of Swindon will just have to make do with antidepressants and the placebo effect, at least for the time being.

Although the B.B.C. brass have axed Swindon, replacing it with Slough, I seem to have survived the in-house execution. Apparently, one of the commissioners liked my screen test and, should I be agreeable, I can become the resident psychotherapist for this television programme and use my clinical skills to transform the mental health of the Sloughians in just ten short weeks. I should be ecstatic that such a visionary project will now become a televisual reality at long last, but as the waitress brings our sushi, our salmon teriyaki, and our Kirin Ichiban beer, I find myself quaking, wondering how I shall manage to turn the neurotic misery of Slough into extraordinary happiness, especially as I work full-time in clinical practice, with barely a ten-minute lunch break. Pat and Ben assure me that filming days can be planned carefully in order to accommodate my restrictive clinical timetable but that I should be prepared to work late into the evening as well as every weekend. Fortunately, a fast train from Paddington Station can spirit me to Slough in a mere twenty minutes or so; thus, I should be able to make frequent appearances.

Thereafter, an endless round of television-related activities begins: meetings with the Producer, meetings with the Executive Producer, a meeting with the Assistant Producer, photo sessions with the B.B.C., additional photo sessions with the local newspapers in Slough, appearances on B.B.C. Radio 2, as well as broadcasts for the local Slough Radio station, Star F.M., hosted by the impossibly beautiful Angie Walker who looks like a young Marilyn Monroe. The Production Manager of the programme, Sarah Gowers, who has the thankless task of coordinating all of the administrative details of this increasingly behemoth project, telephones me six or seven times a day in order to pin me down to a raft of filming dates, experts' meetings, and such like. Our conversations always begin thus: "Can you manage Friday morning the 12th, Brett?" "No, sorry, Sarah, I am with my patients all morning." "What about Tuesday afternoon, the 16th – any good for you, Brett?" "No, sorry, Sarah, I'm with patients all afternoon." "Well, Brett, can you do the following Wednesday, late in the evening? We'll send a car for you and pick you up from your office." "Yes, Sarah, actually, that works quite well. It's a deal." Ten minutes later, the telephone rings again: "Sorry, Brett, it's Sarah. One of the other experts can't manage next Wednesday. Any chance we can go back to the Tuesday?" "No, sorry, Sarah, I still have my patients." "I just thought that maybe some of them could be cancelled, Brett." "No, sorry, Sarah, you must understand that these people have been coming to see me for years, at these regular times, and I cancel only for funerals, health scares, and family emergencies." "Oh, Brett, I see. Well, I'll have to get back to you."

Eventually, we select a date on which to begin filming, or rather, the Production Manager has selected a date – a Saturday in May – and she tells me in no uncertain terms that because all of the other team members can manage this particular time, it simply cannot be altered. Unfortunately, I have already registered to attend a three-day conference in Dublin that very weekend – the annual meeting of the International Association for Forensic Psychotherapy. I know, however, that I will have to find a way to make this work; and although I have already paid my subscription and booked my flight and, also, my hotel room, I will have no choice but to leave the conference mid-way through in order to fly to England, and then, once back home, wend my way to Slough.

I travel to Dublin, deliver my pre-conference dinner speech on the Thursday night, catch up with long-standing colleagues in the forensic mental health field, and then attend most of the conference papers on the Friday, during which time the Executive Producer bombards me with hourly faxes and telephone calls at my hotel room in order to brief me on the running order of our first day of filming. I elect to stay in Dublin for the main conference dinner on the Friday, especially as the incoming President has asked me to make a speech praising the contributions of the outgoing President. All my forensic colleagues, many of whom I have not seen for years, decide to party into the small hours of the morning, but, by 10.00 p.m., I return reluctantly to my hotel, as I must catch a 7.20 a.m. flight from Dublin in order to arrive in Slough by 10.00 a.m. And in order to catch the 7.20 a.m. departure, I must be at the airport by 6.00 a.m. And in order to be at the airport by 6.00 a.m., I must be in a taxi by 5.00 a.m. Thus, I request a wakeup call for 4.00 a.m. Of course, owing to the excitement and anxiety of the forthcoming shoot – a major four-part B.B.C. television series – I cannot fall asleep easily, and so I read through my briefing notes again and again in preparation for the filming, and I iron my shirts with care, as there will not be time to do anything domestic once I will have arrived in Slough. By 3.00 a.m., I drift into semi-consciousness, only to be awakened by the shrill ring of the telephone one hour later. I feel wretched and groggy, rather like a frightened first-year undergraduate who has "pulled an all-nighter" in order to finish my term paper minutes before the deadline. As I revive myself in the hotel shower, I curse Pat and Ben, I curse the B.B.C., and I curse myself for having agreed to undertake some thirty days of filming, which will absorb every hour of my non-clinical time over most of the next three months – intruding upon precious domestic time – and all for a social experiment with a very uncertain outcome.

After a worryingly bumpy flight, albeit a mercifully short one, I arrive at Heathrow Airport at 8.50 a.m. to be met by a very fancy car which Sarah Gowers has dispatched in order to shepherd me directly to Slough. Sarah had hoped that by providing me with a private driver, I would arrive "fresh" for the first day of filming. Sadly, she did not reckon on the fact that I have had only one hour of sleep. Perhaps I should have left the conference the night before, but having already booked, and having yearned to see many lifelong colleagues, I opted for this particular arrangement. As an experienced television contributor, I actually own a 25-millilitre tube of concealer makeup – *Fond de Teint Effet Velours 07* – and a small compact hand-mirror; and so, as the car nears our destination, I apply a dollop on each of the dark rings beneath my tired eyes and try to look reasonably sparkly, not least because the B.B.C. has told me that they chose me over the other possible psychotherapy contenders because I seem to have "life behind the eyes"!

Before I meet the residents of Slough, fifty of whom have signed up for a course of intensive life-transformation, I must film a series of "travelling shots" of me arriving in Slough for the very first time. The airport limousine driver has received strict instructions to drop me off on the motorway where I meet Sam Maynard, one of the two Producer-Directors, along with a fleet of his assistants. Martin, the soundman, laces a microphone through my shirt, which clips onto my tie, and then shuttles me into a B.B.C. hired car. Sarah, the Assistant Producer (one of three Sarahs on the core team), drives us onto the motorway, while Sam, perched in the front seat, turns round and shoves his camera right up against my face for a close-up and then asks me, "So, Brett, are you nervous?" I know that Sam would like me to answer "Yes", so that when he comes to edit the footage, he can build up some dramatic tension; and I already know from past experience with editors that the voice-over (which for this programme will be provided by the Academy Award-winning actor Jim Broadbent) will probably sound something like this: "To help make the residents of Slough happier, we've called in leading psychotherapist Brett Kahr. No stranger to helping people in trouble, Brett is the Resident Psychotherapist on B.B.C. Radio. But can he work his magic on the people of Berkshire?" So, to play along, I reply that I *do* have butterflies in my stomach, never having undertaken a project of this magnitude before. Actually, I am not particularly nervous, but having slept only one hour, and having just disembarked from a choppy flight, I am, instead, exhausted, though trying to be as buoyant as possible.

Because television directors fear technical hitches, such as passing airplanes that interfere with the sound quality, or film that becomes somehow damaged, every sequence must be shot, and re-shot, and then re-shot once again, until we have several "takes" in the "can". I spend the next half-hour explaining to Sam, over and over, in different intonations, that I have butterflies in my stomach, never having participated in a project of this magnitude before. It all seems very silly, not least because Sam then jumps out of the car and positions himself on the side of the motorway with his camera. He then instructs Sarah, the driver, to turn back on herself and to travel up the road at least two more times, so that Sam can shoot a sequence of my car arriving in Slough. Apparently, a mere shot of me in the back seat, speaking about my apprehension of curing Slough, will not provide the viewers at home with sufficient evidence that I have actually come all the way from London. In television land, my arrival in the county of Berkshire must be *seen*. And though the shot of my car arriving in the chosen town of Slough will occupy merely two or three seconds of on-air time – certainly no more than that – we spend yet another half hour driving up and down and up and down the motorway once again until Sam satisfies himself that he has captured a glimpse of me through a smoky-glass window, dashing by at lightning speed.

Eventually, I arrive at a huge mansion not far from Slough itself – Caversham House – once home to the G.C.H.Q. (Government Communications Headquarters) during World War II and, subsequently, the offices of B.B.C. Radio Berkshire. Once there, I meet my fellow experts (now six in total): a talented young economist who believes that governments should devote their time to improving subjective wellbeing rather than to gross national product; a social entrepreneur who received the O.B.E. decoration – Officer of the Most Excellent Order of the British Empire – from Her Majesty The Queen for having turned the downtrodden London satellite of Bromley-by-Bow into a thriving creative community; two glamorous workplace consultants who have made quite an impact by transforming the culture of various office environments; a statistically-minded research psychologist who will have the onerous task of conducting empirical work throughout our project, testing and retesting the levels of happiness of the natives of Slough on a number of standardised and, also, newly-created questionnaires; and yours truly as the provider of a depth-psychological contribution, whose precise nature we have not yet quite determined. Nicola Moody, a former Commissioner within the B.B.C. and now a freelance Executive Producer for Optomen Television, greets us and briefs us on our task. For the first day of filming, we must meet the "Slough 50", those men and women who have volunteered to work with the six of us at close quarters over the next few months, during which time we, the experts, must improve their lives, almost beyond recognition, and boost their baseline happiness ratings to states of near delirium.

Dr. Richard Stevens (1983a), the research psychologist, and, also, the author of a very good student guide to the work of Sigmund Freud, as well as a comparable tome about the contributions of the noted psychoanalyst Erik Erikson (Stevens, 1983b), has already administered one round of pre-questionnaires to the Slough 50. Apparently, according to the initial data, quite a number of these people suffer from so much depression that their baseline happiness levels before the project seem to be on a par with the inhabitants of most Third World countries. We certainly have our task cut out for us as we must now spread joy and sunshine, change the culture of their offices, improve their family relationships, work on their sex lives, lift their depressions, and get the residents of Slough to hum together like a creative community. The Slough 50 will serve as ambassadors and they will be our links to the remaining 119,950 or so residents of Slough, many of whom will feature in the programme as well.

As the sole mental health clinician among the six experts, I have negotiated that I will provide as much off-camera individual psychotherapy and group psychotherapy to the Slough 50 as I can manage in the time available – in all likelihood, short-term psychodynamically orientated psychotherapy. We have not quite yet established which residents will come to see me, nor where, nor, indeed, at what frequency. Nicola has decided, quite rightly, that I must meet them first.

But in the view of the fact that I cannot, and will not, practise actual psychotherapy on camera in front of a potentially limitless audience of multiple millions of Britons, the producers have insisted that we must find another role for me which will utilise my psychological knowledge and skills and which will also be "visual" and, above all, not compromise my professional code of clinical confidentiality in any way.

Nicola Moody, the Executive Producer, tells me that a "little bird" has informed her that in my spare time I occasionally compose songs and play the piano and sing, and that I have written music for the theatre – all true. Perhaps, she proposed, I could create a Slough Choir? After all, I could use my psychotherapeutic capacities to promote group cohesion, and I could deploy my musical skills to help the people of Slough to find their voices. I suddenly remember that throughout much of the 1990s, I did serve first as Musical Director, and next as author, of several annual Tavistock Clinic pantomimes, and then, in 1997, I became the first Musical Director of the Tavistock Clinic Choir. I reasoned that if I could manage to extract some tuneful sounds from a group of predominantly silent British National Health service psychoanalysts and psychotherapists and psychiatric nurses, I might just stand a chance of getting the residents of Slough to warble as well.

And so, after some coaxing, I agree that I shall attempt to become a singing psychotherapist of sorts, and, in my first meeting with the Slough 50, I invite them all to join me in learning the jaunty anthem of happiness, "Put On a Happy Face", from the popular Broadway musical *Bye Bye Birdie*. After our first rendition, with me on piano, the previously grey group of Sloughians suddenly erupts in peals of laughter and jubilation, and the heights of happiness seem within immediate reach. By the end of the first day of filming, I have had good conversations with all fifty key participants, and we have established a date for the first rehearsal of the Slough Choir. It seems that I have also agreed to write a pop song which will be performed at a big concert in the Slough town centre on the final day of filming and which will serve as the climax to the television series.

As I head back to London at the end of the day, this time on the train (as Sarah Gowers needs to keep a tight eye on the budget and cannot always afford to transport me by luxury limousine), I can just about hear Jim Broadbent's voice-over narration in my mind: "Well, Brett has rashly agreed to write a pop song for the residents of Slough. But can he pull it off? Will the Slough 50 disappoint him? Will they be able to sing on key? Will it all prove to be a great disaster? Tune in at nine o'clock next week."

For those people who did not have a chance to watch the television series, I shall now provide a *very* brief overview of what we actually did in Slough. As I write this sometime after my visits to Berkshire, I have elected to pen this portion of the narrative in the past tense, in contrast to the first part of this chapter, which I had written more freshly in the present tense during the early days of filming.

***

Although Optomen Television had originally engaged me to introduce the residents of Slough to the art of psychotherapy, it soon became apparent that owing to the very large number of Sloughians – roughly 120,000 in total – any free treatment that I could provide would be merely a token gesture. However, the producers and I thought that it might be worthwhile to see whether psychotherapy could, in fact, be undertaken outside of the familiarity and security of my London consulting room.

At the very outset of my sojourns, one of the "Slough 50", a robust and charming young man, approached me and asked me for a psychotherapy consultation. The producers found us a private office, and, in due course, he and I sat down to talk. This gentleman, whom I shall call "Mehmet", told me that although he enjoys his family life, his job, his relationship with his girlfriend, as well as a broad circle of friends, he decided to apply for a spot on this television programme because he hoped that one of the experts could help him conquer a crippling fear, namely, a terror of stepping into the London Underground. Although he lived in Slough for his entire life, he felt that his phobia of the "tube" prevented him from ever moving to London and had kept him a virtual prisoner in Slough.

Mehmet began to discuss his fear of travelling by public transport in our nation's capital and explained that although he and his family rarely visited London, due to financial restrictions, he did, on occasion, ride the tube during his boyhood. I asked Mehmet *when*, precisely, the fear of the underground first emerged, and he responded in no uncertain terms, "Oh, maybe seven years ago." Naturally, I wondered aloud what had occurred in his life seven years previously, and he revealed that he could not recall much of any note, claiming that, back in 1998, he simply went about his business, working, socialising, and getting on with life, much as he did in 2005, the year in which we made *Making Slough Happy*. In spite of numerous investigations on my part, I could not find any particular trigger that would have accounted for the onset of Mehmet's phobia at that particular time.

In the absence of being able to provide an instant or clever answer, I simply permitted the free-associative process to unfold during our initial conversation, and I entreated Mehmet to talk about whatever thoughts and images popped into his mind. A very engaging person, he spoke freely and happily, painting a very helpful portrait of his current life, of his colleagues at the office, of his partner, and of his relatives. At one point, Mehmet mentioned that he had a large constellation of siblings, describing himself as "one of eight". But half an hour later in the conversation, Mehmet spoke again about his many brothers and sisters, and, at that moment, he made a passing reference to "the seven of us". As someone who enjoys obsessing over tiny, seemingly insignificant details in the psychotherapeutic narrative, I wondered whether I had misheard Mehmet the first time round. Did he have six siblings ("the seven of us"), or did he have seven brothers and sisters ("one of eight")? This seeming discrepancy troubled me, and, consequently, I asked for clarification.

Mehmet replied with hesitation, "Ah, did I confuse you? Well, I'm not surprised. You see, we *were* eight, but *now* we're seven. So, I guess that means that I have six brothers and sisters. But sometimes, I still think that I have seven siblings. Sorry to have confused you." In a soft, understated voice, I asked Mehmet what had happened, having hypothesised already that he must have suffered a sibling bereavement somewhere along the line. Mehmet turned his head downwards and told me that, several years ago, his eldest sister, "Zofia", had dropped dead of a heart attack at the age of only twenty-five. This death came as huge and sudden shock, and the family still missed her greatly, although, according to Mehmet, his relatives still find it very difficult to talk about Zofia.

I asked whether Mehmet could tell me anything more about the circumstances of Zofia's death. "Yes, of course," he replied, "she was just coming back from her first day in her new job." "In Slough?" I wondered. "Oh no", he rebutted, "in London." Apparently, Zofia had only recently relocated from Slough to London to take up a position in a financial institution, and her parents and siblings all bristled with pride, not least as she had become the first person in the family to work in such a highly paid position. I commiserated with Mehmet on this loss and commented that I could see from his expressions and hear in his voice that he still felt quite sad at the loss of his big sister, understandably so. Mehmet nodded in appreciation of my very simple comments, acknowledging his bereavement. I then inquired if he knew precisely *where* Zofia had died, and *when*? He responded, "Yes, she died on Wednesday, 18th March, 1998, at about 6.30 in the evening." Mehmet's description struck me, and I underscored, "The date is still very much at the forefront of your mind." "Very much so," he replied, "I will never forget her."

I continued to engage Mehmet on this matter and commented that if Zofia had died on a Wednesday, at 6.30 p.m., perhaps she had only recently finished her work day. "Yes, she was walking on the street, back towards her new flat," he explained, "and then, the heart attack took her from us." "Where did she work?" I inquired. "Oh, in some big banking house in the City of London", he told me. "And where was her flat?" I asked. "Oh, in Stoke Newington, in North London", he clarified.

With all of this important information to hand, I then asked Mehmet whether he knew exactly *how* Zofia travelled to and from the office. He explained that, to the best of his knowledge, she might have taken a taxi, or that she might, perhaps, have walked. As a Londoner, I hypothesised to Mehmet that a daily taxi from Stoke Newington to the City would be quite expensive, and that the walk would take an extremely long time. I wondered, perhaps, whether she took public transport. Suddenly, Mehmet burst into tears, and blubbed, "I suppose she took the underground. Do you think she took the underground?" I told him that I could not be certain, but I mentioned that most people newly arrived in London from the provinces, especially young people who cannot yet afford a car, will ride the tube and that it seemed to me highly possible that his sister might have done so as well. Tears streamed down Mehmet's cheeks as he reflected about Zofia, but, to my surprise, he still made no connection whatsoever between his own phobia of the underground and the possibility that his sister might have died from a heart attack shortly after having disembarked from a tube station.

I then reminded Mehmet, rather gently, that at the outset of our conversation he had told me that he stopped going to London approximately seven years ago – in 1998 – the very year of Zofia's death. At last, Mehmet's eyes brightened, and he gasped, "My God, I never thought of that. Jesus Christ, the timing is exact. But I never thought about this. You think I can't tolerate the tube because of my sister?" I explained that I could not be certain, but that we might well consider this possibility. He cried a bit more, and then he wiped his face, and turned to me, "Wow, they told me it might be a bit intense to talk to the 'shrink'. I really didn't see this coming."

Mehmet took a sip of water, and then breathed a deep sigh. He thanked me for speaking to him, and he told me that he would like to try an experiment. Next week, he would take his girlfriend to London for a romantic adventure, and, at some point, he would be brave and would purchase tickets for the underground. I wished him well, told him that I would be very happy to speak to him again in future should he find that useful, and I thanked him for his candour and for his hard work during what I knew to be his very first conversation with a mental health professional.

Two weeks later, one of the assistant producers of the television programme came running towards me, and clapped me on the back, describing me as a "miracle worker". Apparently, Mehmet had indeed gone to London with his partner; and, as promised, he braved the tube with few difficulties, for the first time in seven years. He took his girlfriend all over London and it seems that they had a ball.

I certainly did not feel like a miracle worker. Although moved by my consultation with Mehmet, I could not believe the simplicity of our conversation. His sister died seven years ago, after having left Slough, while working in London; and shortly thereafter, Mehmet developed a tube phobia which prevented him from seeking employment in the capital, and which kept him imprisoned in Slough. It all made great sense, and I did not have to engage in any particularly deep analysis. Of course, in the context of this private consultation, sponsored by a B.B.C. television project, formal psychoanalysis would be neither possible nor desirable; but, in one simple, confidential conversation, I helped a young man to talk about a painful bereavement which still caused him great anguish, understandably so.

In many respects, I had not appreciated that Slough, though separated from London by merely a short train ride, could not be more different from the cosmopolitan, sophisticated world that I inhabited daily in Hampstead, North West London, and had done so for years and years. Although that part of London boasts a veritable army of psychotherapists and psychologists, Slough had at that time, to the best of my knowledge, only one properly trained psychotherapist, and he actually spent most of his time working at a clinic in London! Thus, many Sloughians had but meagre emotional vocabulary and, like Freud's early patients, felt very psychologically starved. Hence, a simple conversation about a sibling death provided immense relief and allowed a young man to resolve a long-standing symptom. If only the rest of my psychotherapeutic practice proved so simple and straightforward.

Having undertaken this consultation with Mehmet, it soon became clear to me that although I could try to offer forty-nine more consultations of this variety to the "Slough 50", that would prove to be a very time-consuming endeavour, and, moreover, none of this material could be shown on the television programme, owing to the demands of clinical confidentiality. If the B.B.C. wished to use me, we would have to find something for me to do which would not involve psychotherapeutic sessions. One of the producers, trained initially as a classicist and hence quite fluent in Greek and Latin, jested with me that I had to do something "on camera" as opposed to "*in camera*" (i.e., in private).

Music, of course, became the vehicle, and after many discussions, the producers and I decided that I would indeed establish a special Slough Choir. Nicola Moody and the other television executives knew that music brought me much happiness and creative pleasure, and they hoped that I would be able to share this enthusiasm with the participants in this four-part series. All of the choir sessions would be filmed, and we would not be restricted by confidentiality.

Having already established choirs in a number of different psychiatric in-patient and out-patient settings, and having inaugurated the Tavistock Clinic Choir, I felt confident that I would be able to conjure something useful for our television programmes, and so, several times a week, I took the train to Slough after I had finished work with my regular analytical patients in London and I would then facilitate an evening choir with approximately fifteen of the Slough 50. The group consisted of a nice mixture of men and women, including the very old and the very young, as well as the enthusiastic and the depressed. The producers had found me a marvellous large room in a nearby nunnery, replete with an excellent, freshly tuned baby grand piano; and, twice-weekly, I seated myself at the keyboard and attempted to encourage the eager members of this newly consecrated choir to sing.

With one exception, most of the participants in the Slough Choir had virtually no musical training, and many of them had tiny, wafer-thin voices, inhibited by anxiety, and by lack of experience in being heard. So, I proceeded slowly and gently, just as I had done with the psychiatric choirs that I had facilitated, and just as I had done with the staff at the Tavistock Clinic, none of whom could sing especially well, even though all of these people yearned to do so.

As the weeks unfolded, confidence began to grow, and the *pianissimo* voices gradually swelled to a *mezzo forte*. Naturally, we had to navigate some dramas along the way. One of the members of the choir, a young housewife, threatened to drop out, as she believed that she could not possibly compete with the other members in terms of volume, pitch, or vocal dexterity. The producers seized upon this woman, and filmed her extensively, and I could readily foresee that they hoped to shape a really compelling storyline around her: "Will she continue with the choir and satisfy her dream of singing "Happy Birthday" to her child, or will she bottle out? And can Brett help?"

Although one might hypothesise that the fear of singing out loud, of using one's throat, and of enjoying one's voice, can be linked to depressive affects and to early discouraging experiences, I had to be careful not to expose this woman's psychological history on television. But I could help her in an ordinary way by offering private singing lessons at the piano. To my delight, and to the pleasure of the producers (who had, at last, found a way to use footage of me that did not violate confidentiality at all), this sweet lady readily took up the offer and, step by step, I coached her through "Happy Birthday to You" until she had the confidence to stand on a rostrum, all by herself, and sing the song loudly and proudly at the top of her lungs. Tears and laughter followed in equal amounts as she marvelled at her achievement, something which she regarded as a major breakthrough. Eventually, she returned home and sang happy birthday to her son for the first time ever (Kahr, 2020c).

During the upcoming weeks and months, in which I focused on the Slough Choir, the other experts did magnificent work in their own areas of specialisation. Richard Reeves, a multi-talented graduate of the University of Oxford, who had worked, *inter alia*, as a correspondent for *The Guardian* newspaper, as an author, and also as a policy adviser, launched himself into the revitalisation of Slough in the most creative and fearless manner, preaching sermons in a house of worship, lecturing on the virtues of happiness with a megaphone on the open streets, and launching a campaign to remove television sets from the homes of the Slough 50 to help them to progress beyond their stagnant lives as "couch potatoes". A man of immense popularity and personal charm, he made a big impact in Slough, and he turned his hand to anything and everything with zest and good cheer. Andrew Mawson, a social entrepreneur, had, as we noted, received an O.B.E. from Her Majesty Queen Elizabeth II in the Millennium New Year's Honours List for his work on revitalising the downtrodden district, Bromley-by-Bow, in the London Borough of Tower Hamlets, having turned that part of the East End into a thriving example of "healthy living". A warm-hearted Yorkshireman, Andrew worked vigorously with the members of local government in Slough to advise on certain structural changes which might be implemented in order to improve transport, industry, economy, and lifestyle. Jessica Pryce-Jones, a dynamic, super-smart woman, who founded a high-level workplace consultancy organisation called "iOpener Institute", and her affable colleague Philippa Chapman, ventured into many of Slough's family businesses and did wonders to sort out conflicts on the factory floor. And Dr. Richard Stevens, the distinguished academic psychologist and sometime Head of the Psychology Department at the Open University, undertook a number of activities to engage the people of Slough, launching wonderful outdoor exercise programmes and such. He also designed and supervised the research project which allowed us to collect pre-intervention, peri-intervention, and post-intervention data about the impact of our efforts on the levels of happiness in Berkshire. I felt very privileged to collaborate with such a formidable team of experts, and I learned an immense amount from all of them.

As the months of filming proceeded, Dr. Stevens offered us encouraging news. His mid-term research data revealed that, according to the self-report measures of the participants themselves, happiness ratings had increased dramatically. Based on his intensive study, conducted throughout the project (which included the administration of a number of tests, not least his very own "Happiness Domains", his "Slough Questionnaire" and his "Affectometer"), Dr. Stevens (2005) demonstrated that the average level of happiness among the residents of Slough increased by approximately thirty-three per cent, thus rendering the happiness ratings of life satisfaction even higher than the already impressive results among the residents of Scandinavia. In fact, the people in our television programme no longer regarded themselves as depressed or apathetic. The Slough 50 and their families now felt seen and heard, respected and encouraged, and richly involved in a project that became increasingly community-based and impactful. Buoyed by these encouraging results, the experts and the production team became more and more hopeful that we might actually achieve something uplifting, worthwhile and, perhaps, enduring.

Travel and timetabling proved to be a challenge for all of the experts. None of us lived in Slough, and all of us had other professional commitments and, of course, family responsibilities, which prevented us from moving to Berkshire for the three months of filming. As a practising clinician, I had perhaps the most restricted timetable of all, as I could not, and would not, cancel any of my regular patients to undertake filming; thus, as I have already indicated, the producers thoughtfully accommodated my availability, and arranged for me to be filmed during the evening and on weekends as much as possible. In consequence, I often missed seeing Andrew, Jess, Philippa, and the two Richards – my fellow experts – except for our occasional team meetings in which we would review our ongoing progress. It soon became very clear that each of us had embarked on completely separate interventions. At one team meeting, I wondered whether the time had come for us all to join forces and to plan a large "closing" event which would integrate our skills and capacities, and which would serve as a hopefully inspiring ending to the final episode of this four-part television series. Drawing upon my musical training, I suggested that we might put on a show!

With tremendous enthusiasm and encouragement, the other experts agreed that we should join forces and, thus, we set about creating a day of celebration. Andrew Mawson would supervise the physical transformation of the Slough town centre into a giant performing space with a large, raised stage. Richard Reeves and Richard Stevens would mobilise individuals and groups from the town to participate as street entertainers, acrobats, dancers, and vendors. Jessica Pryce-Jones and Philippa Chapman would enlist the help of the local industries. And I would take responsibility for composing a special song for the Slough Choir and for its rehearsal and staging. Thankfully, the accomplished team of B.B.C. television executives and researchers provided fantastic encouragement and administrative support of this unusual project.

Over the years, in my rare spare time, I have written songs for West End theatre artists and for performers overseas, all of whom have excellent, professionally trained voices with a wide vocal range. I knew that, on this occasion, I would have to create something far simpler for the Slough Choir – a song which would encapsulate the essence of *Making Slough Happy*, a televisual experiment in psychological and social transformation. My frequent train journeys from Paddington Station in London to Slough, and back, afforded me some protected time in which to compose a hopefully catchy tune with singable lyrics. Eventually, it occurred to me that if we could bring people together in a large community project, if we could offer special support and carefully tailored interventions to people in need, and if we could boost happiness ratings in Slough, why could this model not become a template for other towns and cities throughout the United Kingdom and beyond? Perhaps, over time, we *could* make Slough happy, and then Swindon, and then Basingstoke, and then Crewe. (After all, Pat Llewellyn, the head of Optomen, had already expressed a hope that *Making Slough Happy* might one day become a franchise). Perhaps, therefore, in due course, we could change the world. And so, in a moment of arguably hypomanic enthusiasm, I penned the following song. The printed lyrics hardly do justice to the peppiness of the tune, and to the rich vocal harmonies, but hopefully, in the absence of being able to hear the music, readers might still be able to gauge something of the rhythm.

WE'RE GONNA CHANGE THE WORLD.

Though we are facing a planet that's troubling,
Pulses are racing, adrenaline's bubbling,
We are ablaze with unbeatable energy,
Ready to change the world.

Battered and bruised but our soul is uncrushable,
Crazed and confused but our voice is unhushable,
Singing in unison, singing in harmony,
Ready to change the world.

We're gonna change the world,
Aren't we?
We're gonna change the world.
Turning our town into something terrific
By helping our sisters in need,
Embracing our brothers of every colour and creed.

In spite of our scars, we will not let them censure us.
Reach for the stars, we are bold and adventurous.
Maybe we'll stumble, but nevertheless,
We're going to give it a try.

We're gonna change the world,
Aren't we?
We're gonna change the world.

Turning our town into something terrific
By helping our sisters in need,
Embracing our brothers of every colour and creed.

We can improve each acre that we inhabit,
Life is a banquet with bounty beyond compare.
Jump out of bed, there's plenty of love so grab it.
People, it's time to declare:

Stand and be heard even though you are ill at ease.
Passions are stirred, we have great possibilities.
Poised on the brink of a brighter horizon,
Ready to change the world.

We're gonna ...
We're gonna change the world,
Aren't we?
We're gonna change the world.
Turning our town into something terrific
By helping our sisters in need,
Embracing our brothers of every colour and creed.

We're gonna ... change ... the ...
We're gonna change the world,
Change the world.

After setting the song to music, and polishing the lyrics, I then demonstrated the number to my fellow experts, on camera; and, to my delight, Andrew, Jess, Philippa, Richard, and Richard all agreed to participate in a final event which would culminate in a huge outdoor performance of "We're Gonna Change the World". Jessica Pryce-Jones, with whom I had developed a fond connection, confessed that she had previously trained as a flautist, and that although she had not had much time to make music in recent years, she would unearth her flute from the back of the cupboard and would join us as one of the musicians. We then set about our various tasks, giving ourselves approximately two weeks to prepare for what we hoped would be a climactic finale.

Shortly thereafter, I met once again with the Slough Choir, and I taught them the song. I think they enjoyed the fact that I had written something especially for them, and they all sang with bravura. Regrettably, in spite of their valiant efforts, the dozen or so members of the Slough Choir would hardly make a sufficiently impactful sound to fill the large town square. And it soon became quite clear that our tiny group would look rather sparse on the enormous stage which Andrew Mawson and his team would be constructing. Needless to say, we would need reinforcements, and so, we decided to recruit citizens from the wider Slough community to supplement our numbers, and to make this finale more full, more theatrical, and more group orientated. The participants in the Slough Choir began co-opting their relatives and friends; the members of the production team started to round up people from the streets; and we all gently twisted arms. Before long, our tiny Slough Choir had swelled into a large group of approximately 100 singers, including a bevy of angelic-voiced youngsters from the local primary school.

I knew that I would need help at this point, as one lone clinician-musician could not possibly manage to rehearse a choir of this size, especially as I had to return to London for my next day of sessions with patients. And so, I spoke to our ever-cheerful Production Manager, Sarah Gowers, and told her that I needed to enlist the services of an extremely talented full-time musician to help rehearse, conduct, orchestrate, and co-ordinate this big number. After hemming and hawing, Sarah managed to work wonders with the programme budget, and she succeeded in earmarking a fee for a musical consultant to support me and the Slough Choir. With funding in place, I telephoned my old friend, John Gladstone Smith, one of the most accomplished musicians in London's West End, and one of the most psychologically healthy to boot. We had first met at a West End song competition many years ago, and we became firm friends soon thereafter. During his long and distinguished career, John has worked for Andrew Lloyd Webber, and has served as Musical Director for many of Baron Lloyd Webber's productions. I, too, have had the privilege of working with John on a number of more modest projects, as has my wife, a professional singer. I trust John unreservedly, and I knew that the Slough Choir and its new recruits would warm to him greatly and that he would deliver exactly what we needed.

John and I convened at Paddington Station, and we took the train to Slough, planning our rehearsal programme en route. I then introduced him to the members of the Slough Choir, waiting eagerly for us at the nunnery, and I seated him behind the piano, and let him begin to work his magic. As a West End musical director, John often has the task of taking a group of extremely talented professional singers and making them sound even better. He brought all of that extraordinary know-how to bear upon the Slough Choir, and, after several rehearsals, he helped me to turn those meagre voices into bountiful instruments. He also assembled a team of local musicians to create a band, and he even found time to work personally with Jessica Pryce-Jones who would be joining us on flute.

A few weeks later, the big day finally arrived. John and I travelled in the very early morning by train to Slough, and then we headed straight for the town centre. To my delight, the television production crew had worked throughout the night with the local Berkshire residents and, together, they had already transformed an otherwise dreary public square into the most impressive of performing spaces, replete with stage, banners, streamers, audio speakers, and lights. Eventually, the crowds started to arrive, with dancers of every ethnicity, street musicians, jugglers, clowns, and men on stilts. The sleepy town soon came to life in the most starburst-like fashion, and everyone immersed themselves in the increasingly cheerful party atmosphere. Towards the end of the afternoon, the Slough Choir took to the stage, in front of an audience of several thousand local people, with the cameras recording our every move and our every sound. I made a short speech introducing the choir and the *Making Slough Happy* project, and then, joined by my fellow experts and by the members of the choir, we launched into our song, "We're Gonna Change the World". The enthusiastic crowds greeted our little musical effort with loud cheers, and I took immense pleasure in seeing the happy faces of the members of the Slough Choir, many of whom never thought that they would have the courage to sing out loud, let alone to do so in public.

Did we make Slough happy? Apparently, we did.

After we had completed our ten weeks of filming, Dr. Richard Stevens re-interviewed the Slough 50 to evaluate whether our "intervention" had helped, and it pleases me to report that, in every case, the participants in this unusual project claimed to have benefitted hugely, and their self-ratings on Richard's various specially designed questionnaires revealed large, statistically significant increases in levels of happiness. Apparently, we had done something right.

After several months of feverish, round-the-clock editing, the British Broadcasting Corporation trailered the programme and then launched a large-scale publicity campaign. As an experienced radio psychotherapist, the B.B.C. invited me to appear on dozens of radio programmes in the days leading up to transmission, talking about the project, about the importance of happiness for long-term mental and physical health, and about what can be done to ameliorate sadness and depression. Eventually, *Making Slough Happy* aired over four successive weeks, beginning on Tuesday, 15th November, 2005. We enjoyed the highly visible and popular 9.00 p.m. slot on the television channel B.B.C. 2, which guaranteed a very large number of viewers – nearly two million in total for each episode.

I confess that, after the airing of the first instalment, we received a very mixed reaction from the notoriously cynical British press. Although we garnered many favourable reviews, a number of journalists made some rather cutting remarks about the programme, attacking the London-based experts as somewhat imperialistic for having descended upon the unsuspecting residents of Slough. Others found us too peppy and accused us of shoving happiness down peoples' throats. However, as the series progressed across the next three weeks, some of the more jaded reporters began to revise their views and, after the transmission of the fourth and final episode in this series, one of our most outspoken critics apologised to us all in print in a major national newspaper for having misjudged our efforts so abruptly. This reporter had now watched our work over four hour-long episodes and had become increasingly immersed in these touching human stories of transformation and, moreover, had even enjoyed our finale concert. It seems that people could at last appreciate that rain-sodden British misery need not be a permanent state of mind.

After the programme ended, Jessica Pryce-Jones invited me and the other "experts" to facilitate a training day at the Saïd Business School at the University of Oxford, where we talked about our methodology to a group of very intelligent professionals from a variety of disciplines who wished to develop our contributions further. We discovered that happiness, though at first derided as a rather sappy concept, had now become part of the public discourse.

The B.B.C. produced a book as a "tie-in" with the television series, entitled *How to Be Happy*, written by the highly respected journalist Liz Hoggard (2005), based heavily upon interviews with the six Slough "experts". Designed to be read by the general public, the front cover bore a shiny orange "smiley" face with the inscription: "LIFE-CHANGING INSIGHTS FROM THE TV SERIES MAKING SLOUGH HAPPY". Not having read this book since its initial publication, I recently opened up a page at random, and I found myself staring at a chapter on the promotion of greater happiness in families, which contained an extract from one of Ms. Hoggard's (2005, p. 121) many conversations with me: "The key element in raising happy children is to love them unconditionally, but also offer boundaries. 'Children need boundaries, but boundaries are very different from discipline,' says BBC happiness expert Brett Kahr. He believes that the word 'discipline' has an inherently punitive quality to it, and overtones of a master-slave relationship. Truly loving parents will always want to set boundaries rather than discipline their child. In practice, this means granting them considerable autonomy while setting clear rules about what is and isn't permissible, then stepping back and letting them get on with it. All children find it easier to develop their potential if they know that, no matter what happens, they have a safe emotional base in the family." Mostly Hoggard, spurred by a thought or two from Kahr, this book reached a very wide audience and offered, hopefully, some sage advice. At any rate, having treated so many depressed patients crushed in childhood in the name of "discipline", it pleases me that I could speak out in this way.

In the wake of the broadcast of our experiment in Slough, serious discussions about happiness continued to filter into British public discourse. Eventually, in 2010, shortly after his election as Prime Minister of the United Kingdom, The Right Honourable David Cameron (2010) announced that happiness would actually constitute an official component of his political platform, and that his government would devote itself to the study of this topic, including its economic and medical benefits, as well as its psychological advantages. The subject even attracted serious attention in medical publications such as *The Lancet* (e.g., Easterly, 2011). In our small way, we had made an impact by alerting millions of members of the general public to the newly emerging field of "positive psychology" (e.g., Carr, 2004; Layard, 2005; Gilbert, 2006; Linley, Joseph, Harrington, and Wood, 2006; Diener and Biswas-Diener, 2008; Layard and Ward, 2020), and, moreover, by demonstrating that happiness can be boosted by a number of means, whether musical, psychotherapeutic, or what have you.

My fellow experts on the four-part television series all went on to undertake distinguished work in the public sphere. Richard Reeves (2007) published a major biography of John Stuart Mill, having always admired the writings of that great nineteenth-century thinker – a true champion of women's rights – and then, in 2010, Richard became a Special Adviser to The Right Honourable Nick Clegg, the Deputy Prime Minister of the United Kingdom. Eventually, Reeves received an appointment as a Senior Fellow at the Brookings Institution – a venerable public policy body in Washington, D.C. One can but hope that Richard's experiences in Slough will have informed his important contributions to government. And Andrew Mawson, already an O.B.E., became elected as a life peer in the House of Lords in 2007, now styled as Baron Mawson of Bromley-by-Bow in the London Borough of Tower Hamlets. He also published a very powerful study of *The Social Entrepreneur: Making Communities Work* (Mawson, 2008). Richard Stevens continued his important teaching in psychology at the Open University, while Jessica Pryce-Jones and Philippa Chapman made "iOpener" increasingly successful as a consulting agency, and Jess eventually produced a lovely book on *Happiness at Work: Maximizing Your Psychological Capital for Success* (Pryce-Jones, 2010). I continue to remain speechless with admiration of the very important public contributions made by each of these visionary individuals, and I feel quite honoured to have had this opportunity to collaborate with them.

After I finished my consulting work on the Slough project, I received a number of very kind invitations to speak at national conferences, most of which I had to decline, with great regret, having decided that I had already done quite enough juggling for the time being. Instead, I returned to my full-time clinical practice, and I have remained thus ensconced ever since. I certainly know that one can improve someone else's happiness by singing songs, by dancing, by exercising, by eating good food, and by relating to loving people; but I also know that *profound* characterological change often requires more intensive psychological intervention, of the sort that I have trained to provide, and thus I have come to the conclusion that I can best contribute to the growth of happiness in the United Kingdom by persevering with my daily psychoanalytical practice. I still work on various media projects from time to time, but the core of my diary and of my efforts will always be my clinical psychotherapeutic treatments.

I did have one very amusing experience post-Slough that I would like to share. Perhaps three or four weeks after the broadcast of the final episode, I delivered an evening lecture to a group of opera students at the University of London in the heart of Bloomsbury. The group consisted of twelve young people: eleven women and one man. At the end of this class, which met on a Friday evening, the students invited me out to have a short drink at a nearby pub frequented by undergraduates from University College London. I accepted the offer with pleasure. The sole male student on the course had to leave early to catch his train, and thus I found myself, a middle-aged man, surrounded by eleven engaging young women. We perched ourselves at a large table on the upstairs floor of the pub, and we all began to talk animatedly about music, singing, and related matters. Nearby sat three young men in their rugby jerseys, all looking rather miserable, devoid of any female companionship on a Friday night. These lads kept staring at me and whispering to one another in a conspiratorial manner. I felt rather uncomfortable as I imagined them wondering, "How the hell does that balding, bespectacled man manage to attract eleven female groupies?"

Eventually, we had all finished our drinks, and I got up from the table to leave the pub. As I walked past the three single men, one of them called out, "Hey, Brett!" I panicked, wondering how on earth this person could possibly have known my name. "Nice job in Slough!" he shouted above the din of the pub. I smiled, thanked this chap, and felt very pleased to know that our television programme had reached a young audience.

Randolph Churchill (1955, p. 213), son of Sir Winston Churchill, once wrote to his father, "by being happy, make those who love you happy too." Though easy to lampoon as a sentimental concept, happiness has now become an object of serious study, and it has also become a key policy item on the agenda of many presidents and prime ministers worldwide. I feel pleased to have made a very small contribution to the public foregrounding of happiness, and I take great satisfaction knowing that others with more vision and talent can now develop this subject further in such a multitude of creative ways.

5

On Stage at the Royal Opera House

Nowadays, in 2023, the United Kingdom boasts literally hundreds of very well-trained and highly experienced couple psychoanalytical psychotherapists, but back in 2007, we had merely *thirty-five* fully accredited *marital* psychotherapists in total. It might seem rather striking to learn that, in the latter decades of the twentieth century, when I had undertaken my own training in couple mental health, many colleagues within the classical psychoanalytical world regarded marital psychotherapy as a waste of time in view of the fact that one simply could not force a couple to lie down upon a couch five days per week.

Fortunately, the reputation of couple psychotherapy has progressed substantially during the last fifteen years and more. But, when, in 2007, I became Chair of the Society of Couple Psychoanalytic Psychotherapists and, subsequently, of the British Society of Couple Psychotherapists and Counsellors – the accreditation bodies of the London-based Tavistock Marital Studies Institute and, subsequently, the Tavistock Centre for Couple Relationships (now known simply as Tavistock Relationships) – our community certainly needed to participate in a bold public relations event in order to promote our important profession, designed to save couples from murdering one another and from ruining the lives of their offspring!

As couple psychotherapists in the United Kingdom, we do important work, helping often deeply troubled partners by providing long-term psychoanalytically orientated psychotherapy, hoping thereby that these struggling individuals may recapture the joys that they had once experienced in their marital relationships. But why, then, did we have only *thirty-five* fully accredited clinical members in our professional organisation, especially when we have a population of some 50,000,000 adults, most of whom live in a marital or co-habiting arrangement? Our training – part of the Tavistock Institute of Medical Psychology – demanded a great deal of time and effort, like any intensive psychoanalytical training. Our clinical students would generally undergo five or six years of study – and often longer – in order to complete their postgraduate diploma, treating at least six couples successfully in long-term psychoanalytical psychotherapy. Many of the students

DOI: 10.4324/9781003327240-8

who undertook our training would already have graduated from an individual psychoanalytical training, and so, on the whole, we did not attract young energetic students; rather, we would appeal primarily to older, hopefully wiser, trainees, who would, however, also be burdened with extensive domestic and professional commitments. This would explain, to a certain degree, our relatively small numbers as well as the suspicion which many practitioners of *individual* psychoanalysis had long harboured towards *couple* psychoanalysis.

One might well attribute the dearth of marital practitioners in the United Kingdom to various external factors (such as age, time commitment, and cost), but I suspect that there may be a far more important reason why colleagues would often neglect marital work as a possible field of specialisation. Not only does couple work force us to question the strength and creativity of our own personal marital relationship, but, as psychotherapists, we must spend a great deal of our professional lives in the presence of warring couples, depressed couples, hypersexual couples, hyposexual couples, unfaithful couples, mentally ill couples, forensic couples, bereaved couples, physically violent couples, and the like. Not only does the nature of the work stretch our psychological digestive capacities, but, also, it requires us to tolerate being a "third" party in an oedipal triangle; and as many of us may already have felt excluded from such triangular experiences as infants and children, we might wish to avoid immersing ourselves in a clinical marital situation as a defence against having to tolerate the vicissitudes of being part of a threesome of sorts.

Whatever the ultimate explanation for the sheer paucity of couple psychoanalytical psychotherapists in the United Kingdom, those few of us who have made a life-long, passionate commitment to such a profession continue to struggle to find ways to generate interest in our field, both among our individual psychoanalytical colleagues, and, also, among members of the public alike, many of whom might require our services, or might benefit from our clinical expertise, yet who, because of our small numbers, do not even know of our existence.

Some years ago, my very warm-hearted and charismatic colleague Pauline Hodson, then Chair of the Society of Couple Psychoanalytic Psychotherapists, twisted my arm and encouraged me to serve on the Executive Committee of our teeny, tiny group of marital practitioners. Knowing of my involvement in the media, as a presenter of both radio programmes and television programmes dealing with mental health issues, Pauline thought that I might be able to contribute to the "public face" of couple psychoanalytical psychotherapy. With gratitude, I accepted Pauline's kind offer.

At the very first committee meeting that I attended, one of my colleagues suggested that we should mount an academic conference for the general public, full of worthy papers about "What is Couple Psychotherapy?", "Why Should One Undergo Couple Psychotherapy Instead of Individual

Psychotherapy?", "How Do Transference and Countertransference Issues Become Manifest in Marital Work?", and so forth. I realised that such a conference would be highly meritorious – a sober parade of up-to-the-minute British psychoanalytical clinical thought about the marital relationship – but that such a day-conference would hardly pull punters in off the streets. I humbly suggested that if we wished to prize people away from their e-mails, their television sets, their laptops, their iPods, and their health clubs, we would have to create a more cunning, more inviting means of exploring the world of marital woe.

Having organised theatrical events in the past, including a charity gala, designed to raise money for a child mental health organisation, hosted in the presence of Prince Charles, His Royal Highness The Prince of Wales (Kahr, 1999a) – the future King Charles III – I felt confident that I could draw upon my earlier experiences in order to concoct a more novel means of introducing psychoanalytical marital concepts to the general public than the typical academic–clinical conference. After extensive planning and discussion with colleagues in both the psychoanalytical community and the theatrical community, I stumbled upon what I thought might be a rather interesting idea.

It occurred to me that the world of the arts contains many fine representations of rich, intricate, and often troubled couple relationships, ranging from "Romeo" and "Juliet" in William Shakespeare's timeless play *The Tragedie of Romeo and Ivliet*, [1] to "George" and "Martha" in Edward Albee's drama *Who's Afraid of Virginia Woolf?* And from a musical perspective, one cannot help but wonder about the unconscious nature of the attraction between "Alfredo", the aristocrat, and "Violetta", the courtesan, in Giuseppe Verdi's and Francesco Maria Piave's opera *La Traviata*; or perhaps similarly, one might wish to theorise about the powerful dynamics that prompted "Maria" and "Tony" to become so enmeshed with one another in Leonard Bernstein's, Stephen Sondheim's, and Arthur Laurents's Broadway masterpiece *West Side Story*. I reasoned that if we could engage a talented core group of actors and singers to perform highlights from several of these great works of drama, opera, and musical theatre, we could thus better immerse ourselves in the complexities of convoluted couple relationships; and, moreover, we might understand more fully the vicissitudes of such spousal interactions if we could also assemble a team of qualified couple psychoanalytical psychotherapists who might offer the audience some clinical commentary.

I had trained as a musician in early childhood, long before I became a mental health professional, and although I have always worked full-time in the psychological field, I have continued to devote a small percentage of my time to music, either as a composer, répétiteur, or lecturer on musical topics; therefore, I know a great many people in the musical world, and I decided that in the spirit of being a loyal couple psychotherapist, I would attempt to forge a marital alliance between psychoanalysis and music, thus bringing these two often disparate worlds into closer collaboration.

I presented my notion of producing a "musico-psychological" concert evening to some of my contacts at London's Royal Opera House; and although such a performance would be rather a far cry from their usual fare, the enlightened officials at Covent Garden responded with cheeriness and enthusiasm to my suggestion for a "special event", to be hosted in the Royal Opera House's smaller space, the Linbury Studio Theatre (known as R.O.H. 2), which boasts 394 seats and fifty-six standing room places. If only we could manage to sell tickets to a psychoanalytical event at the United Kingdom's preeminent cultural institution and thus obtain a certain amount of press coverage in the process, we would then be in a strong position to publicise couple psychoanalytical psychotherapy more broadly to a hitherto untapped audience.

With the Royal Opera House on board, allowing us to use their studio theatre on a Sunday evening, and thereby not interfering with any of the opera company's ongoing productions, it took little persuading to enlist the services of a talented team of singers, actors, directors, musicians, and psychotherapists to mount an evening entitled "Couples in Counterpoint", during which we would explore the psychodynamics of couple relationships in a hopefully creative and unusual manner – a far cry from the typical, "old school" academic-style gathering to which we had all become so accustomed over the last century.

I thus formed a working party, spearheaded by the West End theatre director Lisa Forrell, the daughter of the American psychoanalyst Mildred Forrell, a senior member of the New York Freudian Society;[2] and after much creative and spirited dialogue, we eventually decided that we would focus our evening on the nature of couple interactions as portrayed in the American musical theatre, in part, because Lisa had worked extensively in the musical theatre world, and because she and I had developed many helpful and willing relationships with comrades in this field. Before long, we had organised a very exciting series of auditions and soon assembled a dream cast of talented West End performers to assist us in our endeavour. Jessica Martin, a well-known star of theatre and television in the United Kingdom, perhaps best remembered for her leading role in the West End musical *Me and My Girl*, came on board at once, followed swiftly by Andy Morton, a brilliant operatic tenor. Andy agreed to participate in the exhausting rehearsal period, even though he had already committed himself to appearing as "Nemorino" in Opera North's production of Gaetano Donizetti's classic opera *L'Elisir d'Amore*, based in Leeds, many miles away from London. A true trouper, Andy took the train to London on his days off and immersed himself enthusiastically in these extra rehearsals on our behalf.

John Addison and Lydia Griffiths, two juvenile leads who had starred respectively as "Marius" and "Éponine" in the West End production of Sir Cameron Mackintosh's long-running musical *Les Misérables* at the Palace Theatre, rounded out our singing ensemble. And Nigel Lilley, an outstanding musician who had, most recently, worked on the London production of the hit Broadway musical *Wicked*, based at the Apollo Victoria Theatre, supervised the vocal coaching and served as our musical director.

We all enjoyed a stroke of extremely good fortune when we succeeded in securing the participation of the Broadway and West End diva Kim Criswell, an American-born singer who has recorded over forty albums during the course of a distinguished international career. Across the decades, Miss Criswell has performed in many of the world's greatest opera houses and concert halls, ranging from the Teatro alla Scala in Milan, to the Théâtre du Châtelet in Paris, to La Fenice in Venice, to Carnegie Hall in New York City, to the Royal Albert Hall and the Wigmore Hall in London. A specialist in the American musical theatre songbook, Miss Criswell has played the leading role of "Ruth Sherwood" in Leonard Bernstein's *Wonderful Town* with the Berliner Philharmoniker, conducted by Sir Simon Rattle, and has starred in the West End revival of Irving Berlin's *Annie Get Your Gun*, to great acclaim.

In conjunction with Lisa Forrell, our vivacious director, we put together a compelling line-up of songs:

1 "Together" (from the musical *Gypsy*, with music by Jule Styne and lyrics by Stephen Sondheim), performed by John Addison, Lydia Griffiths, Jessica Martin, and Andy Morton.
2 "One Hand, One Heart" (from the musical *West Side Story*, with music by Leonard Bernstein and lyrics by Stephen Sondheim), performed by John Addison and Lydia Griffiths.
3 "On My Own" (from the musical *Les Misérables*, with music by Claude-Michel Schönberg and lyrics by Alain Boublil, Herbert Kretzmer, Jean-Marc Natel, Trevor Nunn, and John Caird), performed by Lydia Griffiths.
4 "Could I Leave You?" (from the musical *Follies*, with music and lyrics by Stephen Sondheim), performed by Jessica Martin.
5 "I Won't Send Roses" (from the musical *Mack and Mabel*, with music and lyrics by Jerry Herman), performed by Andy Morton, and reprised by Jessica Martin.
6 "Soliloquy" (from the musical *Carousel*, with music by Richard Rodgers and lyrics by Oscar Hammerstein II), performed by John Addison.
7 Medley (from the musical *Annie Get Your Gun*, with music and lyrics by Irving Berlin), performed by Kim Criswell and Andy Morton, comprising, "The Girl That I Marry" (Andy Morton), "You Can't Get a Man with a Gun" (Kim Criswell), "They Say It's Wonderful" (Kim Criswell and Andy Morton), "Anything You Can Do" (Kim Criswell and Andy Morton), and "An Old Fashioned Wedding" (Kim Criswell and Andy Morton).
8 Surprise Finale.

Essentially, we decided that we would invite the actors to perform these wonderful, iconic musical theatre songs and then provide commentary from a team of marital psychotherapists who would be seated on the stage, near the singers, as a means of helping the audience to acquire a better sense of how we, as clinicians, speak and, also, how we think. Fortunately, I managed to recruit three distinguished, senior marital psychotherapeutic colleagues to join me on stage: Dr. Christopher Clulow, the recently retired Director of both the Tavistock Marital Studies Institute and the Tavistock Centre for Couple Relationships, as well as Pauline Hodson, past Chair of the Society of Couple Psychoanalytic Psychotherapists, and Helen Tarsh, past Chair of the Society of Psychoanalytical Marital Psychotherapists.

In order to illustrate the sort of interaction which unfolded on stage, let me describe one of the songs. After an opening number performed by four of the singers, our talented juveniles, John Addison and Lydia Griffiths, then recreated the classic roles of "Tony" and "Maria" from *West Side Story* and sang a beautiful, poignant rendition of the well-known ballad "One Hand, One Heart". Lisa Forrell, the Director of "Couples in Counterpoint", explained to the audience that, from a theatrical point of view, "Tony" and "Maria" represent the very epitome of "romantic love" – two young teenagers who triumph over parental prejudice and heal the bonds of racial hatred by forging a passionate liaison. Lisa then interviewed the panel of couple psychotherapists and asked us whether we would agree with that interpretation. Straightaway, the four couple clinicians disagreed with one another, albeit in a friendly manner.

I inaugurated the discussions by acknowledging that although "One Hand, One Heart" cannot fail to grip the listener with its tenderness and sweetness, one must not forget that Tony winds up dead, with Maria bereaved, at the conclusion of *West Side Story*, and that perhaps their romantic connection may not be a simple expression of "love", but rather, an attempt to forge a primitive symbiotic merger, as a means of avoiding a terrifying external and internal world and, also, as a defence against an accurate perception of an impending tragedy. Famously, Tony and Maria intone: "Make of our hands one hand, / Make of our hearts one heart". As a romantic sentiment, it would be difficult to surpass the wish to meld into one's lover; but as an expression of a characterological state, their desire to turn two hands into one and two hearts into just one might indicate something more psychologically vulnerable and fragile, namely, the need to merge as a means of combating depression, emptiness, and persecutory anxiety. My colleague Pauline Hodson expressed an alternative viewpoint. She argued that in order for healthy adult love to emerge, one *must* immerse oneself in a period of losing one's bodily boundaries, falling in love in such a primitive, teenage manner. With our stall thus set out, the other panellists joined us in a vibrant fashion as we all discussed such couple psychoanalytical concepts as shared defence structure, unconscious marital wishes and fears, shared marital phantasy, splitting and projective identification, and so forth.

As the evening unfolded, we examined "tender love" from *West Side Story*, "unrequited love" from *Les Misérables*, "bitter love" from *Follies*, "defensive love" from *Mack and Mabel*, as well as "anticipatory parental love" from *Carousel* as the character of "Billy Bigelow" contemplates the arrival of his first child in the famous "Soliloquy". We particularly wished to include a song about a young man becoming a father, because the birth of the first baby represents one of the most common family events which often disequilibrate the very fabric of marital life, and in our work as couple psychotherapists, we see a very large number of partners whose marriages begin to founder in the immediate aftermath of the transition to parenthood.

Our marital psychotherapy team offered a variety of psychoanalytical observations about all aspects of the songs. At times we agreed and at times we disagreed in a thoughtful, collegial manner, thus modelling for the members of the general public the ways in which psychotherapists have a capacity to learn from one another and to reconsider our thinking. We also hoped to portray ourselves as independent-minded professionals, thus quashing a popular cultural anxiety that psychoanalysts and psychotherapists blindly apply a stock-standard theory to every single patient in a repetitive, dogmatic manner.

In addition to providing clinical commentary on each of the songs, Pauline Hodson and I also conducted a mock-marital therapy session with Andy Morton and Jessica Martin who portrayed the silent film director "Mack Sennett" and the silent film star "Mabel Normand" in the Jerry Herman musical *Mack and Mabel*. After they sang their song "I Won't Send Roses", about two people who "love" each other but who cannot move beyond the "dating" phase and thus risk real intimacy, Pauline and I engaged "Mack" and "Mabel" in a recreation of a psychoanalytical session, on stage at the Royal Opera House. We "worked" with the actors for approximately ten minutes, during which time we offered the audience a small taste of how we welcome couples into the consulting room, how we formulate interpretations, how we speak, how we interact, and how we conceptualise. This segment proved one of the most popular and most successful of the whole evening, providing a very detailed glimpse into the nature of our work, without any risk of breaching confidentiality.

The evening climaxed with a medley of songs from the infectiously melodic Broadway musical *Annie Get Your Gun*, featuring our diva-for-the-evening, Kim Criswell, who took the West End by storm when she appeared in the revival of the Irving Berlin masterpiece, years previously, in 1992–1993, receiving a Laurence Olivier Award nomination in the process. Based on the true story of a nineteenth-century Midwestern sharpshooter Annie Oakley and her rival Frank Butler, *Annie Get Your Gun* represents the apotheosis of healthy, tender romance. After listening to magnificent performances of

Frank Butler's ballad, "The Girl That I Marry", a paean to idealised love, and Annie Oakley's charm number, "You Can't Get a Man with a Gun", a communication about her often phallic, castrating posture, the audience then had the privilege of watching the plot unfold further as "Frank" began to remove women from the pedestal while "Annie" began to drop her rifle, so that, bit by bit, the two characters could, at last, risk the vulnerability of trusting one another. The characters of Annie and Frank then engaged in a more meaningful way in the sweeping romantic ballad, "They Say It's Wonderful". Frank and Annie could, at last, retract their projections and examine one another in a more reality orientated fashion; and they could also embrace the challenge of envy and competition, expressed in the exuberant duet, "Anything You Can Do", which facilitated the resolution of their aggressivity. As the plot continued to unfold, these two lovebirds performed a deeply thoughtful and highly lilting number, "An Old Fashioned Wedding", thus demonstrating their capacity to forge an intimate coupling. Kim Criswell and Andy Morton brought down the house with their medley – brilliantly sung and magnificently acted.

We concluded the evening with a rendition of one of my own compositions, a comedic number entitled "The Divorce Song", which I sang with Miss Criswell, with yours truly on the piano. Afterwards, the entire cast returned to the stage for a reprise of Irving Berlin's classic song, "They Say It's Wonderful", with the audience joining us in the most unexpectedly enthusiastic fashion. I must confess that, apart from my foray some years previously as Director of the Tavistock Clinic Choir, I had never before heard a group of several hundred mental health professionals singing together with such bravura. For the first time, my colleagues sported happy faces, rather than the more traditional scrunched up ones, so familiar to anyone who has ever spent more than five minutes in a consulting room.

In spite of the uncertainty of such an unusual theatrical venture, we succeeded in filling each of the 394 seats, as well as the fifty-six standing places; and, with regret, we had to turn away large numbers of keen individuals who had not managed to book in time. I suspect that we might well have sold double the number of tickets if only the Royal Opera House studio had more seats to offer. The audience included not only colleagues from other psychotherapeutic institutions such as the Association of Child Psychotherapists, the British Association for Sexual and Relational Therapy, the British Association of Psychotherapists, the British Psychoanalytical Society, the London Centre for Psychotherapy, Nafsiyat, the Oxford Psychotherapy Society, Relate, the School of Psychotherapy and Counselling at Regent's College, the Tavistock Society of Psychotherapists, and the Wessex Psychotherapy Society, as well as American colleagues from the New York Freudian Society and from other psychoanalytical groupings, but we also attracted prominent members of divergent professions, including a brace of barristers and Queen's Counsels from the law, distinguished practitioners of medicine, numerous enterprising television producers, representatives from some of the nation's leading newspapers, as well as noted figures from cultural life such as Candace, Lady Rattle (the former wife of Sir Simon Rattle) and, also, Clive Hollick (Lord Hollick), the Chair of London's South Bank Centre. Chris Smith (Lord Smith), the former Arts Minister in Prime Minister Tony Blair's Labour government, had also purchased a ticket, but sadly, could not attend at the last minute. Generously, he sent us a donation, nevertheless. So, at least two peers of the realm had now come to possess a much more intimate knowledge of the Society of Couple Psychoanalytic Psychotherapists.

All in all, the event exceeded our expectations. Not only did we achieve our primary aim of publicising marital psychotherapy as a discipline and as a modality, but we also managed to garner some goodly press coverage, and we even earned a profit for the coffers of the Society of Couple Psychoanalytic Psychotherapists, which we used to sponsor future educational events. As a direct result of our opera house evening on "Couples in Counterpoint", our training body, the Tavistock Centre for Couple Relationships, received a number of new requests from potential students, and the Couple Psychotherapy Service, our clinical outreach arm, fielded a number of potential new referrals from partners eager to embark upon a course of marital psychotherapy. We even created a new committee within the Society of Couple Psychoanalytic Psychotherapists, namely, Couples Centre Stage, which assumed the responsibility for organising future events for members of the general public.

Although I cannot speak with any authority about the public perception of psychoanalytical mental health professionals in the United States of America or in other countries, I can confirm that, in the United Kingdom, psychotherapists still remain objects of suspicion and derision among many people, in spite of our nearly century-long existence. I remain committed to the notion that mental health professionals must become more accessible, more approachable, and more available; and although we must never lose our dignity or our gravitas, we must endeavour to find ways of publicising our organisations and our services, mindful of the fact that our future patients will all have grown up in the post-internet age. One young colleague, for instance, told me that he would never visit a psychotherapist who did *not* have his or her own website, for example. I suspect that this view will become increasingly common among the patients of tomorrow and, therefore, we should not be embarrassed about drawing upon our reservoirs of creativity in an attempt to design newer and, even, more theatrical means of reaching the man and woman in the street.

I trust that this brief account of a "musico-psychological" experiment – a marital collaboration between psychotherapists and singers – may serve as a small piece of inspiration to colleagues in other branches of the mental health field who might wish to explore different means of transmitting our knowledge, other than the long-standing tried-and-tested (and perhaps somewhat fatigued) model of the conference and the journal article. We could even surprise ourselves by attracting some new friends and some new sources of inspiration for our work.

Section III

Television in the Consulting Room

6
Television as Rorschach
The Unconscious Use of the Cathode Nipple

What Do Suicide Bombers Watch on Telly?

At precisely 8.50 a.m., on Thursday, 7th July, 2005, Mohammad Sidique Khan, a thirty-year-old al-Qaeda sympathiser, detonated an organic-peroxide bomb concealed in his rucksack, while riding on the London Underground, somewhere between Liverpool Street and Aldgate stations. He died instantly, killing six fellow passengers in the process. During the next hour, three of Khan's comrades exploded their own homemade bombs, murdering a total of fifty-two women and men, and injuring approximately 700 others. Some three days before the perpetration of these grotesque atrocities, Mohammad Sidique Khan sent a poorly spelled text message to fellow conspirator, nineteen-year-old Germaine Maurice Lindsay, which stated, "'I aint getting on no plain fool'" (quoted in Godwin, 2010, p. 5), a catchphrase used, apparently, by the television character "Sergeant Bosco Albert (B.A.) Baracus", portrayed by the actor "Mr. T." in the long-running American series *The A-Team*. After receiving this text message, Germaine Lindsay sent a reply, which read, "'Fuck u bitch dats my line'" (quoted in Godwin, 2010, p. 15).

In view of the horror that Khan, Lindsay, and their accomplices would inflict on the residents of London some seventy-two hours later, one might have imagined that they would have had other preoccupations, rather than spouting dialogue from a 1980s television programme. As Richard Godwin (2010, p. 15), a columnist for the *London Evening Standard* newspaper, hypothesised, the revelations of these text messages and of the bombers' obsession with "Mr. T." and *The A-Team* might well prompt us all to describe these young jihadists as little more than "hapless goons", and that the carnage executed by these assassins "was less to do with Islam, more to do with a group of dysfunctional, childish idiots" (Godwin, 2010, p. 15).

If anyone still harboured doubts about the way in which television and its discourse often sears itself into the very fabric of our unconscious minds and into the labyrinth of our neuronal pathways, then this revelation of text messages, reported in the 7/7 Inquest, certainly dispels any questions in this

DOI: 10.4324/9781003327240-10

respect. The mind and the media do, of course, enjoy a relationship of reciprocal influence, but how best might we describe this set of interconnections? Does the media merely reflect the contents of the human unconscious, or does the media actually shape the nature of the unconscious over time?

No doubt educationalists, critics, politicians, religious leaders, and broadcasters alike will all have strong viewpoints on these vexing matters, as do mental health professionals. In the pages which follow, I hope to offer a clinician's perspective on the ways in which television seeps into the unconscious mind, as the well as the manner in which that very same unconscious mind filters, absorbs, edits, and identifies with the media and its offerings in order to satisfy a series of very basic, often very primitive, wishes and desires.

Since its inception, psychoanalysts have served as consultants to a considerable number of filmic and dramatic and televisual productions, even musical ones. As early as 1926, the Austrian cinema director Georg Wilhelm Pabst, a representative of the 1920s movement in German art known as "Die Neue Sachlichkeit" ["The New Reality"], made a movie entitled *Geheimnisse einer Seele* [*Secrets of a Soul*] which debuted at the Gloria Palast, the lavish cinema-house in Berlin. Pabst's masterpiece has earned a beloved place in psychoanalytical history as the first feature-length film about the new psychology created by Professor Sigmund Freud. This extraordinary work explored the journey of a patient, portrayed by the German actor Werner Krauss, who suffered from compulsions and from a knife phobia, and who then underwent treatment with a psychoanalyst, played by the Russian actor Pavel Pavlov.

One might have thought that Sigmund Freud would have welcomed such cinematic publicity for his new psychological science of psychoanalysis. But, in fact, he expressed great displeasure about Georg Wilhelm Pabst's project, concerned about the potentially vulgar popularisation and bastardisation of his discoveries (e.g., Freud, 1925c).

Sigmund Freud's great suspicion towards the media also prompted him to snub the Hollywood film mogul Samuel Goldwyn, who, on a visit to Vienna, had hoped to recruit Freud as a well-paid psychological consultant to a movie about great lovers from history (Jones, 1957). Similarly, Freud turned down a series of other lucrative offers to appear as an expert witness in the 1924 murder trial of the American juvenile killers Nathan Freudenthal Leopold, Jr. and Richard Albert Loeb (Jones, 1957; cf. Marx, 1976; Kahr, 2005d, 2005e, 2007b).

And yet, in spite of Freud's reluctance to engage with the media, numerous filmmakers, journalists, broadcasters, producers, and other media practitioners, by contrast, certainly endeavoured to engage with Freud. Indeed, since Pavel Pavlov's portrayal of a compulsion-curing clinician in *Geheimnisse einer Seele*, psychoanalysts and other mental health professionals have ultimately appeared in, or consulted to, a whole range of films, novels, plays, and even Broadway musicals (cf. Sievers, 1955; Fleming and Manvell, 1985; Conroy, 1986; Gabbard and Gabbard, 1987; mcclung, 2007[1]), ranging from the benign "Dr. Alexander Brooks" in the Moss Hart – Ira Gershwin – Kurt Weill musical drama *Lady in the Dark* (Hart, 1941; cf. Kahr, 2000), to the more recent incarnation of "Dr. Paul Weston" in the television programme *In Treatment* (Kahr, 2011a).

Professor Caroline Bainbridge, the distinguished scholar, delivered an important presentation about the portrayal of psychoanalysts in popular culture, examining how the media might revere, celebrate, denigrate, or satirise both the analyst and the analytical process, subsequently published under the title "Psychotherapy on the Couch: Exploring the Fantasies of *In Treatment*" (Bainbridge, 2012, cf. Bainbridge, 2014b). In this spirit, I wish to approach the subject of media psychoanalysis from the other direction, exploring the ways in which television programmes, in particular, appear in the course of sessions with patients undergoing intensive psychoanalytical treatment. Apart from a very small number of communications, precious few psychoanalytical writings have yet considered how the patient's television viewing actually penetrates the consulting room (cf. Anonymous, 1927; Ekins, 1994; Kahr, 2011a). I hope that, by examining the ways in which our analysands discuss their television-viewing habits, we might be able to understand something about the interrelationship between the mind and popular culture rather more fully.

Television Programmes in the Consulting Room

Approximately forty years ago, I began to treat my first case in three-times-weekly psychotherapy, under the supervision of a senior psychoanalytically orientated psychiatrist. The patient, whom I shall call "Mr. A.", a middle-aged man who had spent more than twenty years on the back wards of a provincial hospital with a diagnosis of paranoid schizophrenia, used to scream in pain at night because he believed that the British Broadcasting Corporation would transmit his secret sexual thoughts to the nation each evening as part of the 9.00 p.m. news. The patient would often cry out, in German, "Das B.B.C. ist ein Scheisser", which he translated as "The B.B.C. is a shit-house", and then, he would clutch his anus protectively, fearing that each news broadcaster on the screen might somehow come to sodomise him. As a very young and inexperienced psychologist, these ostensible paranoid delusions of persecution by the B.B.C. made little sense to me, until one day, while reading through the patient's extensive case records in the hospital archives, I had come to learn that, during Mr. A.'s early childhood, his father had actually worked for the B.B.C. as an employee. When I shared my archival discovery with the patient, he began to reveal a long history of sexual activity between himself and his father; and, eventually, the references to the B.B.C. as a *"Scheisser"* and sodomiser began to make infinitely more sense (cf. Kahr, 2012a).

As the years unfolded, and as I became an increasingly experienced mental health practitioner, I began to notice more readily the ways in which patients would introduce their television viewing into the very fabric of the psychotherapeutic session. Often, my analysands would present their television habits in a rather off-hand manner, explaining, for example, "Last night, while I was watching such-and-such a programme, I suddenly remembered ..." In fact, they would frequently refer to television programmes in a disposable, throwaway manner. But as I became more and more savvy, one hopes, I began to focus in greater depth on the precise nature of their programme choices and what their viewing habits might teach us about the underexplored, or indeed *unexplored*, aspects of their psychological state.

Another one of my patients, "Ms. B.", a forty-five-year-old female, had never in her life enjoyed a full sexual relationship with a man, in spite of her attractive appearance. Ms. B. used to watch the medical drama *E.R.* quite compulsively, again and again, and eventually she confessed to me that she harboured a huge crush on the actor who portrayed the chief medical resident. Sheepishly, Ms. B. reported that she would watch this telly doctor on video cassette and would then rewind all the scenes in which he appeared, masturbating to a very pleasurable, if somewhat guilt-stricken, climax.

In our work, Ms. B. and I examined the multiple functions of *E.R.* within her mental world. Her overwhelming crush on the young physician communicated, first and foremost, an important relational striving. In spite of her ongoing, multi-decade failure to have a sexual relationship with a real man, her passion for the telly doctor gave us some sense of hope that, in spite of her fears, she actually craved true masculine contact. We also explored the shadow side of this wish, however, examining the ways in which her masturbatory preoccupation with a television actor, who probably lives in California, might be a very safe way of having sex with a man without having to endure any of the risks attached to actual in-person intimacy. But, of course, as the intensity of the patient's crush on the doctor increased, I also wondered whether we might consider the fact that she found herself fantasising about a *doctor*, as opposed to a lawyer, or a policeman, or a cowboy; and that perhaps she hoped to find someone who could heal her. On one occasion, I even dared to make a transference interpretation, suggesting that her preoccupation with the television doctor might in fact provide some indication of her affectionate feelings towards me, a *psychological* doctor, who, by the way, had sometimes appeared on television. The patient replied, "Don't be ridiculous. The guy from *E.R.* looks nothing like you. And besides, he's hot!"

Some years later, I worked with a young male patient, "Mr. C.", who had perpetrated many horrific sexual crimes against young girls, including rape and other forms of sexual assault. As a consequence of his forensic history, he lived in a secure institution outside of London which lacked any psychological treatment resources. Consequently, the patient spent virtually the whole of each day watching soap operas. He gorged himself on *Coronation Street*, *Doctors*, *EastEnders*, *Hollyoaks*, and many other regular drama series, and he used to arrive at my consulting room for his sessions under escort and would then regale me with detailed plot summaries of each of these programmes. At first, I struggled to make arguably crude connections between certain characters in *EastEnders* and certain key figures in Mr. C.'s early history; but eventually, I realised that one could not reduce his television viewing to a simple *roman à clef*. Rather, I came to understand that Mr. C.'s indulgence in these many television programmes represented his very creative and yet rather desperate attempt to deal with a life of extreme loneliness in a psychiatric institution, one whose naked corridors and chilly dormitories mirrored the desolation of his internal world. As a young, convicted rapist, Mr. C. felt that he had no future, and so he watched an endless parade of soap operas, not only as a means of soothing his chronic isolation but, also, as an attempt to project his own hopelessness and despair into the plethora of miserable, tragedy-stricken characters who appeared daily and nightly on his tiny black-and-white hospital ward television screen.

"Mrs. D.", a middle-aged lady who had sought treatment for depression, began to improve after one year of sustained analytical sessions. She soon became a zealot for the psychoanalytical process and spoke with all of her friends about our psychotherapeutic work. One day, Mrs. D. told me that she had recently watched an episode of the American television drama *Mad Men*, set in the 1960s, and, during the course of the viewing, this person had become very disturbed to see that the Freudian psychiatrist depicted in the programme, who uses a couch, as I do, would often breach confidentiality by talking about one of his patients, "Betty Draper", to her husband, "Don Draper", on the telephone, behind the patient's back. We explored Mrs. D.'s anxieties about any violations of her own privacy, and whether she nursed a fear that I might breach her confidentiality with a third party. Consciously, she replied that she knew me to be too professional to do that. But I then reminded Mrs. D. that, only two or three days earlier, she had asked me whether I might undertake the psychoanalysis of her best girlfriend, who suffered from depression. Although I offered to recommend a colleague who might treat the friend, I refused to do so myself for obvious reasons; but in Mrs. D.'s unconscious mind, she had already established a psychoanalytical *ménage à trois* in which she and I and her best friend would all share secrets indiscriminately. In this instance, the reference to a particular moment from a specific television programme provided me with a most important clue to Mrs. D.'s fear that I might break boundaries, which actually masked a wish that I might do so by treating her friend as well. This mirrored various blurry boundary situations across the generations in Mrs. D.'s childhood and adolescent history. Certainly, the anxiety about whether I might resemble the psychiatrist in *Mad Men* served as a useful springboard for exploring these memories and fears.

"Ms. E.", a young, unwed, single mother, also suffered from depression and from comorbid alcoholism. After she put her child to sleep at night, she would drink five or six whiskies on the trot while viewing back-to-back episodes of the American police thriller *CSI: Crime Scene Investigation*. In one very teary psychoanalytical session, Ms. E. confessed to me that she always enjoyed watching the bloody murders portrayed in *CSI* a very great deal and that she had become convinced that this programme allowed her to project her own murderous wishes towards her unwanted child, and, also, towards the child's absconding father, thus freeing her, she felt, from perpetrating any gross child abuse. On one occasion, Ms. E. arrived at my office quite forlorn. She told me that, on the previous evening, her television set had exploded, and that, in consequence, she could not enjoy her nightly fix of *CSI*. To her shock and horror, Ms. E. had become anxious and aggressive, and, soon thereafter, she started to yell at her child who had in fact already gone to bed. The television had always functioned as a sedative, and as a vehicle for the projection of murderous rage; but, on this occasion, in the absence of this drug, the patient felt greatly at risk.

References to television programmes, and, also, fantasies about television programmes, appear frequently, not only in work with individual patients but, also, with couples who attend for marital psychotherapy. "Mr. F." and "Mrs. F.", two former "hippies" from the 1960s, endured a very fractious, sexless marriage, but as ex-"flower power" participants who had protested against the war in Vietnam, they felt extremely ashamed to admit that they harboured murderous feelings of any kind, let alone towards one another. Every time I attempted to explore their unconscious hostility, my interpretations, alas, fell upon seemingly deaf ears.

Fortunately, on one occasion, television came to our rescue. At the start of a particular session, Mrs. F. entered the consulting room first, while Mr. F. nipped into the toilet. During the short period in which she waited for her husband to join her in my office, Mrs. F. ostensibly made "small talk" and asked me if I had watched the aforementioned *Mad Men* on television the previous night. Keen to remain as neutral as possible, I did not reply. I waited, instead, for Mrs. F.'s husband to join us, and then, after they had taken their seats, each of them became unusually silent. Mrs. F. asked, "Well, what shall we talk about today?" I opined that, perhaps, in view of the fact that Mrs. F. had just spoken to me about *Mad Men*, she had, in fact, already begun the session while her husband had gone to urinate. I queried whether both Mr. F. and Mrs. F. felt like "Mad Men" at times but that they found it very hard to discuss these non-flower-powery feelings. To my surprise, the usually placid Mrs. F. unleashed a barrage of anguish, enumerating the many ways in which her seemingly peaceable husband, Mr. F., resembled the duplicitous, schizoid, adulterous, corporate "Don Draper". After having made this comparison, Mrs. F. then confessed that she hated her husband greatly. Mr. F. simply could not understand how his wife had arrived at such a formulation, and, before long, the three of us entered a fuller, richer, deeper phase of the marital psychotherapy, in which the *Mad Men*-like features of their personalities could now emerge more wholeheartedly.

Other couples also presented media-related material, sometimes in a much more concrete way. "Mr. G.", a television writer, and "Mrs. G.", a housewife, attended for marital psychotherapy after Mr. G., an author who had struggled to write for many years, finally succeeding in scripting a runaway success for one of the major networks. As a consequence of his landmark achievement in the entertainment industry, he soon received a flurry of very time-consuming commissions for further work and had begun to meet some very glamorous actresses as a result. Mrs. G. became increasingly envious of her husband's newfound accomplishments and, also, very heartbroken in the wake of his subsequent flirtations. Unsurprisingly, Mrs. G. revealed that, although she used to enjoy watching television during the evenings, she now hated doing so. In fact, the television set had literally become the hated third person in this marriage.

"Ms. H." and "Ms. I.", a long-standing lesbian couple, arrived at my office after Ms. H., a budding television producer, had made her first feature-length documentary, but, worryingly, her girlfriend, Ms. I., still had not bothered to take the time to watch the D.V.D. of Ms. H.'s film. Once again, television had become both a concrete and a symbolic object which highlighted the ubiquitous themes of competition and sibling rivalry which scar many a marriage.[2]

Sometimes, television appears in psychoanalytical sessions not as a third party, and not as a piece of free-associative material, but, rather, as the very heart of a dream report. "Mrs. J.", a multiply bereaved woman who had suffered for many years from the symptoms of borderline personality disorder, reported a dream in which she had attended a recent annual B.A.F.T.A. Awards ceremony. Mrs. J. had actually watched the broadcast on her television the previous night; hence, it hardly surprised her that she then dreamed about the ceremony. This patient, by the way, had no formal connection to the film or television industry. In her dream, she found herself dancing with Richard, Lord Attenborough, and she reported that the two of them had had a very nice time indeed. At first, the dream made very little sense; certainly, it did not evoke any particular resonances. Mrs. J. told me that she had enjoyed the dream, as well as her dance with Lord Attenborough. Fortunately, I too had seen the B.A.F.T.A. awards on television the previous night, something that I would not have done under ordinary circumstances, but I had a friend who had received a nomination for an award, and, hence, I watched the programme as a gesture of support. Having done so, I knew of course that Lord Attenborough had planned to attend the B.A.F.T.A. event in order to present a lifetime achievement award to the iconic actress Vanessa Redgrave, but that, owing to illness, he had to pull out, and, at the last minute, His Royal Highness Prince William of Wales deputised, to great applause, and then handed the prize to the talented Redgrave. I restrained myself from saying too much in the session, as I wanted to ensure that I would foreground the patient's private free associations, and not my own. In spite of Mrs. J.'s reluctance to reflect upon her dream narrative, I persevered, and I asked again about her thoughts on Lord Attenborough. Eventually, the patient told me what I already knew, namely, that Attenborough had not participated in the actual, real-life broadcast, but that he did make a guest appearance in her dream. This incident reminded Mrs. J. of her father who had died on the evening before her graduation from university, and who could not, therefore, watch his daughter receive her prized parchment. Eventually, through further elaboration of the dream and its elements, and of the day residue of the B.A.F.T.A. awards ceremony itself, broadcast on television, we both came to realise that *all three* of the celebrities involved in this segment of the programme, namely Lord Attenborough, Miss Redgrave, and Prince William, had lost very near and dear relatives in sudden, traumatic circumstances. Prince William, of course, had endured the death of his mother, Princess Diana, in a ghastly road traffic collision in Paris in 1997; Lord Attenborough had suffered the drowning of both his daughter, Jane Holland, and his granddaughter, Lucy Holland, in the Asian Tsunami of 2004; and, several years thereafter, Vanessa Redgrave had lost her daughter, the actress Natasha Richardson, in a tragic skiing accident in Québec, Canada, in 2009. Once we had realised these interconnections, the dream took on a very rich texture, and provided us with a wealth of psychoanalytical material which we explored over several forthcoming sessions, examining, *inter alia*, Mrs. J.'s wish to bring back her dead father, as well as her propensity to hide her pain beneath the ostensible glamour of being a compulsive shopper who would drape her body in extremely expensive clothing whenever she felt depressed.

References to television programmes can also be very helpfully humbling for the psychotherapist. "Mr. K.", a young man in his early twenties, spent a great deal of time watching the "fantasy fiction" television series *Game of Thrones*, based on the novels of George R.R. Martin. Mr. K. would often speak about this programme in detail and would paint very vivid portraits of many of the actors. During one psychotherapy session, Mr. K. devoted at least ten or even fifteen minutes to a very elaborate description of a scene between two of the leading characters, namely "Tyrion Lannister", a dwarf, and "Jon Snow", an illegitimate son. Mr. K., a very tall young man, suffered, nevertheless, from feelings of pusillanimity and pronounced castration anxiety and often struggled to find a girlfriend. After he had finished reciting copious sections of dialogue between "Tyrion Lannister", the dwarf, and "Jon Snow", the illegitimate son, I offered a very simple comment, noting that although Mr. K. stands over six feet tall, and although he has two married parents, who had recently celebrated their thirtieth wedding anniversary, perhaps he often feels like both "Tyrion Lannister" and "Jon Snow", namely, small and also lacking in parental love. Mr. K. agreed with my comment, but he admonished me, "You know, Brett, I am more of a bastard than you know. I think I never told you that my parents conceived me some months *before* they actually married. So, technically, I *am* a bastard, just like "Jon Snow"." This interchange reminded me very powerfully that a tall man can still feel like a "dwarf", and the child of two long-standing parents can still be a "bastard".

Tony Soprano's Swimming Pool

Thus far, I have provided a smattering of case material which offers some indication of the ways in which television imagery appears within the clinical psychoanalytical situation, underscoring how the small screen serves as a source of wish fulfilment, as a protection against loneliness, as a means of communicating internal psychic reality, as a method of obtaining sexual pleasure, as evidence of rivalry between the members of a couple, as way of communicating hitherto preconscious or unconscious material, and, also, as a barometer of the transference. But television can provide, moreover, important information about structural change in the mind of a patient over a long period of time. Most analysands who discuss television programmes do so in an episodic or sporadic fashion, but I did, however, work with one patient over a protracted period of time who had become completely obsessed by the American television programme *The Sopranos*, and who referred to this series in virtually every single one of her sessions. Let us explore the way in which "Ms. L." and her relationship to *The Sopranos* became transmogrified over the course of time.

During the first year of treatment, Ms. L. spoke again and again about a key scene in *The Sopranos* in which the teenage son of the protagonist "Tony Soprano" attempts to drown himself in the family swimming pool. In the television version, the young son jumps into the pool, intent on suicide, but, fortunately, "Tony Soprano" leaps in afterwards and rescues his child. Ms. L. had made a very serious suicide attempt during her own adolescence, not by drowning, but, rather, with razor blades. Sadly, however, no one discovered her bleeding arms, and, in consequence, she had to transport herself to the casualty department at the local hospital for emergency treatment.

In our second year of work, this patient no longer needed to refer to the drowning scene from *The Sopranos* in such a compulsive fashion. As a result of our intensive, five-times-weekly work, she had become much less destructive, and she eventually told me that, in spite of her adolescent suicidality, she had now decided to live a long and non-destructive existence. She explained that although she no longer considered herself at risk for self-harm, she did begin to experience some panic attacks at the thought that her favourite television series would soon come to an end. Apparently, the producers of *The Sopranos* had decided to terminate this multi-year series, and, in consequence, no new episodes would be made. Ms. L. did not know how she would cope. Partnerless, childless, and virtually friendless, Ms. L. lived a rather bleak and arid existence; therefore, *The Sopranos* had become very much a new family for her. At times, I actually found myself facilitating bereavement counselling for this patient who continued to mourn the loss of all the characters of a fictional television series. In this respect, "Tony Soprano" and his family had become honorary objects with whom Ms. L. could enjoy a sort of intimacy; likewise, the programme also served as a transitional object or linking object to help this patient mollify her feelings of loss and desolation.

By the time we had embarked upon our third year of analysis, Ms. L. had recovered from the fact that the American producers would no longer offer any new episodes; happily, she took much comfort from the fact that she could now purchase the entire series on D.V.D., and, thus, she would always have *The Sopranos* near to hand. Also, during this year of further mourning work, Ms. L. began for the first time to recognise that although she grew up in Yorkshire, far from the Sicilian coast, she too had a Mafioso-like father who terrorised her in various ways, and that, as a result, she also had a Mafioso-like aspect within her own character, which often provoked violence in her relationships. This proved a particularly fruitful year of understanding in our work.

Thereafter, the analysis entered a fourth phase, in which *The Sopranos* had now become fully internalised in Ms. L.'s mind. She had watched the complete series on television and, subsequently, on D.V.D. so many times that even she had begun to become a little bit bored. In due course, I noticed that, in some of her sessions, she would not mention *The Sopranos* at all – quite a novelty in view of her long-standing commitment to this programme. Towards the end of our fourth year of analysis, Ms. L. had now embarked on a fifth phase in relation to this iconic television programme. The patient told me that she had recently begun to host regular pizza and spaghetti evenings at her tiny flat for a newly cultivated group of friends and neighbours. Previously, the patient had refused to let anybody into her bedsit under any circumstances, frightened of penetration and other forms of aggression. When Ms. L. realised that she feared her own potential for violence towards any strangers who knocked on the door, she became immediately more available for social relationships and she now began to fancy herself as a "Mrs. Soprano" of sorts, cooking large Italian meals for the masses. Perhaps, in this respect, Ms. L. had finally begun to internalise some of the more nurturant aspects of *The Sopranos*, as opposed to the more violent and suicidal components which characterised this televisual family.

We ultimately commenced the sixth and, perhaps, final, phase of the psychoanalysis in which Ms. L. made absolutely no mention of the programme at all. For the first time in many years, she had begun to date a man, she had held down her first job, and she had started to think about returning to university, having dropped out of education many years previously. Extraordinarily, this patient had also developed what struck me as a very healthy and creative interest in Italian opera, especially the music of Giuseppe Verdi and Giacomo Puccini. Strikingly, the patient had intuited, quite correctly, that I deeply admire the opera, and so she eventually began to regale me with details of her new compact disc purchases. One day, I noted that she seemed to have developed a true penchant for compilations of the great female singers (e.g., Maria Callas, Leontyne Price, Joan Sutherland, and others), and I wondered aloud whether she had now replaced *The Sopranos* with the *sopranos*.[3] Ms. L. giggled with deep pleasure and satisfaction that she seemed to have relinquished her addiction to the Mafia in favour of some far more tender Italian artists.

Conclusion: Eleven Years of Television Viewing

Television insinuates itself into the deepest recesses of our minds. It also serves as a cyber-Rorschach, which paints a picture of what already lurks in our secret thoughts. Nowadays, we use television not only to entertain us, to inform us, and to soothe our loneliness, but, also, we rely upon it to help our minds function. Recently, a new patient, "Mr. M.", had asked me whether I could recommend any really good books about the impact of parents on their children. As I work in a consulting room lined with books and journals, it seemed disingenuous to provide an evasive answer or to wonder why the patient wished for such bibliographical assistance. In fact, I recommended an excellent book written by the psychologist Dr. Oliver James (2010), *How Not to F*** Them Up: The First Three Years*. I merely mentioned the title of the book, but I did not lend an actual physical copy of the book to the patient. Quite intrigued by my bibliophilic reference, Mr. M., expressed his thanks, while lying on the couch, and then began to articulate: "Oliver James ... Oliver James ... ah, good ... it sounds like the perfect book. I shall have to buy a copy. But I don't have a pen. How will I remember that name? Oh, I know, I'll just think of Jamie Oliver, the chef ... but backwards." Even basic cognitive information becomes communicated, processed, and remembered through references to stars of television.

On 20th May, 2010, a television documentary about the work of the Freud Museum of London appeared on B.B.C. 4, broadcast as part of a four-part series entitled *Behind the Scenes at the Museum*. A very pugnacious patient, "Ms. N.", came to her session the following day and told me how she had watched the first episode of this programme and how she had taken a great dislike of all the staff members portrayed therein. The patient's calumniations against the Freud Museum became increasingly vitriolic, and I felt very torn between allowing Ms. N. to use the session in a fully verbally unrestricted fashion and my loyalty towards the Freud Museum and its staff members, many of whom I had known for decades. I listened silently, without interruption, and then dared to wonder out loud about the extreme vehemence of Ms. N.'s hostility towards the mild-mannered archivists who work at Maresfield Gardens. I also knew that Ms. N., a compulsive Googler, had already learned that I myself had many ties to the Freud Museum, some of which could be found quite readily through a cursory search of the internet.

In an effort to explore the deeper aspects of Ms. N.'s transferential feelings, I suggested that her odium for the museum staffers might, in fact, represent a displacement of angry feelings towards me for all sorts of reasons, and perhaps, principally, for not having cured her fully as yet. To my surprise, and to my secret delight, the patient returned for another session following the weekend break. After reclining on the couch, she told me that she had decided to watch that inaugural episode of the Freud Museum documentary once more on the B.B.C. iPlayer, and, having done so, she realised that she may have misjudged the staff. After the second viewing of the documentary, the curatorial and archival staff did not seem quite so bizarre to Ms. N.; in fact, this time, she even warmed to some of them. This change of heart gave me ample material to think with the patient about all of the relationships and opportunities that she had sabotaged in her life by having executed people within seconds of meeting them, and sometimes *before* she had even met them. The patient, an English literature graduate with a detailed knowledge of the works of Jane Austen, then confessed that her "first impressions" (i.e., a reference to the original title of Austen's masterpiece, *Pride and Prejudice: A Novel. In Three Volumes*) might often be quite inaccurate, and that she would, in future, devote more time and energy to better reality-testing and assessment of other people. It seemed extraordinary that Ms. N. and I needed to reach this discovery through the analysis of a television programme, but, once again, such anecdotes provide powerful evidence of the way in which the remote-control device and, moreover, the television set itself – which we might describe as a sort of "cathode nipple" – have begun to shape, and continue to shape, the very structure of our internal and external lives.

According to the statistics of B.A.R.B., the Broadcasters' Audience Research Board, during a period of four weeks in October 2010 – more than one decade ago – the average Briton watched approximately 27.95 hours of television per week (Anonymous, 2020a).[4] Based on that figure alone, one can readily calculate that, over the course of seventy years, an ordinary Briton might well devote approximately eleven years or more of his or her life to the television. These figures have risen in more recent years with the increasing popularity of streaming services such as Amazon Prime and Netflix.

And, of course, during the dreadful coronavirus pandemic which exploded in 2020, large numbers of the world's population worked from home with even greater access to television. One report from the regulator Ofcom – The Office of Communications in the United Kingdom – has speculated that, more recently, many Britons might have spent approximately forty per cent of their waking hours watching television and related streaming services (Anonymous, 2020b); and a further update has revealed that the average person in the United Kingdom has begun to watch at least forty-seven minutes more of television and streaming services (such as Netflix and YouTube) in 2020 compared to the pre-pandemic year of 2019, thus constituting an average of five hours and forty minutes per person per day (Anonymous, 2021a, cf. Anonymous, 2021b).

In view of the technologically enhanced increase in "binge-watching", it should hardly surprise us that television has become a growing topic for discussion within the consulting room and that the content and the format of free associations, dreams, unconscious wishes, and sexual fantasies reported in psychoanalysis should be shaped and moulded by televisual culture, as I have indicated in the aforementioned clinical vignettes.

Strikingly, in the wake of the COVID-19 pandemic, the very practice of psychoanalysis and psychotherapy has become equivalent for many to the art of watching television, as countless numbers of clinical practitioners and patients worldwide have seated themselves in front of a computer screen or laptop, while engaging in Zoom psychoanalysis or Zoom psychotherapy, owing to the necessity of social distancing. Thus, many of our fellow mental health workers and our clients will have spent even more time staring at a screen than ever before (Duarte, 2021; cf. Kahr, 2021a, 2021d, 2021–2022).

In this brief communication, I do not wish to pass judgement on the nature of binge-watching, but I have merely endeavoured to report its existence, in the hope that subsequent discussion and reflection will help us to understand the impact of television on the unconscious mind much more fully. Television remains a source of entertainment and education and, for some, a necessary form of self-prescribed medication which reduces the horrid impact of loneliness and isolation and, often, depression; therefore, this cathode nipple object offers much primitive comfort and intellectual enhancement to many people (cf. Bainbridge and Yates, 2007, 2014; Yates, 2007, 2014; Bainbridge, 2012, 2014a, 2014b, 2019a, 2019b). But, moreover, the way in which we watch television, and the manner in which we discuss our viewing habits in the consulting room, provides mental health practitioners with an immense amount of extremely useful data about the structure of the unconscious mind. Consequently, clinicians must become increasingly sensitive to the impact of our television-watching behaviour, so that we can better understand the ways in which we might help some of our troubled patients to transform themselves from the more Mafia-like *Sopranos* into the more musically pleasing *sopranos*.

7
Dr. Paul Weston and the Bloodstained Couch
Some Critical Comments on *In Treatment*

Dr. Paul Weston has blood on his couch ... quite literally. In the midst of a marital psychotherapy session with a warring couple, the pregnant wife miscarries her foetus and leaves a mark on Dr. Weston's sofa. Afterwards, as Dr. Weston attempts to scrub away the stain, his own wife enters the consulting room in his home-office and promptly confesses that she has begun to have an extramarital affair and will soon be jetting off to Italy with her new lover for a romantic tryst. Enraged and distraught, Weston decides to sleep in his consulting room, on the aforementioned blood-stained sofa.

Having now forsaken his marital bedroom, Dr. Weston places his toiletries in the bathroom adjoining his office – the one used by his patients. These items include a bottle of prescription sleeping tablets. Soon thereafter, a suicidal adolescent girl who has ridden her bicycle headlong into oncoming traffic, and then arrives at Dr. Weston's office for an assessment, excuses herself mid-session and enters the bathroom. Of course, this teenager cannot resist the urge to rummage through her psychotherapist's medicine chest, and, before long, she discovers Weston's bottle of sleeping pills and promptly swallows the contents. Shortly after emerging from the bathroom, this adolescent patient collapses on the floor of Dr. Weston's consulting room, necessitating immediate hospitalisation.

Shockingly, Weston now has blood not only on his couch but, also, on his hands ... quite literally. Fortunately, this adolescent patient does eventually recover from her overdose, but to complicate matters even more so, two of Weston's adult patients, a sexy female anaesthesiologist and a male fighter pilot, have begun to sleep together, having met, by "chance", outside Weston's house. Dr. Weston becomes completely disequilibrated by this news because he harbours a barely contained erotic attraction for the female patient, and he has even gone back into supervision-cum-personal therapy in an effort to manage his own malignant countertransference reaction.

Meanwhile, amid one very heated session of psychotherapy, the male fighter pilot, who had recently dropped a bomb on a group of Iraqi civilians, then hurls a bomb of a different sort at Paul Weston. An accomplished snoop, with access to confidential information, this pilot informs Dr. Weston that he knows all about Mrs. Weston's infidelity and all about her trip to Rome. Moreover, he has discovered that Weston's teenage daughter has had sexual encounters with various drug-addicted boyfriends. But, worst of all, the pilot then gloats about his own sexual exploits with the attractive anaesthesiologist, who, he describes, rather contemptuously, as little more than a slut. These invasive and provocative comments unleash Dr. Weston's volcanic rage and, mid-session, this mental health professional then becomes quite berserk, hurling the contents of his coffee cup in his patient's face and then shoving him brutally. The coffee cup smashes and lacerates Weston who now has even more blood on his hand as well as on his couch.

Readers of this book who might not recognise the name of Paul Weston need not rush to file a professional complaint with the nearest ethics committee or with the Professional Standards Authority for Health and Social Care. As a fictional character – the protagonist of the popular Home Box Office television series *In Treatment* – Dr. Paul Weston falls outside the formal jurisdiction of the psychoanalytical community.

Although many mental health professionals might be inclined to dismiss Paul Weston's completely inexcusable and grossly unethical behaviour as little more than a salacious soap opera designed to seduce viewers with such heightened, indeed exaggerated, clinical drama, one cannot help but wonder whether Weston's unsanctionable conduct might in any way influence current public perceptions of those who practise the "talking therapies". After all, what would a prospective patient think about psychotherapy or psychoanalysis after having watched an episode of *In Treatment*? Perhaps a sensible person would dismiss Dr. Weston as simply a fictional construction. And perhaps a cautious person might stay away from mental health professionals altogether. But one must wonder whether a masochistic or a sadistic person might sign up immediately and book an appointment! As the psychosocial studies scholar and film expert Professor Caroline Bainbridge (2012) has argued, we must take *In Treatment* very seriously indeed. Although many television "shrinks" have already appeared on our screens, notably the kindly, if romantically muddled, "Dr. Frasier Crane" from *Frasier*, and the thoughtful and well-meaning "Dr. Jennifer Melfi" from *The Sopranos*, these tele-psychological practitioners have now disappeared from the small screen (except of course in re-runs), not to mention "Dr. May Foster", the relationship therapist in the popular American television series *Tell Me You Love Me*, as well as "Dr. Craig Huffstodt", the psychiatrist in the so-called "dramedy" *Huff*. But, as Bainbridge has remarked, "Dr. Paul Weston" has attracted considerable attention as well as rave reviews. Indeed, thanks to the riveting scripts, the tight direction, the gripping performances, and the multiple awards, *In Treatment* will likely continue to appear on our televisions in one shape or form for quite some time to come, not only in terms of re-runs, but, also, with further incarnations and spin-offs.

Based on the Israeli television programme *Be'Tipul*, which debuted in 2005 and which received several prestigious awards, the Americanised version, *In Treatment*, has garnered immense international acclaim, featuring well-known film stars such as Gabriel Byrne, Dianne Wiest, and Debra Winger in principal roles, accumulating major prizes at the Primetime Emmy Awards, and at the Golden Globe Awards; moreover, it received an accolade from the venerable Writers Guild of America. Additionally, the American Film Institute voted *In Treatment* as one of the Ten Best Television Programs of 2008. In fact, *Be'Tipul* and *In Treatment* have since become an international franchise, with a Serbian version having premiered in 2009, a Dutch version having launched in 2010, and many more versions which followed suit in other languages, including the much-discussed French edition, *En Thérapie*, launched in 2021, which many of my French-speaking analysands referred to in sessions on numerous occasions.

Indeed, the impact of *In Treatment* has since surpassed even *Frasier* and *The Sopranos*, and Dr. Paul Weston has become far better known than any of his tele-psychological predecessors. In fact, to youngsters steeped in popular, contemporary celebrity culture, Dr. Weston will certainly be better known to many than even Carl Gustav Jung and, possibly, Sigmund Freud.

Eventually, *In Treatment* became available for viewing on Netflix, thus increasing its influence significantly. And, in 2020, the broadcasters Home Box Office announced that they would soon be releasing a new, rebooted fourth series of the American version of the programme (Anonymous, 2020c), which eventually graced our screens in 2021.

In view of the unethical behaviour of the fictional Dr. Weston, and in view of his immense appeal, how might mental health professionals make sense of *In Treatment*? Much as we may wish to do so, we cannot simply dismiss *In Treatment* as a poorly researched television programme or as an act of revenge perpetrated by an insufficiently psychoanalysed television executive whose analyst had failed to cure his or her presenting symptoms. Indeed, many of the writers of *In Treatment* have themselves undergone psychotherapy and have spoken or written publicly about their helpful experiences of the talking cure (e.g., Bunin, 2010). In fact, the American programme makers had even engaged the services of an experienced psychoanalyst, a member of the American Psychoanalytic Association, to serve as its script consultant for both the second season and the third season of episodes, in which Dr. Weston seeks further help for his own personal difficulties, if not psychopathologies. Regrettably, its hero, Paul Weston, did operate as more of an anti-hero, especially in the first season (prior to the engagement of the psychoanalytical consultant), having shoved one of his patients with brute force and having declared his erotic attraction for another patient.

And yet, even though mental health colleagues would unquestionably frown upon, indeed, condemn Dr. Weston's comportment, I know of numerous individuals who have become very attracted to the discipline of psychotherapy, in part, as a direct result of having watched this compelling programme with great interest. In fact, in 2010, during a first consultation with a prospective patient, I queried whether this person had ever had any experience of therapy previously. To my surprise, the new patient replied, "No, but I've watched *In Treatment*. Does that count?"

Should we be worried that a television programme which portrays the psychotherapist in such a troubling fashion might inspire potential masochistic patients to embark upon analysis or therapy (in the hope of being mistreated), or should we celebrate the fact that this programme has generated an interest in the confidential and unpublicised work that we do in our cloistered cabinets? *Be'Tipul*, the Israeli precursor to *In Treatment*, certainly exerted a strong impact on private practice, at least in the financial sense. Apparently, after the psychotherapist in *Be'Tipul* revealed in one episode that he would charge his clients 400 shekels per session, large numbers of Israeli colleagues purportedly raised their real-life fees in consequence (Bainbridge, 2010).

In Treatment differs greatly from *Frasier* and *The Sopranos*, which few psychoanalysts and psychotherapists seem to have minded in quite the same way. For starters, both Dr. Crane and Dr. Melfi had certainly never engaged in violent outbursts or erotic enactments in the clinical setting. Moreover, the actual detailed practice of "therapy" often occupied a far more marginal position in those television programmes. In the situation comedy *Frasier*, psychotherapy *per se* played a relatively tiny role by comparison with Dr. Frasier's romantic entanglements with countless girlfriends; and Dr. Melfi, though an important character in *The Sopranos*, still occupied only a supporting role compared to that of the ubiquitous and highly dramatic members of the Soprano family. But with *In Treatment*, the psychotherapist occupies pride of place in the central, *starring* role. Across the first three series, the figure of Dr. Paul Weston appeared in virtually every single scene, and much of the action occurred in his consulting room, in his home, and in his very presence. And herein lies a problem. Intelligent, thoughtful viewers can easily dismiss the completely insane "killer psychiatrists" who have appeared in films, such as the gun-toting "Dr. Murchison" in Alfred Hitchcock's classic movie *Spellbound*, or the transvestite, knife-wielding "Dr. Robert Elliott" in Brian de Palma's erotic thriller *Dressed to Kill*, knowing full well that most psychiatrists do not, as a rule, carry weapons with deadly intent. But the psychotherapy sessions conducted by Dr. Paul Weston seem so very life-like that the line between clinical truth and televisual embellishment often becomes very blurred indeed.

After all, Dr. Weston did not train at the ridiculously named "Psychoneurotic Institute for the Very, *Very* Nervous" lampooned in Mel Brooks's comedic film about psychiatry, *High Anxiety*. But we do learn that Weston did in fact train at "the Institute". And we know that he had undertaken both personal psychotherapy and clinical supervision. We hear him use terms such as "projection" and "transference". And we know that he has read the works of the eminent clinician Dr. Christopher Bollas. Thus, we cannot simply toss Weston aside as a Brooksian buffoon or as a de Palman psychopath. In fact, if he has read the works of Bollas and has made reference to transference at the Institute, he could, indeed, be a psychoanalyst, especially if a proper member of the American Psychoanalytic Association had served as a script consultant.

Of course, we have no textual evidence to suggest that Dr. Weston works as a classical psychoanalyst as such. He practises, it would seem, more generically, as a psychotherapist informed by psychodynamic ideas. But one could forgive a member of the general public for confusing the two professions, because Weston does make the occasional Freudian-style interpretation, and he does trace symptoms back to childhood traumas, and he does analyse dreams – all hallmarks of classical psychoanalytical work. Thus, the muddling of psychoanalysis and psychotherapy may evoke a mixture of divergent responses from various different communities within the mental health profession, each group keen to disown Weston, quite concerned that we might all become tarred by his brush through association.

Weston has certainly presented viewers with a great challenge, evoking both loathing and, also, admiration in equal measure. Yes, he does, of course, work in a blood-stained consulting room, breaking coffee cups, shoving patients, and leaving pills within easy reach of the suicidal. But, Dr. Weston can also be incredibly kind, often listening deftly with intense concentration, gently eroding pathological defences, ably allowing his patients to cry cathartically, assisting these men and women to articulate hitherto unverbalised family secrets, and so on. In fact, throughout the course of the drama, Dr. Weston had often proved himself to be extremely effective clinically by using traditional methods that every honourable mental health professional would recognise. He does lust and he does shove; *but*, with other patients, he also achieves great results. This paradox prompts the question as to whether television writers have unwittingly created a modern-day Masud Khan (Cooper, 1993; Willoughby, 2005; Hopkins, 2006), often brilliant by day but destructive by night.

Psychoanalysts may derive some small comfort from the fact that Weston does not practise classical Freudian psychoanalysis at all. His patients certainly do not recline on a couch in order to free-associate. Instead, they sit across the room on the blood-stained sofa. Weston often wears jeans, and he has decorated his consulting room with private family memorabilia. He shares his own dream material with his clients. He keeps a football in his office. He makes coffee for patients. He informs a married couple of the approximate dollar value of his own house. He displays many photography books on his shelf, but, as far as I could ascertain, none whatsoever by Sigmund Freud. Certainly, while watching these programmes, I saw no signs of a certain collection of twenty-four well-known, highly recognisable texts with light-blue covers or dark-blue bound spines, namely, the English-language edition of the complete works of Freud (1953a, 1953b, 1953c, 1953d, 1955a, 1955b, 1955c, 1955d, 1957a, 1957b, 1958, 1959a, 1959b, 1960a, 1960b, 1961a, 1961b, 1962, 1963a, 1963b, 1964a, 1964b, 1966, 1974).

Fortunately, Weston seems sufficiently differentiated from most traditionally dressed and classically orientated psychoanalysts. But, in the mind of the general public, all mental health professionals – whether psychiatrists, counsellors, psychologists, social workers, psychotherapists, or psychoanalysts – all become proverbial "shrinks". Has the television series *In Treatment* therefore frightened away potential patients? Might the programme even have enticed new patients, perhaps those with a sadomasochistic underbelly who wish to engage in coffee cup-throwing? Or has the programme actually attracted earnest patients who wish to seek genuine assistance, keen to alleviate their psychological turmoil?

In discussing this television programme with many psychological colleagues and with many people who work in other professions, a trend has certainly emerged among the responses. Most non-mental health professionals have deeply admired *In Treatment* and have found it quite gripping. These may well be the people who have boosted the ratings of the programme, who have purchased the D.V.D.s, and who have voted for the awards, thus ensuring the long-term commercial success of this franchise. Fortunately, many of these fans had already undergone psychotherapy themselves and possess, therefore, a great capacity to differentiate between real-life therapy or analysis and "television therapy". None of the non-professionals with whom I spoke harboured serious worries that their own psychotherapists might splatter coffee upon their faces. The mental health colleagues, by contrast, have reacted in rather a different fashion. Although some of my fellow professionals told me that they had enjoyed watching the programme, many more had expressed extreme revulsion at what they experienced as a contemptuous, denigratory, evil portrayal of the dedicated, compassionate, psychologically orientated work that we aspire to undertake, and for which many of us have trained over several decades. In view of these reactions, should psychoanalytical workers lobby to ban *In Treatment*, or should we play clips from these episodes in our seminars as a means of cautioning our trainees, *or* should we rejoice that the "talking cure" has become, at last, such a central point of focus in world media, regardless of the ways in which Paul Weston might comport himself?

I must confess that I had put off watching *In Treatment* for the longest time and I then immersed myself only after I had received a formal invitation to participate in a panel discussion about the programme. Eventually, I sat down in front of the television with some trepidation, prepared for a veritable busman's holiday, and I immediately became quite cross with the fictional Paul Weston and kept wishing to become his very punitive supervisor: "No, Dr. Weston, don't say *that* to the patient. Hold the silence. Don't interrupt the free associations. And for heaven's sake, don't serve coffee in the middle of the session." But as I watched the entire first series of *In Treatment*, my attitude toward Weston began to change over time, in spite of my growing concern about, and disrespect for, his extremely unboundaried, unprofessional, and violent qualities. Of course, I did at times wish that he had pursued another profession, but, on other occasions, when he practised in a more contained, more thoughtful manner, I marvelled at the sensitive way in which he would make affective contact with some of the painful parts of his patients' narratives. In many respects, my reactions to Weston mirror those of the forensic psychotherapist who certainly never condones the patient's violence, but who can, nevertheless, develop a sense of compassion for the offender's tremendous difficulties and vulnerabilities, which have stemmed, invariably, from childhood traumata.

Will the programme *In Treatment* have damaged the public face of psychotherapy, psychoanalysis, and the talking therapies in general? I very much doubt so. As we know, Professor Sigmund Freud's detractors dismissed him as a "Casanova" (Weiss, 1970, p. 2) and as a veritable pornographer deserving of imprisonment (Ferenczi, 1911; cf. Jones, 1955; Kahr, 2009, 2021a). Attacks on the probity and integrity and utility of psychoanalysis have persisted since its inception and have continued unceasingly ever since. And yet, in spite of these innumerable anti-Freudian assaults, the professions of psychoanalysis and psychoanalytical psychotherapy and psychodynamic psychotherapy have survived and have continued to blossom worldwide.

I recently encountered a little-known letter, which appeared in the distinguished British medical weekly, *The Lancet*, on 14th October, 1939, only three weeks after the death of Sigmund Freud. Mr. Andrew Rugg-Gunn (1939, p. 854), one of Great Britain's most distinguished ophthalmic surgeons at that time, a Fellow of the Royal College of Surgeons of England and, also, a Senior Surgeon at the Western Ophthalmic Hospital in London, wrote from his private practice on Harley Street, "It is both appropriate and necessary to record that Freud's unhealthy obsession with sex has been responsible to an overwhelming extent for the depravity of mind and perversity of taste that has affected, among others, English people and particularly English women since the last war. In itself a sufficiently grave evil, this result has had consequences immeasurably malignant, for it undoubtedly paved the way for wide acceptance of that complete Jewish ideology out of which sprang bolshevism [*sic*], nazism [*sic*] and the present war." By contrast, on 7th October, 1939, only one week previously, Dr. John Rickman (1939, p. 813), a pioneer of British psychoanalysis, wrote to *The Lancet* that Freud "made one feel to be in the company of a new kind of being – an ideal for human nature." Of course, many of us often succumb to splitting and polarisation, creating both an idealised Freud and a denigrated Freud; so, it should hardly be surprising, therefore, that a large percentage of the television viewership became so entranced by Dr. Paul Weston, a modern-day psychotherapeutic sinner-saint.

Viewers have watched *In Treatment* for both conscious as well as unconscious reasons. For those curious about the art of psychotherapy, *In Treatment* provides an intimate glimpse into a very particular clinical practice, albeit not necessarily *our* clinical practice. For others, the programme serves as a confirmation that one has to be mad to visit a psychological professional, and mad to be one as well. For those in the mental health field keen to damn all heretics who do not practise exactly as we do, *In Treatment* offers a field day of boundary violations that one can lambaste. But as Bainbridge (2012) has noted, the strong political subtext of the script has also afforded each of us an opportunity to work through shared national and international traumata. For example, one of Weston's patients, the aforementioned fighter pilot who bombed a group of civilians in Iraq, sought consultation from Weston in order to receive assistance so that he might cope more successfully with the horror of what he had done. Although few ordinary television viewers will ever have bombed Iraq, those of us living in the very Western countries which orchestrated such real-life attacks can obtain vicarious relief from our conscious and unconscious guilt by watching Dr. Weston treat the traumatised bomber pilot.

The case of Paul Weston raises many crucial issues about ethics, about the public perception of psychoanalysis and psychotherapy, and about the relationship between mental health professionals and the media. Dr. Weston also serves as a televisual Rorschach test onto whom viewers can project any number of concerns, anxieties, wishes, and superegoic restrictions. For some colleagues, Paul Weston represents a reprehensible blot on the psychoanalytical escutcheon, and these practitioners might well insist that all professionals ought to distance ourselves from Weston's nefarious doings. For others, Paul Weston serves as a reminder that human beings – even healers – can be complex, creative, healthful and, also, damaged at the same time, and that Weston provides a true, honest portrait of a simultaneously strong and, also, wounded post-modern person (cf. Cotter, 2011; Izod, 2011). To date, many psychoanalytical organisations around the world have devoted seminars, panels, conferences, and symposia to *In Treatment*. In fact, I have had contact with a group of psychoanalytically trained couple psychotherapists in South Africa who convened a study group in which the members reflected upon Dr. Weston's marital therapy sessions in detail and then discussed the technical issues which arose therein. The programme certainly cannot be ignored.

But whether we decide to send Dr. Weston to the Ethics Committee for a reprimand, or whether we ship him back to his training therapist or training analyst for further personal work, or whether we merely remind ourselves of Weston's status as a purely fictional character and thus treat the matter with good humour, we might wish to consider one other dimension of the story, namely, the place of Weston and of *In Treatment* within a broader history of the representation of mental health professionals in the media.

In 1941, a very pioneering musical play opened on Broadway and took the United States of America by storm. As we indicated in the previous chapter, the formidable team of Moss Hart, the librettist, as well as Ira Gershwin, the lyricist (and, also, the elder brother of George Gershwin), and Kurt Weill, the composer, had joined forces to create *Lady in the Dark*, the first Broadway musical properly devoted to psychoanalysis. Moss Hart, a sometime patient of the eminent American psychoanalytical pioneer, Dr. Lawrence Kubie (1962), had experienced his own personal analysis as so very deeply rewarding that he transformed aspects of that psychological undertaking into a thrilling theatre piece about the editor of a fashion magazine who cannot make a commitment to any of the men in her life (Brown, 2006). Fortunately, the protagonist of this iconic Broadway musical eventually embarks upon a course of psychoanalysis and succeeds in uncovering the traumatic childhood roots of her erotic ambivalence and, ultimately, enjoys being cured and then settles down to domestic bliss (Hart, 1941). Although the portrayal of such old-fashioned gender stereotypes might seem rather simplistic to a twenty-first century audience, *Lady in the Dark* certainly captured the public imagination in the World War II era and created a huge upsurge of interest in psychoanalysis among the intelligentsia of New York (Farber and Green, 1993; Hale, 1995; Shorter, 1997).

Lady in the Dark ran for 777 performances on Broadway, a rarity in that era, rather akin to the success of *Les Misérables* today. It proved so popular that the Hollywood moguls at Paramount Pictures paid the princely sum of $285,000 for the film rights and transformed the intimate Broadway musical into a lavish 1944 blockbuster film starring Ginger Rogers as the fashion magazine editor. And the character of "Dr. Alexander Brooks", the fictional psychoanalyst in both the stage play and the screenplay, helped to increase the popularity of Freudian psychology across the entire country (Kahr, 2000; mcclung, 2007). Although one cannot easily compare mid-twentieth-century theatre and cinema with early-twenty-first-century global television, one could argue that *Lady in the Dark*, the most prominent artistic depiction of psychoanalysis in the mid-twentieth century, may well have played a cultural role equivalent to the more recent television series *In Treatment*.

By studying the Broadway script and the Hollywood screenplay of *Lady in the Dark*, one soon discovers that although psychoanalysis occupies a very important role in the story, one meets Dr. Alexander Brooks only very sparingly, here and there. In fact, Dr. Brooks does not even have the opportunity to sing a song of his own – extremely unusual for a significant character in a Broadway musical. Indeed, he remains mostly silent and offers only a small amount of dialogue from time to time. In other words, Dr. Brooks, the psychoanalyst, actually functions as a relatively minor character in the world's first full-length all-singing, all-dancing, all-psychoanalysing musical.

If one studies the many portrayals of psychoanalysis and psychiatry in theatre during the first decades of the twentieth century, one would be very hard pressed to find many works of art which feature a proper, grown-up psychoanalyst. Freudians and Jungians often appeared as passing characters, offering merely a frisson of psychological culture, but they almost never starred in major roles (Sievers, 1955). *In Treatment*, by contrast, has provided modern art with one of the first truly serious portrayals in which the psychotherapist functions at all times as the central character in quite a serious way – not as a serial killer, not as a comic, but, rather, as a professional talking therapist (cf. Fleming and Manvell, 1985; Gabbard and Gabbard, 1987).

As I have suggested, although the lead character in *Frasier* works as a radio psychiatrist, the detailed clinical practice of psychotherapy as such occupies only a marginal role in that television series. And, in *The Sopranos*, Dr. Melfi does facilitate a form of psychotherapy that we would recognise today, but she does not function as a chief protagonist in the drama. By contrast, *In Treatment* has proved to be a far more impactful portrayal of the clinical psychotherapist-psychoanalyst. Thanks to the superb acting of Gabriel Byrne as the lead character, we now witness the placing of the psychotherapist in the most central position. Both Dr. Paul Weston's private life and his working life take centre stage; and whereas the patients come and go, never to return after the end of each successive season, Weston always remains. Whatever we may think about Weston as a practitioner or as a representative of our profession, he certainly serves as positive proof that the era of the psychotherapist has moved from the *side* to the *centre*, stimulating unparalleled scrutiny of our field and endless opportunities for vicious criticism, as well as a myriad of possibilities for creative and healthful influence.

Section IV

Celebrity and the Psyche

8

Fame and the Unconscious
Toxic and Inspiring Aspects of Celebrity Culture

Are All Celebrities Mad?

Some years ago, I attended a very lavish dinner party in London's Notting Hill. The guest list consisted of a noted theatrical director, a nationally renowned broadcaster, a best-selling novelist, a multi-millionaire financier, an astronaut who had commanded one of the Apollo rocket ships, and an internationally venerated musician, who, for reasons of confidentiality, I shall call "Maestro X." The assembled personalities proved so glittering that I recognised all the names beforehand, bar my own.

In spite of the elegant decor and the delicious food, prepared meticulously by our gracious and beautiful hostess, I had a dreadful evening. Whenever any particular subject arose in conversation, Maestro X. dominated the discussion. In the midst of debating the crises in the Middle East, we soon learned that Maestro X. had performed there many times and knew more about Israeli politics than Benjamin Netanyahu. When we progressed to a discussion of cinema, Maestro X. regaled us with his recent work in Hollywood and told us exactly what inner forces had prompted Steven Spielberg to film *Schindler's List*. And when our attention turned to psychoanalysis, the Maestro certainly knew more about Sigmund Freud than I did, and he proceeded to pontificate in emphatic tones about why Freud had become a dinosaur.

I sat next to the astronaut, and, never having previously met anyone who had walked on the surface of the moon, I dared to switch the topic of conversation in an effort to include this rather timid and understated space voyager, who looked very bored. Before the astronaut could clear his throat, Maestro X. launched into a disquisition about the future of space travel and about his hopes of conducting, one day, an interplanetary concert. Indeed, Maestro X., an undeniably accomplished gentleman, supreme in his craft, and by far the most celebrated figure at the dining room table, held court all evening, but he did so in the most grandiose manner, and he turned what might otherwise have proved to be a truly enjoyable supper party into a cross between a Shakespearean monologue and a press conference.

Throughout the course of this meal, Maestro X. displayed far more narcissistic psychopathology than patients with whom I have worked who had actually received a formal psychiatric diagnosis of narcissistic personality disorder. Indeed, the Maestro reminded me very much of the famous anecdote concerning the screen star Marlene Dietrich. Apparently, when some friends came backstage to see Miss Dietrich after one of her live, cabaret performances, she reputedly boasted how magnificently she had performed in the first act, how brilliantly she had sung in the second act, and how stunning she looked in her shimmering dresses. Then, turning to her friends, she intoned, "But enough about me, what did *you* think of my performance?" In spite of being one of Marlene Dietrich's greatest friends and admirers, the actor, playwright, songwriter, and novelist Noël Coward (1955, p. 277) found Miss Dietrich "fairly tiresome", and later remarked, "It is sad to think how many of our glamorous leading ladies are round the bend" (Coward, 1958, p. 384).

Shortly after I had begun to work in the media, a very eminent psychologist forewarned me that I would soon come to discover that every famous individual suffers from borderline personality disorder. He told me that I would not believe this fact at first, but that, after a period of years, I would have no option but to accept the veracity of this hard-won clinical observation.

Having now worked in the media for nearly forty years, I have had the privilege of meeting, and often collaborating, with those who have achieved international fame, as well as with those who have had walk-on parts in crowd scenes; and although I have interviewed several people who have met the diagnostic criteria for borderline personality disorder and narcissistic personality disorder, I must confess that I have come to know many more in the entertainment industry whom I have come to regard as rather sane. Indeed, I have discovered that working with "famous" people and with "celebrities" in a psychotherapeutic context often proves to be a most fulfilling experience because famous people invariably become excellent psychotherapy patients, and they usually work extremely well in treatment. Having already survived the pains and the pleasures of being scrutinised by the entire world, they experience the benign camera lens of the psychotherapist as a tremendous relief.

I could of course speak at greater length about the psychology of the celebrity, addressing questions concerning grandiosity, exhibitionism, and related topics, but I shall not do so for two reasons. First of all, the pledge of confidentiality that each psychotherapist promises implicitly or explicitly to each client must be sacrosanct, and should remain so, even after the death of the psychotherapist. Second of all, some of us may well experience a sense of titillation hearing about Sir Paul McCartney's preoedipal conflicts, about Madonna's psychosexual development, or about Lady Gaga's struggles with the rapprochement sub-phase of the separation-individuation process, but I rather suspect that we might be able to pose a much more interesting set of psychological questions, as part of a broader cultural analysis.

In the pages that follow, I will address no further the question of whether celebrities might be psychopathologically disturbed, attention-seeking, maternally deprived exhibitionists. In fact, I shall focus *not* on the celebrities at all but, rather, upon the audience – *you and I* – to begin to understand why we as onlookers become so obsessed with the lives of our celebrities. What function or functions do celebrities serve within our inner worlds, and what function or functions do celebrities fulfil in terms of the unconscious life of the large group which we inhabit?

The Celebrity Worship Syndrome

One need be neither a mental health professional nor a cultural commentator to appreciate our deep preoccupation with fame, with the famous, with those who wish to become famous, as well as with those who had once been famous, and with those earmarked for fame, and, moreover, with those who *had* enjoyed fame, then plummeted into obscurity, and then became famous once again, such as Gloria Stuart, a huge American film star of the 1930s, who retired and virtually disappeared from sight, before resurfacing, decades later, in James Cameron's 1997 blockbuster film *Titanic*, for which she received an Academy Award nomination at the age of eighty-seven years. We have become obsessed with those who have achieved fame for their magnificent deeds, as well as those who have become famous for their shocking crimes, as well as those who have acquired notoriety simply by virtue of being famous. We relish details of the lives of those who acquire fame overnight, such as the British television songbird Susan Boyle, as well as those who had toiled for a lifetime, such as Mother Teresa. We cannot escape the famous. They fill our stages and our screens, our radios, newspapers, magazines, advertisements and, most especially, our television sets, which I have come to think of as our "cathode nipple". As we indicated in Chapter 6, many of us watch so much television per day, per week, per month, and per year, that the activity becomes virtually a full-time job.

So much of our television content revolves around fame and celebrity. We can neither turn on our television sets nor open a copy of the *Radio Times* without being bombarded by an avalanche of programmes which exalt celebrities, or which promise that ordinary men and women might become celebrities too. These include: *The X Factor, Popstars, Pop Idol, American Idol, American Idol: Idol Gives Back, America's Got Talent, Britain's Got Talent, Britain's Got More Talent, When Will I Be Famous?, Stars in Their Eyes, Star Search, Star Academy, Star Academy Arab World, Celebrity Fit Club, Celebrity Fat Camp, Celebrity Detox, Celebrity Juice, Celebrity Duets, Celebrity Bedlam, Celebrity Four Weddings, Celebrity Wife Swap, The Celebrity Apprentice, Celebrity Big Brother, National Celebrity Games, Drop the Celebrity, Stars Behind Bars, Celebrity Alcatraz, Celebrity Go Home, Celebrity MasterChef, Celebrity MasterChef Australia, Celebrity Come Dine with Me, Celebrity Deal or No Deal, Celebrity Exposed, Celebrity Pressure Cooker, Pointless Celebrities, Celebrity First Dates, 40 Most Shocking Celebrity Divorces, 10 Cutest Celebrity Babies: The Shortlist, 40 Naughtiest Celebrity Scandals, America's Next Top Model, Fame Academy, Comic Relief Does Fame Academy, How to Be Famous,* and literally hundreds and hundreds of similar programme titles (Kahr, 2020a).

Some years ago, the theatrical impresario and composer, Andrew Lloyd Webber, Baron Lloyd Webber of Sydmonton, courted enormous controversy in both the press and the entertainment industry for having subverted the conventional casting process of four major West End musicals by recruiting newcomers from the ranks of the general public and by turning them into overnight stars, at taxpayer expense, courtesy of the British Broadcasting Corporation, with his television programmes *How Do You Solve a Problem Like Maria?, Any Dream Will Do,* as well as *I'd Do Anything,* and *Over the Rainbow.*

One television programme, in particular, has perhaps best captured the imagination of the public, and, moreover, its wish to promote celebrities, and also to humiliate them, namely, *I'm a Celebrity ... Get Me Out of Here!,* which has now graced British television screens over twenty seasons (with potentially more in the pipeline), attracting average viewing figures which have ranged between approximately seven million and twelve million people (nearly one-third of the adult population of the United Kingdom), and sometimes more. The programme has become so popular that it spawned versions in many other countries, including Australia, Denmark, France, Germany, Hungary, India, The Netherlands, Romania, Sweden, and the United States of America.

Celebrities have become so absorbing that even already immensely famous people have the capacity to become entranced. For instance, in 1965, Noël Coward, one the most venerated public figures in Great Britain, succumbed to the lure of several celebrities more popular than himself, namely, the Beatles. Coward (1965a, p. 602), by no means a lover of rock and roll, lambasted the Beatles as "talentless"; nevertheless, in spite of his odium, Coward (1965b, pp. 602–603) pontificated, "To realize that the majority of the modern adolescent world goes ritualistically mad over those four innocuous, rather silly-looking young men is a disturbing thought. Perhaps we are whirling more swiftly into extinction than we know. Personally I should have liked to take some of those squealing young maniacs and cracked their heads together." Yet in spite of his loathing for both the Beatles and their fans, Coward insisted on meeting those Liverpudlian singers and, after greeting Paul McCartney, he lied through gritted teeth and told the moppet-haired rock and roll superstar how much he had enjoyed the performance.

Celebrity even infuses our sexual fantasy life, perhaps unsurprisingly. In my own work as Principal Investigator for the British Sexual Fantasy

Research Project, conducted between 2002 and 2008, I surveyed over 25,000 British and American adult sexual fantasies. As part of this research, I asked participants whether they had ever experienced either masturbatory fantasies or coital fantasies about celebrities, and I discovered that approximately twenty-five per cent of British adult participants will have had an orgasm while imagining a sexual scenario with a film star, a pop star, a television star, or a sports star, with young people between eighteen years of age and twenty-four years of age being three times more likely to do so than those over sixty years of age (Kahr, 2007a; cf. Kahr, 2008a).

In 2003, Dr. John Maltby, a psychologist at the University of Leicester, even identified a so-called "Celebrity Worship Syndrome", noting that approximately one third of the British population suffers from this constellation of symptoms (cf. Chapman, 2003; McCutcheon, Maltby, Houran, and Ashe, 2004). In fact, failure to be a celebrity has even become a crime. On 23rd March, 2003, while hosting The 75th Annual Academy Awards, the American actor Steve Martin cried out in mock horror to the crowd of stars, "Oh, I'm sorry, I thought I saw a non-celebrity."

As we know, back in the 1960s, Noël Coward suspected that the planet might soon become extinct, and he attributed the demise of modern civilisation to the Beatles. Indeed, each of us assumes that the younger generation should be held responsible for the rise of crass celebrity culture. After all, our parents and grandparents never salivated over daily doses of gossip about unfaithful golf professionals such as Tiger Woods, or ostensibly domestically violent actors such as Johnny Depp. Or did they? Can we dismiss the preoccupation with famous people as a predominantly modern, twenty-first-century symptom, driven by technologised social media, or might we come to discover that the fetishisation of celebrity had already occupied an important role in our psychological landscape for many centuries?

Towards a History of Fame

I hope that, in the preceding sections, I have begun to dispel the prevailing myth that all celebrities suffer from exhibitionism and grandiosity. Although certain famous people do struggle with these challenging psychological dynamics, I would argue that a far greater intrapsychic conflict exists in the mind of the audience – the "civilians", as model and actress Elizabeth Hurley (former girlfriend of Hugh Grant) has called us – namely, those of us who pay to sustain and fuel the fame industry.

I now wish to scotch a second myth, namely that the so-called Celebrity Worship Syndrome represents a thoroughly modern phenomenon, and an indication that our culture has begun to deteriorate in an invidious manner, especially in the wake of the proliferation of so-called "reality television" programmes. This could not be further from the truth, as even the most perfunctory scrutiny of historical data provides us with evidence that the preoccupation with fame and celebrity has featured as a vital part of human psychological life for thousands of years, if not longer. Let us examine merely a few landmarks from ancient times.

According to Professor Leo Braudy (1986), a distinguished American *littérateur* and cultural historian at the University of Southern California in Los Angeles, one can trace the history of fame back to the reign of the Macedonian monarch, Alexander the Great, who ruled during the fourth century B.C.E. and who represents, for Braudy, the first true celebrity, in view of Alexander's sustained campaign to preserve his own image on coins and in statuary.

But one can readily find substantial references to a preoccupation with fame long before Alexander. In ancient Greece, Homer spoke of the concept of "kleos aphthiton" ["imperishable fame"] in the *Iliad*. Furthermore, in his epic poem, the *Aeneid* (Book X, 468), the ancient Roman author Publius Vergilius Maro, better known as Virgil, enshrined the very notion of "famam extendere factis" ["to extend fame by deeds"]. Other classical writers who came to engage with this subject have included Herodotus and Hesiod as well as Plutarch and Xenophon (Boitani, 1984).

As the centuries unfolded, the admiration of fame persisted and one could, of course, refer to literally hundreds of historical examples of people seeking notoriety. Even the late-fifteenth-century Cornish blacksmith, Mighell Ioseph (later known as Michael Joseph an Gof) – who stirred rebellion, protesting against the levy of taxes by the English king, Henry VII, in order to fight the Scots – proclaimed, while en route to his execution that, "he should haue a name perpetual and a fame permanēt and immortal"[1] (Hall, 1548, p. 479).

The Tudors also boasted a crop of overnight celebrities, notably three ostensibly holy maidens, such as the Holy Maid of Leominster, who claimed that she could survive on nothing more than daily communion and, consequently, became a superstar during the reign of Henry VII, attracting large crowds, until the king's mother, Lady Margaret Beaufort, the Countess of Richmond and Derby, unmasked the Leominster maid as a fraud who actually ate several meals daily, assisted by a deceptive curate (Rex, 1993). Another woman, the Holy Maid of Ipswich, who flourished in 1516, claimed to be cured, miraculously, of epilepsy, as did Elizabeth Barton, the Holy Maid of Kent, who prophesied her own recovery from epilepsy on Annunciation Day (Rex, 1993). These Tudor religious performers became instant sensations, and one suspects that if they had lived several centuries later, they would, no doubt, have launched their own Twitter campaigns. Even Henry VIII himself, already one of the most famous men in the world, and certainly the most notorious in England during the sixteenth century, prompted William Blount, Lord Mountjoy[2] (1509, p. 450), to write to Desiderius Erasmus, the distinguished man of letters, "Noster Rex non aurum, non gemmas, non metalla, sed virtutem, sed gloriam, sed aeternitatem concupiscit" ["Our King's heart is set not upon gold, or jewels, or mines of ore, but upon virtue, reputation, and eternal fame"].

The Elizabethans also pursued notoriety with considerable fervour. In his play *As You Like It*, written circa 1599 to 1600, William Shakespeare pontificated about the dangers of young men "Seeking the bubble Reputation", [3] as part of the famous "All the world's a Stage"[4] speech, delivered by the melancholy character "Jaques" in the seventh scene of the second act.

By the mid-eighteenth century, the English novelist Laurence Sterne, best remembered as the author of *The Life and Opinions of Tristram Shandy, Gentleman*, had also embraced the wish for celebrity. As he explained, in a letter to an unknown correspondent, dated 30th January, 1760, he had embarked upon writing "not to be *fed*, but to be *famous*" (Sterne, 1760, p. 22). Contemporaneously, the French philosopher and *encyclopédiste* Denis Diderot and the sculptor Étienne Maurice Falconet engaged in a debate, known as the "*dispute sur la postérité*" – the dispute about posterity – arguing whether it would be preferable to strive for fame in one's lifetime or, by contrast, to become renowned after one's death (Diderot, 1765–1767). Strikingly, Diderot (1766, p. 218) emphasised that, "*Tant de grands noms oubliés! tant de grands hommes dont les ouvrages sont perdus ou détruits!*" ["*So many great names forgotten! so many great men whose works are lost or destroyed!*"]. Falconet, who advocated the former position – pre-mortem celebrity – published their correspondence and became quite famous at the time, though his name has since plummeted into obscurity, whereas Diderot, who endorsed the latter position – post-mortem fame – has become a legendary figure in the pantheon of great philosophers.

Fame even penetrated the eighteenth-century prison system. During the *Règne de la Terreur* in France, notorious penal institutions such as the Conciergerie in Paris offered special provision for wealthy, so-called celebrity prisoners, who awaited their executions by guillotine in private cells fitted with a small cot and a bed. By contrast, the more ordinary prisoners, known as the "*pailleux*" (Bijaoui, 1996, p. 30) [i.e., those who slept on straw], had to share vermin-infested cells.

The lust for fame persisted across the nineteenth century as well. For instance, in 1812, the appearance of the first section of the narrative poem *Childe Harold's Pilgrimage*, written by George Gordon, Lord Byron, exerted such an impact that Thomas Moore (1833, p. 255), who became Byron's biographer, remarked, "the impression which it produced upon the public was as instantaneous as it has proved deep and lasting", and that, "The effect was, accordingly, electric; – his fame had not to wait for any of the ordinary gradations, but seemed to spring up, like the palace of a fairy tale, in a night" (Moore, 1833, p. 258). Indeed, Lord Byron himself exclaimed, "'I awoke one morning and found myself famous'" (quoted in Moore, 1833, p. 258).

The publication of *Childe Harold's Pilgrimage* and the captivating personality of the poet himself unleashed a veritable flood of "'Byromania'" (MacCarthy, 2002, p. 160;[5] cf. Moore, 1838; Quennell, 1935). Byron's observation about overnight fame became sufficiently well known among men of letters, so much so that composer Arthur Sullivan, the future collaborator of William Schwenk Gilbert, found himself deploying much the same phrase when, after having conducted a performance of his first seminal musical composition, *The Tempest*, at London's Crystal Palace, on 5th April, 1862, noted, "'It is no exaggeration to say that I woke up the next morning and found myself famous'" (quoted in Baily, 1973, p. 17).

In 1878, the year in which the social-climbing Oscar Wilde left the University of Oxford, he wrote to his friend David Hunter Blair: "'I won't be a dried-up Oxford don, anyhow. I'll be a poet, a writer, a dramatist. Somehow or other I'll be famous'"(quoted in Von Eckardt, Gilman, and Chamberlin, 1987, p. 1; cf. Ellmann, 1987).

With the dawning of the twentieth century, fame and celebrity fairly exploded, much assisted by the new media at that time, especially motion pictures. In the era of silent films, actors such as Mary Pickford and Douglas Fairbanks became the new gods of the Western world. According to the *American Magazine* of May, 1918, Mary Pickford received more letters daily than even President Woodrow Wilson (Barbas, 2001). And when silent screen icon Rudolf Valentino died in 1926 at the premature age of thirty-one years from peritonitis and pleuritis, fans became completely hysterical with grief. In faraway London, England, a young woman called Peggy Scott, inconsolable at the news of Valentino's passing, penned a desperate note, "'I am only a little butterfly made for sunshine and I cannot stand loneliness and shadow'" (quoted in Barbas, 2001, p. 169). Miss Scott then promptly swallowed a bottle of poison and died.

Americans and Britons alike not only idolised celebrities, but they yearned to become them, desperate to launch their own 1920s-style *Pop Idol*-like careers. In 1921, the fourteen-year-old Clara Gordon Bow of Bay Ridge, in Brooklyn, New York, borrowed one dollar in order to have a photo session so that she could enter the "Fame and Fortune" contest sponsored by *Motion Picture, Motion Picture Classic*, and *Shadowland* magazines (Stenn, 1988). As a result of the competition, Miss Bow catapulted to stardom, and then went on to feature in the 1927 film *It*, playing the role of "Betty Lou", a shop girl on the rise – yet another example of art imitating life. Everyone had to become famous in Depression-era America. In the blockbuster Warner Brothers Pictures musical film of 1933, *42nd Street*, director "Julian Marsh", played by Warner Baxter, pleads with understudy-turned-leading lady "Peggy Sawyer", portrayed by Ruby Keeler, "Sawyer, you're going out a youngster, but you've got to come back a star." This oft-quoted line of dialogue became the *cri de coeur* for 1930s America, underscoring that celebrity had now become no longer an *option*, but, rather, a *necessity*.

Contrary to popular opinion, Great Britain did not remain immune to this seemingly crass American bid for overnight celebrity. In 1939, a British film called *Let's Be Famous* graced the local screens, all about an Irish singer who craves celebrity and ends up featured on a quiz programme. The film showcased Sonnie Hale, a well-known star of British stage and screen (once married to fellow performer Evelyn Laye, and then to the actress Jessie Matthews), as well as Betty Driver, who eventually became a star of the popular television soap opera *Coronation Street*.

One could provide an endless stream of comparable examples of the search for fame in both American and British culture and, also, in other countries, but I hope that these aforementioned instances will suffice as a means of demonstrating the long-standing interest in celebritisation. This all too brief "history" of fame and celebrity should provide at least an inkling that such notions have entranced human beings for century upon century and that, perhaps, such an obsession indicates what an important role fame has long occupied in our inner world. We may come to discover, in fact, that the lust for fame represents not only an expression of pathological narcissism but, also, perhaps, a very basic human need to be seen.

The Roots of Celebrification

We have no shortage of theories which explain the perseverance of the phenomena of celebrity and fame. Some have argued that modern celebrity culture has developed as one of the legacies of the late-nineteenth century rise of universal literacy and the success of the growing press and, ultimately, the emergence of radio, film, and television, establishing celebrities as internationally recognisable and bankable commodities who generate income for capitalistic bureaucrats. Others have suggested that the declining popularity of the Church and other organised world religions, as well as the collapse of the omnipotent European Royal houses (e.g., the Habsburgs, the Hohenzollerns, the Romanovs, and the Wittelsbachs) have created a void in public consciousness, once filled by priests and princes, and that our film stars, pop stars, and sporting stars have become the new potentates at whose thrones we worship. Did not football hero David Beckham and his "Spice Girl" spouse Victoria Adams sit, famously, on *faux* thrones, at the fifteenth century Luttrellstown Castle, on the outskirts of Dublin, at their much-publicised wedding celebrations in 1999?

But although the rise of the media and the fall of the monarchy and the growing de-Christianisation of the Western world have all provided us with an historico-political backdrop to the proliferation of celebrity culture, one wonders whether modern depth psychology might have any contribution to make to the study of this perennially engaging polemic?

In spite of having achieved international fame in his own right as the founder of psychoanalysis, Professor Sigmund Freud (1909a) wrote virtually nothing on the subject in his vast corpus, except perhaps a brief observation in his infrequently quoted paper "Der Familienroman der Neurotiker", composed, in all likelihood, in 1908, and published as a short insert in a book written by his young colleague and protégé Otto Rank (1909). These remarks ultimately appeared in English translation, known as "Family Romances" (Freud, 1909b, 1909c). In this modest communication, Freud noted a widespread phenomenon among children, namely, the tendency to imagine oneself in fantasy *not* as the child of Herr X. and Frau X., but, rather, as the son or daughter of a member of the aristocracy. According to Freud (1909c, p. 238), these daydreams and imaginings serve as "the fulfilment of wishes"[6] and as "a correction of actual life"[7] (Freud, 1909c, p. 238). In other words, "the child's imagination becomes engaged in the task of getting free from the parents of whom he now has a low opinion and of replacing them by others, who, as a rule, are of higher social standing"[8] (Freud, 1909c, pp. 238–239). Sigmund Freud (1909c, p. 238) referred to this phenomenon as the "'family romance'"[9] (cf. Kahr, 2002d).

Who among us has not harboured a fantasy of living in a palace and having servants to wait on our every need? And when we gawp at the luxurious photographs of wealthy people in *Hello* magazine, do we not do so, at least in part, to indulge a private fantasy that we too might one day have a comparable country estate?

Although intended merely as a modest *pièce d'occasion*, Freud's short communication on the family romance serves as an important insight into the psychology of celebrity culture. Regrettably, Freud wrote no further about this phenomenon, certainly not in any direct fashion, and neither had the vast majority of his followers, with the slight exception of the English psychoanalyst, child psychiatrist, and paediatrician, Dr. Donald Winnicott, who, in his little-quoted paper on "The Manic Defence", presented to the British Psycho-Analytical Society in 1935, made a passing, and completely overlooked, comment about the preoccupation with the Court Circular published in stolid newspapers such as *The Times*, which provided an itinerary of the comings-and-goings of the monarchy. As Winnicott (1935, p. 131) observed, "in order to account for the existence of the Court and Personal column of our newspapers we must postulate a general need for reassurance against ideas of illness and death in the Royal Family and among the aristocracy; such reassurance can be given by reliable publication of facts." Winnicott (1935, p. 131) added further that, "In these Court and Personal columns the movements of the aristocracy are reported and predicted, and here can be seen in thin disguise the omnipotent control of personages who stand for internal objects."

This short essay – Winnicott's very first official psychoanalytical paper, in fact, presented in order to obtain membership in the British Psycho-Analytical Society – contains many important nuggets which will help us to create a psychological theory of our obsession with celebrity culture. First of all, Winnicott posited that famous people – in this case, the Royal Family and other aristocrats – become symbolic substitutes in our minds for early parental figures. Second of all, Winnicott noted that we, as citizens, seem to have a need to keep tabs on the whereabouts of these honorary parents, reassuring ourselves that they have not died. After all, do we not refer to the eldest female in the Royal Family as the "Queen *Mother*", and does the Monarch not always keep the flag flying at Buckingham Palace to indicate her or his presence or absence? (cf. Winnicott, 1970). In other words, scouring the Court Circular or *Hello* magazine or internet fan sites allows us to identify the whereabouts of our symbolically venerated celebrities and, in doing so, we both delight in the fact that they have not yet died, and we take pleasure, further, in the fact that we gain some degree of surreptitious control over them, knowing all about their private lives.

Although few commentators have remarked upon this fact, Winnicott's 1935 paper on "The Manic Defence" actually contains the kernels of one of his most important contributions to psychoanalysis, one which he would not publish more explicitly until 1969, namely that of "The Use of an Object" (Winnicott, 1969a), a much better-known essay, yet one still not fully appreciated by the psychoanalytical community at large. In this article, originally delivered before the New York Psychoanalytic Society in 1968, Winnicott proposed that the dedicated psychoanalyst must allow himself or herself to be used by the patient as an object, and that this experience of being used might include a ruthless co-opting of the analyst as a vehicle for the discharge of unneutralised, murderous rage.

Winnicott's concept of "The Use of an Object" certainly merits a fuller exegesis, but in this context, we can certainly draw upon his idea and conceptualise the celebrity as an object used by a fan and, similarly, appreciate that the fan may be an object which will be used, likewise, by the celebrity. Thus, when a fan indulges in a sexual fantasy about a celebrity, or vilifies a celebrity in conversation, he or she has engaged in the use of the celebrity as an object for the fulfilment of certain unconscious needs. Likewise, when a celebrity performs before a large audience in order to be seen, and heard and, indeed, remunerated, said celebrity has used fans as objects who serve a variety of very basic needs.

In my extensive studies, I have discovered only one other small Freudian-type contribution of direct value to our understanding of celebrity, namely, a passing remark made in 1937 by the distinguished American psychiatrist and psychoanalyst Dr. Karl Menninger of Topeka, Kansas, after visiting the plush Vendôme restaurant on Hollywood's Sunset Boulevard, an eatery often frequented by movie stars. Reflecting on his experiences, Dr. Menninger (1937, p. 235) boasted that he had seen several film personalities "at close range". He also explained that, "Trying to see these movie stars in the flesh is a game here and seems to be related to the impulse to see Mama getting out of the bathtub in the nude. Anyway they all do it and we follow suit" (Menninger, 1937, p. 235).

Karl Menninger's letter deserves our attention for at least two reasons. First of all, he has drawn successfully upon early Freudian theories of the so-called "'Urszene'" (Freud, 1918a, p. 617) or "'primal scene'" (Freud, 1918b, p. 39), namely, the wish of the young infant to enter the parental bedroom in order to avoid painful feelings of exclusion. Menninger had appreciated that the wish to stare at celebrities and to learn about their private lives represents a sublimation of this quite primitive, archaic impulse to see our parents *in flagrante*. And yet, interestingly, in spite of Menninger's own psychoanalytical training, he still found himself quite compelled by a deep-seated voyeuristic urge to gawp along with all the other tourists ("Anyway they all do it and we follow suit"), as though he had lost all sense of discernment or agency. So, the wish to learn about the private lives of celebrities may represent something extremely fundamental to human nature, namely, a sublimation of the wish to watch Mummy and Daddy up close.

Apart from these brief, though seminal, contributions from Sigmund Freud, Donald Winnicott, and Karl Menninger, the classical psychoanalytical literature on celebrity culture remains rather sparse.

Towards a More Comprehensive Theory of Celebrity

Having benefited enormously from the foundation stones of Freud and his followers, I shall now elaborate a more integrated and comprehensive theory which, I trust, will help to explain our deep-seated, never-ending preoccupation with celebrity and fame, encompassing both our very human wish to become widely revered ourselves and, also, our desire to align ourselves with those who have already done so. I shall draw not only upon a century of psychoanalytical thinking, both classical and modern, but also upon my own experiences as a clinician who has worked with those who have achieved fame, as well as those who have aspired to fame, as well as those who have claimed to have no interest in fame at all.

Synthesising a variety of observations, I have arrived at the following hypotheses:

Celebrity Worship and the Family Romance

I strongly concur with Sigmund Freud's concept of the "family romance" as a key ingredient in the lust for fame and celebrity, based upon his clinical psychoanalytical experience, and, also, upon his direct observations of youngsters. As we have already noted, the universal childhood wish for more exalted and more celebrated parents serves as a correction of a disappointing reality. As Freud (1909c, p. 239) noted, many children indulge "in a phantasy in which both his parents are replaced by others of better birth", [10] a fantasy which takes root, in part, due to the child's ignorance of the nature of sexual procreativity, thereby allowing him or her to fantasise more readily about having other parents.

Freud also commented, with great prescience, that, in certain cases, a youngster will imagine having not only a new set of parents, but, also, a new childhood altogether in which he or she will no longer be persecuted by pesky siblings. As Freud (1909c, p. 240) explained, "An interesting variant of the family romance may then appear, in which the hero and author returns to legitimacy himself while his brothers and sisters are eliminated by being bastardized."[11] Perhaps this fleeting remark from 1909 can help us to understand more readily the profound popular cultural preoccupation with so-called "reality television" programmes such as *American Idol*, *Big Brother*, *I'm a Celebrity ... Get Me Out of Here!*, and so many others, in which viewers vote to evict a member of the television family each week, as though indulging in the symbolically transmogrified act of eliminating our sibling rivals one by one. If this insight contains any validity, it may well contribute to a better appreciation of the pervasive appeal of this highly rated genre of entertainment.

Celebrity Worship, Object Loss, and Object Use

Building upon Freud's studies in child psychology, Winnicott enriched the terrain quite considerably as the veritable "cartographer of infancy" (Kahr, 2002b, p. 1), who fleshed out the map in exquisite detail. In terms of the psychology of celebrity lust, Winnicott (1935) has helped us to comprehend more fully our attraction to famous people based, in part, on our need to know the whereabouts of important figures in our lives, as a means of minimising object loss. Additionally, Winnicott (1969a) wrote with frankness about our need to use objects, to control objects, and to allow ourselves as clinicians to become objects who might be used by our patients in exactly the same way in which fans use celebrities, and likewise, celebrities use fans. Winnicott's notion of object use provides us with ample material for theorising about the nature of popular culture. One doubts, however, whether Donald Winnicott, who died long before the introduction of the personal computer or the internet, would have appreciated just *how* fully we have come to use celebrities. For example, consider the B.B.C.'s one-time computerised celebrity trading service Celebdaq, which allowed participants to delight in watching the monetary value of a particular celebrity rise and fall like so much stock (Hensher, 2003). Of course, we have the capability of using celebrities in far more sinister ways, and we shall examine some examples of a more sadistic use of the famous in due course.

Celebrity Worship and the Primal Scene: Mother's Face, Voice, and Scent

In addition to the contributions of Sigmund Freud and Donald Winnicott, one must not omit Karl Menninger's (1937) simple, but profound, aforementioned remark, based on his experience in Hollywood's Vendôme restaurant, namely, that we stare at movie stars in order to indulge our "primal scene" wishes to see our mother's naked body, which contemporary psychoanalytical workers would understand perhaps more accurately as a wish for primitive skin contact with our primary caregiving attachment figure. Having practised psychiatry and psychoanalysis before the flourishing of the experimental developmental psychological research on facial recognition, which appeared throughout the 1960s and beyond, Menninger would not have known the extent to which each infant craves his or her mother's face and develops the capacity to differentiate one's own mother's visage from that of other women of similar age and appearance within hours after birth (e.g., Bower, 1989). Similarly, we know from the important neonatological research of Dr. Aidan Macfarlane (1975) and others that newborn infants can also discriminate the smell of the breast milk of their biological mothers from that of other lactating women who have recently given birth, and that newborn infants can do so almost immediately. Similarly, infants can also appreciate the sound of mother's voice, and might even be able to identify and recall specific maternal tones while still *in utero* (e.g., deMause, 1981, 1982, 2002b).

Just as a grown-up might sit down with a D.V.D. or a book for entertainment, the infant amuses himself or herself with an *Ur*-D.V.D., namely, the sight, the smell, and the sound of the preoedipal mother of earliest infancy, the first celebrity worshipped by each of us. Our preoccupation with the mother's body parts manifests itself in our endless desire to see the faces of young celebrities in their late teens and early twenties, the age of most mothers at the time of birth. Advertising companies and film production companies appreciate this insight quite intuitively, and thus, by parading posters of Betty Grable, Marilyn Monroe, Farah Fawcett Majors, Taylor Swift, or Rihanna in front of us at every possible moment, through a process now known as "branding" or "marketing", they have succeeded in indulging our wish to see the face of one very special young woman with sparkling eyes, lustrous hair, and all the other characteristics of the young, idealised, primiparous mother.

By staring at the faces of our celebrities, by listening to their voices on compact disc or in concert or on the radio, and by sniffing their scent (through the purchase of the growing barrage of celebrity perfumes such as *Heat* by Beyoncé Knowles, *Fantasy* by Britney Spears, and *In Bloom* by Reese Witherspoon), we indulge an archaic wish to become reunited with the nurturant mother of infancy. Furthermore, we yearn not only to obtain renewed access to the face, voice, and scent of our mothers, but, additionally, we hope for *exclusive* access, hence our wish to penetrate the bedrooms of our celebrities by snooping into their private lives in the most relentless and, often, invidious manner.

Celebrity as a Defence Against Impotence and Castration Anxiety

In the Hollywood film *Bonnie and Clyde*, released in 1967, and based upon the lives of the infamous American gangsters, Bonnie Parker and Clyde

Barrow, we discover that Barrow, portrayed by the film actor Warren Beatty, struggles with erectile dysfunction. However, upon reading a poem written about him in a newspaper – in other words, upon discovering himself to be famous – Barrow becomes aroused and then engages in sexual intercourse. One cannot of course confirm with certainty that the real Clyde Barrow, as opposed to the Hollywood version, actually struggled with impotence, but the film's director, Arthur Penn, a graduate of a long Freudian analysis with the German-American refugee clinician Dr. Rudolph Loewenstein, one of the founders of classical ego psychology (Farber and Green, n.d.), suggested this as a psychologically plausible contribution to the script, one which might also explain, perhaps, Barrow's need to carry an enormous gun.

Becoming famous serves as a temporary remedy for feeling ineffective and pusillanimous. Similarly, worshipping someone famous provides a cure through identification with the phallic potency of another. How many billions of flabby, out-of-shape, arthritic middle-aged and old-aged men have jeopardised their marriages to devote long weekends to watching vigorous, young, orthopaedically potent sporting heroes kicking a ball across a stadium? Only through the process of fame worship, or *identification with the celebrity*, can one experience a temporary sense of thrill, of power, of vitality, and of triumph over an experience of being castrated either physically or psychologically (cf. Kahr, 2018b, 2019a).

Fame and Celebrity as Defences Against Loneliness and Misattunement

The preoccupation with the fame of others provides an illusion of connection with those in the public eye. In this way, immersing oneself in the lives of others serves as a very powerful defence against solitariness. Indeed, countless numbers of television viewers develop private worlds peopled only by themselves and by the cast of such television and radio programmes as *EastEnders*, or *Coronation Street*, or *Desperate Housewives* or, indeed, *The Archers*. Of course, it would be naïve to deny that these dramas provide pure entertainment to many. Part of the pleasure, however, stems, not from the intellectual stimulation or entertainment value inherent in these soap operas but, rather, from the fact that these dramas offer lonely people a sense of community and continuity.

Years ago, I had the privilege of attending clinical supervision with a very senior child psychoanalyst called Dr. Susanna Isaacs Elmhirst, who had inherited Donald Winnicott's post at the Paddington Green Children's Hospital upon his retirement. During the course of my supervision with Dr. Elmhirst, I presented the case of a profoundly intellectually disabled person who spent the entire day watching soap operas. I shall never forget Dr. Elmhirst's wise observation: "Do you know why people love soap operas? Because the *same* people keep coming back and back and back in episode after episode." Although soap operas and other dramas do kill off some of their characters from time to time, they do so rather sparingly for the most part, allowing viewers to develop cyber-relationships with the denizens of "Albert Square" or "The Rovers" on a regular basis, thus mitigating against the dreadful pain of object loss.

In states of loneliness, we track celebrities, we collect their autographs, we purchase items of their clothing at auctions, and we even pretend to *become* them (witness the adolescent impersonating a pop star, replete with hairbrush and bedroom mirror); and we do so, in part, as a form of admiration, in part as a shrewd financial investment perhaps, but, also, and most fundamentally, as a means of correcting early experiences of loss and misattunement and of not quite feeling famous enough ourselves in our families of origin. Staring at the celebrity may, in fact, represent a displacement of our own more primeval wish to be seen.

Fame Worship as a Defence Against Death and Death Anxiety

In 1980, the American film *Fame* burst onto cinema screens around the world. A finely wrought movie about the struggles of young performing arts students desperate to find a niche for themselves in show business, the film will perhaps best be remembered nowadays for Irene Cara's electric rendition of the title track, "Fame", which won the Academy Award for Best Song. As Ms. Cara and her comrades danced with abandon on top of New York taxicabs, they exulted, "Fame! / I'm gonna live forever", thus encapsulating a universal unconscious desire. One need not be a psychologist to appreciate that the lust for fame (i.e., immortality) represents the primitive wish to live forever and to avoid death at all cost.

Not only do we crave fame as a means of cheating the unbearable inevitability of death, but we also delight in controlling the process of death to the best of our ability. In the United States of America, certain office workers have, apparently, created a phenomenon which has come to be known as the "'death pool'" (Gritten, 2002, p. 54), using either aged celebrities or self-destructive celebrities as part of a game, betting money on which famous person will die first, for example, Katharine Hepburn versus Bob Hope, or Robert Downey, Jr. versus Eminem. These office death pools represent not only the expression of death wishes directed at famous, wealthy, talented celebrities but, also, serve as a primitive means of projecting all deathliness into someone else. By turning the anticipated death date of a celebrity into a betting matter, we burden celebrities with yet one further task, not only that of entertaining us in life, but also in anticipated death. Perhaps the death pool also allows us to attain some primitive control over the deeply unpredictable nature of human mortality, especially its timing.

Celebrities as Targets of Envy, Destructiveness, and Murderous Rage

As we have already noted, Dr. Donald Winnicott wrote creatively about the way in which each of us will use someone else, or a part of someone else, as an object, often for our own primitive purposes. We might perhaps kick our dog, for example, as a means of discharging primitive destructive affect. In this way, the dog becomes a target for externalisation, an object for use. Similarly, we might scream at our psychotherapist, because we know that a decent, well-trained mental health professional will not, in all likelihood, retaliate, and will also consent – perhaps therapeutically, perhaps masochistically – to tolerate this discharge, which no one else would do.

One special case of "object use" concerns the deeply primitive affect of human envy, a subject of special interest to psychotherapists and psychoanalysts, as envy becomes a source of deep pain and destructiveness in the human mind and within human relationships. Melanie Klein (1957, p. ix), the noted Austrian-British psychoanalyst and author of the foundational textbook on envy, described it as "a most potent factor in undermining feelings of love and gratitude at their root".

According to Mrs. Klein and her successors, we express our enviousness in a multitude of attacks, sometimes of a verbal nature, sometimes of a physical nature. With reference to famous people, one need not search very far for evidence of envy throughout the history of celebrity. For instance, virtually every famous individual has had to endure verbal assaults, often of a most cruel nature. In his *Naturalis Historiae*, Gaius Plinius Secundus, better known as the first-century Roman historian Pliny the Elder, took great delight in calumniating the empress Messalina, somtime wife of the emperor Claudius, as a rank prostitute, claiming that she had participated in an all-night sex orgy, servicing large numbers of customers. Some centuries later, Marie Antoinette, the deposed queen of France, had to endure similar public humiliations, including accusations from the scandalmonger Jacques-René Hébert, of having engaged in an incestuous relationship with her young son, Louis Charles, the former *dauphin* (Haslip, 1987; Dunlop, 1993; Fraser, 2001). And, in more recent times, the Tsaritsa Alexandra of Russia endured many envious assaults, lambasted for her ostensible sexual liaison with the monk Grigori Efimovich Rasputin (King, 1990; Cook, 2005).

These calumniations invariably exert a very powerful effect. Having served as psychotherapist to many people in the public eye who have had to read vicious falsehoods about themselves in the press, I can confirm that such stories lacerate most deeply.

But envious attacks can appear in a more concrete, physical form. In the most severe cases, the so-called "love" of celebrity can become perverted into the forensic phenomenon of stalking or, even, murder, the ultimate manifestations of a deadly envy. Celebrity stalking occurs with great frequency in the upper echelons of show business; indeed, I have heard more than one famous person explain with pride that one can only regard oneself as truly famous when one can claim to have a deranged stalker in tow. Ursula Reichert-Habbishaw, a mother of four children, bombarded the film star Richard Gere with approximately 1,000 e-mails, faxes, and telephone calls. Shockingly, this represents the *less* extreme form of stalking. Tragically, envious stalking can become manifest in much more vicious forms (cf. Mullen, James, Meloy, Pathé, Farnham, Preston, Darnley, and Berman, 2009). In 1995, for example, the beautiful, twenty-three-year-old Mexican American singer "Selena" [Selena Quintanilla-Pérez], suffered a fatal gunshot wound to her back, fired by none other than Yolanda Saldívar, the president of the Texas branch of Selena's fan club.

On 8th December, 1980, at approximately 5.00 p.m., a twenty-five-year-old Texas-born, sometime security guard, one Mark David Chapman, caught the attention of Beatle John Lennon outside the latter's lavish apartment building, The Dakota, on the Upper West Side of New York City. Chapman entreated Lennon to sign a copy of the English singer's recently released album *Double Fantasy*. Some hours later, Chapman met Lennon again as he returned to his home and, at 10.49 p.m., fired five shots, killing Lennon instantly (Norman, 2008). Afterwards, while in prison, Mark David Chapman confessed to the television journalist Barbara Walters that, by killing Lennon, he had hoped to acquire the singer's fame. This murder in particular reveals not only the horrors of envy towards the famous but, also, the painfully easy erosion between idealisation and denigration, between autograph-hunting fanship and the act of murder, an act which can never be undone.

Celebrity and the Urge to Commit Infanticide: The Bedrock of the Human Mind

Thus far, I have identified some seven explanatory strands which help us to comprehend the urge to engage in a relationship with celebrities: (1) a manifestation of the "family romance", substituting our drab, ordinary parents with more spectacular, fantasmatic parents; (2) an expression of our need to control object loss and to engage in "object use"; (3) a concretisation of the "primal scene", and, consequently, a celebration of the face, voice, and scent of the preoedipal mother of infancy; (4) a defence against impotency and castration anxiety; (5) a defence against loneliness; (6) a defence against death and death anxiety; and (7) a form of envious attack, often of a murderous nature. According to my clinical experience, these seven strands will often overlap, and, in so doing, will contribute to the potency of the wish to use and abuse our celebrities. In other words, we might scream and shout and rant when watching a pop star at Wembley Arena or a sports star at Old Trafford, not only because the celebrity entertains us, but because we also have seven further, often unconscious, reasons to engage in a connection with said celebrity.

But in addition to these aforementioned contributory factors, I wish to highlight yet one more. This particular factor may have the greatest pull of them all, namely, the wish to commit ritual infanticide of the youngest members of our civilisation.

According to ancient Greek legend, the mythical king Minos of Crete, son of the god Zeus and the Phoenician-born mortal Europa, waged war against the Athenians and proved victorious. As part of his spoils of war, Minos demanded that every nine years the Athenians would have to select seven of their most beautiful maidens and seven of their most handsome boys, equivalent in age to young teens, and send them by ship to Crete where, imprisoned in the king's diabolical labyrinth at Knossos, they would be devoured, sacrificially, by the infamous creature – half-bull, half-human – known as the Minotaur, who fed on flesh and blood. The ritual sacrifice of the young Athenians continued unabatedly until one potential victim, young Theseus, a brave hero, vanquished the Minotaur. As the winner of the competition, Theseus became, accordingly, the founder-king of Athens.

This iconic tale of ancient sacrifice, of a bloody competition in which only one youthful participant rises victorious, has occupied an archetypal place in both Western and Eastern civilisation, and students of mythology will find elaborated versions of this very thematic in the stories of the Mesopotamian bull-man Shedu, in the tales of the Middle Eastern bull-man Moloch [Molech], in the legend of the Egyptian bull-man Apis, as well as in the exploits of the Japanese bull-man Ushi-oni. Later representations of the Minotaur persist into the Middle Ages and Renaissance, notably as the *"infamia di Creti"* in Dante Alighieri's *Inferno*, which constitutes the first part of *La Divina Commedia*, written in the early fourteenth century.

Myths do not originate out of thin air. They derive from long-standing, primitive experience. In this case, the sacrifice of the young in mythology can be traced to infanticidal child-rearing practices perpetrated by the ancient Africans, Celts, Chinese, Egyptians, Etruscans, Greeks, Hebrews, Hindus, Japanese, Magyars, Mesoamericans, Romans, and others, studied extensively by contemporary historians and psychohistorians, notably the American scholar Lloyd deMause (1974, 1990, 1991, 2002a) and by numerous other historians (e.g., Kellum, 1974; Langer, 1974; Lyman, 1974; McLaughlin, 1974; Helmholz, 1975; Kahr, 1991, 1993, 1994a, 1994b, 1994c, 1996c, 1996d, 1997, 2001d, 2002c, 2007c, 2007d, 2012a; Miles, 2010) as well as by archaeologists (e.g., Stager and Wolff, 1984; Brown, 1991; cf. Miller, 2001). Psychoanalytical clinicians have also written widely about the ubiquity of parental death wishes towards babies, which will be enacted by more fragile parents, resulting in either the physical or the psychological destruction of the infant (e.g., Winnicott, 1949b; Lidz, 1973; Bloch, 1978; Sinason, 2001, 2020).

Throughout history, our predecessors have compulsively repeated the Minotaurean destruction of young people, often in ritualised, repetitive ways. The ancient Carthaginians sacrificed their infants to the gods, and placed their bodies in the Tophet, an ancient burial ground which survives to this day, containing numerous urns full of charred infant remains (Stager and Wolff, 1984; Brown, 1991). Often infants would be sacrificed, but, sometimes, those slain might be teenagers. The ancient Moche of Northern Peru, a Pre-Colombian people who flourished in the first millennium of the Common Era, sacrificed newly pubescent youngsters, and a contemporary archaeologist-anthropologist, Professor Steve Bourget (2006) of the University of Texas at Austin, has uncovered the osteological remains of these ritual killings (cf. Bourget and Jones, 2008; Hocquenghem, 2008; Uceda, 2008; Verano, 2008; Gaither, Kent, Bethard, Vasquez, and Rosales, 2016; Klaus and Shimada, 2016), thus offering further proof of the human need to kill our offspring.

Minotaur-style executions, in group formations, have occurred in virtually every epoch of human history, and in every culture, ranging from the gladiatorial combats of ancient Rome, to the Colonial witch trials in Salem, Massachusetts, to the guillotines of Revolutionary France, to contemporary warfare, which involves the transportation of young members of our community, often on ships or planes, to meet their deaths overseas. Sometimes, these tribal group murders will take the form of actual slaughter, as with the ancient child sacrifices, and sometimes, the executions will occur more symbolically. In 513 B.C.E., Cleisthenes, an Attic Greek aristocrat from Athens who claimed grand descent from Herakles, introduced a new form of public execution, the *ostrakon*, from which the word "ostracism" derives. The *ostrakon* refers literally to a piece of broken pottery, and Cleisthenes, one of the founders of modern democracy, devised a system whereby Athenians would inscribe the name of the person they most wished to evict from the city on the *ostrakon* pottery, usually a person of fame and fortune. This may well be the first historical instance of calling an 0800 number to evict one's most despised celebrity from a television programme.

Ancient infanticide, Minotaurean sacrifices of the teenagers, and Athenian *ostrakon* voting persist to this day in one form or another. And they certainly appear in our current crop of reality television programmes such as *American Idol* and *The X Factor* and others too numerous to mention, in which viewers sacrifice one or more youngsters each week, until a winner can be chosen. Often, the public executions will be assisted by youthful women – attractive presenters such as Cheryl Cole or Alesha Dixon or Dannii Minogue or Nicole Scherzinger – who represent the infanticidal, preoedipal mothers of infancy, facilitating the sacrifice of the modern equivalent of the beautiful Athenian virgins.

The Roman author Plutarch [Lucius Mestrius Plutarchus] and the Christian Berber writer Tertullian [Quintus Septimius Florens Tertullianus] had reminded us that, often, those children selected for sacrifice would be required to offer their own consent beforehand. Perhaps the long queues of young girls who yearned to play the role of "Dorothy" in Lord Lloyd Webber's stage production of *The Wizard of Oz* represent the modern reincarnation of the ancient children chosen for sacrifice. In terms of the notion of *object use*, perhaps we still have a deep, unconscious need to create celebrities and then worship them, so that we can ultimately assassinate them, as our ancestors had done, in a highly symbolic ritual, swamped by beautiful music and costumes, in order to hide the execution waiting in the wings.

Conclusion

The world of celebrity and fame might well be described as one of great toxicity. Some writers have suggested that fame produces breakdown (e.g., Wallace, 1986). Others have argued that its practitioners all suffer from histrionic personality disorder (Gritten, 2002). At least one researcher has discovered that celebrities live shorter lives, suffer from a higher likelihood of cirrhosis of the liver, kidney disease, and ulcers, and will be more likely to commit suicide or to be murdered than the average citizen (Fowles, 1992).

Perhaps Dante Alighieri described fame best in his admonition, inscribed in the *Purgatorio*, the second part of *La Divina Commedia*: "Non è il mondan romore altro ch'un fiato / di vento, ch'or vien quinci e or vien quindi" ["Your earthly fame is but a gust of wind / that blows about, shifting this way and that"]. Or perhaps we might remember the wariness of Emily Dickinson, conveyed in a brief poem, written circa 1861:

> "How dreary – to be – Somebody!
> How public – like a Frog –
> To tell your name – the livelong June –
> To an admiring Bog!"

And yet, in spite of the horrors of the world of fame and celebrity, this phenomenon continues to exert the most primitive of influences upon the famous, upon those who crave fame, and upon those who fan the flames of fame. Indeed, fame and its worship will not disappear, even when subjected to a penetrating psychoanalytical investigation.

We know that celebrity culture contains many malignant components, and we need not repeat these here. But might we identify any *positive* aspects of celebrity culture? Although I have not focused on these features as comprehensively as I have concentrated upon the negative ones, I have come to the conclusion that celebrity culture has immense benefits for fans. Celebrities entertain us, they help us to laugh, they facilitate play, and they provide us with non-prescription antidepressant medication. As "Lina Lamont", the intellectually challenged screen goddess, brilliantly portrayed by Jean

Hagen in the 1952 musical film *Singin' in the Rain*, chirped to her fans: "If we bring a little joy into your humdrum lives, it makes us feel as though our hard work ain't been in vain for nothing. Bless you all."

Our celebrities function as aspirational role models to young people and, perhaps, to the not so young as well. They provide us with stories of success, of conquest over adversity, of survival from cancer and other painful diseases. They also offer us a sense of community, and furnish us so-called "water cooler" moments, which allow us to feel part of shared experience, as we go to the office the next day and compare the previous evening's news items, or offer our reviews of a popular, much-watched television programme.

But old-timers might balk that fame should be accorded only to the Marie Curies, the Albert Einsteins, and the Nelson Mandelas of the world, mindful of the ancient Latin epithet *"famam extendere factis"* ["to spread abroad his fame by deeds"]. The Victorians embraced this philosophy of fame, and those of us who live in North London can drive past the William Ellis School in Highgate and might well derive satisfaction from the school's motto, chiselled on its outer wall: "Rather Use Than Fame". Clearly, the institution of fame will always have its proponents and its critics, and each of us will pursue a different model of fame, some craving international acclaim, some desirous of recognition by colleagues within a peer community, others requiring only the appreciation of their spouses, parents, and children.

Whatever our final view about fame and its healthfulness or, indeed, its malignancies, modern fame – early twenty-first-century fame – has adopted new contours. Dr. Brendan MacCarthy (2003), the distinguished British child psychiatrist and psychoanalyst, told me that when he began to practise child psychiatry in the 1950s and 1960s, he did not remember any youngsters expressing a wish to become famous. Little boys hoped that they might perhaps train as astronauts, or be rich, while little girls planned to become wives and mothers, but they certainly did not fantasise about careers in film and television. Contemporary youngsters, however, have a rather different experience and, for many, fame has become a career choice that threatens to sit alongside medicine, the law, psychotherapy, academia, accountancy, and graphic design. Should this phenomenon of fame as a profession cause alarm or, indeed, celebration?

Some would argue, of course, that fame should never be a goal, merely an unexpected outcome of having achieved great works. Others would suggest that the endless stream of minimally educated men and women and children from economically straitened backgrounds who appear on our television screens in search of two minutes of fame on *Britain's Got Talent* represents not a *deterioration* of civilisation as we know it, but rather, its *democratisation* – a watershed era in human history akin to the emergence of women, the disabled, the ethnic minorities, and the sexual minorities from the shadows and margins of our culture. For years, we prevented anyone who could not speak the King's English, or more recently, the Queen's English, from broadcasting on our radio sets or from appearing on our television screens. But through this democratisation of fame, everyone now has permission to join the party.

Although we might lambaste the fame seekers as hysterical and narcissistic and exhibitionistic, and although we might diagnose the modern media as corrupt and perverse, perhaps the fame seekers, the fame producers, and the fame supporters serve, above all, as a reminder that each of us not only craves a platform but *deserves* one. As the eighteenth-century Irish philosopher, Bishop George Berkeley, sloganised, *"Esse est percipi"* ["To be is to be perceived"]. Perhaps it may not be accidental that just as the popularity of reality television programmes continues to swell, so too does the demand for psychotherapy. Once considered an American-style indulgence, or the last resort for seemingly "crazy" people, Britons everywhere have finally begun to embrace the potentialities and benefits of psychotherapy and psychoanalysis with increasing seriousness and sympathy, not least in the wake of the coronavirus pandemic of 2020 and 2021 and beyond. It may be that British men and women have finally begun to recognise that psychotherapy provides a profound opportunity for clients or patients to feel not only rescued and saved but, also, at times, famous and celebrated. The psychotherapist, after all, provides a spotlight for each client, placing him or her centre stage for fifty minutes, with no competition from irritating understudies or cut-throat members of the chorus. Psychotherapy offers those in search of richer peace of mind and greater meaning in their lives an opportunity to star in their own autobiography, instead of observing it from the sidelines, as so many billions of people still seem to do.

Before we ossify our final views on celebrity and fame, let us recall not only our wish but, also, our *need* and *necessity* to be perceived, whether on screen, in the lecture theatre, in the consulting room, or, more pressingly, at the family supper table. Perhaps we may come to recognise that the craze for international celebrity speaks symptomatically to the failure of so many parents and partners and children to celebrate their nearest and dearest sufficiently at home.

On Not Being Shakespeare, Mozart, or Picasso

Creativity, Bereavement, and the Wish to Be Famous

Beyond Bodily Bereavement

In recent years, mental health professionals, social care workers, medical and nursing practitioners, and those who toil in the field of grief counselling have undertaken an enormous amount of pioneering work to develop the theory and practice of bereavement studies. Our growing sensitivity to bereavement has helped many of us who have lost a spouse, a child, a parent, a sibling, a friend, a colleague. Similarly, bereavement specialists have also supported us as we prepare for our own deaths, whether through disability, illness, or ordinary old age.

But, as we know, bereavement exists in many forms, and it need not involve the actual death of a loved one. Grief reactions can ensue from other deprivations as well, such as the loss of a body part, or the loss of one's employment, or the loss of one's reputation in the wake of a humiliation or scandal, or indeed the loss of one's freedom as a result of imprisonment or enforced migration.

In my own work as a clinical psychotherapist, I have, over the decades, endeavoured to help my patients process and, ultimately, surmount these manifold losses, all of which constitute the ordinary, though painful, bread and butter of daily human experience. But I also encounter another form of bereavement which may perhaps be more invisible, namely, the loss of creativity, and, more painful still, the loss of the *fantasy* that one day, in some way, one might still become creative, but then have to face the mortifying reality that this wish may never come true.

In the pages that follow, I wish to explore how a psychotherapist deals with four types of bereavement involving the creative process, what we might come to refer to as the *creativity bereavements*, namely:

1 The development of a block or an inhibition in a person who has already demonstrated artistic creativity in one or more forms, and yet who, for a whole variety of reasons, now finds himself or herself completely stagnant, unable to be productive and, therefore, quite depressed as a result.

2   The sense of disillusionment and meaninglessness in a creative artist who, in spite of his or her continued capacity to be fertile, now finds the creative work utterly devoid of meaning or purpose, and, hence, becomes bereaved and depressed.
3   The loss of creativity due to disability, illness, or ageing.
4   And, finally, perhaps the most painful form of creativity bereavement, namely, the loss of a fantasy of what I have come to understand as a grandiose creativity: the long-held wish that, one day, one might become a rival to William Shakespeare, Wolfgang Amadeus Mozart, and Pablo Picasso, and hence, dominate media coverage in an unprecedented manner.

I shall now endeavour to provide a sketch of each of these four forms of creativity bereavement, with reference to clinical material. In particular, I shall focus on the least studied and least understood, yet possibly the most ubiquitous, form of creativity bereavement, namely, the loss of the fantasy that at some point, one will burst onto the stage, or into print, or onto the sports pitch, or in the press, as a person of huge importance who will be loved and cherished and who will vanquish all one's enemies, making them suffer a deep and unrelenting envy.

Creativity Bereavement: Type One – The Writer's Block

In the course of a lifetime career as an artist, one invariably encounters periods of great fecundity and productivity, and, likewise, periods of significant inhibition and stagnation (Leader, 1991; Bergmann, 1997; Kramer, 1997; Olinick, 1997; Kahr, 1998). The late Professor Peter Ostwald (1985), a distinguished psychiatrist from San Francisco, California, wrote a marvellous book about the nineteenth-century composer Robert Schumann, who suffered famously from manic-depressive illness. Professor Ostwald explored with meticulous care the intimate interrelationship between Schumann's musical compositions and his affective illness. One will hardly be surprised to discover that during periods of pronounced mania, Schumann created music extensively, whereas during periods of melancholia, he produced far fewer compositions. Thus, we may appreciate that creative inhibitions may be linked to one's psychological state of mind. However, not every case of inhibition or blockage will be as dramatic or as clear-cut as that of Robert Schumann.

Often, a creative block will ensue in the wake of a very invisible psychological conflict, invariably unconscious in nature, which will remain obscure to the artist himself or herself and will often emerge only in the course of psychotherapeutic investigation. "Albert", a writer who had recently turned fifty years of age, consulted me because, in spite of a sterling and lucrative track record as the author of several screenplays for motion pictures, he had run aground and found himself unable to write at all. Albert explained that although he had never had difficulty writing previously, in recent months he had begun to stare at his computer screen in a state of utter paralysis, incapable of crafting a single sentence. Although numerous film companies had paid Albert handsomely for his writings, in the wake of his fiftieth birthday, he simply could not write any more, and he found himself in deep distress, unable to understand why he could no longer manufacture a finished product as he had done so many times previously.

Although he had often earned impressive sums of money, Albert regarded most of his screenplays as "pap", mere drivel which permitted him to pay his monthly mortgage. But even though he knew that he had not yet produced a *Gone with the Wind* or a *Citizen Kane*, he persevered and still managed to support a wife and three children in a comfortable style. Some six months before his psychotherapy began, he had received a commission for what seemed to be an ordinary, straightforward screenplay about a troubled relationship between a woman and a man. He assumed that he would be able to polish off this project in no time at all; and yet, as soon as he sat down at his computer terminal, he found himself empty of all creativity, explaining that he felt as though his brain had actually died.

Albert used the language of bereavement to describe his creative inhibition. He would often tell me that his inspiration had "dropped dead" and then explained that the world had become "as bleak as a graveyard". He would often stare fixatedly at his computer screen and hallucinate pictures of coffins and tombs. Although no one had actually died in his external world, something certainly seemed to have died in his internal world.

In the context of a brief communication, I cannot hope to convey the complexity of the psychoanalytical process: a slow, unfolding piece of work in which gradually, bit by bit, the origins of one's unconscious conflicts become increasingly lucid and hence available for discussion and understanding. But in our three-times-weekly sessions in which Albert reclined on the Freudian couch, it soon became clear that this man's recent fiftieth birthday had activated a long-buried conflict, one which had a direct bearing on his capacity to be productive.

At the age of two, Albert's father, whom he described as a lazy, derelict man with no regular source of income, walked out on the family, leaving Albert alone in the care of his overly burdened mother. The father moved far away to the North of England and made absolutely no attempt to see his son or to speak to him ever again. Life thereafter proved extremely hard for Albert's mother who had to work exceptionally long days in order to earn enough money to care for herself and for her child. Indeed, at one point, the mother left Albert with his maternal grandparents for a lengthy period of two full years, while she moved to a city in another county in order to work at a more lucrative job. Mother did not take Albert with her, explaining that his presence would impede her capacity to focus on her employment. Somehow, in spite of all of this loss and deprivation, Albert managed to become a good student, and eventually graduated from university, and soon became quite an adept writer.

One day, during the very early years of his unfoldingly successful writing career, Albert appeared on television in order to promote one of his films. Apparently, his father had watched the interview and, soon thereafter, had somehow managed to track down his long-lost son by telephone for the very first time in decades. Although Albert spoke to his father briefly on the phone, he refused to accede to the father's request for a face-to-face meeting. Later that day, Albert became consumed with regret, changed his mind, and then telephoned the father, suggesting that they could, in fact, meet after all. Albert found his father quite a broken man: unkempt, unhygienic, penniless, and forlorn. The meeting left Albert with a sense of morbidity and, afterwards, he made no further attempt to communicate with his father. Several months later, this estranged parent died, due to complications of alcoholism, and Albert experienced a deep sense of grief, feeling as though he had lost his father, and then found him at last, and then lost him again, all within the space of a very short period of time.

During the course of one of our psychoanalytical sessions, I asked Albert whether his current project – the "stuck" screenplay which prompted his arrival at my office – contained any interactions between a son and a father. He told me that the story had no parent-child scenes, only those between a husband and a wife.

What then made this particular screenplay so difficult for Albert?

Naturally, as Albert had only recently turned fifty years of age – a watershed period in everyone's biography – we focused a good deal of our psychological discussions on the meaning of having entered the second half of life. Albert seemed pleased to have managed to create a reasonably successful marriage, and somehow, to his great surprise, he had even become a good father to his three children, although he claimed that in view of the fact that he had absolutely no male role model during his own growing-up years, he could so easily have become an absent father. Albert sometimes quipped, "I never saw a man being nice to a woman. It's amazing that I did not become gay. You see, while growing up I had absolutely no heterosexual template in my life."

As our three-times-weekly conversations continued to unfold over time, it became increasingly apparent that Albert felt not only an enormous amount of grief at having endured so much parental abandonment but, also, immense guilt at having succeeded where his own father had failed. One day, Albert estimated that he had earned more money from just one of his own screenplays than his father had earned in a whole lifetime. Although Albert often experienced tremendous rage towards his wastrel father, and sometimes fantasised about killing him off, he now began to feel as though he really had vanquished his father through his great achievements as a writer of some renown.

One day, Albert arrived at his session, having just watched a film which contained a tender scene in which an estranged father meets his son for the first time in years. Albert felt that he and his father could easily have starred in this film since it seemed so uncannily autobiographical. In true Hollywood style, the reunion between the filmic father and son concluded quite happily, whereas Albert's own reunion with his father some twenty years previously had ended so miserably, followed soon thereafter by the father's death, rendering Albert deeply depressed and forlorn. While Albert compared himself to the protagonist in the film, he began to weep copiously, mourning for the relationship that he had never had with his own absent parent.

Naturally, I sympathised with Albert's sadness, and I certainly appreciated the great significance of his mention of the fact that his father died *twenty* years ago – the very first time that Albert had provided such details of the timing of his father's death. I asked Albert how old his father would have been at that time. After a quick calculation, Albert told me that his father had only just turned fifty!

As one might imagine, I had always assumed that Albert's father had passed away at rather an older age, as he had always described his father as a failing, decrepit man; but, in fact, he died relatively young, having attacked his liver through excessive alcohol consumption. I wondered whether Albert felt awful at having reached his own fiftieth birthday in good health, with a fine family and a prominent career, whereas his father had no family and no career whatsoever at the very same age.

This rather simple observation stimulated many more tears of deep pain and regret. The very intelligent Albert realised quite quickly that his writing block and his loss of creativity had become a means of preventing himself from becoming even more successful on the eve of his own fiftieth birthday. Struggling mightily between the unconscious conflict of shaming his father through further triumphs, and protecting his father likewise from such imagined humiliation, Albert managed quite unconsciously to attack himself and to create a symptomatic block which prevented him from writing at all. By failing to complete his screenplay, he succeeded in safeguarding his internal father from further failure, and thereby shielded himself from guilt and from vanquishing this unsuccessful parent any further. In his unconscious mind, Albert may well have hypothesised, "If I become a failure at fifty, I will in no way eclipse my father or cause him any more heartbreak."

Over the next few weeks, Albert gradually developed the courage to return to his computer and, before long, he succeeded in writing once again without much inhibition or conflict. Eventually, he finished his screenplay, and then he received a commission for another one and, soon thereafter, for yet another one still. These sorts of creative inhibitions, which feel like bereavements, occur quite frequently in the life of every writer, composer, artist, or craftsperson. With skilled psychological cradling, these blocks can be resolved quite successfully in most instances when one helps the client to untie the invisible knot which often prevents the successful completion of the creative endeavour. One often discovers that a piece of unresolved bereavement contributes to the development of the block in the first place, and, consequently, with the solicitude of the non-bereaved psychotherapist or psychoanalyst, a resolution of the conflict may be achieved.

Creativity Bereavement: Type Two – Disillusionment

Often, a creative practitioner will manage to avoid blocks and inhibitions and will be able to generate products (whether books, dances, drawings, poems, screenplays, symphonies, or even scientific discoveries and inventions) in an unfettered way; yet, at other times, the practitioner will experience a sense of disillusionment and meaninglessness and will feel bereaved. "Bradley", a painter, came to my office one year after he had mounted a reasonably successful exhibition of his artwork. Although he had continued to paint since the closing of his exhibition, he did so without joy or verve, and although he still produced good work, it all felt rather frivolous. Bradley even considered leaving his career and wondered whether he should actually retrain as a counsellor or psychotherapist – something which would allow him to be of immediate assistance to people. As Bradley intoned, "A fucking painting never helped anybody in distress."

From our psychotherapeutic discussions, it became quite clear to me that Bradley's sense of disillusionment had developed in the immediate aftermath of his art exhibition, and so, naturally, I devoted a great deal of time and attention to exploring the many precise details of that experience. I soon learned that Bradley had completed approximately fifty-five paintings of various shapes and sizes, and that the paintings had won the praise of a well-known gallery owner who decided to champion Bradley as a promising young protégé. Bradley spent five years producing his body of work, and, eventually, he invited *le tout Londres* to his opening ceremony. He received a great deal of enthusiastic paeans, including some very favourable reviews in the national press, and, to his delight, he even sold some of his larger pieces at huge prices. All in all, one could consider Bradley's debut a great success.

Sadly, however, one particularly "fiendish" critic from a prominent art magazine had slated Bradley in a deeply excoriating review, which many members of the local art community would have read. Bradley's friends and colleagues told him that he should just forget about that nasty review, and they urged him to develop a thicker skin. Well-meaning, though platitudinous, in their attempts to cheer him up, none of Bradley's friends quite appreciated the deep sense of narcissistic injury that he experienced upon reading in print an assessment of his so-called "tasteless" paintings. Suddenly, none of the favourable reviews that he had received seemed to have registered at all, and Bradley identified himself quite powerfully with that sole vicious review, believing this to be the true and final assessment of half a decade of work.

Fortunately, the owner of the gallery at which Bradley had displayed his efforts soon invited him to begin assembling material for a further exhibition to be mounted in two years' time. And so, Bradley set about creating more paintings. But although he could still start a picture and finish it, the process had suddenly lost all its lustre and *joie de vivre*. Bradley often compared himself to a widower who had buried his greatest love. A single man with no partner, Bradley viewed his paintings as a mistress of sorts, and now he felt like a wizened old husband married to a frumpy *Hausfrau* who no longer brought him pleasure.

In our psychotherapeutic work, Bradley and I devoted a great deal of attention to the impact of that "fiendish" review, recognising that such a negative evaluation of his work from a harsh critic provoked a great deal of murderous rage. As a well-behaved church-going child, Bradley's parents had prevented him from using foul language of any sort, and this ban on cursing persisted into adult life. Thus, Bradley found it almost impossible to scream and shout about the evil critic. One day, however, in the context of our discussions of his hatred for this man, Bradley finally managed to call him a "fucking piece of shit", and this outburst proved transformational. As soon as Bradley realised that, unlike his parents, I would be neither shocked nor disapproving of his "filthy" language, he gradually began to enjoy ever more colourful verbal expressions of his venom. He even began to report dreams in which he would kidnap the art critic, tie him to a chair, and then flay him with a knife. Bit by bit, Bradley became increasingly adept at transforming his sad and humiliated feelings into vicious words, which created a great sense of cathartic relief.

Not only did Bradley use psychotherapy quite well to articulate his pent-up murderous rage, but he also began to examine the loss of the fantasy that his art exhibition would be a magical cure for everything in his life. He had secretly hoped that millions of people would come to the gallery and fall madly in love with him and with his paintings, and that all of the guests would wish to have sex with him, and would, therefore, come to admire him more than his mother and father had ever done. Although Bradley had received much affection from his parents, he also knew that they had conceived him "accidentally", some twelve years after the birth of his brother, and some fourteen years after the birth of his sister. I hypothesised that when he arrived in the world, he might have felt that his mother and father did not give him an entirely favourable "review", and that any subsequent unfavourable assessment or evaluation of his art might underscore this much more invisible and subterranean feeling.

My interpretation produced quite a few tears and, eventually, Bradley began to mourn the loss of having staged an art exhibition which, though successful, did not quite compare to the arrival of the Messiah. Gradually, Bradley could appreciate that he had achieved something meritorious, which evoked a range of reactions, and that he had not gratified his omnipotent infantile fantasy of creating paintings which would become so alluring that everyone would love him beyond compare and would never utter a harsh word against him.

Bradley persevered with his psychoanalytical work over several years, and it pleases me to report that, over time, he became more and more robust, and he eventually recaptured the joy that he had previously experienced about his artistic achievements. In fact, he came to appreciate that painting could represent an expression of creativity and that it need not function as his primary source of love. Eventually, Bradley committed himself to a woman, with whom he embarked upon a reasonably successful marriage, something that he had not managed to achieve before. Perhaps of greatest importance, Bradley came to understand that he must paint primarily for himself and not, predominantly, for the admiration of others.

Creativity Bereavement: Type Three – Disability and Ageing

Often, an artist or writer will cease production, not because of any block or sense of disillusionment, but, quite simply, due to the incapacities which follow in the wake of ordinary ageing. Although most of us enter life in reasonably good physical health, unhampered in our ability to use our bodies, advancing age often scuppers our fantasy of corporeal immortality, and, as the decades unfold, each of us must grieve as we become bereaved of our eyesight, our hearing, our dexterity, our speed, and our memory. So many examples of disabled artists come to mind, such as the singer Julie Andrews, whose magnificent voice became damaged after a failed surgery designed to remove non-cancerous nodules from her throat.

"Clarissa", a seventy-four-year-old sculptress, entered once-weekly psychotherapy, having developed a mild depression in the wake of deeply crippling rheumatoid arthritis. Clarissa had sculpted since the age of ten, and now, having reached her seventies, she could no longer shape clay as she had done over the previous sixty years, because her fingers had become gnarled and full of excruciating pain which required frequent, but ultimately fruitless, cortisone injections. Although still married to her loving and long-standing husband, Clarissa nevertheless felt that she had become an "honorary widow", having lost her capacity to relate to sculpture. In fact, she had even gone so far as to place a padlock on the door to her studio, as she could not bear to enter that once-fertile space any longer. Thus, the studio had become a coffin, and the clay, perhaps, a representation of the buried body parts which she could no longer use.

An essentially healthy woman with no history of severe mental illness, Clarissa had the sense to seek out psychotherapeutic engagement as a means of mourning the loss of her fingers, much as an amputee might have to do. Owing to the fact that her lack of capacity to sculpt stemmed from essentially physical causes of recent origin, rather than from psychological ones of ancient origin, Clarissa soon came to realise that although she missed the sensual and creative pleasure of touching and moulding the clay, she had enjoyed the privilege of a very long lifetime of working in this medium, and had achieved a great deal, and that she still possessed a sense of being a sculptress deeply internalised inside her; consequently, even though she no longer visited her studio, she still felt herself to be a sculptress in the depth of her soul and even believed that, in her own small way, she had made a contribution to British art through her many statues. Thus, Clarissa felt both creatively dead with a locked studio door and, also, artistically alive, with the capacity to remember and to enjoy the vitality within her mind and soul.

Eventually, Clarissa developed the idea that she might offer her services as a teacher at a local art college; and, happily, the head of department greeted this generous proposal with great cheer. Clarissa soon began to teach a weekly course on pottery and proved herself to be a most popular teacher. She also took up a number of other creative pursuits which did not require the use of her fingers, and she derived great satisfaction from having begun to learn Italian – the language of her revered idol Michelangelo Buonarroti – the man whom Clarissa regarded as the greatest sculptor of all time. By speaking Italian, she felt herself to be closer to Michelangelo than ever before, and this experience brought her a sense of comfort and satisfaction of the most quiet and private variety.

In many ways, I found working with Clarissa such a treat that I often felt that *I* should be paying *her*, rather than the other way round. She taught me that one can bear physical losses in adulthood, perhaps even the death of a body part or of a spouse, so much better when one has had the privilege of a strong foundation of mental health in the first instance. Clarissa also helped me to appreciate, perhaps more fully than ever before, that the loss of one's artistic productivity will not automatically constitute what I have come to refer to as a "creativity bereavement". One can remain internally creative and engaged without having to manufacture sculptures and sonatas and essays; instead, one can embrace creativity as a state of mind and enjoy one's thoughts as well as one's actions.

Creativity Bereavement: Type Four – The Loss of the Fantasy of Genius

Throughout the course of my psychotherapeutic career, I have encountered a surprisingly large cohort of analysands who have suffered from a profound battle with narcissistic rage (Kohut, 1971; Kernberg, 1975), and, particularly, from that extreme variant of narcissistic pathology which the American psychoanalyst Dr. Helen Tartakoff (1966, p. 236) had christened as the "Nobel Prize complex", a phrase which characterises those patients who might harbour covert wishes and desires to become Prime Minister of the United Kingdom, even though they may be a retired ditch-digger, or those who yearn to win the Academy Award for Best Actress, even though they have never set foot upon a film set. Although many of us do fantasise about extraordinary achievements, such as discovering the cure for cancer, or being the monarch, we generally do so only fleetingly, aware of the realities of our own lives. Such a grandiose fantasy may be aspirational, prompting us to maximise our current potentialities; but, in most cases, we know that the likelihood of discovering a vaccine for the coronavirus overnight, or succeeding Her Majesty Queen Elizabeth II to the throne, may be very, very slim indeed. But for the patient who struggles with the proto-narcissistic Nobel Prize complex, such fantasies not only persist gnawingly throughout the life cycle, but they also become incredibly powerful motivating forces. For instance, in the large-scale study which I undertook on the psychology of sexual fantasies, I interviewed an elderly man – a failed scientist, alas – who claimed that he could achieve orgasm *only* by fantasising that he had actually won the Nobel Prize (Kahr, 2007a).

Whereas most of us abandon our grandiose childhood fantasies as we progress through the life cycle and begin to develop other sources of satisfaction, the Nobel Prize complex patients cling to their secret desires most vociferously. Over the years, I have worked with some very seemingly reasonable adult men and women who have confessed to me from the psychoanalytical couch that if only they could enjoy a break, or if only they could quit their jobs, then they would be able to show the world that they could write a play as good as, if not better than, William Shakespeare's *The Tragedie of Hamlet, Prince of Denmarke*, or, that they could compose a masterpiece infinitely more stirring than Wolfgang Amadeus Mozart's *Requiem*, or, that they could paint a canvas more impactful than Pablo Picasso's *Guernica*.

Among these Nobel Prize complex patients, I have found two sub-groups, namely, those who *do* have demonstrable skills and talents – often very highly honed – yet who still believe that they can outstrip the greatest figures of global history, and those who have *no* overt creative capacities at all, and yet still claim superiority, or crave superiority, over Shakespeare, Mozart, and Picasso. Some years ago, I worked with a member of the performing arts industry who achieved great fame in both the United Kingdom and beyond, and who garnered many coveted prizes, and who "almost received an Academy Award nomination". In spite of these achievements, this patient claimed privately that he knew himself to be the greatest actor in history, certainly much better than Sir Laurence Olivier, whose work he found pedestrian. Similarly, I once provided psychotherapy for another patient who had never even participated in an amateur dramatics group, let alone a professional production, and yet still clung to the fantasy of being the best actor in the world.

Many men and women navigate their entire lives by clinging to an almost delusional belief in their own genius and magnificence, constantly staving off the likely reality that someone else might have outstripped them in some way. Another one of my patients – a long-standing unemployed actor – refused to go to the theatre or to the cinema, as such an experience would then confirm that his rivals had succeeded where he himself had failed. In this way, by remaining at home and by refusing to watch television, this person managed to maintain a grandiose fantasy, albeit tenuously, that he could outstrip all of his competitors. Alas, in having done so, this man denied himself a great source of learning and of pleasure.

I must confess that at the outset of my work with an analysand called "Damian", I had no inkling of the depth of his Nobel Prize complex or of his narcissistic fantasies, although, in retrospect, I can now see the many signs which might have provided some indication of his preoccupations with world domination. On the surface, Damian appeared to be a cheerful, charming, affable, intelligent, likeable gentleman of forty-three years of age who had become very successful in the business world. He first attended psychotherapy because of marital concerns which became more pronounced after the birth of his third child. Our work proceeded very successfully, and Damian engaged himself deeply with the psychoanalytical process, often finding the sessions very helpful indeed. In many ways, I could not have asked for a more satisfying patient. He always attended punctually, and he free-associated while reclining on the couch, thus generating rich material. Moreover, he listened to my interpretations with interest and gratitude, and he often cried and laughed. And he always paid his bills on time. Above all, Damian claimed that I really *did* understand him, and that he felt so much better in all aspects of his life as a direct result of having embarked upon regular psychoanalytical work.

It took some time, nearly two years in fact, to discover that beneath the demonstrably successful exterior of Damian's life lurked a much more troubled interior, one suffused with profound dissatisfaction, envious rage, and murderous competition with siblings. In spite of having reached the pinnacle of success in the business world, having already become a multi-millionaire by the age of twenty-five, Damian now found that business no longer excited him, and he told me that he felt increasingly depressed, having come to appreciate that, in truth, he would never be a celebrated *football player*. Apparently, ever since boyhood, he had yearned to be a sports star like David Beckham, Gary Lineker, or Diego Maradona, but he claimed that his parents never knew of the intensity of his desires and that, alas, they never encouraged him in the least. Regrettably, this childhood wish would never materialise.

As our conversations about his long-standing passion to become a champion athlete unfolded, I soon learned, with some surprise, that during the time in which we had worked together, Damian had spent a great deal of money purchasing sporting memorabilia at auctions or through the internet. He invested a huge amount on a football signed by one of the most iconic British athletes, and he also bought an old jersey once owned by yet another football superstar. I certainly admired this man's industry and hypervigilance in obtaining these fetishised items, but, above all, I became worried that this successful, middle-aged man had begun to live his internal life through the successes of others, rather than by enjoying his own very considerable achievements in the world of business.

When confronted with material of this sort, the psychoanalytical practitioner can approach these communications from a variety of perspectives. Could there be a latent homosexual element in Damian's fascination with another man's used shirt and another man's big ball? Might he be suffering from homeovestism, the obverse of transvestism, wherein one dresses up in the clothes of someone else of the same sex (e.g., Zavitzianos, 1972)? The interpretative possibilities seemed endless. Although we did consider the homoerotic subtext of Damian's preoccupation, our work soon deepened when he confessed to me that not only did he think about these footballers all day long – so much so that these thoughts often interfered with his concentration at work – but, also, that he *knew* in his soul that if his parents had only encouraged him during childhood then he could have become a much better champion than Beckham, Lineker, or Maradona.

On the surface, my account of Damian's internal life seems like a classic case of narcissistic personality disorder topped with a Nobel Prize complex – and I would not dispute this – but I have found it much more useful to conceptualise this man's psychological situation as one of creativity bereavement. And as our work unfolded, we came to conceptualise his endless fantasies of winning a championship not only as an expression of grandiose pathology, but, more fruitfully, as an attempt to enliven his deadened creative capacities and to deal with his monumental rivalry towards siblings.

The eldest of nine children – six boys and three girls – all tightly spaced, Damian grew up loathing his younger brothers; and he denigrated his sisters so much that he often pretended that they did not even exist, and he frequently neglected to mention them for weeks and weeks at a time. Above all, he hated his brothers in particular – his fellow male rivals – and he fought with them over toys, over physical space, and over parental affection. As Damian aged, he transferred his loathing for these boys onto his professional colleagues, describing all the other men in his office as "fucking idiots" and as "shithead losers". His considerable success at work, driven in a cut-throat manner by rivalry and rage, made it much easier to despise these men, because he could readily produce hardcore, forensic evidence which proved that he had earned more money for the company and, ultimately, for himself through pay raises. Therefore, Damian managed to create a situation in which his external financial superiority on the ledger confirmed his hoped-for internal psychological superiority.

But, in relation to football, Damian found it much harder to dismiss David Beckham as a "fucking idiot" or as a "shithead loser" who could not do his job properly. Rather than denigrating Beckham and his comrades, he purchased their balls and their clothing – quite literally – thus attempting to achieve some imaginary sense of victory over these athletic superstars. Yet, in spite of his fantasmatic football victory, Damian still had to face the fact that he had never, ever set foot on a professional pitch.

Once, a business colleague gifted Damian several tickets for an important football match, and although he had worshipped the game in his own way for decades, he had never allowed himself to attend in person, though he could easily have afforded the high-priced seats in the stadium. On this occasion, however, Damian did do so, and, while there, he experienced a most odd sense of "derealisation" and could not quite believe that he had actually entered the football arena. In his mind, he simply could not differentiate between the *reality* of himself as a forty-something-year-old man sitting in a wide-brimmed hat with sunglasses on the sidelines, and, by contrast, the *fantasy* of himself as a young twenty-year-old stallion claiming victory in front of the world's television cameras. This momentary psychotic-like state allowed Damian to tolerate the very evident knowledge that he had come to the stadium as an ordinary punter, not as a champion, and that he would leave as an ordinary punter, and, moreover, that no one would interview him afterwards on the B.B.C.

With my assistance, Damian eventually began to mourn the loss of his long-standing childhood fantasy of vanquishing his father and his sibling rivals, which had become displaced onto the international football pitches. As he grieved for the sporting career that he would never have, he decided that, for the first time in his life, he would hire a football coach and thus enjoy some elementary sports lessons, rather than simply sneer at those heroic athletes from the sidelines. As a forty-plus-year-old man, he did struggle to play amateur football, frequently experiencing breathlessness; and, at last, he came to appreciate that he would never beat David Beckham. As the months unfolded, Damian began to lose interest in football, and we talked about how he might find other creative arenas in his life, which might not require such an immense expenditure of draining and time-consuming grandiosity. Eventually, Damian identified another arena in which he could use his not inconsiderable intelligence in his own unique way, without having to engage in a losing battle with his internal persecutors.

Conclusion

When confronted with the extremely impressive creative talents of other people, most of us find it difficult to express true gratitude and appreciation, or even enjoyment. More often, we find ourselves either idealising or denigrating the famous, public artist as a way of removing ourselves from a more direct, more potentially painful competition. For instance, when the famed nineteenth-century Italian violinist Niccolò Paganini used to perform with lightning speed, onlookers claimed that the Devil must have taken control of his bow (Blanning, 2008). In other words, Paganini could not possibly be an ordinary mortal like the rest of us; he had evidently received assistance from the supernatural. Similarly, Franz Liszt played the piano so extremely well that one contemporary observer wrote in 1832, "'Such a talent, or rather, such powers, would make you believe in miracles!'" (quoted in Blanning, 2008, p. 52). In similar vein, Ludwig II of Bavaria regarded the music of Richard Wagner as so supremely celestial that he dealt with his own rivalry by exclaiming to the composer, "'You are a god-man'" (quoted in Blanning, 2008, p. 58). In other words, by interpreting Paganini's violin-playing as the work of the Devil, by conceptualising Liszt's piano-playing as a "miracle", and by exalting Wagner as a "god-man", each one of us can better manage the pain of not being quite as proficient as these distinguished creative celebrity practitioners. To quote a more prosaic example, I recently worked with a concert pianist who played fantastically well. This talented man told me that one of his fans had once exclaimed, "Look at that dexterity... you must have fifty fingers", thus implying that if each of us had fifty fingers, instead of a mere *ten*, then we, too, would have no trouble performing with such brilliance. Suggesting that a pianist possesses fifty fingers might well be a form of compliment but, above all, it represents a desperate attempt to minimise envy.

Bearing the pain of someone else's accomplishments presents us with a challenge. First, we must face the powerful envy which forms a part of everyone's mind (Klein, 1957). Next, we must face our own despair and thus experience the sense of loss and bereavement, knowing that our own artistic juices may have died or may never have developed at all. And finally, we must stretch ourselves to discover our own creativity and then dare to have it judged. It really would be easier to remain at home in one's armchair lambasting the singers, musicians, and sports figures whom we watch on television, confident in our private fantasies that if only we had chosen to do so, or if only we had fifty fingers, we would manage infinitely better than those brave men and women who did rise to the frightening challenge of success.

Recognising the death of one's creativity may often be as painful as an actual bodily bereavement. We all remember the playwright Peter Shaffer's (1980) stirring portrait of the Italian composer Antonio Salieri who lived his entire professional life in anguished competition with Wolfgang Amadeus Mozart. According to Shaffer's depiction in his drama, *Amadeus*, and in the subsequent film version, Salieri had no alternative but to attempt suicide, thereby avoiding the horror of his own creativity bereavement.

Few of us will ever become as skilled a writer as William Shakespeare, as breath-taking a composer as Wolfgang Amadeus Mozart, or as gripping a painter as Pablo Picasso. And perhaps, few of us would want to be or need to be. After all, one can easily idealise such individuals and lionise them for their art, ignoring the enormous suffering that each experienced during his lifetime. Shakespeare, after all, wrote *The Tragedie of Hamlet, Prince of Denmarke* in the aftermath of the death of his own son Hamnet Shakespeare (e.g., Holden, 1999); Mozart suffered from crippling illness for much of his life and died penurious (e.g., Solomon, 1995); and Picasso painted *Guernica* in order to work through the trauma of having survived an earthquake in childhood (e.g., Miller, 1988). Perhaps as one learns of the challenges of another person's life, the desire to trade places diminishes. Although many women might yearn to be as classically beautiful as the actress Marilyn Monroe, and although many men might wish to be as famous and wealthy as the pop star Michael Jackson, the brutal truths behind these idealised lives may give us some food for thought.

I recently had the pleasure of reading the autobiography of the late Margaret Torrie, founder of Cruse – the United Kingdom's leading bereavement counselling service. In her well-written memoir, *My Years with Cruse*, Mrs. Torrie (1987) revealed that, before she founded this irreplaceable organisation, she had studied painting at the St. Martin's School of Art in London. Additionally, before creating Cruse, she had given birth to another organisation, the International Arts Centre, which flourished during World War II, providing a community for distinguished practitioners such as the playwright Maxwell Anderson, the choreographer Frederick Ashton, the sculptor Henry Moore, the poet Stephen Spender, and the actress Sybil Thorndike. As Torrie (1987, p. 8) explained, "I wanted to find a growth factor in all the daily destruction of war and the negative news that killed the creative spirit." In similar vein, she wrote, "It was, I believe, this demand for growth factors in a situation of destruction, that found its echo in my work many years later for those battling with the life of widowhood" (Torrie, 1987, p. 9).

Nothing feels more painful than loss, especially the loss of a loved one. But that loved one may include not only family and friends, but, *also*, our own potentialities and capacities. Until we face the reality that we may be bereaved of our creative abilities and that we may suffer crippling competition with those who have embraced their creative skills already, we will find it difficult to move forward, or to experience pleasure and joy to the fullest.

For those of us who engage with the topic of media psychoanalysis, we must consider the role of celebrity culture, not only in the press and on television, but, also, in the consulting room, because our wish to become famous geniuses can, in fact, exert a painful impact upon our state of mind. When engaging with popular culture, we must understand not only the powerful wish to be famous but, also, the potentially crippling cost of *not* being famous and how, precisely, psychotherapy and psychoanalysis can help us to navigate such a mediatised planet.

Section V

Uneasy Bedfellows

Freud and His Progeny
Confront the Media

10

Media Monasticism and Media Whoredom

The Uncomfortable Marriage Between Psychoanalysis and Popular Exposure

"PSYCHOANALYZE BY RETURN MAIL": Freud and the Media

In 1924, the sixty-eight-year-old Viennese psychoanalyst Professor Sigmund Freud received a most unexpected invitation from the faraway American State of Illinois. Colonel Robert Rutherford McCormick, the formidable publishing tycoon, known as the "Duke of Chicago" (Seldes, 1953, p. 85), instructed his *Chicago Daily Tribune* staff reporter George Seldes, then based in Europe, to offer Freud an enormous fee to come to the United States of America to testify in the sensational murder trial of two wealthy Jewish teenagers, Nathan Leopold, Jr. and Richard Loeb, who had abducted, and then murdered, a fourteen-year-old schoolboy, Bobby Franks, by having bashed in his skull with a chisel (Baatz, 2008). Anxious to sell newspapers, Colonel McCormick hoped that Freud's presence on the witness stand would create a tidal wave of publicity, and, in consequence, he cabled his employee Seldes (1953, p. 107) to "OFFER FREUD $25000 COME CHICAGO OR ANYTHING HE NAME PSYCHOANALYZE BY RETURN MAIL".[1]

Although eager to collect funds for the growing psychoanalytical movement, and keen to support his Internationaler Psychoanalytischer Verlag [International Psycho-Analytical Press] – Freud's own publishing house – the ailing Viennese physician nonetheless refused. On 29th June, 1924, Freud (1924b, p. 103) replied to Seldes, "'Your telegram reached me belatedly because of being wrongly addressed. In reply I would say that I cannot be supposed to be prepared to provide an expert opinion about persons and a deed when I have only newspaper reports to go on and have no opportunity to make a personal examination. An invitation from the Hearst Press to come to New York for the duration of the trial I have had to decline for reasons of health.'"[2] It seems that not only had Colonel McCormick attempted to entice Freud, but so, too, had the impossibly wealthy publishing tycoon William Randolph Hearst – the real-life model for Orson Welles's "Charles Foster Kane", depicted in the film *Citizen Kane* – who offered to charter an ocean liner for Freud's express use in order to transport him westward (cf. Pizzitola, 2002).

DOI: 10.4324/9781003327240-16

Although Freud provided no detailed explanation as to why he had refused to accept these lavish offers which would have secured not only his own financial future but also that of his children and grandchildren, as well as that of the psychoanalytical movement, we can but speculate (cf. Kahr, 2005d, 2005e, 2007b). Never a fan of the United States of America, a country which he regarded as "a gigantic mistake" (Freud, 1921, p. 419; cf. Hale, 1971; Roazen, 1995a; Prochnik, 2006), Freud had also begun to undergo treatment for carcinoma of the jaw (Schur, 1972; Romm, 1983), and he may have feared leaving his Austrian physicians for such an extended period of time. But, in spite of his cancer, Freud still maintained an active life and treated a full complement of patients; thus, it seems unlikely that his health anxieties constituted the sole deterrent against travelling overseas. Furthermore, Freud had already refused at least one previous lavish offer from the Americans when, in 1919, four years *before* the onset of his carcinoma, the New York publishers Boni and Liveright offered him $10,000 for an American lecture tour. Writing to his Berlin colleague Dr. Karl Abraham, Freud (1920b, p. 416) sneered, "I have no intention of accepting" (cf. Jones, 1957).[3] In view of Freud's track record of suspiciousness towards American publicity, it seems unlikely that he would have refused the invitations from Seldes, McCormick, and Hearst exclusively on health grounds.

But Freud may also have shied away from testifying in an American court for a host of quite unconscious reasons (Kahr, 2005e), which may have included the fear of being in the presence of two Jewish youths who had killed an even younger boy, something which may have activated Freud's long-standing unconscious guilt over the death of his baby brother, Julius Freud. Having portrayed "Brutus" in a school play, Sigmund Freud identified heavily with the murderous Brutus who killed "Julius" (Freud, 1900; cf. Shengold, 1971; Blum, 1977); and Freud believed that, in his own mind, he had caused the death of his younger brother, much as Nathan Leopold and Richard Loeb had orchestrated the death of the fourteen-year-old Bobby Franks.

Additionally, Freud may have feared the media circus which might have ensued in the wake of the Leopold and Loeb trial. The *Chicago Tribune* had proposed to broadcast the proceedings on radio – a shocking innovation at that point in time (Baatz, 2008). The elderly Freud, sequestered in Vienna, may, of course, not have known about such plans for massive publicity, but he might well have sensed the scope and penetration of the growing American advertising machine nonetheless; and so, he declined.

Shortly after the Leopold and Loeb murder trial, Freud received yet another handsome offer from America. The Hollywood film mogul Samuel Goldwyn, keen to capitalise on Freud's reputation as a guru of sexuality, wrote to the father of psychoanalysis, offering him $100,000 to serve as a consultant on a silent film about the great lovers of history, beginning with Antony and Cleopatra (Jones, 1957). Goldwyn journeyed to Vienna but, shockingly, Freud refused a meeting, provoking a huge scandal, which received considerable press attention (Sachs, 1944).

Having now declined a spate of lucrative media invitations from the Americans, Freud responded in similar fashion when offered opportunities from his fellow Europeans; and in 1925, he expressed great consternation when his Berlin-based disciples, Dr. Karl Abraham and Dr. Hanns Sachs, had begun to consult to Georg Wilhelm Pabst's film about psychoanalysis, the now classic *Geheimnisse einer Seele* [*Secrets of a Soul*], produced by U.F.A., the Universum Film Aktiengesellschaft (cf. Chodorkoff and Baxter, 1974; Ries, 1995). Freud became infuriated that his trusted epigones should lend their support to such a project, which, Freud feared, "would have an absurd rather than an instructive impact"[4] (Freud, 1925b, p. 547). Indeed, in a contemporaneous letter to another cherished German colleague, Dr. Ernst Simmel, Freud (1925c, p. 99) cautioned, "In my opinion, psychoanalysis does not lend itself in any way whatever to the medium of the motion picture."

According to Dr. Ernest Jones (1957, p. 115), the newspapers lambasted this film about a patient undergoing treatment for a knife phobia, and claimed that, owing to Freud's inability to secure support for psychoanalysis from fellow medical professionals, he "had in despair fallen back on the theatrical proceeding of advertising his ideas among the populace through a film. This accusation was typical of the bad feeling which was attacking psychoanalysis in every possible manner." Dr. Sándor Radó, the Hungarian psychoanalyst, then practising in Berlin, believed that many colleagues, especially those in Vienna, became jealous of the publicity that Hanns Sachs had received as a result of his involvement in this cinematic project. Such attitudes would have contributed to the suspicion towards the media among Freud and many of the early psychoanalysts (Roazen, 1995b).

As a man who grew up in the era of inkpots and quills, long before the proliferation of the modern medias, Freud would have regarded newspaper barons, commercial publishers, filmmakers, and scriptwriters as vulgarians; and when producers and authors approached Freud with a view to dramatising his own life story, he flatly refused (Schur, 1972). In fact, according to his eldest son, Dr. Martin Freud (1957), the founder of psychoanalysis virtually never listened to the radio, except, on 11th March, 1938, when Kurt von Schuschnigg delivered his resignation speech as the Austrian *Bundeskanzler*, shortly before the Nazi *Anschluß*.[5]

Freud craved scientific respectability; and, as the founder of a new discourse, namely, psychoanalysis, he had to ensure that his creation would not be diluted or corrupted in any way.

Across the decades, Sigmund Freud fought a huge battle, struggling to protect psychoanalysis from media denigration, but, at the same time, he also endeavoured to create a trademark and an international movement, constantly recruiting disciples and often encouraging the creation of new psychoanalytical training institutions throughout the world (Jones, 1957; cf.

Makari, 2008; Falzeder, 2012; Shamdasani, 2012; Skues, 2012). Keen to protect his growing psychoanalytical brand, Freud harboured mistrust towards the media. Nevertheless, he did, at times, recognise its possibilities and its potentialities.

As early as 1875, the nineteen-year-old Freud (1875b, p. 127) wrote to his school friend Eduard Silberstein that, "A respected man, supported by the press and the rich, could do wonders in alleviating physical ills, if only he were enough of an explorer to strike out on new therapeutic paths."[6] Certainly, as he aged, Freud did offer interviews to the press from time to time, including one of five-minutes' duration, on 18th December, 1921, to Hans von Kaltenborn, foreign correspondent of the *Brooklyn Daily Eagle*, published under the title "A Talk with Dr. Freud, Psycho-Analyst". Kaltenborn reported, no doubt erroneously, that he observed some thirty to forty people in Freud's Berggasse 19 waiting room, and claimed that Freud had cautioned him, "'One should have nothing to do with self-styled psychoanalysts who have not had direct contact with me'" (quoted in Hale, 1995, p. 78).

Certainly, Freud did not oppose the popularisation of psychoanalysis entirely. When his Polish colleague, Dr. Gustav Bychowski, paid Freud a final visit in 1935, prior to the emigration of most European psychoanalysts in order to escape the Nazi menace, the two men discussed the fate of civilisation. As Bychowski (1948, p. 9) recalled, "I asked him what contribution he thought psychoanalysis might eventually make to the solution of the appalling crisis with which our civilization was threatened. "How can we," I said, "devote our time and energy to curing a few individuals at a time like this when our entire civilization, our very existence, is imperiled?" Freud replied that in his opinion we could not hope to save mankind but could best help by advancing and popularizing our psychoanalytic knowledge, so that eventually it would become public property, a part of universal thought, so to speak. Then, in the distant future, the day might come when these horrifying reactions of the collective psyche would no longer be possible."

In fact, from time to time, Freud wrote pieces for the noted liberal Viennese newspaper, the *Neue Freie Presse*, a publication which often provided coverage of psychoanalytical activities (Tichy and Zwettler-Otte, 1999). Freud even permitted extracts of several of his later books to appear in that paper, including sections of *Hemmung, Symptom und Angst* (Freud, 1926a) [*Inhibitions, Symptoms and Anxiety* (Freud, 1926b)], *Die Frage der Laienanalyse: Unterredungen mit einem Unparteiischen* (Freud, 1926c) [*The Question of Lay Analysis: Conversations with an Impartial Person* (Freud, 1926d)], *Das Unbehagen in der Kultur* (Freud, 1930a) [*Civilization and its Discontents* (Freud, 1930b)], and the *Neue Folge der Vorlesungen zur Einführung in die Psychoanalyse* (Freud, 1933a) [*New Introductory Lectures on Psycho-Analysis* (Freud, 1933b)]. Freud also permitted the *Neue Freie Presse* to conduct an interview him with in 1933, in which he praised psychoanalysis as a beneficial treatment for schizophrenia and other psychoses (Le Rider, 1992).

Freud loathed the media, and yet, he also recognised its usefulness, if not its necessity, in the promulgation of psychological ideas worldwide. And on 7th December, 1938, only months before his death, Professor Freud allowed his voice to be recorded by the British Broadcasting Corporation, albeit for only a few short minutes.

But in spite of Freud's (1926f, p. 161) efforts to engage from time to time, he did confess to a Hungarian-born colleague, Dr. Sándor Radó, "I have nothing to communicate to the public".[7] The American psychoanalyst, Dr. Martin Peck (1940, p. 206), referred to this aspect of Freud's relationship with the outside world as his "isolation policy".

In view of Freud's tremendously ambivalent attitudes towards publicity, how could psychoanalysis and the media possibly become tolerable bedfellows? And what impact did Freud's contradictory viewpoints towards the media exert on subsequent generations of psychoanalytical practitioners?

"Growing tendency towards shallowness": Fear among the Freudians

In the 1920s, the burgeoning Viennese psychoanalytical community endeavoured to become better known and to expand its services to the wider public by establishing an *Ambulatorium* – a free clinic – for the treatment of the poor (Sterba, 1982; Danto, 1996, 2005). In fact, the Viennese psychoanalysts created a "propaganda committee" (Bronner, 2011, p. 15) in 1925, in order to popularise psychoanalytical ideas. But, by the 1930s, the members of the Wiener Psychoanalytische Vereinigung [Vienna Psycho-Analytical Society] had made a pact to become more self-effacing, by necessity, in the face of the growing Nazi menace (Aichhorn, 1995). For those Viennese and Berliners who ultimately survived Hitlerism and who fled to the United States of America and to Great Britain for sanctuary, many endeavoured to create an insular version of psychoanalysis, which kept its doors closed (cf. Gibeault and Gougoulis, 2011).

The refugees had developed, unsurprisingly, a strong wish for privacy and, hence, they did not publicise their work, fearful that the Nazis could then target them for their prominence. Anna Freud, the veritable queen of the refugee psychoanalysts, set the tone for most of her international colleagues by refusing to collaborate with the press as much as possible. Nobly, she concentrated on her important clinical work with children; and she studiously avoided granting newspaper interviews about her famous father, although towards the end of her life she did speak to selected historians from time to time (Roazen, 1969, 1975; Peters, 1979; cf. Young-Bruehl, 1988). She did also submit to an interview by the American writer Ralph Ingersoll for his left-wing magazine *PM*, published in 1940, discussing the impact of air-raids on London during World War II, as well as the survival measures undertaken in the Freud household (Roazen, 2000b).

When less frightened, less inward-looking, less *Jewish* psychoanalysts such as Dr. Edward Glover or Dr. Donald Winnicott – both native Britons from Gentile backgrounds – began to appear on the B.B.C., their activities caused a great deal of suspicion and scepticism among their fellow psychoanalytical colleagues. Dr. Brendan MacCarthy (2002), former President of the British Psycho-Analytical Society, recalled that Winnicott's pioneering work as the first consummate mental health broadcaster in Great Britain produced a backlash of hostility within the Freudian community. Apparently, many British psychoanalysts, even as late as the 1960s, regarded Winnicott's pioneering talks to health visitors as somewhat sacrilegious, and they feared a dilution of the purity of five-times-weekly psychoanalytical work. In contrast to many of his colleagues, Dr. MacCarthy admired Winnicott's attempts to counteract the massive public hostility towards psychoanalysis during the 1940s, 1950s, and 1960s in Great Britain, and he described Winnicott as a lone voice in this campaign towards popularisation (Kahr, 2002e). MacCarthy recalled that the British Psycho-Analytical Society had adopted a posture of monasticism, which he viewed as a protective defence against attacks from the outside world. Indeed, when MacCarthy submitted his dissertation for his advanced medical degree at University College Dublin in 1965, his colleagues advised him to remove all reference to his extensive psychoanalytical training from his accompanying curriculum vitae, as the external examiner, a certain psychiatrist from Bristol, had vowed that he would never award a higher degree to a psychoanalyst (Kahr, 2002e).

The hesitancy of the Jewish refugee psychoanalysts to engage with the broader world persisted across the decades. Dr. Jeffrey Moussaieff Masson (1984), a young and controversial psychoanalyst, became embroiled in a huge scandal when he questioned Freud's motivations for having abandoned the so-called seduction theory. Dr. Kurt Eissler, Secretary of the Sigmund Freud Archives, summoned Masson for questioning before a meeting of the board of this organisation, at which one psychoanalyst upbraided Masson for having permitted his photograph to be published in *The New York Times*: "'Your picture appeared in the *Times*. No decent analyst would let his picture appear in the *Times*.'" (quoted in Malcolm, 1983, p. 127; cf. Malcolm, 1984).

Of course, this more hidden, even secretive, approach to Freudian psychology can be understood not only as a phobic protection against hostile assaults, but, also, as a stance that makes great sense, owing to the very private, very confidential nature of the psychoanalytical enterprise. When patients present for treatment, they both expect and deserve a pledge that the very intimate, very exposing, often quite shaming, content of their material should remain secret. Only through the provision of a completely confidential setting will analysands dare to reveal the true contents of their fantasies, their histories, their fears and, even, their acts of criminality. Thus, any attempts to publicise the psychoanalytical enterprise must be treated with great care and caution.

In view of the fact that psychoanalytical clinicians receive neither the training nor the encouragement to work with media, and in view of the fact that the mental health professions tend to attract those of a more introverted disposition (which would be required in order to sit in a chair in relative silence for the bulk of one's working life), it should not surprise us that, even today, most mental health professionals have avoided collaboration with the media in any form. During the 1990s, when I worked as a Course Tutor in the Child and Family Department at the Tavistock Clinic in London, journalists would ring up all the time, eager for a quotation from a staff member at this eminent mental health out-patient facility, which could then be included in a newspaper article or a magazine feature. Journalists generally did not know which specialists to approach, and so, in most instances, they spoke first to the departmental secretaries who would then scribble a note on a small piece of paper which would be thumb-tacked to a bulletin board in the post room with a handwritten inscription above it, "Is anyone interested in speaking to this journalist?" Most members of staff walked by the notice board without even glancing at the request. And although a very small number of us did have an interest in collaborating with the media, by the time we had clocked that piece of paper, the story would have then become "old hat", and the journalist would already have filed his or her copy. The Tavistock Clinic lacked a plan to collaborate with the media in any way; consequently, these potential opportunities became deeply destroyed.

Of course, psychotherapists and psychoanalysts do not have a monopoly on sabotaging the publicisation of Freud's work and legacy. Sometimes, media practitioners themselves have wished to steer clear of mental health matters, especially those of a psychoanalytical nature. In 1951, Lucy Freeman, a brilliant and prolific American journalist who had undergone several successful courses of personal psychoanalysis, wrote a one-time best-selling memoir about her experiences on the couch, the now much-overlooked *Fight Against Fears* (Freeman, 1951). Having bravely "outed" herself as a psychoanalytical patient, one of the first people to do so proudly in a book-length study, Mrs. Freeman began to write a large number of serious and appreciative articles on psychoanalysis for a host of American publications, not least *The New York Times*, having worked there as a staff reporter for many years (Kahr, 1999b, 1999c). In spite of her formidable track record as arguably the world's very first full-time mental health correspondent, *The New York Times* eventually issued a ban on all coverage of psychoanalysis. When I had the privilege of meeting Mrs. Freeman (1986) during the mid-1980s, she told me that the prohibition of this subject matter took place after the wife of the newspaper's managing editor had issued divorce proceedings following a period of psychoanalytical treatment! Clearly, the obstacles to a fuller collaboration between the media and psychoanalysis can stem from a multitude of sources and will sometimes even result from a none too thinly disguised personal vendetta.

Throughout the century-long history of psychoanalysis, thousands of practitioners have remained silent, failing to work with the media, and focusing instead, as Anna Freud had done, on their clinical work with patients. But many of the leaders of the field – those with much to say – had found creative ways of contributing to newspapers, to radio, and, even more recently, to television and to film, without compromising their ethical positions. To the best of my knowledge, no previous scholar has attempted to sculpt the contours of the history of media psychology or media psychoanalysis. Owing to limitations of space, it will not be possible to do justice to such a topic in this context, other than to indicate, at least, some of the highlights, demonstrating that one can indeed identify, and study, and perhaps celebrate, a discipline of media psychology or media psychoanalysis, as practised by workaday mental health clinicians.

From Radio Berlin to the B.B.C.: Psychoanalysts as Broadcasters

We cannot possibly know whether Professor Sigmund Freud would have allowed himself to appear on television had he lived into the 1940s and 1950s or beyond. Perhaps with the encroachment of more modern media technology, Freud might have relented, whereas during his lifetime, he regarded electrical devices with considerable suspicion (Freud, 1957). But Freud's one-time disciple and consequent rival, Professor Carl Gustav Jung, a longtime broadcaster on Radio Berlin and also on B.B.C. Radio, appeared on no fewer than two television programmes and one filmed conversation during his lifetime. In July of 1955, Jung submitted to an interview conducted by Stephen Black as part of a *Panorama* television programme for the B.B.C., designed to honour Jung's eightieth birthday. And then, in August of 1957, Jung permitted the American psychologist Professor Richard I. Evans (1964) to interview him for an educational film which would be used in American colleges and universities. In 1959, the distinguished broadcaster and former Labour Party Member of Parliament, John Freeman, chatted with Jung on camera at his home in Küsnacht, in Switzerland, for Freeman's (1959) popular programme *Face to Face*, broadcast on 22nd October, 1959 (cf. Shamdasani, 2005; Schoenl, 2009).

Dr. Alfred Adler, one of the earliest Viennese psychoanalysts who, like Carl Gustav Jung, fell foul of Sigmund Freud, engaged with the media in an even more receptive manner. Adler appeared frequently in newspaper interviews and, on one occasion, in the 1930s, he met two colleagues, Professor Dr. Anitra Karsten, a Gestalt psychologist by training, and Dr. Susanne Liebmann (1977), one of his disciples, at a café in London's West End to discuss the possibility of making a film about Adler's newly branded individual psychology. Professor Dr. Karsten enjoyed a connection to a film studio, and Adler seemed delighted to pursue the idea and even offered to write the script himself. But owing to the incursions of Nazism, the project did not materialise.

Dr. Wilhelm Stekel (1949, 1950), like Alfred Adler, one of the founding members of the Viennese psychoanalytical community, whom Sigmund Freud also excommunicated, engaged with the press quite often. Indeed, when Stekel opened a new clinic for the practice of what he referred to as active-analytical psychotherapy, he warmly encouraged newspaper reports, and he welcomed a radio broadcast about his work as well. Other early members of Freud's most intimate circle, such as Dr. Karl Abraham and Dr. Hanns Sachs, collaborated with the creators of the film *Geheimnisse einer Seele*, as already indicated; and Freud's Hungarian disciple, Dr. Sándor Ferenczi (1922), published a book of overtly accessible lectures on psychoanalysis, the *Populäre Vorträge über Psychoanalyse [Popular Talks on Psychoanalysis]*, which treated such subjects as dreams, suggestion, jokes, philosophy, mythology, and criminology. Ferenczi (1922) described these chapters in his "Vorwort" ["Foreword"] as "psychoanalytical themes for medical and non-medical lay people."[8]

Dr. Franz Alexander, the first person in history to graduate from a psychoanalytical institute, certainly had a capacity to engage with the media. On 27th March, 1926, the Berliner Psychoanalytische Vereinigung [Berlin Psycho-Analytical Society] hosted a meeting on the theme of psychoanalysis and publicity, and both Franz Alexander and Dr. Siegfried Bernfeld contributed to the discussion.

Dr. Montague David Eder, Dr. Ernest Jones, and Dr. Edward Glover, three pioneers of psychoanalysis in Great Britain, each made strong contributions to the nascent field of media psychology. David Eder, a politically active physician with strong leftist leanings and an impressive track record in social medicine (Thomson, 2011), wrote for a number of popular publications. Eder's article on "Doctors and Dreams" appeared on 7th August, 1913, in the *Daily Dispatch* (Glover, 1945); and, he also penned pieces for *New Judea* (Hobman, 1945a), as well as for *The Jewish Chronicle* newspaper (Jones, 1936), and for the *Nation, Eye-witness*, the *Westminster Gazette*, and the *Daily Herald* (Hobman, 1945b), and, also, quite frequently, for *New Age*, a radical literary magazine for which Eder served as a consultant from 1907 until 1915 (Hobman, 1945b; Ellesley, 2004).

Dr. Ernest Jones, the founding President of the British Psycho-Analytical Society, made a very large number of contributions to the media during his years of prominence. To quote but a few instances, in 1932, both Dr. Jones and Professor Cyril Burt (also a pioneering member of the British Psycho-Analytical Society, though much better remembered nowadays for his contributions to academic psychology) participated in a series of further B.B.C. radio talks on *How the Mind Works*, published first in *The Listener* (Burt, 1932a, 1932b; Anonymous [Ernest Jones], 1932a, 1932b, 1932c; Anonymous [Ernest Jones] and Burt, 1932) and then in book form (Burt, 1933a,

1933b; Jones, 1933; cf. Burt, Jones, Miller, and Moodie, 1933). In his report to the Institute of Psycho-Analysis, Jones noted with pride that the B.B.C. had actually dared to invite a psychoanalyst to appear on the radio (The Institute of Psycho-Analysis (The London Clinic of Psycho-Analysis), 1934). Additionally, he lectured to the Sociological Society (Jones, 1924), and he wrote at least one letter to *The Times* (Jones, 1934).

Perhaps Jones made his greatest contribution to media psychology when he granted a consultation to Laurence Olivier, then a young actor, preparing his now legendary 1937 production of *Hamlet* at the Old Vic theatre in London. Olivier met with Jones in order to discuss the unconscious motivations of William Shakespeare's characters,[9] and he brought the Old Vic stalwart actress Peggy Ashcroft and the director Tyrone ("Tony") Guthrie along as well. Olivier (1982, p. 79) recalled his meeting with Jones, years later, in his autobiography, *Confessions of an Actor*, noting, "He had made an exhaustive study of Hamlet from his own professional point of view and was wonderfully enlightening. I have never ceased to think about Hamlet at odd moments, and ever since that meeting I have believed that Hamlet was a prime sufferer from the Oedipus complex – quite unconsciously, of course, as the professor was anxious to stress. He offered an impressive array of symptoms: spectacular mood-swings, cruel treatment of his love, and above all a hopeless inability to pursue the course required of him. The Oedipus complex, therefore, can claim responsibility for a formidable share of all that is wrong with him. There is great pathos in his determined efforts to bring himself to the required boiling point, and in the excuses he finds to shed this responsibility." Olivier (1982, p. 79) went to visit Jones because, as he says, "For my generation, determined upon realism, the burning question was, of course: 'What makes him what he is?'" Jones's consultation must have proved useful and contributed to the psychological veracity of Olivier's work, so much so that, in 1948, he received an Academy Award for Best Actor for his starring role in the film version of *Hamlet*. Under Olivier's splendid direction, the movie also won the Academy Award for Best Picture.

It seems that Laurence Olivier must also have discussed his upcoming 1938 production of *Othello*, in which he would play "Iago", while Ralph Richardson would portray the title character, and Tyrone Guthrie would direct once again. According to Olivier (1982, p. 82): "Tony Guthrie and I were swept away by Professor Jones's contention that Iago was subconsciously in love with Othello and had to destroy him. Unfortunately there was not the slightest chance of Ralph entertaining this idea. I was however, determined upon my wicked intentions, in cahoots with Tony; we constantly watched for occasions when our diagnosis might be made apparent to the discriminating among an audience, though I must say I have never yet discovered any means of divulging something that is definitely *subconscious* to any audience, no matter how discerning they may be. In a reckless moment during rehearsals I threw my arms round Ralph and kissed him full on the lips. He coolly disengaged himself from my embrace, patted me gently on the back of the neck and, more in sorrow than in anger, murmured, 'There, there now; dear boy; *good* boy ....' Tony and I dropped all secret connivance after that." Olivier's psychologically orientated performances in two of Shakespeare's most classic tragedies certainly helped to promote psychoanalytical ideas in cultural spaces on a more widespread basis; and Jones played a critical role in that process (cf. Jones, 1910, 1947, 1949).

Dr. Edward Glover, Jones's amanuensis – a much-maligned and much-overlooked figure in the history of British medical psychology, criminology, and psychoanalysis – made vast contributions to the promulgation of mental health ideas in the press and on the radio. Before World War II, Glover appeared several times on air for the Talks Department at the British Broadcasting Corporation. His 1936 book, *The Dangers of Being Human*, even contains a "Preface" on "Science and Broadcasting" (Glover, 1936). He also wrote for many popular publications, including *Horizon*, *The New York Times*, *The Spectator*, and *The Times* (Roazen, 2000a), as well as *Cavalcade* and the *Daily Mail* (Stephen, 1944). And, during World War II, he gave a number of shortwave radio broadcasts to North America on *Inside the Nazi Mind* to which his psychoanalytical colleagues Professor John Carl Flügel and Ella Freeman Sharpe also contributed (Roazen, 2000a, 2000b).

One would require an entire monograph in which to survey the full scope of psychoanalytical collaborations with the media. Briefly, one must not forget other brave, pioneering, early contributions to this interdisciplinary endeavour, which many people, at the time, regarded as daring, even shocking. Freud's analysand and leading French disciple, the Princesse Marie Bonaparte, wrote frequently for newspapers and magazines such as *Evidences*, *Marianne*, *Le Matin*, *Les Nouvelles Littéraires*, *L'Ordre*, *Paris Soir*, and *Le Petit Parisien*; and she enjoyed lecturing to public institutions such as L'Alliance Israélite universelle, as well as to the more traditional psychoanalytical institutions (Bertin, 1982a, 1982b).

Dr. Abraham Arden Brill, the leader of the American psychoanalytical movement, also enjoyed the media. In 1930, Brill granted an interview to the *New York Post* newspaper about John L. Balderston's popular 1929 Broadway play *Berkeley Square*, describing the character of "Peter Standish" as a classic case of schizophrenia with a mother fixation (Sievers, 1955). He even spoke in Hollywood, California, at the famous women's group, the Friday Morning Club, which convened in the Hancock Park mansion of socialite Adeline Jaffe Schulberg, wife of the eminent film producer Benjamin Percival Schulberg [B.P. Schulberg] (Farber and Green, 1993). Most spectacularly, Brill provided consultation to Freud's nephew, the shrewd founder of the modern profession of public relations, Edward L. Bernays, who, in 1929, had organised an Easter Sunday parade on New York City's Fifth Avenue in which glamorous ladies walked while smoking, all part of Bernays's (1965) work for the American Tobacco Company, promoting the sexiness of cigarettes (cf. Tye, 1998).

Dr. Karl Menninger (1973, 1988), the celebrated American psychiatrist and psychoanalyst, exemplified the more outward-facing breed of clinician (cf. Friedman, 1990; Hatcher, 2004) and, before World War II, the Menninger Clinic had employed the services of a public relations consultant, one Laura Knickerbocker, a sometime reporter for *The New York Times* (Grotjahn, 1987).

Other early psychoanalysts who collaborated with the general public in active ways, whether as lecturers at cultural institutions, as broadcasters on radio or television, as authors of popular books and articles, or as theatre or film consultants, included: Professor Grete Bibring (Gifford, 1978), Frieda Fordham (Postle, 1977); Dr. Michael Fordham (Postle, 1977); Dr. Erich Fromm (1956); Harry Guntrip (later Dr. Harry Guntrip) (1951); Dr. Karen Horney (Willig, 1991); Dr. Susan Isaacs (1932, 1948); Dr. Heinz Kohut (Strozier, 2001); Dr. Ernst Kris (Kris, Speier, Axelrad, Herma, Loeb, Paechter, and White, 1944); Dr. Lawrence Kubie (Brown, 2006; mcclung, 2007); Barbara Low (Anonymous, 1927; MacGibbon, 1997; Maddox, 2006); Dr. Theodor Reik (Selznick, 1983; Farber and Green, 1993; Laurents, 2000); Dr. John Rickman (*Institute Board Meetings: 16.1.1925 to 30.4.1945*, 1925–1945; MacGibbon, 1997; cf. Cameron and Forrester, 2000); Dr. May Romm (Farber and Green, 1993); Helen Ross (Hunter, 1979); Dr. Adrian Stephen (Berenson, 1934; MacGibbon, 1997); Dr. Karin Stephen (Kahr, 1984); Adolf Josef Storfer (Blowers, 2004); and countless others, too numerous to mention.

In addition to this bespoke litany, the particular contributions of such titans of media psychoanalysis as Dr. Donald Winnicott in Great Britain and Dr. Jacques Lacan (1974) and Dr. Françoise Dolto (1977, 1989) in France, all of whom made frequent radio broadcasts, as well as occasional television appearances, merit a more full-length investigation. Winnicott became the voice of psychology on the British Broadcasting Corporation throughout most of the 1940s and 1950s (Kahr, 1996a, 1996b, 2002b, 2018a; cf. Karpf, 2014); and Lacan, and especially Dolto, performed similar roles for the French (Roudinesco, 1993, 1994; cf. Lumbroso, 2007; de Mijolla, 2010). Winnicott, in particular, penetrated the culture entirely, whether speaking about the unusual subjects of the use of the toothbrush and religious ritual on the B.B.C.'s *Brains Trust* programme (Rich, 1948), or about his more stalwart work on mothers and babies (e.g., Winnicott, 1949a, 1987, 1993); and, in doing so, Winnicott truly captured the public imagination. Aided and abetted by his long-standing producer, Isa Donald Benzie (Donovan, 2004), who promoted Winnicott's (1949a, p. 2) concept of the "ordinary devoted mother", Winnicott's reputation and influence as a broadcaster grew, and he exerted a huge impact on a young generation of mental health professionals who listened to him with great delight (Kahr, 1994e). In spite of Winnicott's (1967e) belief that psychoanalysts do not, on the whole, broadcast well, he persevered and developed a great skill for reaching members of the public at a time when even basic information about childcare proved difficult to acquire. In 1952, a woman called Florence Bantin wrote to congratulate him on his radio talks. Mrs. Bantin explained that she regarded Winnicott's compassionate and non-directive approach to child psychology to be a most helpful antidote to the prevailing views which included: "'*Never* give feeds at night'" (quoted in Bantin, 1952), "'Let him scream'" (quoted in Bantin, 1952), "'Babies should not be picked up'" (quoted in Bantin, 1952), and "'Babies are very cunning, and will master you if you don't master them'" (quoted in Bantin, 1952).

Among the subsequent generations of psychoanalytical clinicians who have worked in media, one might mention briefly that two noted practitioners made either a cameo appearance or undertook a small role in major films directed by none other than Woody Allen. Professor Bruno Bettelheim featured in Allen's 1983 movie, *Zelig*, and Professor Martin Bergmann, noted for his conservative, careful historical scholarship (e.g., Bergmann, 1976, 2004), played the role of "Professor Louis S. Levy" in Allen's 1989 film, *Crimes and Misdemeanors*, each helping to make psychoanalysis more visible and more accessible, and, perhaps, more playful as well. Bergmann's colleague, Dr. Arlene Kramer Richards (1994, p. 34) described Martin Bergmann's film work for Woody Allen as an opportunity "where he pithily embodied psychoanalytic thinking into art", and that, "Few analysts would have been bold enough to attempt such a thing. Only Bergmann would have the understanding of its importance to do it proudly and the vision to do it well" (Richards, 1994, p. 34).

In 1999, London's Tavistock Clinic authorised the British Broadcasting Corporation to film some of its patients and staff members in sessions – a bold and controversial enterprise – but one which reaped rich rewards in terms of the dissemination of mental health information. Certainly, a member of the administrative staff at the Tavistock Clinic, the much-admired Joe Hynes, once told me that, in the wake of this six-part series, entitled *The Talking Cure* (Taylor, 1999), the telephones rang off the hook with people wishing to have psychotherapeutic consultations!

Popularisation or Plebification: Sigmund Freud or Dr. Phil?

But in spite of this catalogue and, also, celebration of the heroes and heroines of media psychology, let us remember that only a tiny percentage of the larger membership of the mental health community has actually contributed to these activities. Most prefer to remain silent, whether owing to their concentration on clinical work, or due to an incapacity to communicate more clearly and broadly, or as a result of their destructive envy at not having had the opportunity to express their views on air or on camera, or for a whole host of other reasons. Often, even those who have made great strides in the field of media psychology, such as Dr. Ernest Jones, had attempted to quash the efforts of their colleagues from doing likewise, either out of a wish to protect the field, or to prevent other sibling rivals from achieving too much prominence. In 1922, Barbara Low, a loyal Freudian psychoanalyst, allowed herself to be interviewed by *Lloyd's Weekly Newspaper*, a Sunday periodical. Regrettably, the article which featured Miss Low bore the unfortunate title: "Psycho-Analysis Dangers: Need for Protection Against Quacks Who Exploit Hysterical Women" (Maddox, 2006). As a result, Jones expressed great displeasure. Thereafter, he strove to prevent colleagues from speaking about psychoanalysis outside of the confines of the British Psycho-Analytical Society. As Dr. John Bowlby recalled, Ernest Jones admonished Dr. Karin Stephen for lecturing at the Tavistock Clinic (Kahr, 1984) – at that time a rival institution which housed Jungians and Adlerians on its staff (Dicks, 1970). In fact, Jones objected so much to Stephen's proposed lectures that he actually threatened her career (Kahr, 1984). As Bowlby (1985, p. 5) recalled, "Jones maintained that no one should give lectures on psychoanalysis anywhere without his permission, which was rarely given." Intimately aware of Jones's restrictive policies and tendency towards insularity, Bowlby declaimed to the Annual Meeting of the British Psycho-Analytical Society, "'We find ourselves in a rapidly changing world and yet, as a Society, we have done nothing, I repeat nothing, to meet these changes, to influence them or to adapt to them. That is not the reaction of a living organism but of a moribund one. If our Society died of inertia it would only have met the fate that it has invited'" (quoted in King, 1989, p. 19).

Paradoxically, Ernest Jones prevented colleagues from working with the media, and yet, he also lamented that psychoanalysis did not have a better public profile. Only one year after having founded the British Psycho-Analytical Society, Jones (1920, p. 5) complained, "In addition to the deeper and more permanent sources of opposition to Psycho-Analysis, there have been two practical reasons why knowledge of it has spread slowly in England in particular. One of these has been the relative inaccessibility of the standard works on the subject".

It would not be unreasonable to speculate that Jones's anti-media stance developed from at least two sources. First of all, Jones wished to preserve his own terrain, and, as we have indicated, he would prevent potential rivals from stealing the media limelight. But second of all, in spite of his wish to publicise psychoanalysis (and his own role therein), Jones harboured great suspicion towards, and profound fear of, the media, in part, because many years previously, on 20th March, 1906, Jones became exposed in the British press for allegations of acting inappropriately while examining handicapped children at the Edward Street School in Deptford, in South East London, resulting in his arrest. Although Jones would be exonerated of the charges, he did, nonetheless, emigrate to Canada thereafter in an effort to distance himself from this humiliating scandal (Kuhn, 2002; Maddox, 2006).

Psychoanalysts and psychotherapists and other mental health professionals can of course work with the media improperly, scandalously, and unethically. When Dr. Melitta Schmideberg (1981, p. 67), the daughter of Melanie Klein, emigrated from London to New York City, New York, in 1945, she met one psychoanalyst who had, exhibitionistically, engaged his own "public relations man". Of course, such practices would raise eyebrows among those of us who work in this essentially private and confidential profession.

And herein rests the tension between what I have described in the title of this essay as "media monasticism" versus "media whoredom". Do we as mental health professionals seek out opportunities to educate the public? Or do we endeavour to keep a low profile? Do we respond to media inquiries? Or do we refuse them? As a clinician who has worked for the British Broadcasting Corporation as its Resident Psychotherapist and as a Spokesperson for one of the B.B.C.'s mental health campaigns, I can report that colleagues respond to these questions with every possible set of reactions, ranging from admiration and approbation, to envy and jealousy, to a wish to identify and to undertake similar work, to a scathing disapproval, to actual obstreperousness and name-calling.

Collaborating with the media does of course carry risks. One exposes one's thoughts and one's work to national and international scrutiny, which may not always feel comfortable. One becomes prey to the charge of vulgarising our hard-won professional knowledge. One even runs the risk of being accused of rape, as occurred when, in 1975, a woman in Australia levied assault charges against a psychologist called Dr. Donald Thomson. It subsequently transpired that the woman in question had been watching Donald Thomson talking about psychological matters on her television screen (on the Australian Broadcasting Corporation) while an assailant entered her home and actually raped her. During questioning afterwards, the traumatised woman, in a state of confusion, identified Thomson (then speaking live on television – the very *best* of alibis) as the perpetrator (e.g., Baddeley, 1982, 2004).

Of course, mental health professionals can continue to sequester ourselves in tiny, antiseptic, media-free bubbles, refusing to return telephone calls from journalists and television researchers; but if we behave in such uncooperative ways, we run the risk of annihilating our potential for visibility and for accessibility. As a matter of interest, on several occasions, spaced out over quite a number of years, I tapped the names of four of our leading psychoanalytical geniuses into the Google search engine. On 25th January, 2009, the name of Sigmund Freud received 4,000,000 hits, rising to 14,500,000 on 6th July, 2011, and then dropping again to 13,400,000 on 6th October, 2012, but skyrocketing to 16,600,000 hits on 4th July, 2021, and up, even further, to 26,100,000 hits on 6th February, 2022. Carl Gustav Jung earned 1,140,000 hits in 2009, rising to 5,190,000 in 2011, and then slumping to 2,450,000 hits in 2012 and, extraordinarily, to only 1,500,000 in 2017, but bouncing back up to 4,290,000 hits in 2021 and then to 10,200,000 hits in 2022. Melanie Klein's name resulted in 2,870,000 responses in 2009, but dropped, slightly, to 2,350,000 in 2011, rising moderately to 2,970,000 in 2012, and then dropping, alas, to only 1,190,000 in 2021, and then, up a bit more, to 1,430,000 hits in 2022. And Donald Winnicott, likewise, slipped in popularity from 516,000 hits in 2009, to 474,000 in 2011, rising to 540,000 in 2012, but, plummeting, surprisingly, to only 316,000 hits in 2021 and 344,000 hits in 2022.

As a contrast, I then typed in the names of arguably the four most important, culturally iconic, promoters of psychological and psychoanalytical thinking, three of whom – Woody Allen, Oprah Winfrey, and "Dr. Phil" [Phil McGraw] – have disseminated psychological ideas through film or television, and one of whom is a fictional character on a sitcom, but rather famous nonetheless, "Dr. Frasier Crane", protagonist of the popular television programme *Frasier*. Although one cannot accurately compare the Google results of four dead psychoanalysts with those of four contemporary figures who flourish in the popular media, the results still deserve our attention. In 2009, "Frasier Crane" yielded 3,080,000 responses, and in 2011, this rose to 11,000,000 but then dropped to only 403,000 in 2017, long after the end of the *Frasier* television series, but bounced up to 576,000 in 2021 and then down yet again to 492,000 hits in 2022. Dr. Phil earned 5,370,000 results in 2009, rising to 25,400,000 in 2011, and then skyrocketing to 89,800,000 in 2012, but declining to 11,000,000 in 2021 and to 15,000,000 in 2022. Woody Allen's penetrativity escalated from 7,500,000 in 2009 to 35,700,000 in 2011, and then, in 2012, to 49,500,000, dropping slightly to 46,600,000 in 2017, but, up again to 85,800,000 hits in 2020, though falling to 15,800,000 in 2021 and rising once more to 24,300,000 in 2022. And Oprah Winfrey topped the list with 7,220,000 hits in 2009 and, subsequently, received a whopping 52,300,000 hits in 2011, dropping slightly to 43,700,000 in 2012, and then to only 16,700,000 in 2017, but up again to 24,600,000 in 2020 and down to 22,900,000 mid-pandemic, in 2021, and bouncing back to 45,200,000 in 2022.

Indeed, during this period of googling, Freud, at his peak, never achieved the internet penetrativity of some of these media icons, including, at times, Dr. Phil. What, then, can we reasonably conclude, if anything, by examining these search results? Clearly, we as mental health professionals no longer lead the way in promoting our own work. Or, put another way, the progenitors of psychotherapy may no longer be the most famous proponents of this discipline.

In recent years, the number of trainees within British psychoanalytical and psychotherapeutic organisations has declined, and many organisations have had to move to somewhat less plush premises, or have had to suspend their trainings, or have had to amalgamate their organisations. Many psychoanalytical colleagues have few or no patients, and all psychoanalytical workers face stiff competition from the behavioural and cognitive therapies. According to my own large-scale survey, conducted in association with the national pollsters YouGov, less than one per cent of the British population had ever consulted a trained psychotherapist (Kahr, 2007a), though many more had worked with counsellors or with psychiatrists. No wonder Malcolm Allen (2011, p. 1), the former Chief Executive Officer of the British Psychoanalytic Council, had called for "the urgent need for realignment to begin to overcome the debilitating fragmentation" of our profession.

Reminiscing about the history of psychoanalysis on the eve of his ninetieth birthday, the distinguished clinician and administrator, Professor Robert Wallerstein, former President of both the American Psychoanalytic Association and of the International Psycho-Analytical Association, recalled, "Anna Freud said strongly that there is no other discipline that is both a serious intellectual one and a therapeutic one, that tries to do its training on a part-time basis. Like any serious study, it should be full-time, and the fact that we, for historical reasons, still meet at our part-time educational gatherings at night, she said, is analogous to modern churchgoers still doing what the original Christians did, reciting their prayers secretly in a catacomb" (quoted in Di Donna, 2010, p. 656). Perhaps we would do well to heed Anna Freud's concern and warning.

Throughout history, numerous famous and impactful sciences have embraced the press wholeheartedly. Albert Einstein, for instance, enjoyed travelling through the streets of New York City, New York, as part of a parade celebration (e.g., Pais, 1994; Brian, 1996; Schwartz, 1999). And when Marie Curie came to the United States of America, also in 1921, she worked closely with Marie Meloney, known as "Missy", the editor of the women's magazine *The Delineator*, who arranged extensive press coverage for Madame Curie, so much so that the clippings from her American trip now fill some nine huge volumes housed in the Musée Curie in Paris, France (Pflaum, 1989). Neither Einstein nor Curie had damaged their scientific reputation by collaborating with the press and with the public; indeed, their renown soared in consequence, both as personalities and as serious researchers.

Sigmund Freud bequeathed a complicated legacy to his professional grandchildren and great-grandchildren. By refusing to speak to Samuel Goldwyn, by declining the opportunity to testify in a prominent murder trial, and by responding unfavourably when colleagues attempted to create an essentially sympathetic, if not flattering, filmic representation of the psychoanalytical enterprise, Freud had allowed many of his followers to treat the media in a contemptuous manner. But Freud also appreciated the importance of growth, of the creation of an international movement, and of a global trademark of professional excellence.

But in spite of Freud's quite understandable ambivalences and hesitations, many of his successors did, indeed, find ways of representing good, solid mental health work and psychoanalytical thinking in broadsheets, in magazines, on radio, on television, and on film. In doing so, these forward-thinking men and women have helped to make good mental healthcare more available to larger numbers of people and have contributed to the crucial de-stigmatisation of mental illness and help-seeking. Surely, this would be a fine time to celebrate the historical achievements of our forefathers and foremothers in the field of media psychoanalysis. Likewise, this would also be a good time to learn how those of us working clinically might collaborate more interdisciplinarily with media practitioners, with media academics, and with the culture at large, in a much more enthusiastic manner. Should we fail to do so, we will, undoubtedly, imperil ourselves most dangerously.

11

"I think analysts are not very good as broadcasters"

Donald Winnicott's Contribution to Media Psychology

The Unsung Winnicott

Donald Woods Winnicott has earned an everlasting place in the history of the human sciences for his multitudinous contributions to the psychology of childhood and adulthood. Mental health professionals, paediatricians, educationalists, and social welfare workers alike need little reminder of Winnicott's gargantuan achievements in the realms of psychoanalysis, childcare, and related fields. Building upon Sigmund Freud's theories of psychosexual development, Winnicott sculpted undoubtedly the most comprehensive model of normal infant psychology and of infant psychopathology, rooted boldly in the actual vicissitudes of the baby-parent relationship, exploring the detailed ways in which the holding and handling of the newborn will contribute either to safety, security, and mental health on the one hand, or to indescribable fears and anxieties, and ultimately, to psychopathology on the other hand.

Not only did Winnicott elaborate a detailed proto-psychological model of growth and development, based upon more than fifty years of professional clinical experience, but he also facilitated the creation of new methods and styles of treatment, practising not only traditional five-times-weekly psychoanalysis with children and adults, but developing, also, the roots of what we now refer to as parent-infant psychotherapy, of early intervention or preventative psychiatry, of the therapeutic consultation, of brief psychotherapy, of infant observation, and of so much more (cf. Winnicott, 1971b, 1977, cf. Kahr, 2021c). Additionally, in the 1930s, Winnicott did more, perhaps, than any other practitioner to introduce Freudian psychology into the field of children's medicine, thus laying the groundwork for contemporary paediatric psychology (e.g., Winnicott, 1931). Furthermore, one can claim Winnicott as the progenitor of forensic child and adolescent psychotherapy (Kahr, 2001b, 2001c), in view of his many pioneering achievements in the field of delinquency research (e.g., Winnicott, 1943c, 1962c, 1968a, 1984); and likewise, one can thank Winnicott for helping to develop the multidisciplinary team and, even, the field of family therapy, to boot (Kahr, 1996b, 2002b; cf. Kahr, 1996a).

DOI: 10.4324/9781003327240-17

Just as we remember Freud for his rich vocabulary, whether the id, the ego, the superego, the conscious, the preconscious, the unconscious, transference, countertransference, and so forth, we also hold Winnicott warmly in our thoughts for his many neologisms, whether the transitional object, the holding environment, the facilitating environment, hate in the countertransference, the true self, the false self, the good-enough mother, the ordinary devoted mother, the squiggle, impingement, play, and so many more. Winnicott's memorable terms have become, indeed, the veritable hieroglyphs of contemporary child psychology, psychotherapy, and psychoanalysis.

Because Winnicott contributed so much to so many aspects of both psychoanalytical theory and clinical practice, many of his other achievements tend to be overlooked amid the growing number of biographical, psychobiographical, clinical, academic, and critical studies which continue to appear in print. In particular, as we celebrate Winnicott the psychoanalyst, Winnicott the diagnostician, Winnicott the researcher, Winnicott the author, and much else besides, we must recognise that the scholarly community has devoted very little attention indeed to Winnicott the *broadcaster*.

Although every psychoanalytical practitioner and academician knows that Donald Winnicott delivered many radio broadcasts during the middle years of the twentieth century, and most of us will have read his more popular books, intended for members of the general public (e.g., Winnicott, 1957a, 1957b, 1964a, 1965a; cf. Winnicott, 1987, 1993), based largely on these radio talks or popular press articles, no one has yet undertaken a detailed study of Winnicott's contribution to the field of endeavour which has since come to be known as media psychology or media psychoanalysis. Dr. Robert Rodman's (2003) biography of Winnicott, for example, some 459 pages in length, contains only one fleeting reference to the British Broadcasting Corporation, and mentions none of the radio commissioners with whom Winnicott worked so closely over many years. My own biography of Winnicott, only 189 pages in length, and written as a prelude to a much more comprehensive study (currently in preparation), contains a mere two half-pages of information about Winnicott's contributions as a broadcaster, although I do mention some of his principal B.B.C. colleagues, namely, Isa Benzie and Janet Quigley (Kahr, 1996a; cf. Kahr, 2018a). One would be hard-pressed to find many serious or extended references to Winnicott's media work in the broader, now heaving, literature of books, monographs, chapters, and essays on Winnicott's life and work (cf. Karpf, 2014).

In many respects, the relative neglect of Winnicott as a public broadcaster can be understood, in part, as a reflection of the fact that most mental health practitioners have little professional experience of, or interest in, the media; and most clinicians spend all of our time in tiny consulting rooms, engaged in very private, non-public work, with patients, clients, or analysands. Indeed, the very essence of the confidential psychoanalytical enterprise requires that we as practitioners reveal nothing about our patients' lives. In other words, we must *not* be *broadcasters*. And, certainly, we must never broadcast the secrets of our patients. One can appreciate, therefore, that most clinical workers will remain much more engaged with the inside world than with the outside world, and that few psychoanalysts or psychotherapists, on the whole, will work, or have worked, very closely with the media, in spite of some notable exceptions. As we know from the previous chapter, Freud feared the potential of the media to exploit, or cheapen, or caricature the psychoanalytical enterprise, and thus, he resisted many opportunities to collaborate with filmmakers and newspapermen (e.g., Kahr, 2005d, 2007b, 2013).

But at another level, however, the neglect of Winnicott as broadcaster can be described as shocking, in view of the fact that he devoted so many years of his life to speaking on radio and even on television, and to writing for the popular press, reaching audiences of millions, thus making more contact with the wider public than any other mental health professional in Great Britain at that time. One might argue that Winnicott promoted a psychological accent, and thus did more to ensure the survival of psychodynamic ideas and concepts than his colleagues in the British Psycho-Analytical Society, many of whom found his media activities to be provocative or exhibitionistic (MacCarthy, 2002; cf. Kahr, 2002e).

In the following pages, I shall endeavour to investigate Winnicott's contribution to the field of media psychoanalysis, exploring not only *what* he contributed but, also, hopefully, *why* he might have done so, examining the roots of his broadcasting activities within the contours of his personal and professional biography. Finally, I shall conclude with some thoughts on the reasons for our relative marginalisation of Donald Winnicott as broadcaster and public educator.

Broadcasting in Britain

On 10th March, 1876, the Scottish-born inventor Alexander Graham Bell rang his assistant Thomas Watson on the newly minted telephone for the very first time. The following year, on 6th December, 1877, Bell's American-born counterpart, the multi-talented Thomas Alva Edison, recorded the words "Mary had a little lamb" on a tinfoil phonograph, becoming the first person to capture human speech in a permanent form. These two pioneering moments in the history of transmitting sound and, also, preserving sound formed the basis of what would ultimately become the radio (Tritton, 1991).

Shortly thereafter, in 1878, Henry Edmunds, an engineer and inventor from Yorkshire, visited Thomas Edison in Menlo Park, California, and soon acquired sufficient knowledge to build the very first British phonograph (Tritton, 1991). Edmunds's new creation piqued the interest of Queen Victoria herself, who, in 1888, asked to have a recording made of her voice, but as Edmunds could not visit Her Majesty in person, his colleague Sydney Morse went in his stead and brought a special machine to Balmoral, in Scotland, to capture the monarch's vocal tones (Tritton, 1993).

After numerous technological developments and improvements during the last decade of the nineteenth century and the first two decades of the twentieth century, the radio, as we know it, had become established and could at last be transmitted into private homes. On 15th June, 1920, Dame Nellie Melba, the noted Australian operatic soprano, delivered a pioneering thirty-minute recital over the wireless airwaves from the Marconi Company headquarters in Chelmsford, Essex (Street, 2002), inaugurating, for many, the birth of the British radio industry (cf. Pegg, 1983). Two years later, in 1922, radio had become so sufficiently sophisticated that a British Broadcasting Company (the forerunner of the British Broadcasting Corporation) began to transmit regular programmes to the general public (Boyle, 1972), under the supervision of the forward-thinking John Reith, son of a Presbyterian minister, who became the first Director-General of the new organisation, known as the B.B.C. Captain Ernest Beachcroft Beckwith Towse, a hero of the Second Boer War, delivered the very first talk for the fledgling B.B.C. (Briggs, 1985) – a carefully scripted speech, in all likelihood – and soon a Talks Department developed, producing live broadcasts by serious-minded thinkers such as Professor John Hilton, who lectured on unemployment, pensions, and social security, as well as Cecil Henry Middleton, who spoke on gardening (Walker, 1992; cf. Sturmey, 1958; Smith, 1974; Coe, 1996).

By the early 1920s, radio had, at last, become an increasingly well-established feature of modernity, transforming the fabric of daily life in Great Britain. Along with the black-and-white silent cinema, radio contributed to the new phenomenon of mass entertainment (Branson, 1975). But whereas the picture palaces of the 1920s offered *silent* films until the very end of the decade, radio offered *sound*.

In 1927, the B.B.C. acquired a Royal Charter and changed its name from the British Broadcasting Company to the British Broadcasting Corporation. In 1932, the organisation moved from its initial home on Savoy Hill, close to The Strand, in London, to a permanent headquarters on nearby Langham Place – Broadcasting House – built at a huge cost of £350,000 (Anduaga, 2009). This new art deco building, some 112 feet high, with eight floors above street level and three floors below (Chesmore, 1935), designed by the architect George Val Meyer, created immediate controversy owing to the naked statue of "Ariel", placed atop the building, sculpted by Eric Gill, who had to be persuaded to make his work of art appear less well-endowed (Loughran, 2002). Gradually, the B.B.C. expanded its foundational Talks Department, which Reith and his colleagues hoped to develop into the equivalent of an on-air university. Additionally, the B.B.C. created departments for Drama and Literature, as well as Music (both Classical and Popular), Features, Sports, News and Public Affairs, and, perhaps most appealing of all for so many Britons, a department for Vaudeville, Variety and Light Entertainment (Crook, 2004).

The British Broadcasting Corporation flourished, having received not only its Royal Charter but, also, the blessing of many members of the Royal Family throughout its early years. On 7th October, 1922, His Royal Highness The Prince Edward, the Prince of Wales (the future King Edward VIII), delivered the first public radio broadcast by a member of British royalty; and then, in 1924, King George V allowed his voice to be recorded and transmitted at the opening of the Wembley Empire Exhibition, becoming the first reigning monarch to appear on the radio. Although Director-General John Reith had tried to convince King George to prepare a special broadcast for the B.B.C. as early as 1923, the king would not do so until 1932, on the occasion of the launch of the B.B.C. Empire Service (Hajkowski, 2010). By the time Edward VIII delivered his famous abdication broadcast in 1936, radio had become a veritable centrepiece of British daily life, and it would sustain Britons and those in the Commonwealth throughout World War II when the voices of Winston Churchill and other politicians, as well as those of the great wartime entertainers such as Arthur Askey, Joyce Grenfell, and Vera Lynn, became profound sources of hope and inspiration (Parker, 1977).

Winnicott's Wartime Forays

Born in Plymouth, in the county of Devon, on 7th April, 1896, Donald Woods Winnicott entered the world less than one decade after the pioneering developments in the history of sound transmission and recording undertaken by Bell, Edison, Edmunds, and others. Nonetheless, he grew up long before the advent of the commercial radio, during a period of history when Britons entertained themselves more simply by playing a piano in the parlour. Thus, by the time that radio – this new-fangled object of curiosity – arrived in most domestic British homes in the 1920s, Winnicott had already reached physical maturity.

Some adults regarded the transmission of sound from the radio as a passing phase or, even, as vulgar, such as Arthur Hyatt Morse (1925, p. 99), the former Superintendent of the Dom de Forest Wireless Telegraph Company and the United Wireless Telegraph Company, who warned that radio "is likely to prove unprofitable, if not contrary to the public interest". But Winnicott always remained more open-minded and he would, in due course, come to embrace the radio as a magnificent means of communicating to a very large percentage of the country.

We know very little about how Donald Winnicott came to broadcast for the B.B.C., or, precisely, when he first appeared on radio. In all likelihood, he began to work in radio during the very late 1930s; certainly, he had begun to do so by 1939. It seems most improbable that Winnicott would have had a radio presence prior to this time, and probably not as a psychoanalyst, in part, because he had qualified only in 1934, and also, because psychoanalysis evoked too much suspicion among Britons prior to that period and, hence, the B.B.C. would not have regarded Freudian psychology as sufficiently relevant to the population at large.

Indeed, throughout the 1920s, psychoanalysis had no discernible presence at all on the radio in the United Kingdom. At that point in time, the predominantly London-based psychoanalytical establishment boasted very few members, and the press still regarded Freud's ostensibly Jewish sexual psychology as rather suspect, and not fit for the English (e.g., Rapp, 1988, 1990). For example, no less an authority than Sir Robert Armstrong-Jones (1917, p. 219), Winnicott's teacher in mental diseases at St. Bartholomew's Hospital Medical School in London, condemned psychoanalysis as a grotesque form of medicine, ranting that, "The foreign teachers who have been responsible for employing these "sex-mad methods" to reveal the unconscious mind, have, so far as this country is concerned, already received the recognition of a posthumous notice of their labours, and it would not be incorrect to state that among psychiatrists – in this country at any rate – Freudism is dead."

But by the 1930s, however, not only had the British Psycho-Analytical Society begun to become slightly more impactful but so, too, had the broader medico-psychological movement, as evidenced by the founding of the Tavistock Square Clinic for Functional Nervous Disorders in 1920 (Dicks, 1970; Kahr, 2020d, 2021b), by the launching of the Analytical Psychology Club in 1922 (Kirsch, 2000), and by the work of such pioneering but all too frequently neglected figures such as Dr. Paul Bousfield (1920, 1922), Dr. William Brown (1921, 1922, 1923, 1924, 1926, 1929, 1936, 1938, 1939), Dr. Thomas Ross (1932, 1937, 1938), Dr. Emanuel Miller (1933), Dr. James Hadfield (1935), and many others who never held membership in the British Psycho-Analytical Society, yet who occupied important positions of leadership within the medical community more broadly, and who championed non-sectarian and pluralistic approaches to the works of Sigmund Freud, Carl Gustav Jung and, even, Alfred Adler. Thus, in the build-up to World War II, psychoanalysis and dynamic psychotherapy began to enjoy a more serious reception. In fact, in 1935, the B.B.C. had considered engaging the services of Dr. John Rickman, one of the more outward-thinking members of the British Psycho-Analytical Society (King, 2003), but, in the end, they refused to do so as Rickman (1935) had, apparently, an "unsuitable" quality of voice. Winnicott would certainly have understood the B.B.C.'s reluctance to hire Rickman; indeed, years later, he confessed to a correspondent, one Robin Hughes of the B.B.C., that, "I think analysts are not very good as broadcasters" (Winnicott, 1967e).

At the time, Britons knew full well that, "The B.B.C. chooses its staff with great care" (Chesmore, 1935, p. 20); and although John Rickman may not have passed muster, Donald Winnicott certainly did, in spite of the fact that he spoke with quite a high-pitched voice (James, 1991). Even so, Winnicott's vocal timbre did not disqualify him from working for the British Broadcasting Corporation. In point of fact, when one listens to a recording of Winnicott (many of which still survive today), one becomes calmed, in spite of his tessitura, owing to the soothing, measured, steady cadences of his compellingly crafted sentences. One can imagine that the very combination of Winnicott's formidable knowledge about infancy, childcare, and related topics, melded with his idiosyncratic speaking style, made him quite an attractive figure to radio producers at Broadcasting House. And though we cannot confirm the precise details of Winnicott's engagement with the B.B.C., as very little of his correspondence prior to 1948 has survived, [1] we do know that, by the late 1930s and, certainly, during the early 1940s, Donald Winnicott had become an increasingly popular figure in the Talks Department.

When Winnicott joined the B.B.C., he did so in what we might now describe as a "freelance" capacity, providing occasional broadcasts when requested to do so. The B.B.C. would not, in fact, engage a mental health professional in a contracted staff position until the early twenty-first century.

Throughout the 1930s and 1940s, the Talks Department became a seminal unit within the British Broadcasting Corporation, providing a forum for numerous intellectual contributors and for more serious topics of discussion. Early broadcasters for the Talks Department included such noted public figures as Prime Minister Stanley Baldwin, Cabinet Minister Herbert Morrison, diplomat Harold Nicolson, noted economist Alexander Loveday, and writers such as Max Beerbohm, George Bernard Shaw, Herbert George Wells, and William Butler Yeats, among many others (Snagge and Barsley, 1972; Scannell and Cardiff, 1991), not to mention prominent Bloomsbury group figures such as Edward Morgan Forster, John Maynard Keynes, Desmond MacCarthy, and Leonard Woolf (Avery, 2006). The Talks Department, under the successive direction of the pioneering producers Hilda Matheson and Charles Siepmann, sponsored various landmark radio series such as *S.O.S.*, which examined unemployment, and *Other People's Houses*, which exposed the slums, each transmitted in 1933. The Talks Department maintained a strong commitment to social issues, prompting critical comments from the press about the B.B.C. having an overtly left-wing bias (Scannell and Cardiff, 1991; cf. Snagge and Barsley, 1972). As a physician and psychoanalyst committed to working with children and their families from the slums of Paddington and from the impoverished districts of London's East End, Winnicott would have maintained a similar liberal, if not leftist, philosophy, and would, no doubt, have felt honoured to share a platform with such distinguished and respected public figures.

The onset of Winnicott's broadcasting career coincided with the outbreak of World War II. In many respects, the war both ignited and solidified Winnicott's trajectory as a radio personality. After the evacuation of literally thousands of London's children, parents needed thoughtful commentary from a psychologically orientated children's specialist more than ever (cf. Jackson, 1985; Gardiner, 2005; Welshman, 2010; Summers, 2011). On 4th September, 1939, the writer and publisher Leonard Woolf (1939, p. 81) wrote to his younger colleague at the Hogarth Press, John Lehmann, about his experience of children being evacuated: "We have been working like coolies here the last 48 hours. Yesterday 18 pregnant women, accompanied each by 3, 4, or 5 already born children arrived in omnibuses. Half an hour later 11 more pregnant women arrived ditto, but with rather fewer already born children. These had to be distributed in inhabited and uninhabited cottages. We spent hours carrying furniture about. On Saturday we expected 100 school children but they got lost on the way and never arrived." Clearly, specialist advice on the care of the evacuated child would be of enormous use.

Indeed, Winnicott may well have begun his work for the B.B.C. with his radio talk on "The Deprived Mother", dating from 1939, and written at the time of the evacuation (Winnicott, 1957b). Quite fittingly, and in true Winnicottian spirit, he came to realise that before he could address the emotional needs of babies and children – his growing medical and psychological speciality – he would have to speak to the caretakers of these children first, knowing them to be struggling with the loss of their evacuated offspring. "The Deprived Mother" certainly represents a fitting early contribution – and possibly debut – to Winnicott's radio work. In this talk, he challenged the popular notion that mothers of evacuated children must be having a ball, with lots of free time on their hands for visits to the cinema. Winnicott knew, of course, that evacuation caused havoc in the home, not only for the children, but also, without doubt, for the parents themselves, beset by loss and sadness and fear.

Over the next few years, Winnicott delivered several more broadcasts. And, by 1943, although Winnicott had already spoken on the radio on a number of occasions, his social work colleague, Clare Britton (1943) (who would, eventually, become his second wife), appreciated that broadcasting might be a challenging experience, and she wrote, "I hope you will make a *very good* broadcast – + that it won't be too nerve-racking. I hope it will be successful + that you'll be asked again – + will become very famous!"

The following year, in 1944, Winnicott (1945f) delivered a further broadcast, entitled "What About Father?", in which he addressed, in pioneering fashion, the complex, but hitherto neglected, emotional needs of men. One can imagine that Winnicott's radio address must have touched parents quite deeply, and gave them permission to feel bereaved when, at the start of a war, all of his fellow Britons launched themselves into the manic, but necessary, work of protecting the nation.

In order to implement his radio transmissions, Winnicott would have had to enter the bronze doors of Broadcasting House and would have wended his way to one of the fully soundproofed studios, then located in the brick-lined

Central Tower, which also contained a concert hall and a music library. Broadcasting House boasted some 150 miles of electrical wiring during the 1930s, as well as some seven thousand electrical lamps, the height of modernity at the time (Chesmore, 1935).

Thereafter, Winnicott turned his attention, quite naturally, to the problem of the evacuated child, exploring the struggles of those youngsters cleaved from their parents, as well as the plight of the foster parents themselves. Although he had no biological children of his own, Winnicott knew a great deal about evacuation and its consequences, not only from the experience of his thirteen-year-old nephew, Anthony Bradshaw, with whom he enjoyed a very close relationship (Fitter, 2010; cf. Kahr, 1996a), but, most particularly, from his intensive wartime work as a psychiatric consultant to the Government Evacuation Scheme in Oxfordshire, helping foster parents and social workers to understand and to care for several hundred children evacuated from London. From these many strands of experience, Winnicott knew how much the evacuated child could suffer, and how transitions to and from the foster home would have to be handled with sensitivity; and his several radio programmes on evacuation certainly reflected this deep knowledge.

By the time Winnicott had begun to broadcast for the B.B.C., the sound quality of radio transmissions had improved greatly, and listeners could rejoice that they no longer needed to endure the crackling and the fuzziness so common throughout the 1920s and 1930s. As Winnicott's close personal friend, the noted acoustician Hope Bagenal (1942, p. 106), had boasted, "the radio studio is no longer a padded room but a carefully designed concert room". During the 1940s, Winnicott's voice would have travelled into British homes through the popular brands of radio of the time, surrounded by Bakelite casing, such as the KB Model BM20, made in Foot's Kray, Kent; or the Bush Model DAC 90, launched in 1946 – one of the most popular post-war sets – manufactured in Chiswick, West London; or the GEC Model BC 4941, produced in Coventry, Warwickshire, in 1948. Owing to Winnicott's high-pitched voice, some listeners thought that he must be a woman. After all, he spoke about mothers and children with intimate familiarity, in high tenor tones; therefore, one should not be surprised that Clare Winnicott, his second wife, once told the psychoanalyst Dr. Martin James that someone had once referred to Winnicott on air as "'a mother'" (quoted in James, 1991). One cannot help but wonder whether this overtly maternal man proved to be a very attractive figure to the British public – a sort of "combined parental figure" (Yates, 1930, p. 178) or "combined parent-figure" (Klein, 1940, p. 148; cf. Klein, 1945), representing both mother and father, rolled into one. Perhaps that very androgynous quality had helped to contribute to Winnicott's mounting popularity as a broadcaster.

Winnicott must have pleased the authorities at the B.B.C. with his first efforts at speaking on the wireless. If they had not admired Winnicott greatly, they certainly would not have invited him back for further broadcasts and would have had no hesitation in finding him unsuitable (as they had done with Dr. John Rickman some years earlier). Members of the public also appreciated Winnicott's broadcasts greatly. Helen Trevelyan of Inverness, Scotland, the wife of the teacher and progressive educationalist George Trevelyan (son of Sir Charles Trevelyan, the 3rd Baronet Trevelyan), knew Winnicott personally and, after listening to him on air, she sent him a letter offering congratulations. This woman had recently suffered great sadness when her brother died during World War II; and furthermore, she had just adopted a new baby. With much gratitude, Helen Trevelyan (1944) wrote, "At a very bleak moment I turned on the wireless + heard your voice – you can imagine how it sustained me!"

Additionally, Winnicott received praise from at least one psychoanalytical colleague, namely, Dr. Ernest Jones (1944), the long-serving President of the British Psycho-Analytical Society, and a sometime pioneer broadcaster in his own right. Jones, semi-retired in Elsted, in West Sussex, did not listen to Winnicott's transmissions on the wireless, but Winnicott had sent him a copy of one of his scripts, and Jones replied by letter, "I have been reading with great pleasure the broadcast you kindly sent me, which at the time I unfortunately missed. It is really charming and brings out to the full your wonderful gift of empathy. I am sure it must have benefitted many people."

But, without doubt, Donald Winnicott's family of origin – his elder, spinster sisters, Violet Winnicott and Kathleen Winnicott, and his benevolent father, Sir Frederick Winnicott – served as his most fervent admirers. Violet Winnicott (n.d.) wrote to her younger brother from the family home in Plymouth, "We "listened in" at 10.45 with rapt attention. Father + Kathleen recognised your voice. I didn't think it *was* you. It sounded like *your* words read by someone else. It came through perfectly +, as K said "It was a little jewel of a broadcast." Perfect in every way. Father's wireless has gone wrong, so we had to fix up our old set, which probably made your voice sound different." On other occasions, the Devonian Winnicotts invited additional family members around to their home, and they would all listen to a broadcast together, as happened on 11th May, 1944, when a pregnant cousin, Cynthia Sandilands, joined Sir Frederick and his daughters (Kathleen Winnicott, 1944).[2]

In early 1945, Winnicott delivered three broadcasts on wartime topics, for a series on *Difficult Children*, consisting of programmes on "The Only Child" (Winnicott, 1945j), which aired on 2nd February, 1945; "The Evacuated Child" (Winnicott, 1945l), transmitted on 16th February, 1945; and "The Return of the Evacuated Children" (Winnicott, 1945m), which appeared one week later, on 23rd February, 1945. After listening to the first two programmes, his sister, Kathleen Winnicott (1945), wrote to her brother in London, "We very much enjoyed your 2 broad-casts. Your voice comes through so well + so clear." No doubt this appreciation from Winnicott's father and sisters proved hugely fortifying as he developed and refined his skills in this relatively new branch of work.

Winnicott must have struggled to find the time to broadcast for the B.B.C. Scripts had to be carefully prepared in advance and closely edited to fit the exacting time restrictions (usually a slot of fifteen minutes). Winnicott had many other professional commitments which kept him occupied, namely, a private psychoanalytical practice in Central London, a clinical post at the Paddington Green Children's Hospital, his work for the Government Evacuation Scheme in Oxfordshire, not to mention his multiple commitments to the British Psycho-Analytical Society and other organisations, as well as his manifold professional writings for both psychoanalysts and for physicians (e.g., Winnicott, 1941a, 1942a, 1943a, 1943b, 1944a, 1944b, 1944c, 1944d, 1945b). Furthermore, his first wife, Alice Winnicott, a hugely creative and talented potter and painter, suffered from much psychological fragility; and she required a great deal of Winnicott's attention, as did some of his particularly time-consuming private patients (Kahr, 1996a, 2011b). But, somehow, Winnicott managed to complete all of these tasks, working long days and nights. His unpublished log book, detailing his wartime experiences in Oxfordshire, indicates, for example, that on 27th April, 1945, Winnicott (1943–1945) recorded a radio programme for the B.B.C. in the morning and then travelled to Oxford where he spent the remainder of the day.

Broadcasting during World War II could, at times, prove to be quite hazardous, and the B.B.C. certainly took precautions, placing sandbags around the perimeter of its headquarters (Parker, 1977). In 1940, the German *Luftwaffe* dropped a 500-pound delayed-action bomb, which crashed into the seventh floor of Broadcasting House and killed seven B.B.C. staff members (Loughran, 2002). Winnicott did not encounter any bombs directly during his time at the B.B.C., but, years later, he did recall that he would sometimes have to drive his car over broken glass and other rubble from the previous night's air raid in order to reach Langham Place (Bollas, Davis, and Shepherd, 1993).

During the late 1930s and early 1940s, Winnicott broadcast, at the very least, "The Deprived Mother" (1939 [Winnicott, 1940a]), "Getting to Know Your Baby" (1944 [Winnicott, 1945c]), "Why Do Babies Cry?" (1944 [Winnicott, 1945d]), "Infant Feeding" (1944 [Winnicott, 1945e]), "What About Father?" (1944 [Winnicott, 1945f]), "Their Standards and Yours" (1944 [Winnicott, 1945g]), "Support for Normal Parents"[3] (1944 [Winnicott, 1945h]); "The Only Child" (1945 [Winnicott, 1945j]; cf. Winnicott, 1928), "Twins" (1945 [Winnicott, 1945k]), "The Evacuated Child" (1945 [Winnicott, 1945l]), "The Return of the Evacuated Child" (1945 [Winnicott, 1945m]), and "Home Again" (1945 [Winnicott, 1945n]). This steady stream of programmes offered more insight, perhaps, into the psychological education of the nation than any other set of activities undertaken by British mental health professionals at that time. In fact, Winnicott enjoyed such a strong presence on radio, especially in 1944 and 1945, that he very nearly held his own next to Winston Churchill. Indeed, according to the noted biographer Martin Gilbert (1994), Churchill appeared on radio only seven times, for instance, in the 1940 calendar year, subsequent to his election as Prime Minister on 10th May, 1940.[4] In this regard, Winnicott – an increasingly popular broadcaster – would certainly have had a fighting chance to make an impression upon the British psyche.

Janet Quigley, one of the first women to work in radio, became a very loyal champion. She had joined the B.B.C. in 1936 and had only recently received the M.B.E. – Member of the Most Excellent Order of the British Empire – in 1944 for her services to broadcasting. As a producer, Miss Quigley enjoyed a range of interests, including such subjects as fitness, nutrition, and women's issues (Street, 2006). Documentary evidence confirms that Winnicott had met Quigley (1944) at least as early as 1943. The following year, in 1944, Quigley commissioned six broadcasts from Winnicott under the title *Happy Children*, amalgamating material from the aforementioned talks on "Getting to Know Your Baby", "Why Do Babies Cry?", "What About Father?", and "Their Standards and Yours". The series did not include Winnicott's contemporaneous work on "Infant Feeding". Having his own special forum – what media practitioners would nowadays call a "multi-part series" – elevated Winnicott from the ranks of being an occasional freelance radio speaker to becoming one of the more audible presences emanating from Broadcasting House.

In the wake of the transmission of *Happy Children*, Peggy Volkov (1944), then assistant editor of the popular periodical *The New Era in Home and School*, wrote to Winnicott, full of admiration for his radio work: "Your BBC stuff is as simple as the gospel stories". Mrs. Volkov had enjoyed contact with Winnicott prior to this time, having spoken with him about the possibility of serving as his private secretary. But now, she approached Winnicott with a much more ambitious proposition. Not only did she wish to publish Winnicott's talks in her magazine, *The New Era in Home and School*, and then did so (Winnicott, 1945c, 1945d, 1945e, 1945f, 1945g, 1945h), but she also engineered to have those talks printed in pamphlet form as *Getting to Know Your Baby* (Winnicott, 1945a), under the imprint of the distinguished publishers William Heinemann (Medical Books), the firm that produced Winnicott's (1931) landmark psychologically orientated paediatric textbook, *Clinical Notes on Disorders of Childhood*, some fourteen years earlier. Volkov (1945a) negotiated a deal for Winnicott and arranged to have 4,000 copies printed on behalf of *The New Era in Home and School*, each costing one shilling, with a four-and-a-half pence royalty per copy for the author, along with an overall honorarium of approximately £30. She also obtained an agreement that Alice Winnicott's woodblock picture of a mother holding a baby against her chest would be used as the front cover.

The pamphlet proved to be an instant success. A certain Dr. Bick[5] ordered thirty-six copies of *Getting to Know Your Baby* for a postgraduate course for health visitors from Chester, Leeds, and Liverpool (Volkov, 1945b). And the aforementioned Helen Trevelyan, mother of an adopted daughter called Catriona, and an admirer of Winnicott's broadcasts, wrote once again to congratulate him on the publication of this pamphlet. Mrs. Trevelyan (1945) explained, "what you say is right + well put – but for me it would have been more valuable if I had them when I first got Catriona. I should have trusted myself with greater confidence!" She also told Winnicott that her husband had enjoyed the broadcasts as well: "George read them aloud to me of an evening. He was gratified that you had a special word about fathers" (Trevelyan, 1945). Thus, Winnicott had clearly established his capacity to relate to mothers and to fathers, and to be of real use in helping parents to trust their native instincts at a period in time when harsh, often punitive, modes of child-rearing held sway.

In gratitude for having made the pamphlet possible, Winnicott gave Peggy Volkov (1945b) a gift of £20 – a huge sum in 1945 – representing quite a substantial proportion of his fee from the publishers. Winnicott also expressed a wish that Volkov (1945c) might liaise with William Heinemann (Medical Books) to inquire whether the proceeds from the pamphlet could be given directly to the Paddington Green Children's Hospital, the institution where he had worked since 1923. Alas, we do not know whether Peggy Volkov managed to secure such an arrangement.[6]

During this formative period of Winnicott's work as a radio broadcaster, he honed and developed his public presentational skills in other arenas as well. A frequent lecturer to professional and popular organisations alike (Kahr, 1996a), Winnicott felt increasingly comfortable on the lecture podium, capable of addressing diverse groups, whether paediatricians, psychiatrists, psychoanalysts, teachers, or even school children. But additionally, Winnicott wrote extensively for the national press, most particularly for *The New Era in Home and School*; and he did so at the behest of its editor, the French-born Beatrice Ensor, an enlightened educationalist much influenced by the work of Dr. Maria Montessori and, also, by the writings of the pioneers of psychoanalysis. A woman who had, in her time, met both Dr. Carl Gustav Jung and Dr. Alfred Adler, Ensor commissioned many psychoanalysts, psychologists, and educationalists to contribute to her publication, among them, Theodora Alcock (1963) (one of the pioneers in the use of the Rorschach inkblot test in Great Britain), Dorothy Gardner (an important educationalist at the Institute of Education in the University of London), as well as the psychoanalysts Dr. Michael Balint, Dr. John Bowlby, Dorothy Burlingham, Dr. Marjorie Franklin, Anna Freud, Dr. Susan Isaacs, Barbara Low, Marion Milner, Joan Riviere, Dr. Melitta Schmideberg, Ella Freeman Sharpe, and Dr. Sybille Yates. It cannot be said, therefore, that Winnicott had a monopoly on writing for the general public and for the educational profession, although he did maintain a virtual monopoly on broadcasting. His many publications for *The New Era in Home and School* during the early 1940s and mid-1940s included a range of articles (e.g., Winnicott,

1941b, 1942b, 1943c, 1945i), a brace of book reviews and letters (e.g., Winnicott, 1940b, 1941c, 1941d, 1944e), as well as the transcripts of his radio series on *Happy Children* referenced earlier. And perhaps of greatest significance, *The New Era in Home and School* also featured a short piece on "The Problem of Homeless Children", written jointly by Dr. Donald Winnicott and Clare Britton (Winnicott and Britton, 1944), the social worker with whom he collaborated closely on the Government Evacuation Scheme in Oxfordshire. She would, of course, in time, become the second Mrs. Winnicott, following on from Winnicott's divorce from his first wife Alice (Kahr, 1996a, 2019b, 2019c).

Thus, Winnicott ended the war years somewhat emotionally battered in his domestic life, and extremely exhausted in his professional orbit (Kahr, 2011b); but nevertheless, he had established a secure foundation as a public teacher and as a public educator in the field of child psychology. It would not be quite correct to refer to Winnicott as a broadcaster on *psychoanalysis* as such because he succeeded completely in avoiding all of the complex vocabulary employed freely by the Freudian community. Of course, Winnicott used his psychologically inspired knowledge, his clinical experience, and his capacity for empathy and immersion in order to reach mothers, fathers, and even children in both a profound and accessible manner, but he did so without directly acknowledging the cumbersome in-house language employed by his clinical colleagues. In this respect, one could claim that, by the end of World War II, Donald Winnicott had become the undisputed father of British media psychology.

Winnicott in Full Flourish

After the Allied victory, Winnicott continued to broadcast from time to time on the wireless, though not nearly as frequently as he had done in 1944 and 1945. We know that he made one appearance on a very distinguished B.B.C. radio programme called *The Brains Trust* in either 1946 or 1947, and, as we indicated in the last chapter, he talked about such diverse themes as the use of the toothbrush and religious ritual (Rich, 1948). *The Brains Trust*, which debuted on 1st January, 1941, became a very intellectually up-market discussion programme in which resident experts Dr. Cyril Joad, a noted philosopher, Professor Julian Huxley, an eminent scientist, and Commander Archibald Campbell, a distinguished naval officer, interacted with guest experts and responded to queries from the general public. In those early days, nearly one-third of the nation's entire radio listenership tuned into *The Brains Trust* (Harrington and Young, 1978); therefore, to be invited to appear would have proved to be quite a mark of recognition.

In 1948, Donald Winnicott served not as a broadcaster *per se* but, rather, as a consultant to a twenty-one-minute-long film, *Your Child's Sleep*, produced by the Realist Film Unit for the Central Office of Information on behalf of the Central Council for Health Education. This short documentary, detailing the consequences of inadequate sleep among children, appeared in the "Film Programme" of the International Congress on Mental Health, held in London during August, 1948. The noted psychologist and psychoanalyst, Professor John Carl Flügel, served as Chairman of the Programme Committee for this huge gathering of many of the world's most influential mental health professionals; and, in his summing-up address at the end of the proceedings, Flügel (1948) urged that mental health must no longer be regarded as the sole province of physicians; by contrast, members of the general public – whether policemen, architects, plumbers, or income tax officials – must take responsibility as well.

Flügel and his colleagues had organised the International Congress on Mental Health in the wake of the establishment of the United Kingdom's new National Health Service, launched on 5th July, 1948 – one of the great achievements of Prime Minister Clement Attlee's post-World War II government. Winnicott's work as a film consultant, which helped people to understand something more about the vicissitudes of children's sleeping difficulties, coincided with a growing public interest and participation in healthcare. Perhaps Winnicott's unique and pioneering radio addresses to the populace at large during the previous decade might, in some way, have impacted upon the widening conversation around mental health matters. Winnicott's media work had begun as a series of radio broadcasts for Britons but had now expanded to become a part of a highly publicised international mental hygiene policy (cf. Kahr, 2011c).

1949 proved to be a watershed year for Winnicott in a great many other respects. Not only did he have a severe heart attack that nearly killed him (Kahr, 1996a, 2011b), but he also published one of his most important clinical papers – if not *the* most important – namely, "Hate in the Counter-Transference" (Winnicott, 1949b), about the potential for psychoanalysts to despise their patients, owing to the intense challenge of the clinical encounter and to the burden on the psychoanalytical practitioner who must care for an often very ill and, even, aggressive person. But 1949 would be memorable for another reason, as it marked the flourishing of Winnicott's collaboration with Isa Benzie, one of the most influential and dynamic producers at the British Broadcasting Corporation.

Isa Donald Benzie, born in Glasgow, Scotland, in 1902, studied German at Lady Margaret Hall at the University of Oxford; and in 1927, she joined the still youthful British Broadcasting Corporation as a secretary in the Foreign Department, rising to the post of department head in 1933. Benzie became, thus, not only one of the first women in British broadcasting but, also, an important figure in overseas radio to boot. She married fellow B.B.C. employee John Royston Morley, one of the very first producers of television programmes, in 1937 (Donovan, 2004), but, owing to the B.B.C.'s rule that married women could not work alongside their husbands – a ban not removed until after World War II (Street, 2006) – Isa Benzie had to retire. But she did succeed in returning to the B.B.C. in 1943, perhaps owing to the wartime shortage of male personnel, and she became a producer in the Talks Department where she would remain for the rest of her career, keen to help women pursue motherhood and employment outside the home simultaneously (Street, 2006). Benzie would eventually make radio history by founding the B.B.C.'s *Today* programme in 1957 and by serving as its Senior Producer, eventually retiring in 1964 (Donovan, 1997, 2004). Of course, the *Today* programme still graces the airwaves after more than sixty years.

A raven-haired woman of compelling beauty, Isa Benzie had come to know Donald Winnicott (1949d) through his wartime broadcasts, but we do not know precisely how much contact they had enjoyed at that time. Certainly, the pair had become better acquainted by late 1946 (Benzie, 1946).

Throughout the 1940s and beyond, Winnicott (1943a, 1943b, 1943d, 1944b, 1944c, 1944d, 1947a, 1949b, 1949c, 1951a, 1951b, 1951d, 1954a, 1954b, 1956a) became a vocal adversary of electroconvulsive shock treatment and of leucotomy and other types of psychosurgery used in the treatment of mental distress, thus anticipating many of the critiques of the anti-psychiatry movement of the 1960s (e.g., Laing, 1960, 1964, 1976, 1981; Laing and Esterson, 1964; Szasz, 1961; cf. Double, 2002, 2006; Heaton, 2006; Wall, 2018). On 27th November, 1946, Winnicott delivered a talk on "Some Reasons for Personal Prejudice Against the So-Called Physical Therapy of Mental Disorder" to colleagues in the Medical Section of the British Psychological Society. This communication would later be published in abbreviated form in the *British Medical Journal* (Winnicott, 1947a). Miss Benzie (1946) attended the talk as a guest at this otherwise closed meeting for members of the British Psychological Society, and she did so, presumably, at Winnicott's direct invitation. Perhaps Winnicott had hoped to interest the increasingly influential Miss Benzie in developing some further radio work.

We know from subsequent correspondence that Benzie and Winnicott (1949d) had discussed the possibility that he might broadcast his thoughts on leucotomy, but Winnicott seems to have refused, aware of how potentially provocative it might be to criticise the vast majority of Great Britain's somatically orientated psychiatrists openly on public radio. Winnicott may also have felt discomfort at the thought of speaking about physical psychiatric treatments when he had not trained specifically in psychiatry but, rather, in children's medicine and in psychoanalysis; hence for a paediatrician-psychoanalyst who had never held a medical superintendency in a lunatic asylum to broadcast nationwide about psychiatric treatment might well have exposed Winnicott to greater criticism than he had received from having written about psychosurgery and electric shock in the pages of various medical journals with more restricted circulations.

Consequently, to the best of our knowledge, Winnicott undertook little media work between 1946 and 1948. His clinical practice did flourish, however, during this period, as did his extramarital relationship with his social work colleague Clare Britton (Kahr, 1996a, 2019a; Kanter, 2004); hence, he had much with which to occupy himself. But the yen for media work persisted, and, in January 1949, after having listened to a radio programme on leucotomy on the B.B.C., presented by the well-known journalist Nesta Pain, Winnicott (1949d) renewed his acquaintance with Isa Benzie by writing an unsolicited letter, dated, 24th January, 1949, which began:

> Dear Miss Benzie,
> I wonder if you remember me? You were very kind to me when I was giving the talks about Parents and Children, and you came to the British Psychological Society Medical Section when I read a paper there in which I expressed criticism of electric shock therapy and leucotomy. Do you remember that at the time you asked me whether I would be willing to talk on the wireless on this subject? At the time I refused because I felt that it would be better to work in psychiatric circles and not to introduce the subject to the wider public for fear of rousing emotion and making the scientific discussion more difficult.

Winnicott (1949d) then revealed to Benzie that he had spent more time thinking about broadcasting possibilities, and he continued by explaining, "there is now a place wide open for a talk by someone who feels that the tendency represented by leucotomy is a bad one, and one which the public should interest themselves in and have an opinion on. I should be most grateful if you would put me in touch with the right department, or actually put in a word for me to find out whether I could be asked to state my personal view."

Benzie (1949a) replied to Winnicott's letter the very next day, on 25th January, 1949, offering to discuss this matter further; and Winnicott (1949e) responded almost immediately, on 26th January, 1949, admitting that, "Broadcasts about children really interest me four thousand times more than broadcasts about the frontal lobes." Perhaps Winnicott had thought that the recent transmission of the B.B.C. programme on leucotomy had offered a good opportunity for re-establishing links with the Talks Department, and he may have secretly hoped that he could now undertake more broadcasts on childhood, rather than on psychosurgery. But, whatever his motivation, his correspondence with Miss Benzie came to an abrupt halt, because on 28th January, 1949, Winnicott suffered a massive heart attack, and would not return to his office until May, 1949, and then did so only on a reduced basis for quite some months (Kahr, 2011b).

As Winnicott began to convalesce, he ensured that Benzie would be one of the first people with whom he would resume contact and, in the summer of 1949, the two of them met up and began to walk, presumably to a hotel or restaurant, for drinks; and en route, knowing of Winnicott's abilities and capacities as a broadcaster, Benzie immediately offered him the rare opportunity of presenting nine programmes on whatever subject he might wish to discuss. As Winnicott (1966a, pp. 3–4) recalled years later, "She was, of course, on the lookout for a catchphrase, but I did not know this. I told her that I had no interest whatever in trying to tell people what to do. To start with, I didn't know. But I would like to talk to mothers about the thing that they do well, and that they do well simply because each mother is devoted to the task in hand, namely the care of one infant, or perhaps twins. I said that ordinarily this just happens, and it is the exception when a baby has to do without being cared for at the start by a specialist. Isa Benzie picked up the clue in a matter of twenty yards, and she said: "Splendid! The Ordinary Devoted Mother." So that was that."

This brief twenty-yard stroll became a deeply important moment in the development not only of mental health broadcasting, as Winnicott and Benzie set about preparing his new radio series on *The Ordinary Devoted Mother*, but, moreover, their perambulation facilitated the consolidation of Winnicott's position as the professional who dared to allow himself to be a non-expert, thus authorising a parent, or indeed a patient, to become the expert about his or her own life, or about his or her own child, with Winnicott functioning not as the superior medical authority but, rather, as a guide, an aid, and a co-journeyman.

The projected nine-part radio series transmogrified into an eight-part series which began live transmission at 9.30 a.m., on Wednesday, 5th October, 1949. Nowadays, most radio talks about factual topics will be pre-recorded well in advance and will permit the presenter as much time as he or she might require in order to prepare another "take", in case of any errors; but Winnicott had no such luxury. He had to read his scripts straight off, with no opportunity for another recitation or for any fine edits. Fortunately, he had become such an accomplished public speaker by this point that he managed beautifully. Dr. Mildred Creak (1949), one of Great Britain's most seminal child psychiatrists, and a long-time Winnicott admirer, wrote to him afterwards – that very day in fact – to offer congratulations on his radio appearance.

Seven more broadcasts followed each Wednesday thereafter throughout the months of October and November, finishing on 23rd November, 1949. [7] The 9.30 a.m. broadcasts from Langham Place in Central London lasted no more than fifteen minutes; but, in order to manage this carefully timetabled slot in the B.B.C. transmission schedule, Winnicott had to shift his long-standing 9.45 a.m. patient – a very troubled woman indeed – by offering to see her, instead, at 10.00 a.m., at his private consulting room at 47, Queen Anne Street, not far from Broadcasting House. One cannot help but wonder whether Winnicott managed to arrive at his consulting room on time, having boxed himself into a schedule even more restricted than that of the B.B.C.

Donald Winnicott lunched with Isa Benzie on Saturday, 21st October, 1949, presumably to reflect upon the transmissions which had aired thus far and to discuss the scripts for the final instalments in the series.[8] Miss Benzie also engaged Winnicott to serve as a script consultant to a B.B.C. Home Service radio programme, broadcast on Monday evenings, entitled *The Rising Generation* (Benzie, 1949b; Winnicott, 1949f). He soon contributed to the programme as a speaker and wrote to Benzie afterwards, "It was fun noticing odd little bits of me popping in here and there" (Winnicott, 1949g), sharing his relief that he had received only "nice letters" (Winnicott, 1949b) and, fortunately, none which could be described "nasty" (Winnicott, 1949g). For his work on *The Rising Generation*, he earned a fee of seven guineas (Boswell, 1949).

Having recently begun a slow and no doubt frightening recovery from a severe coronary illness, Winnicott's renewed spate of radio appearances may well have helped him to feel that he had truly come back to life. Certainly, he had, by now, reconfirmed his status as Great Britain's premier mental health broadcaster.

The radio talks about the ordinary devoted mother would be published immediately in pamphlet form under the title, *The Ordinary Devoted Mother and Her Baby: Nine Broadcast Talks. (Autumn 1949)*, produced by C.A. Brock and Company of London. With the unparalleled support of his highly efficient private secretary, Joyce Coles, who had begun to work for him in September, 1948 (Kahr, 1994f), Winnicott established a little business selling the pamphlets to members of the public. Winnicott had no doubt inspired so much affection at the B.B.C. that someone, possibly Miss Benzie, arranged for an announcement to appear on the wireless that any listeners who wished to obtain a copy of Dr. Winnicott's pamphlet should send a postal order for one shilling to 47, Queen Anne Street, London W.1 (Bates, 1950) – the address of his private consulting room. Today, such blatant advertising of products for private sale would be strictly prohibited by the British Broadcasting Corporation.

Winnicott received many favourable responses to his radio appearances and to his pamphlet. Dorothy Burlingham (1950), a psychoanalyst who had undergone treatment with Sigmund Freud in Vienna, and who became an intimate friend and collaborator of Anna Freud, wrote, "I cannot remember whether I have told you how much I enjoyed your B.B.C. talks to mothers. I thought your approach was excellent and just what is needed to counteract the everlasting phrase one hears "the mother is to blame"." And Dr. Jean Lawrie, a fellow physician, also wrote to Winnicott, offering intelligent praise of his work. Indeed, she paid Winnicott a supreme compliment by admitting, "Whenever I come across ideas like yours I wish so much I could start my family again reassured that natural love is not the misguided guilty old-fashioned instinct which so many seem to think" (Lawrie, 1951). Sophie Dann (1950), another one of Anna Freud's colleagues, offered to translate these talks into German; and Dr. Gerald Caplan (1950), a child psychiatrist from Jerusalem, in Israel, expressed a wish to have the talks rendered into Hebrew.

Also, in 1950, Donald Winnicott (1950a) delivered further broadcasts on the radio, including his observations about "Knowing and Learning", and, also, about "Instincts and Normal Difficulties" (Winnicott, 1950b). Clearly, Winnicott (1950d) enjoyed his radio work and wrote to his friend Brenda Brennan, "Talking on the radio is a nice way of earning money for a change and I hope they ask me again." Having now found himself on the verge of leaving his wife, Alice Winnicott, and on the brink of marrying his mistress, Clare Britton, as well as thinking about the cost of a new house, Donald Winnicott hoped, perhaps, that broadcasting could become an ongoing source of income which would supplement his private clinical fees.

Winnicott did not restrict himself to radio; indeed, he continued to contribute to magazines and, also, to the newspaper. On 31st January, 1950, he published a short letter to the editor of *The Times* on "Neglected Children", praising the work of the National Society for the Prevention of Cruelty to Children, underscoring, "It is indeed deplorable that there are homes in which children are neglected or cruelly treated" (Winnicott, 1950c, p. 5). But he also took this opportunity to argue against government intrusion into the homes of ordinary, good parents, who, if investigated, might be "afraid to be natural" (Winnicott, 1950c, p. 5).[9]

Throughout the early 1950s, Winnicott battled further coronary episodes but somehow managed to continue to pursue his media activities. He also became a subtle, but persistent, promoter of his own contributions. On 5th December, 1951, Dr. Hilda Abraham (1953), the daughter of Freud's distinguished colleague Dr. Karl Abraham, and a psychoanalyst in her own right who had emigrated to Great Britain from Germany, presented a paper on the psychoanalytical treatment of a twin to colleagues in the British Psycho-Analytical Society and, the very next day, Winnicott (1951e) sent her a copy of his radio programme on that subject: "Just for fun I am enclosing a broadcast on twins which was part of a series given during the war."

In 1951, he appeared twice on *Woman's Hour*, a stalwart B.B.C. programme launched in 1946, and he spoke about "Visiting Children in Hospital" (Winnicott, 1951c).[10] He made further recordings for the B.B.C. on Wednesday, 9th January, 1952, at 1.30 p.m., and on Wednesday, 16th January, 1952, also at 1.30 p.m., and had a subsequent broadcast scheduled for Wednesday, 6th February, 1952, which would be cancelled, owing to the fact that King George VI had died in his sleep earlier that day at Sandringham House in Norfolk at the age of fifty-six years, from a coronary thrombosis.[11] On the evening of 4th April, 1952, Winnicott made a further appearance on the hugely popular programme, *The Brains Trust*. Broadcast on Friday evenings, in a country still straining from post-war austerity, *The Brains Trust* would have attracted a very large stay-at-home audience. Thus,

Winnicott's popularity continued to grow, and this recognition gave him the confidence to approach Isa Benzie (1952) once again to propose a new radio series on the psychology of adoption which certainly resulted in at least one broadcast on that topic in 1955 (Winnicott, 1955a).

No doubt wary of the need to maintain confidentiality, Winnicott managed quite successfully to avoid talking about his psychoanalytical patients on air. Instead, he shared his knowledge about mothers, fathers, and babies in a most general way, based on a huge wealth of professional experience. Often, if he needed to describe a particular aspect of childhood in greater detail, he would speak about those with whom he enjoyed a personal, *non-professional* relationship. His godson, Timothy Bentley, took delight in the fact that Winnicott would, from time to time, refer to him in broadcasts, albeit in disguised form (Kahr, 2010).

Throughout his radio work, Winnicott not only addressed a welter of topics relating to children and parents, but he continued to hone his philosophy that parents should become authorised to consider themselves experts on their own children. In this way, Winnicott tacitly encouraged mothers and fathers to hone their skills as infant observationalists and to learn from their intimate experiences in the home. He also helped to undermine the rigid childcare philosophy of Dr. Truby King and others who advocated strict feeding timetables and who discouraged parents from soothing their children's tears (e.g., King, 1916; cf. King, 1948). As we indicated in the previous chapter, an admirer called Florence Bantin (1952) best encapsulated the nation's gratitude to Winnicott when she wrote to him, expressing her relief upon reading his radio talks, and thanking him for having dared to criticise the prevailing views on childcare.

Winnicott certainly admired mothers and demonstrated public respect for their intelligence, and, moreover, he regarded motherhood as a highly accomplished art rather than as a mere, easy-to-denigrate biological simplicity. He deeply enjoyed speaking to mothers in clear, straightforward language, yet at the same time, he also endeavoured not to be too simplistic: "I dont [sic] want to suggest that mothers are nitt-whitts in thick knitts" (Winnicott, 1961c).

But not everyone found Winnicott's mother-as-expert stance convincing. Dr. Audrey Davidson (1997), a Kleinian psychoanalyst, believed Winnicott to be a "phoney", with false humility, attributing skills and capacities to mothers, which many may have lacked.

Whatever one might conclude about the depth of Winnicott's sincerity, he certainly adhered to his credo about parental expertise, and he always spoke about the strengths of mothers and, also, fathers with persistence and conviction. Certainly, the parents themselves responded enthusiastically to Winnicott's tone and accent. In a post-war world, Britons certainly needed someone like this man. And with so many mothers stuck at home, perched beside their radios, Winnicott enjoyed championing women who became quite eager to listen to a benign physician and childcare specialist speaking to them on the radio.

Winnicott endeavoured to popularise psychoanalysis, not only on the radio but, also, in numerous other quarters. For instance, in 1955, he wrote to Nancy Russ, the Assistant Secretary of the Bollingen Foundation in New York City, New York, "I consider that there is a very strong need at the present time for a spread of the ideas that come from the various kinds of analytical work into the literature which is read by a public of thinking people who do not happen to be involved in therapeutics" (Winnicott, 1955c).

Not only did Winnicott immerse himself thoroughly in the world of broadcasting and public education, but he also had the decency to be generous to others, such as Dr. Lalit Bhandari (1952), an Indian-born man who had trained as a psychoanalyst in London. Upon Bhandari's return to New Delhi, he delivered a radio talk of his own on "Mind and Medicine" and wrote to tell Winnicott of his achievement. Delighted, Winnicott (1952) replied, "I am interested that you gave a broadcast talk and I hope that you will be able to develop work along those lines." Similarly, when, on 28th November, 1952, Winnicott's psychoanalytical colleagues Dr. John Bowlby and James Robertson presented their landmark film about the profound emotional consequences of separation upon young children to the Section of Paediatrics of the Royal Society of Medicine in London, Winnicott praised the film as a "highly successful first effort" (Bowlby and Robertson, 1953, p. 426). Winnicott's words carried great weight, not only because of his well-established reputation, but because Winnicott also held the position of President of the Section of Paediatrics at that time. Soon thereafter, Winnicott (1953a, p. 78) congratulated Bowlby and Robertson further, noting that, "The film, used properly, could have a very big effect."

The Consummate Media Psychologist

Throughout the 1950s, Winnicott continued to appear on air as a radio commentator. For instance, on 7th June, 1955, and on 9th June, 1955, he recorded two segments for *Woman's Hour* on the topic of stepparents (Winnicott, 1955b). On 31st January, 1956, through the ministrations of Isa Benzie of the Talks Department, he broadcast "How Much Do We Know About Babies as Cloth Suckers?" (Winnicott, 1956b), also for *Woman's Hour*. And then, Winnicott contributed to a substantial multi-part series on *The Ordinary Devoted Mother and Her Children*, which would be transmitted in late 1959 and early 1960. Subsequently, he prepared no fewer than three talks on "Saying No" (Winnicott, 1960b), four talks on "Jealousy" (Winnicott, 1960c), three further broadcasts on "What Irks" (Winnicott, 1960d), and one more radio programme on "Security" (Winnicott, 1960a, 1960e).[12]

In 1961, Donald Winnicott worked with a new producer, Barbara Crowther, who facilitated further opportunities. For instance, Winnicott participated in a dialogue with the educationalist and broadcaster Claire Rayner, and spoke about "Guilt Feelings in Young Mothers" (Winnicott, 1961b) for a B.B.C. series on *Parents and Children*. Winnicott rehearsed that talk on 24th February, 1961, from 10.30 a.m. until 11.30 a.m., and he then recorded the programme with Mrs. Rayner from 11.30 a.m. until 12.30 p.m. The producer edited the segment to a mere eleven minutes, which would be broadcast several weeks later on 13th March, 1961, for which Winnicott (1967e) received a handsome fee of fifteen guineas. The following year, Winnicott scripted two more B.B.C. programmes for a projected series called *The First Five Years*, one on "The Development of a Child's Sense of Right and Wrong" (Winnicott, 1962a), and the other on "Now They Are Five" (Winnicott, 1962b).

Having reached the height of his broadcasting powers, Winnicott not only continued to appear on radio programmes, to write scripts, and to offer media consultations, but he had fully caught the ear of the B.B.C. and he could call upon that massive organisation regularly in order to promote psychoanalytical causes or even allow himself to be consulted in more official capacities. For instance, on 6th January, 1956, in the run-up to Sigmund Freud's centenary four months hence, Winnicott lunched with a staff member from the British Broadcasting Corporation, presumably to discuss what kind of coverage could be provided of this important ceremonial date in psychoanalytical history. And, on 19th January, 1959, Winnicott met with Paul Ferris, a radio journalist in his twenties, and with one of Ferris's colleagues, a certain Mr. Vaughan. Ferris had, in fact, attended the Bishop Gore School in Swansea, in Wales, the very school at which Dr. Ernest Jones had studied many decades previously. A further meeting among these men took place at B.B.C. headquarters on 28th January, 1959. Although one cannot be certain, it seems most likely that Winnicott knew that Ernest Jones had become extremely ill with cancer and would not live long, and thus he may have approached Ferris and Vaughan to discuss how the B.B.C. might honour the founding President of the British Psycho-Analytical Society. Jones did, indeed, die two weeks later on 11th February, 1959, at the age of seventy-nine years; and, shortly thereafter, on 15th March, 1959, Paul Ferris collaborated with Mervyn Jones, the son of the deceased psychoanalyst, and prepared a radio tribute in which Winnicott participated, offering reminiscences of Jones as "spiky" (quoted in Jones and Ferris, 1959) but, also, as "extremely friendly eventually" (quoted in Jones and Ferris, 1959). In this broadcast, Winnicott even recalled his very first meeting with Jones in the early 1920s, and he complimented him on his clinical acumen noting, "He knew more about my illness than I did" (quoted in Jones and Ferris, 1959).

In addition to the radio work, Winnicott continued to write articles and to review books for popular publications such as *New Statesman* (e.g., Winnicott, 1961a), and, more regularly, for the left-wing periodical *New Society* (e.g., Winnicott, 1963b, 1965d, 1967a, 1967b, 1968c). But, in later years,

Winnicott's greatest and most permanent contribution to the burgeoning field of media psychology came about entirely through his own persistence.

By 1953, Winnicott (1953c) had already sold some 3,000 copies of the pamphlet based on his radio talks about the ordinary devoted mother (Winnicott, 1949a); but, in spite of this success, he still hoped to find a more impressive and more permanent form of printing, and so, he wrote a letter to the editor of Tavistock Publications, a newly founded press connected to the Tavistock Clinic in London, inquiring whether there might be interest in publishing both of his pamphlets – *Getting to Know Your Baby* (Winnicott, 1945a) as well as *The Ordinary Devoted Mother and Her Baby: Nine Broadcast Talks. (Autumn 1949)* (Winnicott, 1949a) – supplemented with some additional material, under the possible title *Talks on Child Care* (Winnicott, 1953c). After protracted negotiations with the visionary editor, John Harvard-Watts, and with copious editorial assistance from Dr. Janet Hardenberg – a physician in her own right, and the wife of Dr. Herman Hardenberg, a psychoanalyst who had, as a young man, worked for Winnicott at the Paddington Green Children's Hospital – Tavistock Publications repackaged Winnicott's slender pamphlets into two impressive cloth books, namely, *The Child and the Family: First Relationships* (Winnicott, 1957a) and *The Child and the Outside World: Studies in Developing Relationships* (Winnicott, 1957b). These books received very enthusiastic responses, and the anonymous reviewer in *The Times Literary Supplement*, who wrote about the first of the two volumes, crowed, "The best prophylactic against developing neuroses is to possess a pattern of behaviour founded upon sound psychological lines and Dr. Winnicott's book enables parents to know what these sound psychological lines are" (Anonymous, 1957, p. 417).

Penguin Books purchased the rights to both of these books from Tavistock Publications, and, several years later, produced an affordable, amalgamated paperback edition entitled *The Child, the Family, and the Outside World* (Winnicott, 1964a), in their Pelican Books series, priced at four shillings and six pence per copy. This text, which contained approximately two-thirds of the content of the two Tavistock Publications titles, became an instant success, selling thousands of copies. As a matter of interest, the book sold 12,939 copies in 1964, 14,053 copies in 1965, and 14,696 copies in 1966 – a total of 41,688 separate British paperback sales (Palmer, 1967), to say nothing of the overseas editions and translations. In 1968, sales in the United Kingdom had reached 50,000 purchases (Bollas, Davis, and Shepherd, 1993), and this compelling volume has continued to remain in print in one form or another to this very day (Winnicott, 2021). The book even reached interested readers round the world, and a grateful mother in the United States of America, Jacqueline Weber (1966), told Winnicott that she had "worn out" her copy, having read through this text so often.

Although Winnicott will be best known as a writer of books and papers and, also, as a broadcaster of radio talks, he did appear on television as well, albeit on only a tiny number of occasions. At some point in October, 1956, he graced the small screen, perhaps for the first time; but regrettably, we do not know the nature of his contribution. His nephew, John Cranes Taylor (1996), the adopted son of Alice Winnicott's brother, Dr. James Taylor, had not seen his uncle for some time, as Winnicott had distanced himself from the Taylor clan after having divorced his first wife. Nevertheless, John Taylor, the nephew, managed to see his uncle on camera and wrote to him afterwards, "According to the screen, I think you have fattened slightly and your hair is growing more strongly than of late" (Taylor, 1956). Having made a jibe against the uncle who had disappeared from view, the nephew then offered a more complimentary comment and wrote that, "It is to be my privilege, deserved or undeserved, to congratulate the B.B.C. on choosing one so knowledgeable for their program" (Taylor, 1956).

In June, 1968, Winnicott made two of his very final appearances on air, once on radio and once on television.

On 21st October, 1966, Great Britain experienced a horrific tragedy – its very own version of Pompeii – when, sadly, a deadly landslide of thousands of tonnes of colliery waste consisting of sludge and black coal dust broke away and raced down a mountain at great speed, striking the village of Aberfan, south of Merthyr Tydfil, in Wales, killing many schoolchildren and adults. Sometime later, the B.B.C. decided to revisit the Aberfan disaster on its Radio 4 programme, *The World at One*, featuring Donald Winnicott.

On Monday, 10th June, 1968, the British Broadcasting Corporation sent a car to collect him at 12.30 p.m. and whisked him to the studio for a broadcast at 1.00 p.m. so that he could speak to a man who had lost his wife in the Aberfan disaster which had occurred more than one and a half years previously. Regrettably, we do not know what Winnicott had said on that occasion. As this broadcast occurred live, it seems likely that he would have talked directly to the bereaved widower, possibly on air as well, or might have offered some commentary about the psychology of grief and bereavement and, perhaps, its impact on children.

Later that month, on 23rd June, 1968, Winnicott appeared on the popular Sunday-night television show *Meeting Point*, a discussion programme commissioned by the religious affairs department of the British Broadcasting Corporation, which focused on moral and social issues. *Meeting Point* had attracted considerable controversy when, in 1962, the Most Reverend Donald Coggan, the recently enthroned Archbishop of York, confronted the pop singer Adam Faith about the references to sexuality in his songs; and, in 1963, the programme hosted a discussion on premarital sexuality which outraged the self-appointed moralist, Mary Whitehouse. In May, 1968, one month before Winnicott's appearance, Mother Teresa had participated on the programme. On Winnicott's segment, he appeared along with a bishop and with a woman called Mrs. Potts, and he spoke about mourning and death. Apparently, he also talked about a little girl who kicked a wall after the loss of her father, and pontificated about her unconscious death wishes and sense of triumph over her father which contributed to her sense of guilt. Winnicott's brother-in-law Professor Karl Britton, a philosopher, offered compliments. Graciously, he described the programme to Winnicott as a "very good, serious, rather moving broadcast" (Britton, 1968).

Winnicott made one other very important contribution to media psychoanalysis in the late 1960s. As we know, Winnicott had served as President of the British Psycho-Analytical Society on two occasions, first from 1956 until 1959, and then again from 1965 until 1968 (Kahr, 1996a). Although the British Psycho-Analytical Society had sponsored a small number of public lectures during the 1930s, World War II had interrupted any plans for a more consistent series of talks promoting the works of psychoanalysts; and, throughout his presidencies, Winnicott wished to rectify this. During his second term of office, therefore, he encouraged his psychoanalytical colleagues to abandon their somewhat inward and elitist stance by launching a series of Public Lectures which came to be co-ordinated by Dr. Thomas Hayley (1991), an anthropologist who had subsequently become a psychoanalyst, ably supported by Winnicott and, also, by their colleague Dr. Thomas Main. This series of talks, known as the Winter Lectures, convened in the lavish Porchester Hall, in Paddington, West London, not far from the hospital where Winnicott had worked for some forty years. Most of these lectures attracted an audience of approximately 400 people; but, as Winnicott's reputation continued to swell, the Public Relations Directorate of the British Psycho-Analytical Society actually sold more than 600 tickets for his projected talk on 28th January, 1969, on "Some Aspects of Love and Hate", as part of the series on "Sexuality and Aggression in Maturation: New Facets" (Hayley, 1991). The Public Relations Directorate had never before sold so many tickets. Regrettably, Winnicott's recent hospitalisation, due to both an infection from the Hong Kong flu and, also, a heart attack, prevented him from honouring his commitment (Kahr, 1996a; cf. Kahr, 2020f, 2021e, 2021f, 2021g), and Dr. Agnes Main (1969), a child psychiatrist and psychoanalyst, graciously leapt into the fray to present a paper of her own, "On Idealisation and Disillusion in Adolescence". Apparently, "Dr. Main was readily forgiven for not being Dr. Winnicott" (Anonymous, 1969, p. 11).

The Making of a Broadcaster

Thus far, we have reviewed some of the factual highlights of Winnicott's broadcasting and public writing career, examining historically some of the stepping-stones of his development as a media psychologist. But exactly *how* did he acquire the skills and capacities necessary to become a suitable public representative of his profession, and *why* did he elect to cultivate these abilities and tendencies?

In order to provide a deep answer to these questions, one would of course need access to Donald Winnicott's private inner world. Any remarks that one might make about his unconscious motivations must, at this point, be purely speculative. But one can certainly theorise on safer, more evidence-based ground by examining the discernible *influences* upon his outwardly orientated perspective.

First of all, we must not forget that both Winnicott's father, Frederick Winnicott (later Sir Frederick Winnicott), and his uncle, Richard Winnicott, had become very visible public figures in Plymouth and, for the whole of Donald Winnicott's childhood, both of the Winnicott brothers worked tirelessly as justices of the peace and, ultimately as mayors of Plymouth, each for two terms, with Winnicott's uncle having served from 1904 to 1905 and then again from 1924 to 1925, and Winnicott's father having occupied that important position from 1906 to 1907 and then again from 1921 to 1922. Although best known as local Devonian personalities, chairing meetings and opening buildings, the Winnicott brothers would, on occasion, receive recognition in the national press as well. Shortly after the death of Queen Victoria, John Walling, Chairman of the Plymouth Mercantile Association, made a motion, seconded by Frederick Winnicott, expressing profound grief at the monarch's death and offering sympathy to the new king, Edward VII, who also held the post of Lord High Stewart of the Borough of Plymouth. Though a seemingly minor matter, this piece of news received a mention in *The Times* (Anonymous, 1901). Some years later, in 1905, during his first mayoralty, Richard Winnicott had the opportunity of welcoming the new American Ambassador, Whitelaw Reid, to Great Britain after he had arrived in Plymouth on the American Line steamship *Philadelphia*. This event also became national news, reported in *The Times* (Anonymous, 1905).

Not only might the activities of the Winnicott brothers have had an impact on the young Donald Winnicott, allowing him to believe that a man might be entitled to have, or even be *expected* to have, a public voice but, also, the Winnicotts became devotees of Wesleyan Methodism, a type of Protestantism based upon the teachings of the eighteenth-century English theologian, John Wesley, who encouraged public education and public speaking as a means of transmitting its doctrine. Wesley became renowned for his open-air sermons, having preached, reputedly, some 40,000 or 50,000 of them during his long lifetime, not dying until after his eighty-seventh birthday (cf. Simon, 1925; Brailsford, 1954; Baker, 1970; Pudney, 1978; Ayling, 1979; Stone, 2001). Although Winnicott did not, to the best of our knowledge, practise religion formally for most of his adult life, he did attend a Methodist church very regularly during childhood and he even matriculated to a Wesleyan Methodist private boarding school between the ages of fourteen to eighteen years, namely, the Leys School in Cambridge (Kahr, 1996a; cf. Baker, 1975; Houghton and Houghton, 2000). Winnicott would, therefore, have absorbed much of the outward-focused public teachings of John Wesley and his associates.

In his early life, Donald Winnicott certainly identified himself as a Wesleyan Methodist, but, in later years, he also admitted to tremendous sympathy for an even more archaic branch of English non-conformity known as Lollardy, which dates from at least the fourteenth century. The Lollards[13] protested against the strictures of Catholicism, long before the Henrician revolt of the sixteenth century. They regarded the Catholic church as corrupt and, in the words of a modern commentator, came to view the Pope as "a corporate Antichrist" (Rex, 1993, p. 134). The Lollards rejected the ritualistic trappings of Catholicism such as the sacraments and the hierarchies of status, and they resented the fact that only those versed in Latin could read the liturgy. Instead, through the instigation of the leading Lollard theologian, John Wycliffe, this group of radicals became the first to offer translations of biblical texts into English, evoking the wrath of the Catholic Archbishop Thomas Arundel who condemned the Lollard bible by decree in 1408 (Rex, 1993). Sadly, many Lollards would be burned at the stake for their beliefs (cf. Gairdner, 1908; Dickens, 1959; McSheffrey and Tanner, 2003).

In 1969, not long before his death, Winnicott (1969c) confessed to the dramatist Ian Rodger, who had authored a radio play about Lollardy, "My feeling is that I am a natural Lollard and would have had a bad time in the 14th and 15th centuries." He added further that, "the Lollards laid the basis for liberal thinking in England and Europe" (Winnicott, 1969c). It will not be widely appreciated that Donald Winnicott enjoyed a strong identification with the Lollards and with their efforts to make knowledge and learning available to the masses, even at the cost of their own lives; and Winnicott celebrated the Lollard admiration of non-dogmatic, non-sacramental, and non-hierarchical approaches to religion, the very qualities that he endorsed in his politics as the unnamed leader of the independent tradition in British psychoanalysis.

In addition to Winnicott's possible identification with his public-spirited father, Frederick Winnicott, and with his uncle, Richard Winnicott, and, spurred on by the Lollard and Wesleyan devotion to public works preached in the vernacular, Winnicott also became a performer in the arts. At his boarding school, he joined the choir, and as an undergraduate at Jesus College in the University of Cambridge, he entertained people by singing comic songs while playing the piano (Winnicott, 1978; cf. Kahr, 1996a), activities which would have helped Winnicott to develop a public presence. At St. Bartholomew's Hospital Medical School, Winnicott had the opportunity to study with a number of teachers who had a strong public presence, in particular Sir Robert Armstrong-Jones, who taught mental diseases, and Dr. Thomas Horder (later Sir Thomas Horder, and ultimately, the 1st Baron

Horder), a general physician who, in his time, would serve no fewer than five British monarchs: Edward VII, George V, Edward VIII, George VI, and Elizabeth II. Both Armstrong-Jones and Horder enjoyed very public, very visible careers which impacted beyond the milieu of the hospital (Anonymous, 1943a, 1943b, 1955; Horder, 1966; cf. Kahr, 1996a).

After qualifying as a physician at St. Bartholomew's Hospital Medical School, Winnicott came to work for Professor Francis Fraser as his House Physician during 1921 and 1922 (*The Medical Who's Who: Seventh Edition. 1925*, 1925; Kahr, 1996a). Fraser, like Armstrong-Jones and Horder, had many links with the outside world and led an increasingly public career, delivering the Goulstonian Lectures to the Royal College of Physicians of London in 1927. He became the Professor of Medicine at the British Postgraduate Medical School in the University of London in 1934, and then, Director-General of the Emergency Medical Service from 1941, honours and posts which brought him great esteem and national recognition, and which would ultimately result in work with the British Broadcasting Corporation itself (Bearn, 2008). Having such a powerful, outward-focused mentor may also have impacted strongly upon Winnicott and upon his ultimate choice of a career trajectory, which included collaboration with the media.

Not only did Winnicott learn about communicating with the general public – even if only by osmosis – from his father, his uncle, his religious heritage and, also, his musical experiences, and, subsequently, from his more splashy mentors in medical school, but he may also have derived much encouragement from the founders of the psychoanalytical movement, many of whom had worked with the media during the 1920s and 1930s, and many of whom had laid the groundwork for Winnicott's ultimate theoretical contributions, but none of whom would achieve nearly as much as Donald Winnicott would come to do.

As we know, Dr. Ernest Jones (1944) wrote a letter to Winnicott praising him for one of his radio broadcasts during World War II. Nevertheless, in spite of his generosity to Winnicott's work as a media psychoanalyst, Jones, however, had a very complicated personal relationship with the general public. When, in 1922, an article appeared in a Sunday periodical, based on an interview with the London psychoanalyst Barbara Low, bearing the headline "Psycho-Analysis Dangers: Need for Protection Against Quacks Who Exploit Hysterical Women" (Maddox, 2006), Jones became extremely displeased and thereafter forbade members of the British Psycho-Analytical Society from speaking to the press (Kahr, 2013). As Dr. John Bowlby (1985) reminisced, Jones would almost never permit colleagues to work with the media at all (cf. Kahr, 1984, 2012c).

But, as the 1920s and 1930s unfolded, Jones began to recognise the importance of promoting psychoanalysis to the general public in order to defend psychoanalysis from its critics; and so, he began to adopt an increasingly outward-directed stance, lecturing, *inter alia*, on the relationship between psychoanalysis and society more broadly (Jones, 1924), and appearing on radio programmes, often in discussion with his colleague Professor Cyril Burt. Together, Jones and Burt debated "Reason and Emotion" on the B.B.C. in December, 1932 (Anonymous [Ernest Jones] and Burt, 1932) and each contributed to a series of B.B.C. talks (Burt, 1932a, 1932b; Anonymous [Ernest Jones], 1932a, 1932b, 1932c), although on those occasions, Jones did so anonymously, at a time when many did not respect physicians who publicised themselves on air.

As we have already discussed in this book, Jones pressed his psychoanalytical stamp on the theatre-going public when he met with the actor Laurence Olivier, with the actress Peggy Ashcroft, and with the director Tyrone Guthrie, to discuss their forthcoming 1937 production of William Shakespeare's *Hamlet* at the Old Vic theatre in London (Olivier, 1982) and helped them to understand the unconscious aspects of the play and its characters and, in particular, the resonant oedipal aspects of the relationship between "Hamlet" and "Gertrude". Olivier's overtly Freudian-inspired approach to the play earned plaudits, and afterwards, Olivier's production became transformed into a film, *Hamlet*, which won Academy Awards for Best Picture and for Best Actor in 1948. Jones also provided consultation to Olivier and Guthrie in 1938 when preparing their stage version of Shakespeare's *Othello* (Olivier, 1982). Thus, Jones's growing sympathy towards collaboration with the outside world might also have exerted an influence upon Winnicott and may well have given him a sense of permission to collaborate with those in the media.

Not only did Dr. Ernest Jones precede Donald Winnicott as a pioneer of psychoanalytically orientated media psychology in Great Britain, but so, too, did figures such as Dr. Montague David Eder, Dr. Edward Glover, and Dr. Adrian Stephen, as well as others, all early members of the British Psycho-Analytical Society. Although one cannot possibly do justice to their public relations contributions in the context of this brief survey, one might mention that Eder, a physician with a strong commitment to social medicine, wrote for the popular press (e.g., Hobman, 1945a, 1945b). Likewise, Glover wrote for *The Times* and, even, for *The New York Times* (Roazen, 2000a). And Dr. Adrian Stephen, brother-in-law to Virginia Woolf, made several radio broadcasts, including one on "Normal and Abnormal Personalities" (Berenson, 1934). Other important British psychoanalysts who contributed to the public debate during the 1930s and 1940s included Dr. Susan Isaacs (1932, 1948); Dr. Ernst Kris, a Viennese-born and Viennese-trained psychoanalyst who lived briefly in England after the Nazi *Anschluß* of Austria, and who worked at that time for the B.B.C. (Kris, Speier, Axelrad, Herma, Loeb, Paechter, and White, 1944); Dr. John Rickman (*Institute Board Meetings:*

16.1.1925 to 30.4.1945, 1925–1945; MacGibbon, 1997; cf. Cameron and Forrester, 2000); as well as Professor John Flügel (Roazen, 2000a, 2000b) and, also, Ella Freeman Sharpe (Roazen, 2000a, 2000b), to mention but a few (cf. Kahr, 2013).

One must underscore that these towering figures represented very much the exceptions amid the members of the British Psycho-Analytical Society. It would be inaccurate to suggest that the first and second generation of psychoanalysts in Great Britain spent all their time on the radio or writing for the press – quite the contrary – indeed, many expressed virulent opposition and criticism of these media activities. Winnicott, in particular, had to put up with numerous snide and cutting remarks about both his broadcasting activities and his large body of experience addressing non-psychoanalytical audiences (MacCarthy, 2002, 2005).

As we have noted, Winnicott pursued his radio, television, magazine, and public lecturing work because of the encouragement that he may have received from his father, his uncle, his religious heritage, and, also, from his medical mentors. But, moreover, he developed his media psychology *because of* his relationship to certain forward-thinking psychoanalytical teachers and *in spite of* his exposure to certain others.

In thinking about how Winnicott became a broadcaster, one must examine not only the ways in which his predecessors – both personal and professional – had influenced him during his development as a boy, as a young man, as a physician, and as a psychoanalyst, but one must also consider Winnicott's personal qualities, which may have contributed quite independently to his career path. Long before Winnicott met Dr. Thomas Horder or Dr. Ernest Jones, he had already become a performer. A consummate musician (as we have indicated), Winnicott had developed a capacity to feel comfortable on a public stage, whether by singing to entertain his friends at university, or whether by pursuing his love of Gilbert and Sullivan (Milner, 1987). In doing so, Winnicott very much enjoyed being his own playful self. Of course, performance must always raise the question of neurotic exhibitionism (Kahr, 2001a), but Winnicott, like many people who have undergone a lengthy analysis, had found his voice, and he had no inhibitions about using it, much to the benefit of British culture as a whole.

Winnicott boasted a fine mind, a premier education, excellent verbal skills, as well as considerable bravery of character. He also possessed a deep wish to make contact with others, and, on the basis of his clinical experiences with the impoverished of London, he maintained a strong desire to become attuned to the needs of his fellow travellers. All of these factors contributed to the personal resources upon which he drew in order to generate the courage to address millions of people – live – on the airways.

Winnicott completed two lengthy experiences of personal psychoanalysis, first, with James Strachey, throughout much of the 1920s and into the early 1930s, and second, with Joan Riviere, during the late 1930s and early 1940s. My own archival research has revealed that one cannot date these analyses as neatly as some of the textbooks would have us believe. For instance, Winnicott's treatment with Riviere endured many interruptions during the course of World War II. But whatever the precise dates, I can confirm that Winnicott underwent at least fifteen years of personal psychoanalysis as a patient, initially at a frequency of six sessions per week, and later, at a frequency of five sessions per week. I cannot identify any other figure of his generation who completed quite as much personal psychoanalysis as Winnicott had allowed himself to do or had needed to do. It has occurred to me that being a patient undergoing psychoanalysis might be rather akin to the act of broadcasting on radio. One begins by speaking (generally without interruption) to someone whose face one cannot see directly, and, over time, one develops a full and resonant voice. It would not be unreasonable to wonder whether Winnicott's personal psychoanalyses helped to mould and shape his early external and internal influences, offering space for his own character to find its fullest and richest expression. But whatever the sources of Winnicott's interest in broadcasting, he certainly possessed the skills and the capacities to speak to millions and millions of Britons, and later, to those in foreign countries as well, and he used these abilities extremely well.

Winnicott and the Art of Popularisation

We live in a world increasingly imbued with psychological ideas and concepts, so much so that in the American television drama *The Sopranos*, even a Mafia chieftain, "Tony Soprano", attended psychotherapy on a regular basis. We might find it difficult to remember, therefore, that in the early days of psychotherapy and psychoanalysis, many people regarded our work with immense suspicion, and the pioneering practitioners would often shield themselves from public view in order to avoid attacks.

Back in 1946, Professor Cyril Burt, one of Great Britain's leading academic, experimental psychologists and, also, an early advocate of psychoanalysis, prepared a series of three half-hour radio programmes on *The Human Mind* for the British Broadcasting Corporation. Fortunately, some of the transcripts of Burt's programmes still survive. The following excerpt, which dates from the spring of 1946, offers a snippet of dialogue among a number of guests at a dinner party, discussing whether to send a child for a consultation with a psychological expert:

DAPHNE [*first guest*]:	No, dear. That's psychical research. Psychology is something quite different. Isn't that the study of sex? You know, invented by that Austrian Jew – Freud wasn't it?
HUSBAND:	Both equally unpleasant if you ask me. [voices off]
WIFE:	Oh, let's ask them. James what is psychology? Charles says it's the study of spooks, Daphne says it's the study of sex, and Harry says it's just a pack of nonsense.
MALE VOICE:	Sex? Oh, that's psycho-analysis. Psychology is just a study of consciousness; the psycho-analysts study your Unconscious.
HUSBAND:	All sounds horribly morbid to me ...!

(quoted in Overy, 2009, p. 136).

This B.B.C. radio transcript typifies, in many ways, the sort of fear and anxiety with which psychoanalysts and other mental health professionals had to contend during the early decades of this profession. It should not surprise us at all that many of our forebears had great reservations about interacting with members of the general public and with the press. When, for instance, on 29th March, 1911, the Wiener Psychoanalytische Vereinigung [Vienna Psycho-Analytical Society] – the world's first formal psychoanalytical organisation, founded in 1908 – met to discuss whether any outsider, non-members could be permitted to attend meetings, Freud's disciples Dr. Eduard Hitschmann and Otto Rank (1911b, p. 209) advised that guests, including members of the press, might well take part in any discussion, but that they must practise "the utmost discretion."[14]

Unlike the early psychoanalysts who steered shy of the press, Donald Winnicott strove to counteract the anxieties expressed by "Daphne" and the other characters in Cyril Burt's 1946 radio programme. Winnicott did not always like media practitioners; indeed, he once wrote to his secretary Joyce Coles, "Journalism is always in a hurry" (Winnicott, n.d.), emphasising that psychoanalysis, by contrast, takes times. But he tolerated the manic pace of media life, and he used his broadcasting opportunities effectively to introduce his philosophy of attributing experience and expertise to parents, thus shielding them from an undue sense of self-blame.

As a result of his boldness, Winnicott garnered more positive publicity for psychoanalysis than any other clinician of his generation. For instance, after the publication of his book on *The Family and Individual Development*

(Winnicott, 1965a), a review appeared in *The Times Literary Supplement* on 7th October, 1965, which offered the following observations: "Psychoanalysis is out of fashion these days, one accepted view being that it is unscientific, incoherent, at once sentimental and inhumane, and obsessed with sex. To those who have accepted such a caricature, Dr. Winnicott's book (if they will only trouble to read it) will come as a great surprise; for the tone of these essays is realistic as well as charitable; they are beautifully written; and the author plainly cares more than most people about human dignity, scientific truth and the rights of the sane" (Anonymous, 1965a, p. 897). Shortly thereafter, *The Times Literary Supplement* reviewed yet another Winnicott (1965b) book, *The Maturational Processes and the Facilitating Environment: Studies in the Theory of Emotional Development*, praising him as "one of the most original and creative analysts in Britain" (Anonymous, 1965b, p. 1107).

Even after his death on 25th January, 1971, at the age of seventy-four years, Winnicott continued to generate much good publicity for the psychoanalytical cause. On 17th December, 1971, *The Times Literary Supplement* published a joint review of his posthumously published books, *Playing and Reality* (Winnicott, 1971a), and *Therapeutic Consultations in Child Psychiatry* (Winnicott, 1971b). The reviewer praised Winnicott for his ability to make psychoanalysis both approachable and likeable. The anonymous reviewer noted that, apart from Donald Winnicott, "it has been hard for the thinking public to find a middle way between esoteric papers and vulgarizations" (Anonymous, 1971, p. 1579) of psychoanalysis. The author also noted that most people find psychoanalysis and psychiatry to be "recondite, even repulsive" (Anonymous, 1971, p. 1579) as subjects, but observed that Winnicott had the capacity to make these fields accessible. Winnicott also distinguished himself by working with people outside the institutional confines of psychoanalysis and that, in doing so, "he has cut out the mystification and the doctrinaire pronouncements" (Anonymous, 1971, p. 1580).[15]

Throughout history, those who have dared to make knowledge and wisdom accessible have often evoked the wrath of conservative forces. As we indicated earlier in this essay, back in 1408, Archbishop Thomas Arundel refused permission for anyone to translate the Bible from Latin into English and, likewise, prohibited anyone from even reading the Bible in translation (Rupp, 1957). But William Tyndale, a pioneering religious reformer of the early sixteenth century, did produce an English Bible, evoking the wrath of the generally liberal-minded Sir Thomas More, who called Tyndale, ' "the captain of our English heretics" ' (quoted in Rupp, 1957, pp. 16–17). As a result of his work as a populariser, having rendered the Bible into the vernacular, Tyndale would be strangled to death and burned near Brussels (Daniell, 1994). Supposedly, moments before he died, Tyndale exclaimed, ' "Lord, open the King of England's eyes" ' (quoted in Rupp, p. 24).

Even a seemingly conservative figure such as Queen Victoria soon came to recognise the importance of relating to a wider audience. Though often portrayed as a grieving widow in black, shut up in her palaces, Victoria, in fact, became in many ways one of the first media monarchs who, during her long reign, granted permission for the royal image to appear on photographs and engravings, on street ballads, and even at magic lantern shows. As historian Dr. John Plunkett (2003) has argued, Victoria's lengthy queenship coincided with the huge growth in mass print throughout the nineteenth century; therefore, when she allowed herself to be photographed or recorded, unlike many of her predecessors, she would have reached an untold, unprecedented portion of the population.

Like William Tyndale and Queen Victoria, Winnicott strove to be accessible, to be available, and to be readable. In 1984, the American psychoanalyst Dr. Michael Eigen (1984) wrote a letter to Clare Winnicott, discussing the differences between her late husband Dr. Donald Winnicott and his longtime fellow psychoanalyst Dr. Wilfred Bion. As Eigen (1984) reflected, "Bion has one advantage over Winnicott. He scares most readers away, so he is in less danger of being schmaltzed up." Eigen (1984) then reflected, "However, Winnicott has the advantage of potentially reaching a larger audience."

Winnicott has of course achieved legendary status within the fields of psychology and psychoanalysis for his many achievements, insights, inventions, and contributions. But, having brought psychological ideas to countless millions of people during his lifetime and thereafter, it may well come to pass that broadcasting may be the greatest of his innumerable bequests.

Conclusion
The Future of Media Psychoanalysis

In the olden days, many people regarded Sigmund Freud's theories with considerable suspicion, dismissing him as "'Fraud'" (quoted in Stoddart, 1940, p. 191). In consequence, a large number of the early practitioners of psychoanalysis did not advertise the profession too widely, for fear of being lambasted or assaulted. In fact, in the wake of World War II, and the inevitable emigration of Jewish colleagues from Berlin and Vienna to New York City or London, many of those refugees, fearful of being attacked anti-Semitically, kept rather a low profile and created quite ghetto-like psychoanalytical organisations for Continental Jews, reluctant to mix with the outside world. Indeed, when psychoanalytical émigrés to the New World, such as Dr. Karen Horney and Dr. Gregory Zilboorg, wrote popular works and engaged with the mainstream press (e.g., Horney, 1939, 1942, 1945, 1946; Zilboorg, 1935, 1943; Zilboorg and Henry, 1941), they evoked much envy, wrath, and suspicion from their fellow psychoanalysts in Manhattan (e.g., Quinn, 1987; Zilboorg, 2022a, 2022b).

Fortunately, as the decades have unfolded, and as psychoanalysis has survived innumerable assassination attempts, and, moreover, as members of the public have embraced the talking therapies with greater respect and enthusiasm, the level of eyebrow-raising towards media psychology and media psychoanalysis has begun to decrease. Indeed, in recent years, numerous young colleagues have approached me on many occasions, keen for advice on how they might collaborate with broadcasters and filmmakers.

Of course, the mental health profession still boasts some very stuffy and conservative people.

Back in 2007, I lectured to The Squiggle Foundation in London about my work as Resident Psychotherapist for the British Broadcasting Corporation (Kahr, 2007f), and, during the course of my talk, I played a cassette recording of a section from the *Helen Mayhew* programme that I described in Chapter 1 of this book, in which I spoke to "James", the kindly man who, tragically, had recently lost his forty-year-old wife to cancer. The members of The Squiggle Foundation – all very sympathetic to the work of Donald Winnicott and his massive contribution to media psychoanalysis – listened carefully to the recording and seemed to be very moved and touched by James's sudden bereavement and, also, by my conversation with that brave gentleman.

But one colleague in the audience – a very grumpy psychoanalyst – became somewhat agitated and then criticised me for having dared to speak on the radio at all and for having had the presumption to offer emotional support "on air". This psychoanalyst, who has never enjoyed a public profile of any kind and whose name will be known to virtually no one other than a small cohort of conservative colleagues, expressed great disapproval that a trained mental health practitioner should *ever* appear on radio, criticising me thus: "You are exposing the unconscious of these individuals and that absolutely cannot be allowed. We are, after all, a *private* profession."

I tried to explain that, before I talked to James, one of the assistant producers at the B.B.C. had vetted him carefully and had asked him to consider whether he truly wished to speak on the radio about the loss of his wife. As James lived in a faraway town in an obscure part of England, with no mental health professionals in the nearby vicinity, he felt comfortable to communicate with me – indeed, *eager* to do so – as I seemed to have a sympathetic voice and manner. He and I then had a brief and straightforward conversation. I certainly did not expose his unconscious by analysing his dreams or his masturbatory fantasies. I simply facilitated an ordinary human chat with James, expressing my regret at his dreadful loss and my concern for his wellbeing, and I recommended that he might wish to *consider* the possibility of obtaining psychotherapy or counselling. I learned absolutely nothing about his childhood or about his unconscious *per se*; I did not ask him to free-associate; and I certainly did not invite him to recline on a couch! In fact, I merely endeavoured to be kindly, both offering help to this grieving person and, also, endeavouring to destigmatise psychotherapy via the British Broadcasting Corporation. As a result of that radio "session", which reached millions of people, literally hundreds of members of the public contacted me directly via the B.B.C., asking for proper psychotherapy referrals for themselves.

I have shared this anecdote from the year 2007 as a means of confirming that not all of the members of our professional community wish to promote our work or, indeed, our very presence, among the general public.

Fortunately, as the years have unfolded, the somewhat retreated and shy members of our profession have begun to exert less and less influence, and many have since retired or died, and our younger, more open-minded and more outward-reaching colleagues have begun to speak in a much louder and much more impactful voice.

Media psychoanalysis has now become so common that literally thousands upon thousands of fellow psychological workers worldwide have since appeared on radio, on television, on webinars, on podcasts, on social media, and so forth, helping to spread psychodynamic knowledge to the wider population. We have gradually begun to conquer our fear of being seen and we have finally begun to embrace the need for the dissemination of our knowledge more broadly.

In fact, in view of the recent outbreak of the coronavirus pandemic, large numbers of mental health practitioners have had no opportunities to speak in the old-fashioned, crowded lecture theatres of yore and, hence, we have *had* to deliver webinars on-line to large, international audiences, thus disseminating psychoanalytical and psychotherapeutic knowledge even more broadly. For instance, on 19th June, 2020, in the middle of this horrid global emergency, I delivered an on-line lecture as a fundraising event for Freud Museum London. I spoke about "How Freud Would Have Handled the Coronavirus: Lessons from a Beacon of Survival" (Kahr, 2020e), endeavouring to examine what brilliant insights we might all learn from the father of psychoanalysis, who had somehow managed to navigate the so-called Spanish flu of 1918 to 1920, as well as sixteen years of carcinoma, not to mention the Nazis (cf. Kahr, 2021a). I must confess that I found the experience slightly nerve-wracking for the sole reason that I had never before delivered a talk "on-line" from my own consulting room, and I worried greatly about whether I would be able to master the technology of Zoom. Fortunately, the lovely team at Freud Museum London assisted me and, happily, the camera and the microphone seemed to work just fine.

Having spoken at the Freud Museum on numerous occasions, over the decades, to local colleagues and students and friends and other fellow Londoners, I naively assumed that the members of the audience at this on-line Freudian coronavirus webinar would consist of the usual suspects. After the talk, one of the organisers telephoned me full of excitement: "Brett, we raised a lot of money for the museum from this webinar. And guess what? We had people logging on from Germany and France and India and Pakistan and the United Arab Emirates, and, even, Iran! In fact, we had many more people attending from "foreign" countries than from the United Kingdom!"

At one level, this comment should not have surprised me. After all, we now live in a deeply interconnected world, facilitated by extraordinary developments in technology.

But the psychoanalytical community – a group of very softly-spoken, modest, and internally focussed professionals – has certainly never championed external outreach in the way in which members of the film and television and radio and internet industries have done. Thus, when the coordinator of that webinar explained that we had attracted listeners from Pakistan for a Freud Museum London talk about the inner world of the Austrian-born Sigmund Freud, I smiled quietly, relieved to know that I could now introduce my hero to a wider audience, rather than solely to our more regular, local British supporters (cf. Kahr, 2021a).

I cite this vignette as but one tiny example to demonstrate that the appetite for psychological knowledge continues to grow in countries which have not had the luxury or the privilege of hosting psychological events as frequently as we do in the United Kingdom, and that, by encouraging the development of media psychology and media psychoanalysis in its many forms, we now have the opportunity to introduce some of the basic concepts of good psychology far and wide.

For young readers who may be on the verge of entering the mental health profession, I hope that each of you will appreciate that there might be many ways in which psychological practitioners can work in close collaboration with the media. One need not become a Resident Psychotherapist for the British Broadcasting Corporation in order to have an impact. Nowadays, it seems that far more people watch YouTube videos than those who listen religiously to the B.B.C. So, every one of you will have a great many creative options that my generation had never even considered, and I warmly encourage all members of the psychoanalytical and psychotherapeutic communities to think about how we might make ourselves better known to the general public, and more approachable, so that we do not frighten off those who would benefit from our expertise.

Many years ago, Paul Barker, the editor of the influential, progressive British magazine *New Society*, which often championed psychoanalysis and other varieties of social science, wrote about the need for practitioners to present their ideas in readable English. As he underscored, "Fortunately, nothing important in social science is yet at the stage where it cannot be put in reasonably plain language" (Barker, 1972, p. 11). Although *New Society* ceased publication in 1988, after more than a quarter of a century of weekly issues, the forward-thinking editorial team often commissioned psychoanalysts and psychiatrists to contribute essays and reviews.

The noted anti-psychiatrist, Dr. Ronald Laing (1968), wrote about "Liberation by Orgasm" for *New Society* – a shockingly bold and honest contribution for its time. Likewise, the sympathetic psychodynamic psychiatrist and Jungian analyst, Dr. Anthony Storr (1968) – one of my esteemed teachers (Kahr, 2020b) – produced an excellent note for *New Society*, "On Aggression". And, as I indicated in a previous chapter, our shared hero, Dr. Donald Winnicott, the king of media psychology in the 1940s, 1950s, and 1960s, penned numerous short pieces and reviews for this magazine across more than half a decade, reaching large numbers of people who would never have subscribed to *The International Journal of Psycho-Analysis*. In various concise, but illuminating, essays, this genius man taught us about "Struggling Through the Doldrums" (Winnicott, 1963b), about "The Child Behind Society" (Winnicott, 1965d), about "Steps to Good Parenthood" (Winnicott, 1967a), and so much more (e.g., Winnicott, 1964b, 1964c, 1964d, 1965c, 1966b, 1966c, 1966d, 1967b, 1967c, 1967d, 1968b, 1968c, 1969b). Icons such as Laing and Storr and Winnicott could certainly communicate in what the editor, Paul Barker (1972, p. 11), described as "reasonably plain language", and thus, these outward-reaching individuals helped to popularise depth psychology far and wide.

As we embark upon a post-COVID-19 world, full of debilitating climate change, physical unsafety, widespread disease, terrorism, and economic destruction, we certainly need to transmit good psychoanalytical knowledge – good *mental health knowledge* – as effectively as possible. And only through the development of media psychology and media psychoanalysis can our quietly spoken but wise colleagues begin to communicate, not only more plainly but, also, more *loudly*.

Notes

Chapter 5

1. In this instance, I have deployed the spelling utilised in the First Folio edition of William Shakespeare's collected plays, published in 1623.
2. The New York Freudian Society, founded in 1959, in New York City, New York, ultimately changed its name to the Contemporary Freudian Society.

Chapter 6

1. The author of the definitive study of the musical *Lady in the Dark* spells his names without capital letters; hence, I have chosen to honour this preference by referring to him as bruce d. mcclung, rather than as Bruce D. McClung.
2. Shortly after I had completed writing this chapter, yet another couple with whom I work shared some fascinating material about the television and its use within their marriage. Mr. M. and Mrs. M., an elderly couple, entered psychotherapy several years ago, in part, because of Mr. M.'s long-standing depression, which had a profound impact on their marital relations. Understandably, Mr. M. had lost interest in sex, and Mrs. M. became increasingly rageful, in spite of her efforts to be sympathetic. During one session, Mrs. M. explained to me that she and her husband would spend a lot of time watching television, but that they did so in separate rooms. When I inquired about what sorts of programmes they would prefer to watch, Mrs. M. replied that she loves the American mystery drama *Murder, She Wrote*, while Mr. M. enjoys the American comedy-drama *Weeds*. Although I have little familiarity with either of these television programmes, I explored how the television must have served to keep the couple apart, while also communicating something very palpable about Mrs. M.'s *murder-she-wrote*-ish rage, and something about Mr. M.'s depression, which he himself had once referred to as his *"weedy"* feelings. After discussing this subject in detail, the couple

expressed a hope that they could spend more time together watching the same programme at the same time and in the same room; and, happily, three weeks later, they reported their great pleasure at having purchased a new television set which they regarded as an improvement on their old *flat* screen (which, I suspect, represented the depression and flatness within the marriage).
3. Quite some time later, "Miss L." made yet one further reference to *The Sopranos*, not having talked about the series for the longest time. She had eventually married her boyfriend, and they had settled down into a reasonably happy and contented life together. However, shortly thereafter, Miss L.'s mother-in-law died very unexpectedly, and Miss L.'s new husband became somewhat depressed. Miss L. encouraged him to seek psychotherapy of some sort, but he adamantly refused, thinking that it would not be "manly" to cry in front of a stranger. To her surprise, Miss L. found herself returning to her box set of D.V.D.s of *The Sopranos*, and she soon began to watch the entire series once again. She took great comfort from the fact that even the rugged "Tony Soprano" had allowed himself to visit a mental health practitioner, and she used this information as leverage in her discussions with her husband, who eventually relented and found psychotherapy to be a helpful experience.
4. According to these statistics, between 4th October, 2010, and 10th October, 2010, Britons watched 27.15 hours of television per week. Between 11th October, 2010, and 17th October, 2010, that figure rose slightly to 27.48 hours per week, increasing further to 28.05 hours per week between 18th October, 2010, to 24th October, 2010. And, during the later days of that month, from 25th October, 2010, until 31st October, 2010, the average Briton watched as much as 29.13 hours of television per week (Anonymous, 2020a).

Chapter 8

1. Naturally, this phrase deploys the sixteenth-century spelling of "haue" rather than "have", as well as the seemingly unusual rendering of the word "permanēt", with a straight line over the second use of the letter "e", rather than the more familiar spelling "permanent".
2. It may be that William Blount, Lord Mountjoy, wrote this letter by himself. But it might well be the case that Mountjoy's scribe, Andreas Amonius, had actually produced this missive to Desiderius Erasmus on his master's behalf.
3. First Folio, 1623, Actus Secundus, Scena Septima, line 157.
4. First Folio, 1623, Actus Secundus, Scena Septima, lines 144–171.
5. This citation refers to the biography of George Gordon, Lord Byron, written by Fiona MacCarthy, published in 2002. I have inserted this

endnote to differentiate this reference – MacCarthy (2002) – from the reference to a personal communication from Dr. Brendan MacCarthy (2002), mentioned in Chapter 10 and, also, in Chapter 11.
6. The original German phrase reads: "'der Erfüllung von Wünschen'" (Freud, 1909a, p. 65).
7. The original German phrase reads: "'der Korrektur des Lebens'" (Freud, 1909a, p. 65).
8. The original German passage reads: "'die Phantasie des Kindes mit der Aufgabe, die jetzt gering geschätzten Eltern loszuwerden und durch in der Regel sozial höher stehende zu ersetzen'" (Freud, 1909a, p. 65).
9. The original German word reads: ' "Familienromane" ' (Freud, 1909a, p. 65).
10. The original German passage reads: "'in einer Phantasie findet, welche beide Eltern durch vornehmere ersetzt'" (Freud, 1909a, p. 66).
11. The original German passage reads: "'Eine interessante Variante dieses Familienromans ist es dann, wenn der dichtende Held für sich selbst zur Legitimät zurückkehrt, während er die anderen Geschwister auf diese Art also illegitim beseitigt'" (Freud, 1909a, p. 67).

Chapter 10

1. Dr. Ernest Jones misquoted Colonel Robert McCormick's telegram when describing the incident in the third volume of his biography of Professor Sigmund Freud. Jones conveyed the telegram thus: "'Offer Freud 25,000 dollars or anything he name come Chicago psychoanalyze (i.e. the murderers).'" (quoted in Jones, 1957, p. 103). Interestingly, Freud's eldest daughter, Mathilde Freud Hollitscher, confirmed to the Princesse Marie Bonaparte that the Americans had offered Freud a "'nombre incalculable de dollars'" (quoted in Bonaparte, 1926, p. 259) – namely an "incalculable amount of dollars".
2. The original German text of Professor Sigmund Freud's (1924a, p. 107) letter to George Seldes, dated 29th June, 1924, reads thus:

> Sehr geehrter Herr,
> Ihr Telegramm ist mir infolge der unrichtigen Addresse verspaetet zugekommen. Ich beantworte es dahin, dass es nicht in meiner Absicht liegen kann, ein Gutachten ueber Personen und ueber eine Tat abzugeben, wenn ich nur auf Zeitungsberichte angewiesen bin und keine Gelegenheit zur persoenlichen Untersuchung habe. Eine Einladung von Seiten der Hearst-Presse, waehrend der Dauer des Prozesses nach Newyork zu kommen, musste ich aus Gesundheitsruecksichten ablehnen.
>
> Hochachtungsvoll
Prof. Freud

We must appreciate that Seldes had spelled Freud's accented German words without any umlaut accents. I have thus preserved Seldes's version of Freud's missive. Freud had also rendered New York as one word – "Newyork" – no doubt a feature of his traditional Gothic script.
3. Dr. Hilda Abraham and Ernst L. Freud, the editors of the original German-language version of Professor Sigmund Freud's correspondence with Dr. Karl Abraham, had excised this reference from the original published version (Freud, 1920a).
4. The original German phrase reads: "würde eher einen lächerlichen als einen lehrreichen Eindruck machen" (Freud, 1925a, p. 823).
5. We know that Professor Sigmund Freud certainly did not have a complete aversion to the radio. On 7th February, 1934, his eldest daughter, Mathilde Freud Hollitscher, and her husband, Robert Hollitscher, celebrated their silver wedding anniversary, along with some sixty-four guests, at their home in Vienna, Austria. The couple received a radio, a joint gift from Freud and his youngest daughter, Anna Freud, and from two wealthy Freud analysands, Dorothy Burlingham and Dr. Ruth Mack Brunswick, who also contributed to its purchase (Molnar, 1992).
6. The original German phrase reads: "Ein angesehener Mann, von der Presse und den Reichen unterstützt, könnte Wunder tun, um körperliche Leiden zu lindern, wenn er Forscher genug ist, neue Wege der Heilung zu betreten" (Freud, 1875a, p. 144).
7. Interestingly, in the original handwritten letter to Dr. Sándor Radó, Professor Sigmund Freud (1926f) had written, "I have nothing to communicate to the public at the moment", but then he scribbled out the phrase "'at the moment'" (Roazen, 1995c, p. 161). This small piece of self-editing absolutely encapsulates Freud's personal conflict regarding public relations. One can detect a similar conflict in Freud around being seen and being hidden over the impending celebrations of his seventieth birthday in 1926. Freud (1926e, p. 159) wrote, once again, to Radó, "While I am at pains to keep the festivities low-profile, yet I am suddenly appearing to put such a matter on stage. A few days ago I accepted an invitation from Prof. Schmutzer to have my etching made."
8. In the "Vorwort" by Dr. Sándor Ferenczi (1922, n.p.), the original German phrase reads: "psychoanalytische Themen für ärztliche und nichtärztliche Laien." As no one has yet translated this book into English, I have not provided a page number for my own rendering of the phrase.
9. By this point in time, Dr. Ernest Jones (1910) had published an essay about the literary character "Hamlet", which Laurence Olivier may well have read. Jones's (1947, 1949) more substantial studies of William Shakespeare's play would not appear until the late 1940s.

Chapter 11

1. In 1948, Dr. Donald Winnicott engaged the services of a new secretary, Joyce Coles, who would work for him over the next several decades (with only a short interruption) until his death in 1971 (Kahr, 1994f). A woman of remarkable efficiency, Mrs. Coles established a stunningly organised system of carbon copies and filing; hence, contemporary historians can enjoy working on Winnicott's papers which date from 1948 onwards. A small amount of correspondence prior to 1948 does survive but, owing the fact that Winnicott had great trouble keeping a regular private secretary during the 1930s and early 1940s, most of his prior correspondence has not survived.
2. On this occasion, I have referenced this letter as "Kathleen Winnicott, 1944", rather than as "Winnicott, 1944", in order to differentiate this particular unpublished source from the reference to Dr. Donald Winnicott's various 1944 publications or unpublished correspondence (Winnicott, 1944a, 1944b, 1944c, 1944d, 1944e), which I have cited throughout this book.
3. This broadcast, originally styled as "Support for Normal Parents", actually appeared in print under the title "Postscript" (Winnicott, 1945h).
4. According to Martin Gilbert (1994) – subsequently Sir Martin Gilbert – Winston Churchill made broadcasts to the British nation on the following dates: 19th May, 1940; 17th June, 1940; 14th July, 1940; 11th September, 1940; 30th September, 1940; 21st October, 1940; and 23rd December, 1940.
5. As the medical directories of the period contain no listing of a physician by the name of "Bick", this Dr. Bick must refer to Esther Bick, the Polish-born child psychologist who fled to England from Nazism in 1938, by way of Switzerland. After a period in London, Bick spent most of the World War II years as a refugee in Manchester, in the North of England, undergoing psychoanalysis with Dr. Michael Balint, before moving to London (as did Balint). She eventually became the head of the new child psychotherapy training course at the Tavistock Clinic, which launched in 1949. As Peggy Volkov (1945b) had referred to a certain Dr. Bick facilitating a postgraduate course for health visitors in Chester, Leeds, and Liverpool – not far from Manchester – it would not be unreasonable to suppose that Dr. Bick must be Esther Bick. After assuming the reins of the child psychotherapy training programme at the Tavistock Clinic, Esther Bick encouraged her students to listen to Winnicott's radio broadcasts. Mary Boston, one of the very first child psychotherapy trainees in Great Britain, became "enthralled" (quoted in Kahr, 1994e) by Winnicott's talks. She also recalled that she had found Winnicott's broadcasts to be quite impressive, and that she particularly liked the way in which he had described the baby's hunger

pangs as "'lions + tigers inside'" (quoted in Boston, 1994). During the late 1940s and early 1950s, Winnicott made many contributions to the child psychotherapy course at the Tavistock Clinic, but, as Esther Bick became more and more Kleinian in her outlook, she gradually began to sour towards Winnicott (Kahr, 1994d; cf. Kahr, 1996a). In 1953, Winnicott wrote to Bick after she had presented a clinical paper to a meeting of the British Psycho-Analytical Society on "Anxiety Underlying Phobia of Sexual Intercourse in a Woman", chastising her for making too many psychoanalytical interpretations to her patient. He pontificated, "I am thinking of what would happen if you were to give a long period without making interpretations, and perhaps you have done this; but it can easily be that by interpreting you reassure the patient against her anxiety of having annihilated you" (Winnicott, 1953, p. 52). In this respect, Winnicott may have alienated himself from Bick and the other Kleinians who privileged the clinical transference interpretation over holding, silence, play, and other measures which became increasingly associated with Winnicott.

6. By 1947, Peggy Volkov had become the principal editor of *The New Era in Home and School* and, by 1948, she had also acquired a doctorate.

7. It may be that Dr. Donald Winnicott did, indeed, broadcast a ninth talk in the series on 30th November, 1949, as indicated by an unpublished note in his desk diary, but I have not succeeded in clarifying this matter with any certainty.

8. Circa 1962, Dr. Donald Winnicott's recordings for the British Broadcasting Corporation about the ordinary devoted mother appeared in vinyl record form, in a limited edition. We know from a note written in the back of his private desk diary that he had arranged to send copies of the complete sets to:

- Rockville (Winnicott's family home where his sisters, Violet Winnicott and Kathleen Winnicott, still lived).
- Masud Khan (Winnicott's former supervisee and current patient).
- The Institute of Psycho-Analysis, London.
- Anna Freud.
- Dr. Ishak Ramzy (an Egyptian-born psychoanalyst).
- Dr. Clifford Scott (a Canadian-born psychoanalyst who had treated both of Donald Winnicott's wives (Kahr, 1996a, 2019b)).
- The Child Department at the Institute of Psycho-Analysis, London.
- N.S.A. [Nursery School Association of Great Britain and Northern Ireland].
- The Mulberry Bush (a progressive residential school in Standlake, Oxfordshire, which offered psychological treatment for highly disturbed youngsters, headed by Donald Winnicott's supervisee and friend Barbara Dockar-Drysdale).

- Dr. Donald Winnicott himself (a personal reference copy to keep at his home at 87, Chester Square, in Belgravia, South West London).
- Joyce Coles (Winnicott's trusted secretary).
- Dr. Josephine Lomax-Simpson (a psychoanalytical colleague).
- Someone called "Walder" (whose identity cannot be firmly established).

9. Dr. Donald Winnicott wrote this letter to *The Times* in the wake of the famous Curtis Report, published in 1946, to which both he and Clare Britton had contributed expert testimony, which lobbied for better government supervision of childcare provision in Great Britain (*Report of the Care of Children Committee: Presented by the Secretary of State for the Home Department, the Minister of Health, and the Minister of Education, to Parliament by Command of His Majesty: September, 1946*, 1946). Although Winnicott would have supported the spirit of the Curtis Report, he also maintained his stance, developed over many years in his radio speeches, about the potential dangers of experts supervising parents.
10. Dr. Donald Winnicott's two short speeches on "Visiting Children in Hospital" would be transmitted on 16th May, 1951, and on 23rd May, 1951.
11. Regrettably, I have not succeeded in establishing the topics of these broadcasts in 1952.
12. I offer the original titles and dates of transmission of Dr. Donald Winnicott's contributions to this series of talks:

- "Saying No: I", broadcast on 25th January, 1960.
- "Saying No: II", broadcast on 1st February, 1960.
- "Saying No: III", broadcast on 8th February, 1960.
- "Jealousy: I", broadcast on 15th February, 1960.
- "Jealousy: II", broadcast on 22nd February, 1960.
- "Jealousy: III", broadcast on 29th February, 1960.
- "Jealousy: IV", broadcast on 7th March, 1960.
- "What Irks?: I", broadcast on 14th March, 1960.
- "More That Irks – and Why", broadcast on 21st March, 1960.
- "What Irks: III", broadcast on 28th March, 1960.
- "Security", broadcast on 18th April, 1960.

13. The term "Lollard" derives from the Dutch "lollaerd", meaning "mumbler" or "mutterer", first used perhaps in a sermon criticising the Lollard founder John Wycliffe. Critics had accused the Lollards of reciting holy texts by mumbling.
14. The original German phrase reads: "zur strengsten Diskretion" (Hitschmann and Rank, 1911a, p. 201).
15. This book review of *Playing and Reality* (Winnicott, 1971a) and of *Therapeutic Consultations in Child Psychiatry* (Winnicott, 1971b) appeared

under the title "Between the Thumb and the Teddy-Bear: The Psychology of Infancy" (Anonymous, 1971), but when *The Times Literary Supplement* reprinted this tribute in a compendium of pieces, the review of Winnicott's books bore a new title, namely, "Therapy without Mystery" (Anonymous, 1972). In many respects, Dr. Donald Winnicott, as broadcaster, as popular writer, and as media man, allowed psychotherapy to become truly accessible and, thus, no longer quite such a mysterious creature.

Original Sources of Chapters

Several of the contributions published in this book, *How to Be Intimate with 15,000,000 Strangers: Musings on Media Psychoanalysis*, appear here for the very first time. Earlier versions of some of the chapters contained herein have already appeared in print; however, in each case, I have updated and restyled each essay quite considerably. I do wish to convey my warmest thanks to all of the publishers, whom I have identified below, and who had provided me with a welcome forum in which I could share the earlier incarnations of this work.

Preface: How to Publicise Psychoanalysis

This material appears here in print for the very first time.

Chapter 1: The Bulimic Lorry Driver: Championing the Media in Spite of Hesitancy and Envy

This material appears here in print for the very first time.

Chapter 2: "You have five minutes to cure the nation": My Years at the B.B.C.

Over many decades, I have had the privilege of speaking to numerous professional organisations about my work in the field of media psychoanalysis. This chapter, in particular, derives from a series of talks presented between 2005 and 2011, during, and after, my tenure as Resident Psychotherapist for the British Broadcasting Corporation. I wish to convey my gratitude to those hosts and attendees who welcomed me so warmly. In particular, I thank all those colleagues who engaged with my Keynote Address on "How Can We Counsel 15,000,000 People?: Confessions of a Radio Psychotherapist", delivered to the North London Branch of the British Association for Counselling and Psychotherapy, at Avenue House in Finchley, North

London, on 9th November, 2005. Likewise, I offer my gratitude to the many international colleagues who permitted me to lecture on "Can One Practice Psychotherapy on Radio and Television?: The Pleasures and Perils of Media Psychology", at the conference on "'Days of Shaking': Psychotherapy in a Time of Change" – the 14th Congress of the European Association for Psychotherapy, in association with the 10th Professional Conference of the United Kingdom Council for Psychotherapy, delivered at the West Road Concert Hall, part of the Faculty of Music at the University of Cambridge, in Cambridge, Cambridgeshire, on 15th July, 2006. Subsequently, I had the opportunity to talk on "Can One Practice Therapy at 1.45 A.M. with 5,000,000 People Listening In?: Donald Winnicott and the Origins of Media Psychology", as part of the Public Lecture Programme 2006–2007 of The Squiggle Foundation and its Centre for Winnicottian Studies, held at the Primrose Hill Community Centre, in Primrose Hill, North West London, on 12th May, 2007, at the very kind invitation of Dr. Bernard Barnett, who chaired the event with his characteristic graciousness.

I also spoke about my work in a talk on "Media Psychology", delivered to Psychotherapy Sussex at the Aldrington Day Hospital, part of the Sussex Partnership NHS Trust, in Brighton, East Sussex, on 21st September, 2007, and then one further incarnation in a discussion on "Radio Recollections" as part of a Media and the Inner World Radio Seminar, sponsored by the Media and the Inner World Network, held on the Docklands Campus of the University of East London, in Docklands, London, on 6th July, 2011.

Earlier versions of this chapter appeared in print as a short essay, "On Practicing Therapy at 1.45 A.M." (Kahr, 2005a) in the journal *American Imago: Psychoanalysis and the Human Sciences*, due to the generosity of the former editor of the journal, Professor Peter L. Rudnytsky, and the publisher, Johns Hopkins University Press in Baltimore, Maryland, and, also, on the website "All About Psychotherapy: The Online Resource for Psychotherapy" (Kahr, 2005b), courtesy of Einar Jenssen and Dr. Morton Schatzman. A much fuller account of my radio work appeared in my book, *On Practising Therapy at 1.45 A.M.: Adventures of a Clinician* (Kahr, 2020b), published by Routledge/Taylor and Francis Group, of London, and Abingdon, Oxfordshire, whom I thank warmly for their professional work, especially the members of the editorial team with whom I collaborated on that title, most particularly Russell George and Dr. Elliott Morsia.

Chapter 3: How to Dramatise 13,553 Sexual Fantasies in Only Forty-Seven Minutes

I first described the commissioning and the filming of the television documentary that I presented in 2005 in two short essays – "How to Make a Forty-Seven-Minute Television Program in Only Three Years" (Kahr, 2005c), and "Filming Sexual Fantasies" (Kahr, 2006a) – each originally published in *American Imago: Psychoanalysis and the Human Sciences*, courtesy of the

Johns Hopkins University Press, of Baltimore, Maryland. An integrated version of these two chapters appeared in my book, *On Practising Therapy at 1.45 A.M.: Adventures of a Clinician* (Kahr, 2020b), published by Routledge/Taylor and Francis Group, in London, and in Abingdon, Oxfordshire. I owe the most enormous thanks to Dan Chambers, formerly Director of Programmes at Channel Five Television, for having commissioned the television documentary, and to Dunja Noack for having served as the Executive Producer on behalf of Tiger Aspect Productions. I have updated the current incarnation of this chapter quite extensively.

Chapter 4: *Making Slough Happy*: A Television Experiment

A very shortened version of the first half of this chapter appeared originally in a brief essay entitled, "How to Make 120,000 People Happy in Just Ten Weeks" (Kahr, 2006b), first published in *American Imago: Psychoanalysis and the Human Sciences*, courtesy of the Johns Hopkins University Press, of Baltimore, Maryland. I presented a more experiential version, "Can One Practice Winnicottian Play Therapy on National Television?", as part of the Module on "Theoretical Studies 1" of the Music Therapy Theory and Literature Seminars, delivered at the Music Therapy Training Programme in the Department of Music Therapy at the Guildhall School of Music and Drama, in the Barbican, London, on 12th March, 2007, at the kind invitation of Ann Sloboda – a long-standing and much-admired psychoanalytical colleague. I owe deepest thanks to the late Patricia Llewellyn of Optomen Television and to all of the staff at the British Broadcasting Corporation, especially Roly Keating, former Controller of B.B.C. Two, for having commissioned the television documentary, *Making Slough Happy*, which formed the basis of this more expanded chapter. A very much longer version of this essay appeared in my book, *On Practising Therapy at 1.45 A.M.: Adventures of a Clinician* (Kahr, 2020b), published by Routledge/Taylor and Francis Group, London, and Abingdon, Oxfordshire, to whom I extend my ongoing thanks. I also published a far more elongated version of the description of my work with the woman who struggled with her sense of parental confidence, entitled, "The Woman Who Could Not Sing "Happy Birthday": Couple Psychoanalysis at the Baby Grand Piano" (Kahr, 2020c), which appeared in the journal *Couple and Family Psychoanalysis*, edited by Dr. Christopher Clulow and published by Phoenix Publishing House, in Bicester, Oxfordshire. I extend further appreciation to the publisher of that periodical, Kate Pearce.

Chapter 5: On Stage at the Royal Opera House

A much-shortened essay about my adventures at the Royal Opera House first appeared as "A Night at the Opera: The Freudians at Covent Garden" (Kahr, 2007e), published in *American Imago: Psychoanalysis and the Human*

Sciences, courtesy of the Johns Hopkins University Press of Baltimore, Maryland. I provided a fuller account, some years later, in my book, *On Practising Therapy at 1.45 A.M.: Adventures of a Clinician* (Kahr, 2020b), published by Routledge / Taylor and Francis Group, in London, and in Abingdon, Oxfordshire. I owe the most immense thanks to Melvin Cooper, Lisa Forrell, Pauline Hodson, and my colleagues at the Society of Couple Psychoanalytic Psychotherapists, the professional body of the Tavistock Centre for Couple Relationships, at the Tavistock Institute of Medical Psychology in the Tavistock Centre in London (the precursor organisation to the British Society of Couple Psychotherapists and Counsellors, London, and, ultimately, to the Tavistock Relationships Association of Psychotherapists and Counsellors, part of Tavistock Relationships, based at the Tavistock Institute of Medical Psychology, London), for supporting this unusual venture of introducing couple psychoanalysis into the world of opera.

Chapter 6: Television as Rorschach: The Unconscious Use of the Cathode Nipple

I delivered an earlier incarnation of this chapter under the title, "Television as Rorschach: Cathode Nipple, Linking Object, or Transferential Barometer?", as part of a panel on "Television from Both Sides of the Couch" at the conference on "Remote Control: Psychoanalysis and Television", sponsored jointly by the Freud Museum, in Swiss Cottage, London, and by the Media and the Inner World Network – an Arts and Humanities Research Council Research Network – based jointly at the School of Arts, Roehampton University, London, and at the Psychosocial Studies Field in the School of Humanities and Social Sciences at the University of East London, Docklands, London. These organisations hosted this special event at The Anna Freud Centre in Swiss Cottage, London, on 30th October, 2010, under the chairpersonship of Carol Seigel, Director of the Freud Museum. A fuller version of this talk appeared in print under the title, "Television as Rorschach: The Unconscious Use of the Cathode Nipple" (Kahr, 2014), in a book on *Television and Psychoanalysis: Psycho-Cultural Perspectives*, edited by Professor Caroline Bainbridge, Ivan Ward, and Professor Candida Yates (2014), and published by Karnac Books, London, to whom I convey my deepest appreciation.

Chapter 7: Dr. Paul Weston and the Bloodstained Couch: Some Critical Comments on *In Treatment*

Andrea Sabbadini very kindly invited me to write an essay about the television programme, *In Treatment*, entitled "Dr Paul Weston and the Bloodstained Couch" (Kahr, 2011a), for *The International Journal of Psychoanalysis*, published by John Wiley and Sons of Oxford, Oxfordshire (and currently published by Routledge / Taylor and Francis Group, based in

London, and in Abingdon, Oxfordshire), to whom I extend my gratitude. A French translation of that article appeared in a collection of essays, edited by Professeur Louis Brunet, Dr. med. Jean-Michel Quinodoz, Dr. Pierre Dajez, Danielle Goldstein, Dr. med. François Gross, Florence Guignard, Dr. med. Céline Gür, Dr. Marcel Hudon, Dr. Luc Magnenat, Diana Messina Pizzuti, André Renaud, Dr. Michel Sanchez-Cardenas, and Dr. Patricia Waltz, namely, *L'Année psychanalytique internationale: 2012. Traduction en langue française d'un choix de textes publiés en 2011 dans* The International Journal of Psychoanalysis, released by the Paris-based publisher, Éditions In Press (Kahr, 2012b), to whom I also convey my appreciation and regard. These two articles have formed the basis of the revised chapter contained in this volume about this controversial depiction of mental health professionals in the media.

Chapter 8: Fame and the Unconscious: Toxic and Inspiring Aspects of Celebrity Culture

I first presented an extremely preliminary introduction to this chapter as a short talk on "The Psychology of Celebrity" at the kind invitation of Zaki Cooper and his colleagues at the Hampstead Synagogue in West Hampstead, London, on 16th May, 2003. I then delivered a fuller and more formal version of this chapter in a presentation entitled "Fame and the Unconscious: Creative and Malignant Components of Celebrity Culture", as The Eighteenth Annual Lionel Monteith Memorial Lecture, sponsored by The Lincoln Clinic and Centre for Psychotherapy in London, held at Governors' Hall of St. Thomas' Hospital, part of the Guy's and St Thomas' NHS Foundation Trust, in South East London, on 24th April, 2010, at the kind invitation of Serena Heller and her colleagues. Quite a number of years later, I spoke about this very subject in an interview on "The Psychology Behind Your Celebrity Crush", graciously facilitated by the radio presenter Christine Layton on the *Saturday Breakfast* programme for A.B.C. Radio Perth, in Perth, Australia, broadcast on 7th September, 2019. I produced a much more extended version in book form, *Celebrity Mad: Why Otherwise Intelligent People Worship Fame* (Kahr, 2020a), published by Routledge/Taylor and Francis Group, of London and, also, Abingdon, Oxfordshire. For this collection of essays, I have revised and updated and trimmed the contents of that book-length version quite considerably.

Chapter 9: On Not Being Shakespeare, Mozart, or Picasso: Creativity, Bereavement, and the Wish to Be Famous

I first presented a much-shortened version of this paper under the title, "On Not Being Shakespeare, Mozart, or Picasso: Inhibitions of Creativity as a Form of Bereavement", as a plenary address for the National Jubilee

Conference on "Cruse – 50 Years: Restoring Hope", sponsored by Cruse Bereavement Care, and hosted at the University of Warwick, in Coventry, Warwickshire, on 17th July, 2009. This material appears here in print for the very first time.

Chapter 10: Media Monasticism and Media Whoredom: The Uncomfortable Marriage Between Psychoanalysis and Popular Exposure

I first spoke about the early history of media psychoanalysis in a brief presentation entitled, "Why Freud Turned Down an Enormous Fee as an Expert Witness?", at a Pre-Conference Event, part of the Pre-Conference Reception for the Fourteenth Annual Conference on "After Trauma: Within Families and Between Strangers", sponsored by the International Association for Forensic Psychotherapy, held at the Davenport Hotel in Dublin, Ireland, on 19th May, 2005. I wish to extend my warmest thanks to Dr. Estela Welldon (subsequently Profesora Welldon) for her generous welcome and for her kindly remarks. I delivered a revised version on "Why Freud Turned Down an Enormous Fee as an Expert Witness: Heroism and Anxiety in the History of Forensic Psychotherapy" to a group of staff and trainees from the Boston Graduate School of Psychoanalysis of Boston, Massachusetts, during their visit to London, held at the Royal Over-Seas League, in St. James's, in South West London, on 29th March, 2006, at the friendly invitation of Paul Shields. And many years thereafter, I offered a more updated version on "'Psychotherapy is Not a Spectator Sport': The Dissemination of Psychoanalysis from Freud to Orbach" at a conference on "Psychotherapy is a Cultural Issue: The Influence of Susie Orbach's Work on Theory, Practice and Values", sponsored by Confer of Woodbridge, Suffolk, and held at Foyles bookshop in London, on 22nd April, 2017, at the warm invitation of Jane Ryan. This essay appears here in print for the very first time.

Chapter 11: "I think analysts are not very good as broadcasters": Donald Winnicott's Contribution to Media Psychology

As I indicated in the section on original sources for Chapter 2 (see above), I presented some of my research on Dr. Donald Winnicott's work as a media psychologist to The Squiggle Foundation in London, on 12th May, 2007. Some years later, I delivered a more detailed account about Winnicott's radio transmission in a talk entitled, "The Roots of Mental Health Broadcasting", part of a workshop on "Donald Winnicott, the Public Psychoanalyst: Broadcasting Beyond the Consulting Room" – one of the breakout sessions of the international conference on "Donald Winnicott and the History of the Present: A Celebration of the Collected Works of D.W. Winnicott", sponsored by The Winnicott Trust, London, in association with the British Psychoanalytical Society, London, and the British Psychoanalytic Association, London, and, also, the Association of Independent Psychoanalysts, London, held at the Mary Ward House Conference and Exhibition Centre, in Holborn, London, on 21st November, 2015. I extend my thanks to Angela Joyce for the kind opportunity to participate. I also spoke about Winnicott's contributions to the media during my tribute to Dr. Susie Orbach, as indicated in the section on original sources for Chapter 10 (see above). A very abbreviated version of this material appeared in a chapter entitled, "The Public Psychoanalyst: Donald Winnicott as Broadcaster" (Kahr, 2018a) in a book edited by Angela Joyce (2018), *Donald W. Winnicott and the History of the Present: Understanding the Man and His Work*, published by Karnac Books of London. However, the bulk of this chapter appears here in print for the very first time, based, predominantly, on my archival research.

Conclusion: The Future of Media Psychoanalysis

This material appears here in print for the very first time.

Acknowledgements

I owe my greatest thanks to Professor Caroline Bainbridge and Professor Candida Yates – two truly cherished colleagues who, through their own scholarship and through their joint creation of a unique research network – have pioneered the development of psychosocial studies and applied psychoanalysis in the most welcoming of ways.

In 2009, Caroline and Candida founded Media and the Inner World – a remarkable project, funded by the Arts and Humanities Research Council – and sponsored jointly by Roehampton University (later the University of Roehampton), London, and by the University of East London, London, and, more recently, by Bournemouth University, in Ferne Barrow, Poole, Dorset. I had the great privilege of participating as a speaker at the inaugural event of this exciting project, held at Grove House in Roehampton University in South West London, on 7th March, 2009.

Media and the Inner World has flourished greatly over the last decade and more and has become a remarkable venture in which academics, psychoanalytical mental health professionals, and cultural practitioners have all joined forces to explore the deeper unconscious meanings of both popular culture and classical culture, bringing together fine minds and collaborative souls who have the opportunity to communicate with one another in these shared spaces, exchanging rich ideas and decades of experience. As hosts, Caroline and Candida have always proved to be supremely gracious and warmly facilitating to colleagues from all disciplines and all backgrounds, and they have helped to provide a fuller and richer understanding of the meaning and the implications of our psychosocial preoccupations.

I regard myself as quite fortunate to have served as either a speaker or as a chairperson at approximately fifteen Media and the Inner World events since its inception and I have smiled with delight at the wonderful ways in which Professor Bainbridge and Professor Yates have developed their model of psychosocial studies and applied psychoanalysis so refreshingly, forging a warm and stimulating community of people.

Bainbridge and Yates have tackled virtually every subject imaginable, ranging from literature and politics and sexuality, to film and radio and television, and to other topics such as comedy and music and theatre.

I shall never forget the remarkable symposium on "Comedy and Psychoanalysis", held at the Jermyn Street Theatre, just off of Piccadilly Circus in London, on 9th July, 2010, co-sponsored by the entertainment agency, John Noel Management, in which several mental health workers (myself included), teamed up with distinguished academics as well as practising comedians, to explore the unconscious nature of humour and its function in society. I had the pleasant and amusing experience of interviewing three young comedians on stage – Tom Davis, Michelle de Swarte, and Dan Schreiber – as we discussed "The Freudian Approach to Comedy". Two years later, on 21st June, 2012, I participated in another Media and the Inner World panel discussion, held at the Royal Academy of Music in London, after the audience had had the pleasure of watching a student production of the classic 1968 Broadway musical *Promises, Promises.* Rarely do stodgy mental health workers and virtuous academics have the opportunity to enjoy such playful and creative conversations with comedians and musical theatre performers, but, thanks to Caroline and Candida, those of us who live and work in London have had the unique joy of developing partnerships across all of these disciplines.

Media and the Inner World has functioned as a leaping-off point for the creation of many other fruitful projects from Bainbridge and Yates, not least, the inauguration of the set of monographs in which this title appears, namely, the "Psychoanalysis and Popular Culture Series", which these two women have curated so impressively over a number of years.

My gratitude to Professor Caroline Bainbridge and Professor Candida Yates remains eternal and I regard these two inspiring colleagues as the very epitome of original thinking in the development of media psychoanalysis, bringing deeper psychological understanding to every aspect of our lives, whether culture, politics, or basic survival. Thus, I take great pride in sharing this volume of essays in the "Psychoanalysis and Popular Culture Series".

I also wish to express my deep thanks to the publishing team. Oliver Rathbone commissioned this title under the aegis of Karnac Books of London, assisted by his colleagues, Constance Govindin and Dr. Rod Tweedy. Upon Mr. Rathbone's retirement as publisher, I received warm support from many members of the editorial team at Routledge / Taylor and Francis Group in London, and in Abingdon, Oxfordshire, most especially Susannah Frearson, for having kindly steered this project through production. Ms. Frearson has proved the most gracious and professional and collaborative of mental health editors and publishers and I extend my warmest appreciation to her for having facilitated this project in such a pleasant and intelligent manner. I have learned a great deal from her publishing wisdom. I also owe much gratitude to Ms. Frearson's helpful colleagues (present and past), especially Jana Craddock, Ellie Duncan, Russell George, Dr. Elliott Morsia, Alexis O'Brien, Saloni Singhania, and Alec Selwyn, for their kind assistance and encouragement. Furthermore, I convey my deepest appreciation to Nick Craggs, the Senior Production Editor at Routledge, for his kind facilitation of the process, and to Pamela Bertram, the most meticulous and pleasant of copyeditors, for their vital contributions.

As ever, I offer my deepest gratitude and affection to all of my colleagues who have encouraged me and educated me over the years. And I thank my family and friends for their love and support and for providing a secure base.

References

Abraham, Hilda C. (1953). Twin Relationship and Womb Fantasies in a Case of Anxiety Hysteria. *International Journal of Psycho-Analysis*, *34*, 219–227.
Aichhorn, Thomas (1995). Personal Communication to Carol Ascher. n.d. October. Cited in Carol Ascher (2003). The Force of Ideas, p. 169, n. 46. *Luzifer-Amor, 16*, Number *32*, 150–169.
Alcock, Theodora (1963). *The Rorschach in Practice*. London: Tavistock Publications.
Allen, Malcolm (2011). The Hard Choices That Lie Ahead. *New Associations*, Number *6*, p. 1.
Anduaga, Aitor (2009). *Wireless and Empire: Geopolitics, Radio Industry, and Ionosphere in the British Empire, 1918–1939*. Oxford: Oxford University Press.
Anonymous (1901). The Death of the Queen. *The Times*. 25th January, pp. 8–9.
Anonymous (1905). The New American Ambassador: Arrival of Mr. Whitelaw Reid. *The Times*. 5th June, p. 8.
Anonymous (1927). Proceedings of the British Psychological Society. *British Journal of Psychology: General Section, 17*, 266.
Anonymous [Ernest Jones] (1932a). What is Psycho-Analysis? *The Listener*. 30th November, pp. 785–786.
Anonymous [Ernest Jones] (1932b). The Power of the Unconscious. *The Listener*. 7th December, pp. 818–819.
Anonymous [Ernest Jones] (1932c). Have Dreams a Meaning? *The Listener*. 14th December, pp. 850–852.
Anonymous (1943a). Sir Robert Armstrong-Jones, C.B.E., M.D., F.R.C.P., F.R.C.S. *British Medical Journal*. 6th February, p. 175.
Anonymous (1943b). Robert Armstrong-Jones KT, CBE, MD LOND., DSC WALES, FRCP, FRCS. *The Lancet*. 6th February, p. 189.
Anonymous (1955). Thomas Jeeves Horder. Baron Horder of Ashford Bt., G.C.V.O., M.D., B.Sc. Lond., D.C.L., F.R.C.P. *The Lancet*. 20th August, pp. 397–400.
Anonymous (1957). Early Environment. *Times Literary Supplement*. 5th July, p. 417.
Anonymous (1965a). Members One of Another. *Times Literary Supplement*. 7th October, p. 897.
Anonymous (1965b). Growing Up Absurd. *Times Literary Supplement*. 2nd December, p. 1107.
Anonymous (1969). The Directorate of Public Relations. *President's News Bulletin: The British Psycho-Analytical Society and the Institute of Psycho-Analysis*, Number *14*, pp. 10–11.

Anonymous (1971). Between the Thumb and the Teddy-Bear: The Psychology of Infancy. *Times Literary Supplement.* 17th December, pp. 1579–1580.

Anonymous (1972). Therapy without Mystery. *T.L.S.: Essays and Reviews from* The Times Literary Supplement. *1971, 10,* 221–227. London: Oxford University Press.

Anonymous (2020a). Weekly TV Set Viewing Summary (Jan 2010 – Jan 2020). BARB. Broadcasters' Audience Research Board. [https://www.barb.co.uk/viewing-data/weekly-viewing-summary/; accessed on 25th December, 2020].

Anonymous (2020b). Lockdown Leads to Surge in TV Screen Time and Streaming. 5th August. Ofcom [Office of Communications]. [https://www.ofcom.org.uk/about-ofcom/latest/media/media-releases/2020/lockdown-leads-to-surge-in-tv-screen-time-and-streaming; accessed on 6th July, 2021].

Anonymous (2020c). inTreatment. HBO [Home Box Office]. [https://www.hbo.com/in-treatment; accessed on 25th December, 2020].

Anonymous (2021a). Media Nations 2021: Interactive Report. Ofcom [Office of Communications]. [https://www.ofcom.org.uk/research-and-data/tv-radio-and-on-demand/media-nations-reports/media-nations-2021/interactive-report; accessed on 2nd September, 2021].

Anonymous (2021b). Online Nation: 2021 Report. Ofcom [Office of Communications]. [https://www.ofcom.org.uk/__data/assets/pdf_file/0013/220414/online-nation-2021-report.pdf; accessed on 2nd September, 2021].

Anonymous [Ernest Jones], and Burt, Cyril (1932). Reason and Emotion. *The Listener.* 28th December, pp. 930–931.

Armstrong-Jones, Robert (1917). Dreams and Their Interpretation. *The Practitioner.* March, pp. 201–219.

Avery, Todd (2006). *Radio Modernism: Literature, Ethics, and the BBC, 1922–1938.* Aldershot, Hampshire: Ashgate Publishing.

Ayling, Stanley (1979). *John Wesley.* London: William Collins and Sons.

Baatz, Simon (2008). *For the Thrill of It: Leopold, Loeb, and the Murder that Shocked Chicago.* New York: Harper/HarperCollins Publishers.

Baddeley, Alan (1982). *Your Memory: A User's Guide.* London: Sidgwick and Jackson/Multimedia Publications (UK).

Baddeley, Alan (2004). *Your Memory: A User's Guide. New Illustrated Edition.* London: Carlton Books.

Bagenal, Hope (1942). *Practical Acoustics and Planning Against Noise.* London: Methuen and Company.

Baily, Lionel (1973). *Gilbert and Sullivan and Their World.* London: Thames and Hudson.

Bainbridge, Caroline (2010). Lecture on "Psychotherapy on the Couch: Exploring the Fantasies of In Treatment". Conference on "Remote Control: Psychoanalysis and Television". Freud Museum, Swiss Cottage, London, and Media and the Inner World Network, Arts and Humanities Research Council Research Network, School of Arts, Roehampton University, London, and Psychosocial Studies Field, School of Humanities and Social Sciences, University of East London, London, at the Anna Freud Centre, Swiss Cottage, London. 30th October.

Bainbridge, Caroline (2012). Psychotherapy on the Couch: Exploring the Fantasies of *In Treatment. Psychoanalysis, Culture and Society, 17,* 153–168.

Bainbridge, Caroline (2014a). 'Cinematic Screaming' or 'All About My Mother': Lars von Trier's Cinematic Extremism as Therapeutic Encounter. In Caroline

Bainbridge and Candida Yates (Eds.). *Media and the Inner World: Psycho-cultural Approaches to Emotion, Media and Popular Culture*, pp. 53–68. Houndmills, Basingstoke, Hampshire: Palgrave Macmillan/Macmillan Publishers.

Bainbridge, Caroline (2014b). Psychotherapy on the Couch: Exploring the Fantasies of *In Treatment*. In Caroline Bainbridge, Ivan Ward, and Candida Yates (Eds.). *Television and Psychoanalysis: Psycho-Cultural Perspectives*, pp. 47–65. London: Karnac Books.

Bainbridge, Caroline (2019a). Box-set Mind-set: Psycho-cultural Approaches to Binge Watching, Gender, and Digital Experience. *Free Associations*, Number 75, 65–83. Free Associations. [http://freeassociations.org.uk/FA_New/OJS/index.php/fa/article/view/253/304; accessed on 30th October, 2021].

Bainbridge, Caroline (2019b). Television as Psychical Object: *Mad Men* and the Value of Psychoanalysis for Television Scholarship. *Critical Studies in Television*, 14, 289–306.

Bainbridge, Caroline; Ward, Ivan, and Yates, Candida (Eds.). (2014). *Television and Psychoanalysis: Psycho-Cultural Perspectives*. London: Karnac Books.

Bainbridge, Caroline, and Yates, Candida (2007). Everything to Play for: Masculinity, Trauma and the Pleasures of DVD Technologies. In Caroline Bainbridge, Susannah Radstone, Michael Rustin, and Candida Yates (Eds.). *Culture and the Unconscious*, pp. 107–122. Houndmills, Basingstoke, Hampshire: Palgrave Macmillan/Palgrave Macmillan Division of St. Martin's Press.

Bainbridge, Caroline, and Yates, Candida (2014). *Media and the Inner World: Psycho-cultural Approaches to Emotion, Media and Popular Culture*. Houndmills, Basingstoke, Hampshire: Palgrave Macmillan/Macmillan Publishers.

Baker, Derek (1975). *Partnership in Excellence: A Late-Victorian Educational Venture. The Leys School, Cambridge. 1875–1975*. Cambridge: The Governors of the Leys School, Cambridge.

Baker, Frank (1970). *John Wesley and the Church of England*. London: Epworth Press.

Bantin, Florence (1952). Letter to Donald W. Winnicott. 16th March. PP/DWW/B/A/2. Donald Woods Winnicott Collection. Archives and Manuscripts, Rare Materials Room, Wellcome Library, Wellcome Collection, The Wellcome Building, London.

Barbas, Samantha (2001). *Movie Crazy: Fans, Stars, and the Cult of Celebrity*. New York: Palgrave.

Barker, Paul (1972). Introduction. In Paul Barker (Ed.). *One for Sorrow, Two for Joy: Ten Years of New Society*, pp. 11–21. London: George Allen and Unwin.

Bates, Margaret (1950). Letter to Donald W. Winnicott. 6th June. PP/DWW/B/A/2. Donald Woods Winnicott Collection. Archives and Manuscripts, Rare Materials Room, Wellcome Library, Wellcome Collection, The Wellcome Building, London.

Bearn, Alexander G. (2008). *Sir Francis Richard Fraser, 1885–1964: A Canny Scot Shapes British Medicine*. Brighton, East Sussex: Book Guild Publishing.

Benzie, Isa D. (1946). Letter to Donald W. Winnicott. 25th November. PP/DWW/B/B/5/1. Donald Woods Winnicott Collection. Archives and Manuscripts, Rare Materials Room, Wellcome Library, Wellcome Collection, The Wellcome Building, London.

Benzie, Isa D. (1949a). Letter to Donald W. Winnicott. 25th January. PP/DWW/B/B/5/1. Donald Woods Winnicott Collection. Archives and Manuscripts, Rare

Materials Room, Wellcome Library, Wellcome Collection, The Wellcome Building, London.
Benzie, Isa D. (1949b). Letter to Donald W. Winnicott. 19th December. PP/DWW/B/B/5/1. Donald Woods Winnicott Collection. Archives and Manuscripts, Rare Materials Room, Wellcome Library, Wellcome Collection, The Wellcome Building, London.
Benzie, Isa D. (1952). Letter to Donald W. Winnicott. 24th June. PP/DWW/B/B/5/1. Donald Woods Winnicott Collection. Archives and Manuscripts, Rare Materials Room, Wellcome Library, Wellcome Collection, The Wellcome Building, London.
Berenson, Mary (1934). Letter to Judith Berenson. 28th May. In Barbara Strachey and Jayne Samuels (Eds.). (1983). *Mary Berenson: A Self-Portrait from Her Letters and Diaries*, p. 294. London: Victor Gollancz.
Bergmann, Maria V. (1997). Creative Work, Work Inhibitions and Their Relation to Internal Objects. In Charles W. Socarides and Selma Kramer (Eds.). *Work and its Inhibitions: Psychoanalytic Essays*, pp. 191–207. Madison, Connecticut: International Universities Press.
Bergmann, Martin S. (1976). Notes on the History of Psychoanalytic Technique. In Martin S. Bergmann and Frank R. Hartman (Eds.). *The Evolution of Psychoanalytic Technique*, pp. 17–40. New York: Basic Books.
Bergmann, Martin S. (2004). Rethinking Dissidence and Change in the History of Psychoanalysis. In Martin S. Bergmann (Ed.). *Understanding Dissidence and Controversy in the History of Psychoanalysis*, pp. 1–109. New York: Other/Other Press.
Bernays, Edward L. (1965). *Biography of an Idea: Memoirs of Public Relations Counsel Edward L. Bernays*. New York: Simon & Schuster.
Bertin, Célia (1982a). *La Dernière Bonaparte*. Paris: Librairie Académique Perrin.
Bertin, Celia (1982b). *Marie Bonaparte: A Life*. San Diego, California: Helen and Kurt Woolf/Harcourt Brace Jovanovich, Publishers.
Bhandari, Lalit C. (1952). Letter to Donald W. Winnicott. 5th June. PP/DWW/B/A/2. Donald Woods Winnicott Collection. Archives and Manuscripts, Rare Materials Room, Wellcome Library, Wellcome Collection, The Wellcome Building, London.
Bijaoui, Rémy (1996). *Prisonniers et prisons de la Terreur*. Paris: Auzas Éditeurs Imago/Éditions Imago.
Blanning, Tim (2008). *The Triumph of Music: Composers, Musicians and Their Audiences, 1700 to the Present*. London: Allen Lane/Penguin Books, Penguin Group.
Bloch, Dorothy (1978). *"So the Witch Won't Eat Me": Fantasy and the Child's Fear of Infanticide*. Boston, Massachusetts: Houghton Mifflin Company.
Blount, William [Lord Mountjoy] (1509). Letter to Desiderius Erasmus. 27th May. In Desiderius Erasmus (1906). *Opus Epistolarvm Des. Erasmi Roterdami: Tom. I. 1484–1514*. Percy S. Allen (Ed.), pp. 449–452. Oxford: Typographeo Clarendoniano.
Blowers, Geoffrey (2004). Bingham Dai, Adolf Storfer, and the Tentative Beginnings of Psychoanalytic Culture in China: 1935–1941. *Psychoanalysis and History*, 6, 93–105.
Blum, Harold P. (1977). The Prototype of Preoedipal Reconstruction. *Journal of the American Psychoanalytic Association*, 25, 757–785.

Boitani, Piero (1984). *Chaucer and the Imaginary World of Fame.* Cambridge: D.S. Brewer, and Totowa, New Jersey: Barnes and Noble, and Woodbridge, Suffolk: Boydell and Brewer.
Bollas, Christopher; Davis, Madeleine, and Shepherd, Ray (1993). Editors' Preface. In Donald W. Winnicott. *Talking to Parents.* Clare Winnicott, Christopher Bollas, Madeleine Davis, and Ray Shepherd (Eds.), pp. xiii–xvi. Reading, Massachusetts: Addison-Wesley Publishing Company.
Bonaparte, Marie (1926). Diary Entry. 8th January. *Journal d'analyse.* Cited in Célia Bertin (1982). *La Dernière Bonaparte,* p. 259, fn. 2. Paris: Librairie Académique Perrin.
Boston, Mary (1994). Letter to the Author. 2nd October.
Boswell, Ronald (1949). Letter to Donald W. Winnicott. 21st December. PP/DWW/B/B/5/1. Donald Woods Winnicott Collection. Archives and Manuscripts, Rare Materials Room, Wellcome Library, Wellcome Collection, The Wellcome Building, London.
Bourget, Steve (2006). *Sex, Death, and Sacrifice in Moche Religion and Visual Culture.* Austin, Texas: University of Texas Press.
Bourget, Steve, and Jones, Kimberly L. (2008). Introduction. In Steve Bourget and Kimberly L. Jones (Eds.). *The Art and Archaeology of the Moche: An Ancient Andean Society of the Peruvian North Coast,* pp. ix–xiii. Austin, Texas: University of Texas Press.
Bousfield, Paul (1920). *The Elements of Practical Psycho-Analysis.* London: Kegan Paul, Trench, Trubner and Company, and New York: E.P. Dutton and Company.
Bousfield, Paul (1922). *The Elements of Practical Psycho-Analysis: Second Edition (Revised). With a Supplementary Chapter on* Principles of Thinking. London: Kegan Paul, Trench, Trubner and Company, and New York: E.P. Dutton and Company.
Bower, Thomas G.R. (1989). *The Rational Infant: Learning in Infancy.* New York: W.H. Freeman and Company.
Bowlby, John (1985). Notes on Members of the British Psychoanalytic Society, 1935–1945. PP/BOW/G.1/8. (Edward) John (Mostyn) Bowlby (1907–1990) Collection. Archives and Manuscripts, Rare Materials Room, Wellcome Library, Wellcome Collection, The Wellcome Building, London.
Bowlby, John, and Robertson, James (1953). A Two-Year-Old Goes to Hospital. *Proceedings of the Royal Society of Medicine, 46,* 425–426.
Boyle, Andrew (1972). *Only the Wind Will Listen: Reith of the BBC.* London: Hutchinson of London/Hutchinson and Company (Publishers).
Brailsford, Mabel Richmond (1954). *A Tale of Two Brothers: John and Charles Wesley.* London: Rupert Hart-Davis.
Branson, Noreen (1975). *Britain in the Nineteen Twenties.* London: Weidenfeld and Nicolson.
Braudy, Leo (1986). *The Frenzy of Renown: Fame and its History.* New York: Oxford University Press.
Breuer, Josef (1895). Beobachtung I. Frl. Anna O ... In Josef Breuer and Sigmund Freud. *Studien über Hysterie,* pp. 15–37. Vienna: Franz Deuticke.
Brian, Denis (1996). *Einstein: A Life.* New York: John Wiley and Sons.
Briggs, Asa (1985). *The BBC: The First Fifty Years.* Oxford: Oxford University Press.

Britton, Clare (1943). Letter to Donald W. Winnicott. 8th December. PP/DWW/L.4. Donald Woods Winnicott Collection. Archives and Manuscripts, Rare Materials Room, Wellcome Library, Wellcome Collection, The Wellcome Building, London.

Britton, Karl (1968). Letter to Donald W. Winnicott. 27th June. Box 7. File 1. Donald W. Winnicott Papers. Archives of Psychiatry, The Oskar Diethelm Library, The DeWitt Wallace Institute of Psychiatry: History, Policy, and the Arts, Department of Psychiatry, Joan and Sanford I. Weill Medical College, Cornell University, The New York Presbyterian Hospital, New York, New York, U.S.A.

Bronner, Andrea (2011). The Three Histories of the Vienna Psychoanalytic Society. In Peter Loewenberg and Nellie L. Thompson (Eds.). *100 Years of the IPA: The Centenary History of the International Psychoanalytical Association. 1910–2010. Evolution and Change*, pp. 9–24. London: International Psychoanalytical Association.

Brown, Jared (2006). *Moss Hart: A Prince of the Theatre. A Biography in Three Acts*. New York: Back Stage Books/Watson-Guptill Publications, V.N.U. Business Media.

Brown, Shelby (1991). *Late Carthaginian Child Sacrifice and Sacrificial Monuments in Their Mediterranean Context*. Sheffield: JSOT Press/Sheffield Academic Press.

Brown, William (1921). *Psychology and Psychotherapy*. London: Edward Arnold.

Brown, William (1922). *Suggestion and Mental Analysis: An Outline of the Theory and Practice of Mind Cure*. London: University of London Press.

Brown, William (1923). *Talks on Psychotherapy*. London: University of London Press.

Brown, William (Ed.). (1924). *Psychology and the Sciences*. London: A. and C. Black.

Brown, William (1926). *Mind and Personality: An Essay in Psychology and Philosophy*. London: University of London Press.

Brown, William (1929). *Science and Personality*. London: Oxford University Press/Humphrey Milford.

Brown, William (1936). *Mind, Medicine and Metaphysics: The Philosophy of a Physician*. London: Oxford University Press/Humphrey Milford.

Brown, William (1938). *Psychological Methods of Healing: An Introduction to Psychotherapy*. London: University of London Press.

Brown, William (1939). *War and Peace: Essays in Psychological Analysis*. London: Adam and Charles Black.

Bunin, Keith (2010). 'In Treatment': Writing from Life. *New Associations*, Number 4, p. 7.

Burlingham, Dorothy (1950). Letter to Donald W. Winnicott. 16th October. PP/DWW/C.1/2. Donald Woods Winnicott Collection. Archives and Manuscripts, Rare Materials Room, Wellcome Library, Wellcome Collection, The Wellcome Building, London.

Burt, Cyril (1932a). Studying the Minds of Others. *The Listener*. 16th November, pp. 713–714.

Burt, Cyril (1932b). Studying One's Own Mind. *The Listener*. 23rd November, pp. 742–743.

Burt, Cyril (1933a). How the Mind Works in the Adult: The Conscious Mind. In Cyril Burt, Ernest Jones, Emanuel Miller, and William Moodie. *How the Mind Works*. Cyril Burt (Ed.), pp. 17–58. London: George Allen and Unwin.

Burt, Cyril (1933b). How the Mind Works in Society. In Cyril Burt, Ernest Jones, Emanuel Miller, and William Moodie. *How the Mind Works*. Cyril Burt (Ed.), pp. 181–333. London: George Allen and Unwin.
Burt, Cyril; Jones, Ernest; Miller, Emanuel, and Moodie, William (1933). *How the Mind Works*. Cyril Burt (Ed.). London: George Allen and Unwin.
Bychowski, Gustav (1948). *Dictators and Disciples: From Caesar to Stalin. A Psychoanalytic Interpretation of History*. New York: International Universities Press.
Cameron, David (2010). PM Speech on Wellbeing: A Transcript of a Speech Given by the Prime Minister on Wellbeing on 25 November 2010. 25th November. Cabinet Office. Prime Minister's Office, 10 Downing Street. The Rt Hon David Cameron. GOV.UK. [https://www.gov.uk/government/speeches/pm-speech-on-wellbeing; accessed on 24th December, 2020].
Cameron, Laura, and Forrester, John (2000). Tansley's Psychoanalytic Network: An Episode Out of the Early History of Psychoanalysis in England. *Psychoanalysis and History*, 2, 189–256.
Caplan, Gerald (1950). Letter to John Rickman. 21st August. PP/DWW/B/A/4. Donald Woods Winnicott Collection. Archives and Manuscripts, Rare Materials Room, Wellcome Library, Wellcome Collection, The Wellcome Building, London.
Carr, Alan (2004). *Positive Psychology: The Science of Happiness and Human Strengths*. Hove, East Sussex: Brunner-Routledge/Taylor and Francis Group.
Chapman, James (2003). Do You Suffer from Celebrity Worship Syndrome? *Daily Mail*. 14th April, p. 25.
Chesmore, Stuart (1935). *Behind the Microphone*. London: Thomas Nelson and Sons.
Chodorkoff, Bernard, and Baxter, Seymour (1974). "Secrets of a Soul": An Early Psychoanalytic Film Venture. *American Imago*, 31, 319–334.
Churchill, Randolph (1955). Letter to Winston Churchill. n.d. In Martin Gilbert (1994). *In Search of Churchill: A Historian's Journey*, pp. 212–213. Hammersmith, London: HarperCollins Publishers.
Coe, Lewis (1996). *Wireless Radio: A Brief History*. Jefferson, North Carolina: McFarland and Company.
Conroy, Pat (1986). *The Prince of Tides*. Boston, Massachusetts: Houghton Mifflin Company.
Cook, Andrew (2005). *To Kill Rasputin: The Life and Death of Grigori Rasputin*. Brimscombe Port, Stroud, Gloucestershire: Tempus/Tempus Publishing.
Cooper, Judy (1993). *Speak of Me as I Am: The Life and Work of Masud Khan*. London: H. Karnac (Books).
Cotter, Angela (2011). Limping the Way to Wholeness: Wounded Feeling and Feeling Wounded. In Luke Hockley and Leslie Gardiner (Eds.). *House: The Wounded Healer on Television. Jungian and Post-Jungian Reflections*, pp. 101–115. Hove, East Sussex: Routledge/Taylor and Francis Group.
Coward, Noel (1941). *Blithe Spirit: An Improbable Farce in Three Acts*. Garden City, New York: Doubleday, Doran and Company.
Coward, Noël (1955). Sunday 31 July. In Noël Coward (1982). *The Noel Coward Diaries*. Graham Payn and Sheridan Morley (Eds.), p. 277. London: George Weidenfeld and Nicolson.

Coward, Noël (1958). Sunday 17 August. In Noël Coward (1982). *The Noel Coward Diaries*. Graham Payn and Sheridan Morley (Eds.), pp. 383–384. London: George Weidenfeld and Nicolson.
Coward, Noël (1965a). Wednesday 23 June. In Noël Coward (1982). *The Noel Coward Diaries*. Graham Payn and Sheridan Morley (Eds.), pp. 601–602. London: George Weidenfeld and Nicolson.
Coward, Noël (1965b). Sunday 4 July. In Noël Coward (1982). *The Noel Coward Diaries*. Graham Payn and Sheridan Morley (Eds.), pp. 602–603. London: George Weidenfeld and Nicolson.
Creak, E. Mildred (1949). Letter to Donald W. Winnicott. 5th October. PP/DWW/B/A/5. Donald Woods Winnicott Collection. Archives and Manuscripts, Rare Materials Room, Wellcome Library, Wellcome Collection, The Wellcome Building, London.
Crook, Tim (2004). British Broadcasting Corporation: BBC Radio Programming. In Christopher H. Sterling and Michael C. Keith (Eds.). *The Museum of Broadcast Communications Encyclopedia of Radio: Volume I. A–E*, pp. 216–222. New York: Fitzroy Dearborn/Taylor and Francis Group.
Daniell, David (1994). *William Tyndale: A Biography*. New Haven, Connecticut: Yale University Press.
Dann, Sophie (1950). Letter to Joyce Coles. 7th September. PP/DWW/B/A/6. Donald Woods Winnicott Collection. Archives and Manuscripts, Rare Materials Room, Wellcome Library, Wellcome Collection, The Wellcome Building, London.
Danto, Elizabeth Ann (1996). *A Historical Study of Freud's Writings on Free Clinics, Their Implementation in Post-World War I Berlin and Vienna, and Their Repudiation in America*. Ph.D. Dissertation. School of Social Work, New York University, New York, New York, U.S.A.
Danto, Elizabeth Ann (2005). *Freud's Free Clinics: Psychoanalysis and Social Justice, 1918–1938*. New York: Columbia University Press.
Davidson, Audrey (1997). Letter to the Author. 6th May.
de Mijolla, Alain (2010). *Freud et la France: 1885–1945*. Paris: Presses Universitaires de France.
deMause, Lloyd (1974). The Evolution of Childhood. In Lloyd deMause (Ed.). *The History of Childhood*, pp. 1–73. New York: Psychohistory Press.
deMause, Lloyd (1981). The Fetal Origins of History. *Journal of Psychohistory*, *9*, 1–89.
deMause, Lloyd (1982). *Foundations of Psychohistory*, New York: Creative Roots.
deMause, Lloyd (1990). The History of Child Assault. *Journal of Psychohistory*, *18*, 1–29.
deMause, Lloyd (1991). The Universality of Incest. *Journal of Psychohistory*, *19*, 123–164.
deMause, Lloyd (2002a). *The Emotional Life of Nations*. New York: Karnac.
deMause, Lloyd (2002b). The Personality of the Foetus. In Brett Kahr (Ed.). *The Legacy of Winnicott: Essays on Infant and Child Mental Health*, pp. 39–49. London: H. Karnac (Books), and New York: Other Press.
Deputation to the Ministry of Health, Ministry of Education and the Home Office: 21st October 1953 (1953). Typescript. PP/DWW/B/B/4. Donald Woods Winnicott

Collection. Archives and Manuscripts, Rare Materials Room, Wellcome Library, Wellcome Collection, The Wellcome Building, London.
Di Donna, Luca (2010). The Life and Work of Robert S. Wallerstein: A Conversation. *American Imago*, *67*, 617–658.
Dickens, Arthur G. (1959). *Lollards and Protestants in the Diocese of York: 1509–1558*. London: University of Hull/Oxford University Press.
Dicks, Henry V. (1970). *Fifty Years of the Tavistock Clinic*. London: Routledge and Kegan Paul.
Diderot, Denis (1765–1767). Correspondance avec Falconet. In Denis Diderot (1831). *Mémoires, correspondance et ouvrages inédits de Diderot, publiés d'après les manuscrits confiés, en mourant, par l'auteur à Grimm: Tome troisième*, pp. 197–459. Paris: Paulin, Libraire-Éditeur/Alexandre Mesnier, Libraire.
Diderot, Denis (1766). Letter to Étienne Maurice Falconet. n.d. February, pp. 210–268. In Denis Diderot (1765–1767). Correspondance avec Falconet. In Denis Diderot (1831). *Mémoires, correspondance et ouvrages inédits de Diderot, publiés d'après les manuscrits confiés, en mourant, par l'auteur à Grimm: Tome troisième*, pp. 197–459. Paris: Paulin, Libraire-Éditeur/Alexandre Mesnier, Libraire.
Diener, Ed, and Biswas-Diener, Robert (2008). *Happiness: Unlocking the Mysteries of Psychological Wealth*. Malden, Massachusetts: Blackwell Publishing.
Diliberto, Gioia (1987). *Debutante: The Story of Brenda Frazier*. New York: Alfred A. Knopf.
Dolto, Françoise (1977). *Lorsque l'enfant paraît*. Paris: Éditions du Seuil.
Dolto, Françoise (1989). *Autoportrait d'une psychanalyste: 1934–1988*. Alain Manier and Colette Manier (Eds.). Paris: Éditions du Seuil.
Donovan, Paul (1997). *All Our Todays: Forty Years of Radio 4's 'Today' Programme*. London: Jonathan Cape/Random House.
Donovan, Paul (2004). Benzie, Isa Donald (1902–1988). In H. Colin G. Matthew and Brian Harrison (Eds.). *Oxford Dictionary of National Biography: In Association with the British Academy. From the Earliest Times to the Year 2000. Volume 5. Belle-Blackman*, p. 313. Oxford: Oxford University Press.
Double, Duncan B. (2002). The History of Anti-Psychiatry: An Essay Review. *History of Psychiatry*, *13*, 231–236.
Double, Duncan B. (2006). Historical Perspectives on Anti-psychiatry. In Duncan B. Double (Ed.). *Critical Psychiatry: The Limits of Madness*, pp. 19–39. Houndmills, Basingstoke, Hampshire: Palgrave Macmillan.
Duarte, Isabel (2021). Working with Adolescents Virtually During the Covid-19 Period. *Attachment: New Directions in Psychotherapy and Relational Psychoanalysis*, *15*, 98–108.
Dunlop, Ian (1993). *Marie-Antoinette: A Portrait*. London: Sinclair-Stevenson/Reed Consumer Books.
Easterly, William (2011). The Happiness Wars. *The Lancet*. 30th April – 6th May, pp. 1483–1484.
Eigen, Michael (1984). Letter to Clare Winnicott. 2nd February. PP/DWW/H/3/1. Donald Woods Winnicott Collection. Archives and Manuscripts, Rare Materials Room, Wellcome Library, Wellcome Collection, The Wellcome Building, London.

Ekins, Richard (1994). Psychoanalysis, Cinema, and the Role of Film in the Psychoanalytic Process. In Richard Ekins and Ruth Freeman (Eds.). *Centres and Peripheries of Psychoanalysis: An Introduction to Psychoanalytic Studies*, pp. 193–213. London: H. Karnac (Books).

Ellesley, Sandra (2004). Eder, (Montague) David (1865–1936). In H. Colin G. Matthew and Brian Harrison (Eds.). *Oxford Dictionary of National Biography: In Association with the British Academy. From the Earliest Times to the Year 2000. Volume 17. Drysdale-Ekins*, pp. 694–695. Oxford: Oxford University Press.

Ellmann, Richard (1987). *Oscar Wilde*. London: Hamish Hamilton/Penguin Books.

Evans, Richard I. (1964). Jung and Freud. In Richard I. Evans. *Conversations with Carl Jung and Reactions from Ernest Jones*, pp. [25]–116. New York: Van Nostrand Reinhold Company.

Eysenck, Hans J. (1984). Lecture on "How Wrong Was Freud?". Oxford Psycho-Analytical Forum, Corpus Christi College, University of Oxford, Oxford, Oxfordshire, at the Department of Experimental Psychology, University of Oxford, Oxford, Oxfordshire. 30th April.

Eysenck, Hans J. (1985). *Decline and Fall of the Freudian Empire*. Harmondsworth, Middlesex: Viking/Penguin Books.

Eysenck, Hans J. (1990). *Rebel with a Cause*. London: W.H. Allen/W.H. Allen and Company.

Falzeder, Ernst (2012). "A Fat Wad of Dirty Pieces of Paper": Freud on America, Freud in America, Freud and America. In John Burnham (Ed.). *After Freud Left: A Century of Psychoanalysis in America*, pp. 85–109. Chicago, Illinois: University of Chicago Press.

Farber, Stephen, and Green, Marc (1993). *Hollywood on the Couch: A Candid Look at the Overheated Love Affair between Psychiatrists and Moviemakers*. New York: William Morrow and Company.

Farber, Stephen, and Green, Marc (n.d.). Interview with Arthur Penn. n.d. Cited in Stephen Farber and Marc Green (1993). *Hollywood on the Couch: A Candid Look at the Overheated Love Affair between Psychiatrists and Moviemakers*, p. 330. New York: William Morrow and Company.

Ferenczi, Sándor (1911). Letter to Sigmund Freud. 16th February. In Sigmund Freud and Sándor Ferenczi (1993). *Briefwechsel: Band I/1. 1908–1911*. Eva Brabant, Ernst Falzeder, Patrizia Giampieri-Deutsch, and André Haynal (Eds.), pp. 354–355. Vienna: Böhlau Verlag/Böhlau Verlag Gesellschaft.

Ferenczi, Sándor (1922). *Populäre Vorträge über Psychoanalyse*. Vienna: Internationaler Psychoanalytischer Verlag.

Fitter, Alastair H. (2010). Anthony David Bradshaw: 17 January 1926 – 21 August 2008. Elected FRS 1982. In Thomas Wilson Meade (Ed.). *Biographical Memoirs of Fellows of the Royal Society: 2010. Volume 56*, pp. 27–39. London: Royal Society.

Fleming, Michael, and Manvell, Roger (1985). *Images of Madness: The Portrayal of Insanity in the Feature Film*. Madison, New Jersey: Fairleigh Dickinson University Press, and Cranbury, New Jersey: Associated University Presses.

Flügel, John C. (1948). Professor J.C. Flugel's Summing-Up Given at the Final Session. *Preparatory Commissions Bulletin*, Number *11*, p. 3.

Fowles, Jib (1992). *Starstruck: Celebrity Performers and the American Public*. Washington, D.C.: Smithsonian Institution Press.

Fraser, Antonia (2001). *Marie Antoinette: The Journey*. London: Weidenfeld and Nicolson/Orion Publishing Group.
Freeman, John (1959). Interview. In John Freeman (1989). *Face to Face with John Freeman: Interviews from the BBC TV Series*, pp. 62–70. London: BBC Books, BBC Enterprises.
Freeman, Lucy (1951). *Fight Against Fears*. New York: Crown Publishers.
Freeman, Lucy (1986). Personal Communication to the Author. 24th September.
Freud, Martin (1957). *Glory Reflected: Sigmund Freud – Man and Father*. London: Angus and Robertson.
Freud, Sigmund (1875a). Letter to Eduard Silberstein. 9th September. In Sigmund Freud (1989). *Jugendbriefe an Eduard Silberstein: 1871–1881*. Walter Boehlich (Ed.), pp. 142–145. Frankfurt am Main: S. Fischer Verlag.
Freud, Sigmund (1875b). Letter to Eduard Silberstein. 9th September. In Sigmund Freud (1990). *The Letters of Sigmund Freud to Eduard Silberstein: 1871–1881*. Walter Boehlich (Ed.). Arnold J. Pomerans (Transl.), pp. 125–128. Cambridge, Massachusetts: Belknap Press of Harvard University Press.
Freud, Sigmund (1900). *Die Traumdeutung*. Vienna: Franz Deuticke.
Freud, Sigmund (1909a). Untitled Contribution. [Page-Heading Titles: Die Ablösung des Kindes von den Eltern; Die Familienromane der Neurotiker; Die neurotischen Phantasien von hoher Abkunft; Deutung und Rechtfertigung dieser Phantasien; Der Familienroman wird]. In Otto Rank. *Der Mythus von der Geburt des Helden: Versuch einer psychologischen Mythendeutung*, pp. 64–68. Vienna: Franz Deuticke.
Freud, Sigmund (1909b). Family Romances. James Strachey (Transl.). In Sigmund Freud (1950). *Collected Papers: Volume V.* James Strachey (Ed.), pp. 74–78. London: Hogarth Press and the Institute of Psycho-Analysis.
Freud, Sigmund (1909c). Family Romances. In Sigmund Freud (1959). *The Standard Edition of the Complete Psychological Works of Sigmund Freud: Volume IX (1906–1908). Jensen's 'Gradiva' and Other Works*. James Strachey, Anna Freud, Alix Strachey, and Alan Tyson (Eds. and Transls.), pp. 237–241. London: Hogarth Press and the Institute of Psycho-Analysis.
Freud, Sigmund (1918a). Aus der Geschichte einer infantilen Neurose. In *Sammlung kleiner Schriften zur Neurosenlehre: Vierte Folge*, pp. 578–717. Vienna: Hugo Heller und Compagnie.
Freud, Sigmund (1918b). From the History of an Infantile Neurosis. Alix Strachey and James Strachey (Transls.). In Sigmund Freud (1955). *The Standard Edition of the Complete Psychological Works of Sigmund Freud: Volume XVII. (1917–1919). An Infantile Neurosis and Other Works*. James Strachey, Anna Freud, Alix Strachey, and Alan Tyson (Eds. and Transls.), pp. 7–122. London: Hogarth Press and the Institute of Psycho-Analysis.
Freud, Sigmund (1920a). Letter to Karl Abraham. 6th January. In Sigmund Freud and Karl Abraham (1965). *Briefe: 1907–1926*. Hilda C. Abraham and Ernst L. Freud (Eds.), pp. 281–282. Frankfurt am Main: S. Fischer Verlag.
Freud, Sigmund (1920b). Letter to Karl Abraham. 6th January. In Sigmund Freud and Karl Abraham (2002). *The Complete Correspondence of Sigmund Freud and Karl Abraham: 1907–1925. Completed Edition*. Ernst Falzeder (Ed.). Caroline Schwarzacher, Christine Trollope, and Klara Majthényi King (Transls.), pp. 415–416. London: H. Karnac (Books)/Other Press.

Freud, Sigmund (1921). Letter to Ernest Jones. 12th April. In Sigmund Freud and Ernest Jones (1993). *The Complete Correspondence of Sigmund Freud and Ernest Jones: 1908–1939*. R. Andrew Paskauskas (Ed.). Frauke Voss (Transl.), pp. 418–419. Cambridge, Massachusetts: Belknap Press of Harvard University Press.

Freud, Sigmund (1924a). Letter to George Seldes. 29th June. In George Seldes (1953). *Tell the Truth and Run*, p. 107. New York: Greenberg: Publisher.

Freud, Sigmund (1924b). Letter to George Seldes. 29th June. In Ernest Jones (1957). *The Life and Work of Sigmund Freud: Volume 3. The Last Phase. 1919–1939*, p. 103. New York: Basic Books.

Freud, Sigmund (1925a). Letter to Karl Abraham. 9th June. In Sigmund Freud and Karl Abraham (2009). *Briefwechsel 1907–1925: Vollständige Ausgabe. Band 2: 1915–1925*. Ernst Falzeder and Ludger M. Hermanns (Eds.), pp. 823–824. Vienna: Verlag Turia und Kant.

Freud, Sigmund (1925b). Letter to Karl Abraham. 9th June. In Sigmund Freud and Karl Abraham (2002). *The Complete Correspondence of Sigmund and Karl Abraham: 1907–1925. Completed Edition*. Ernst Falzeder (Ed.). Caroline Schwarzacher, Christine Trollope, and Klara Majthényi King (Transls.), pp. 546–547. London: H. Karnac (Books)/Other Press.

Freud, Sigmund (1925c). Letter to Ernst Simmel. 26th October, p. 99. In Frances Deri and David Brunswick (1964). Freud's Letters to Ernst Simmel. Frances Deri and David Brunswick (Transls.). *Journal of the American Psychoanalytic Association, 12*, 93–109.

Freud, Sigmund (1926a). *Hemmung, Symptom und Angst*. Vienna: Internationaler Psychoanalytischer Verlag.

Freud, Sigmund (1926b). *Inhibitions, Symptoms and Anxiety*. Alix Strachey and James Strachey (Transls.). In Sigmund Freud (1959). *The Standard Edition of the Complete Psychological Works of Sigmund Freud: Volume XX. (1925–1926). An Autobiographical Study, Inhibitions, Symptoms and Anxiety, The Question of Lay Analysis and Other Works*. James Strachey, Anna Freud, Alix Strachey, and Alan Tyson (Eds. and Transls.), pp. 87–172. London: Hogarth Press and the Institute of Psycho-Analysis.

Freud, Sigmund (1926c). *Die Frage der Laienanalyse: Unterredungen mit einem Unparteiischen*. Vienna: Internationaler Psychoanalytischer Verlag.

Freud, Sigmund (1926d). *The Question of Lay Analysis: Conversations with an Impartial Person*. James Strachey (Transl.). In Sigmund Freud (1959). *The Standard Edition of the Complete Psychological Works of Sigmund Freud: Volume XX. (1925–1926). An Autobiographical Study. Inhibitions, Symptoms and Anxiety. The Question of Lay Analysis and Other Works*. James Strachey, Anna Freud, Alix Strachey, and Alan Tyson (Eds. and Transls.), pp. 183–250. London: Hogarth Press and the Institute of Psycho-Analysis.

Freud, Sigmund (1926e). Letter to Sándor Radó. 11th February. In Paul Roazen (Ed.). (1995). Freud's Letters to Rado. Tom Taylor (Transl.), p. 159. In Paul Roazen and Bluma Swerdloff. *Heresy: Sandor Rado and the Psychoanalytic Movement*, pp. 151–173. Northvale, New Jersey: Jason Aronson.

Freud, Sigmund (1926f). Letter to Sándor Radó. 14th September. In Paul Roazen (Ed.). (1995). Freud's Letters to Rado. Tom Taylor (Transl.), p. 161. In Paul Roazen and Bluma Swerdloff. *Heresy: Sandor Rado and the Psychoanalytic Movement*, pp. 151–173. Northvale, New Jersey: Jason Aronson.

Freud, Sigmund (1930a). *Das Unbehagen in der Kultur.* Vienna: Internationaler Psychoanalytischer Verlag.
Freud, Sigmund (1930b). *Civilization and its Discontents.* Joan Riviere and James Strachey (Transls.). In Sigmund Freud (1961). *The Standard Edition of the Complete Psychological Works of Sigmund Freud: Volume XXI. (1927–1931). The Future of an Illusion. Civilization and its Discontents and Other Works.* James Strachey, Anna Freud, Alix Strachey, and Alan Tyson (Eds. and Transls.), pp. 64–145. London: Hogarth Press and the Institute of Psycho-Analysis.
Freud, Sigmund (1933a). *Neue Folge der Vorlesungen zur Einführung in die Psychoanalyse.* Vienna: Internationaler Psychoanalytischer Verlag.
Freud, Sigmund (1933b). *New Introductory Lectures on Psycho-Analysis.* James Strachey (Transl.). In Sigmund Freud (1964). *The Standard Edition of the Complete Psychological Works of Sigmund Freud: Volume XXII. (1932–36). New Introductory Lectures on Psycho-Analysis and Other Works.* James Strachey, Anna Freud, Alix Strachey, and Alan Tyson (Eds. and Transls.), pp. 5–182. London: Hogarth Press and the Institute of Psycho-Analysis.
Freud, Sigmund (1953a). *The Standard Edition of the Complete Psychological Works of Sigmund Freud: Volume IV. (1900). The Interpretation of Dreams. (First Part).* James Strachey, Anna Freud, Alix Strachey, and Alan Tyson (Eds. and Transls.). London: Hogarth Press and the Institute of Psycho-Analysis.
Freud, Sigmund (1953b). *The Standard Edition of the Complete Psychological Works of Sigmund Freud: Volume V. (1900–1901). The Interpretation of Dreams. (Second Part) and On Dreams.* James Strachey, Anna Freud, Alix Strachey, and Alan Tyson (Eds. and Transls.). London: Hogarth Press and the Institute of Psycho-Analysis.
Freud, Sigmund (1953c). *The Standard Edition of the Complete Psychological Works of Sigmund Freud: Volume VII. (1901–1905). A Case of Hysteria. Three Essays on Sexuality and Other Works.* James Strachey, Anna Freud, Alix Strachey, and Alan Tyson (Eds. and Transls.). London: Hogarth Press and the Institute of Psycho-Analysis.
Freud, Sigmund (1953d). *The Standard Edition of the Complete Psychological Works of Sigmund Freud: Volume XIII. (1913–1914). Totem and Taboo and Other Works.* James Strachey, Anna Freud, Alix Strachey, and Alan Tyson (Eds. and Transls.). London: Hogarth Press and the Institute of Psycho-Analysis.
Freud, Sigmund (1955a). *The Standard Edition of the Complete Psychological Works of Sigmund Freud: Volume II. (1893–1895). Studies on Hysteria.* James Strachey, Anna Freud, Alix Strachey, and Alan Tyson (Eds. and Transls.). London: Hogarth Press and the Institute of Psycho-Analysis.
Freud, Sigmund (1955b). *The Standard Edition of the Complete Psychological Works of Sigmund Freud: Volume X. (1909). Two Case Histories ('Little Hans' and the 'Rat Man').* James Strachey, Anna Freud, Alix Strachey, and Alan Tyson (Eds. and Transls.). London: Hogarth Press and the Institute of Psycho-Analysis.
Freud, Sigmund (1955c). *The Standard Edition of the Complete Psychological Works of Sigmund Freud: Volume XVII. (1917–1919). An Infantile Neurosis and Other Works.* James Strachey, Anna Freud, Alix Strachey, and Alan Tyson (Eds. and Transls.). London: Hogarth Press and the Institute of Psycho-Analysis.
Freud, Sigmund (1955d). *The Standard Edition of the Complete Psychological Works of Sigmund Freud: Volume XVIII. (1920–1922). Beyond the Pleasure Principle. Group Psychology and Other Works.* James Strachey, Anna Freud, Alix Strachey,

and Alan Tyson (Eds. and Transls.). London: Hogarth Press and the Institute of Psycho-Analysis.
Freud, Sigmund (1957a). *The Standard Edition of the Complete Psychological Works of Sigmund Freud: Volume XI. (1910). Five Lectures on Psycho-Analysis, Leonardo da Vinci and Other Works.* James Strachey, Anna Freud, Alix Strachey, and Alan Tyson (Eds. and Transls.). London: Hogarth Press and the Institute of Psycho-Analysis.
Freud, Sigmund (1957b). *The Standard Edition of the Complete Psychological Works of Sigmund Freud: Volume XIV. (1914–1916). On the History of the Psycho-Analytic Movement, Papers on Metapsychology and Other Works.* James Strachey, Anna Freud, Alix Strachey, and Alan Tyson (Eds. and Transls.). London: Hogarth Press and the Institute of Psycho-Analysis.
Freud, Sigmund (1958). *The Standard Edition of the Complete Psychological Works of Sigmund Freud: Volume XII. (1911–1913). The Case of Schreber. Papers on Technique and Other Works.* James Strachey, Anna Freud, Alix Strachey, and Alan Tyson (Eds. and Transls.). London: Hogarth Press and the Institute of Psycho-Analysis.
Freud, Sigmund (1959a). *The Standard Edition of the Complete Psychological Works of Sigmund Freud: Volume IX. (1906–1908). Jensen's 'Gradiva' and Other Works.* James Strachey, Anna Freud, Alix Strachey, and Alan Tyson (Eds. and Transls.). London: Hogarth Press and the Institute of Psycho-Analysis.
Freud, Sigmund (1959b). *The Standard Edition of the Complete Psychological Works of Sigmund Freud: Volume XX. (1925–1926). An Autobiographical Study, Inhibitions, Symptoms and Anxiety, The Question of Lay Analysis and Other Works.* James Strachey, Anna Freud, Alix Strachey, and Alan Tyson (Eds. and Transls.). London: Hogarth Press and the Institute of Psycho-Analysis.
Freud, Sigmund (1960a). *The Standard Edition of the Complete Psychological Works of Sigmund Freud: Volume VI. (1901). The Psychopathology of Everyday Life.* James Strachey, Anna Freud, Alix Strachey, and Alan Tyson (Eds. and Transls.). London: Hogarth Press and the Institute of Psycho-Analysis.
Freud, Sigmund (1960b). *The Standard Edition of the Complete Psychological Works of Sigmund Freud: Volume VIII. (1905). Jokes and Their Relation to the Unconscious.* James Strachey, Anna Freud, Alix Strachey, and Alan Tyson (Eds. and Transls.). London: Hogarth Press and the Institute of Psycho-Analysis.
Freud, Sigmund (1961a). *The Standard Edition of the Complete Psychological Works of Sigmund Freud: Volume XIX. (1923–1925). The Ego and the Id and Other Works.* James Strachey, Anna Freud, Alix Strachey, and Alan Tyson (Eds. and Transls.). London: Hogarth Press and the Institute of Psycho-Analysis.
Freud, Sigmund (1961b). *The Standard Edition of the Complete Psychological Works of Sigmund Freud: Volume XXI. (1927–1931). The Future of an Illusion. Civilization and its Discontents and Other Works.* James Strachey, Anna Freud, Alix Strachey, and Alan Tyson (Eds. and Transls.). London: Hogarth Press and the Institute of Psycho-Analysis.
Freud, Sigmund (1962). *The Standard Edition of the Complete Psychological Works of Sigmund Freud: Volume III. (1893–1899). Early Psycho-Analytic Publications.* James Strachey, Anna Freud, Alix Strachey, and Alan Tyson (Eds. and Transls.). London: Hogarth Press and the Institute of Psycho-Analysis.

Freud, Sigmund (1963a). *The Standard Edition of the Complete Psychological Works of Sigmund Freud: Volume XV. (1915–1916). Introductory Lectures on Psycho-Analysis. (Parts I and II)*. James Strachey, Anna Freud, Alix Strachey, and Alan Tyson (Eds. and Transls.). London: Hogarth Press and the Institute of Psycho-Analysis.

Freud, Sigmund (1963b). *The Standard Edition of the Complete Psychological Works of Sigmund Freud: Volume XVI. (1916–1917). Introductory Lectures on Psycho-Analysis. (Part III)*. James Strachey, Anna Freud, Alix Strachey, and Alan Tyson (Eds. and Transls.). London: Hogarth Press and the Institute of Psycho-Analysis.

Freud, Sigmund (1964a). *The Standard Edition of the Complete Psychological Works of Sigmund Freud: Volume XXII. (1932–36). New Introductory Lectures on Psycho-Analysis and Other Works*. James Strachey, Anna Freud, Alix Strachey, and Alan Tyson (Eds. and Transls.). London: Hogarth Press and the Institute of Psycho-Analysis.

Freud, Sigmund (1964b). *The Standard Edition of the Complete Psychological Works of Sigmund Freud: Volume XXIII. (1937–1939). Moses and Monotheism. An Outline of Psycho-Analysis and Other Works*. James Strachey, Anna Freud, Alix Strachey, and Alan Tyson (Eds. and Transls.). London: Hogarth Press and the Institute of Psycho-Analysis.

Freud, Sigmund (1966). *The Standard Edition of the Complete Psychological Works of Sigmund Freud: Volume I. (1886–1899). Pre-Psycho-Analytic Publications and Unpublished Drafts*. James Strachey, Anna Freud, Alix Strachey, and Alan Tyson (Eds. and Transls.). London: Hogarth Press and the Institute of Psycho-Analysis.

Freud, Sigmund (1974). *The Standard Edition of the Complete Psychological Works of Sigmund Freud: Volume XXIV. Indexes and Bibliographies*. James Strachey, Anna Freud, Alix Strachey, Alan Tyson, and Angela Richards (Eds.). London: Hogarth Press and the Institute of Psycho-Analysis.

Freud-Marlé, Lilly (2006). *Mein Onkel Sigmund Freud: Erinnerungen an eine große Familie*. Christfried Tögel (Ed.). Berlin: Aufbau-Verlag.

Friday, Nancy (1973). *My Secret Garden: Women's Sexual Fantasies*. New York: Trident Press/Simon & Schuster.

Friday, Nancy (1975). *Forbidden Flowers: More Women's Sexual Fantasies*. New York: Pocket Books.

Friday, Nancy (1980). *Men in Love: Men's Sexual Fantasies. The Triumph of Love Over Rage*. New York: Delacorte Press.

Friday, Nancy (1991). *Women on Top: How Real Life Has Changed Women's Sexual Fantasies*. New York: Simon & Schuster.

Friedman, Lawrence J. (1990). *Menninger: The Family and the Clinic*. New York: Alfred A. Knopf.

Fromm, Erich (1956). *The Art of Loving*. New York: Harper and Brothers Publishers.

Gabbard, Krin, and Gabbard, Glen O. (1987). *Psychiatry and the Cinema*. Chicago, Illinois: University of Chicago Press.

Gairdner, James (1908). *Lollardy and the Reformation in England: An Historical Survey. Vol. I*. London: Macmillan and Company.

Gaither, Catherine; Kent, Jonathan; Bethard, Jonathan; Vasquez, Victor, and Rosales, Teresa (2016). Precious Gifts: Mortuary Patterns and the Shift from Animal to Human Sacrifice at Santa Rita B in the Middle Chao Valley, Peru. In Haagen D. Klaus and Marla J. Toyne (Eds.). *Ritual Violence in the Ancient Andes: Reconstructing Sacrifice on the North Coast of Peru*, pp. 150–177. Austin, Texas: University of Texas Press.

Gardiner, Juliet (2005). *The Children's War: The Second World War Through the Eyes of the Children of Britain*. London: Portrait/Piatkus Books/Imperial War Museum.

Gibeault, Alain, and Gougoulis, Nicolas (2011). Psychoanalysis in France: The "Société Psychanalytique de Paris" and its Relation to the IPA. In Peter Loewenberg and Nellie L. Thompson (Eds.). *100 Years of the IPA: The Centenary History of the International Psychoanalytical Association. 1910–2010. Evolution and Change*, pp. 38–46. London: International Psychoanalytical Association.

Gibson, Hamilton B. (1981). *Hans Eysenck: The Man and His Work*. London: Peter Owen.

Gifford, George E., Jr. (Ed.). (1978). *Psychoanalysis, Psychotherapy, and the New England Medical Scene, 1894–1944*. New York: Science History Publications/U.S.A.

Gilbert, Daniel (2006). *Stumbling on Happiness*. London: Harper Press/HarperCollins Publishers.

Gilbert, Martin (1994). *In Search of Churchill: A Historian's Journey*. Hammersmith, London: HarperCollins Publishers.

Glover, Edward (1936). *The Dangers of Being Human*. London: George Allen and Unwin.

Glover, Edward (1945). Eder as Psycho-Analyst. In Joseph Burton Hobman (Ed.). *David Eder: Memoirs of a Modern Pioneer*, pp. 89–116. London: Victor Gollancz.

Godwin, Richard (2010). The 7/7 Bombers Were Just a Team of Dangerous Idiots. *Evening Standard*. 20th October, p. 15.

Gritten, David (2002). *Fame: Stripping Celebrity Bare*. London: Allen Lane/Penguin Books.

Grotjahn, Martin (1987). *My Favorite Patient: The Memoirs of a Psychoanalyst*. Frankfurt am Main: Verlag Peter Lang.

Guntrip, Harry (1951). *You and Your Nerves: A Simple Account of the Nature, Causes and Treatment of Nervous Illness*. London: George Allen and Unwin.

Hadfield, James A. (Ed.). (1935). *Psychology and Modern Problems*. London: University of London Press.

Hajkowski, Thomas (2010). *The BBC and National Identity in Britain, 1922–53*. Manchester: Manchester University Press.

Hale, Nathan G., Jr. (1971). *Freud and the Americans: The Beginnings of Psychoanalysis in the United States, 1876–1917*. New York: Oxford University Press.

Hale, Nathan G., Jr. (1995). *The Rise and Crisis of Psychoanalysis in the United States: Freud and the Americans, 1917–1985*. New York: Oxford University Press.

Hall, Edward (1548). *The Vnion of the Two Noble and Illustre Famelies of Lancastre & Yorke, Beeyng Long in Continual Discension for the Croune of This Noble Realme, with all the Actes Done in Bothe the Tymes of the Princes, Bothe of the One Linage and of the Other, Beginnyng at the Tyme of Kyng Henry the Fowerth, the First Aucthor of this Deuision, and so Succesfully Proceadyng to the Reigne of the High and Prudent Prince Kyng Henry the Eight, the Vndubitate Flower and Very Heire of Both the Sayd Linages*. In Edward Hall (1809). *Hall's Chronicle;*

Containing the History of England, During the Reign of Henry the Fourth, and the Succeeding Monarchs, to the End of the Reign of Henry the Eighth, in Which are Particularly Described the Manners and Customs of Those Periods: Carefully Collated with the Editions of 1548 and 1550. London: J. Johnson/F.C. and J. Rivington/T. Payne/Wilkie and Robson/Longman, Hurst, Rees and Orme/Cadell and Davies/J. Mawman.

Harrington, William, and Young, Peter (1978). *The 1945 Revolution*. London: Davis-Poynter.

Hart, Moss (1941). *Lady in the Dark*. New York: Random House.

Haslip, Joan (1987). *Marie Antoinette*. London: Weidenfeld and Nicolson/George Weidenfeld and Nicolson.

Hatcher, Jessamyn (2004). *Psychoanalysis and Everyday Life: The Popularization and Popular Use of Psychoanalysis in the United States, 1909–1935*. Ph.D. Dissertation. Department of English, Graduate School, Duke University, Durham, North Carolina, U.S.A.

Hayley, Thomas T.S. (1991). Thomas Forrest Main (1911–1990). *International Journal of Psycho-Analysis*, 72, 719–722.

Heaton, John M. (2006). From Anti-psychiatry to Critical Psychiatry. In Duncan B. Double (Ed.). *Critical Psychiatry: The Limits of Madness*, pp. 41–59. Houndmills, Basingstoke, Hampshire: Palgrave Macmillan.

Helmholz, Richard H. (1975). Infanticide in the Province of Canterbury During the Fifteenth Century. *History of Childhood Quarterly*, 2, 379–390.

Hensher, Philip (2003). Sell Sadie, Buy Zoe. G-2. *The Guardian*. 25th February, pp. 6–7.

Hillman, James, and Boer, Charles (Eds.). (1985). *Freud's Own Cookbook*. New York: Perennial Library/Harper and Row, Publishers.

Hitschmann, Eduard, and Rank, Otto (1911a). Vorschläge zur Regelung des Gästewesens: Erstattet vom Obmannstellvertreter und Schriftführer, p. 201. In Otto Rank (Ed.). Vortragsabend: Am 29. März 1911. In Herman Nunberg and Ernst Federn (Eds.). (1979). *Protokolle der Wiener Psychoanalytischen Vereinigung: Band III. 1910–1911*, pp. 200–208. Frankfurt am Main: S. Fischer/S. Fischer Verlag.

Hitschmann, Eduard, and Rank, Otto (1911b). *Suggestions for the Regulation of the Attendance of Guests*, p. 209. In Otto Rank (Ed.). Scientific Meeting on March 29, 1911. In Herman Nunberg and Ernst Federn (Eds.). *Minutes of the Vienna Psychoanalytic Society: Volume III: 1910–1911*. Margarethe Nunberg and Harold Collins (Transls.), pp. 208–216. New York: International Universities Press.

Hobman, Joseph Burton (1945a). An Introductory Sketch. In Joseph Burton Hobman (Ed.). *David Eder: Memoirs of a Modern Pioneer*, pp. 11–31. London: Victor Gollancz.

Hobman, Joseph Burton (1945b). Social and Medical Pioneer. In Joseph Burton Hobman (Ed.). *David Eder: Memoirs of a Modern Pioneer*, pp. 73–85. London: Victor Gollancz.

Hocquenghem, Anne Marie (2008). Sacrifices and Ceremonial Calendars in Societies of the Central Andes: A Reconsideration. In Steve Bourget and Kimberly L. Jones (Eds.). *The Art and Archaeology of the Moche: An Ancient Andean Society of the Peruvian North Coast*, pp. 23–42. Austin, Texas: University of Texas Press.

Hoggard, Liz (2005). *How to Be Happy*. London: BBC Books/BBC Worldwide.
Holden, Anthony (1999). *William Shakespeare: His Life and Work*. London: Little, Brown and Company/Little, Brown and Company (UK).
Homayounpour, Gohar (2012). *Doing Psychoanalysis in Tehran*. Cambridge, Massachusetts: MIT Press.
Hopkins, Linda (2006). *False Self: The Life of Masud Khan*. New York: Other Press.
Horder, Mervyn (1966). *The Little Genius: A Memoir of the First Lord Horder*. London: Gerald Duckworth and Company.
Horney, Karen (1939). *New Ways in Psychoanalysis*. New York: W.W. Norton & Company.
Horney, Karen (1942). *Self-Analysis*. New York: W.W. Norton & Company.
Horney, Karen (1945). *Our Inner Conflicts: A Constructive Theory of Neurosis*. New York: W.W. Norton & Company.
Horney, Karen (Ed.). (1946). *Are You Considering Psychoanalysis?* New York: W.W. Norton & Company.
Houghton, Geoff, and Houghton, Pat (2000). *Well-Regulated Minds and Improper Moments: A History of The Leys School*. Cambridge: The Governors of the Leys School, Cambridge.
Hunter, Doris, M. (1979). Helen Ross: 1890–1978. *Psychoanalytic Quarterly, 48*, 465–469.
Institute Board Meetings: 16.1.1925 to 30.4.1945 (1925–1945). Archives of the British Psychoanalytical Society, British Psychoanalytical Society, Byron House, Maida Vale, London.
Isaacs, Susan (1932). *The Children We Teach: Seven to Eleven Years*. London: University of London Press.
Isaacs, Susan (1948). *Troubles of Children and Parents*. London: Methuen and Company.
Izod, John (2011). The Physician's Melancholia. In Luke Hockley and Leslie Gardiner (Eds.). *House: The Wounded Healer on Television. Jungian and Post-Jungian Reflections*, pp. 27–42. Hove, East Sussex: Routledge/Taylor and Francis Group.
Jackson, Carlton (1985). *Who Will Take Our Children?* London: Methuen/Methuen London.
James, Martin (1991). Letter to the Author. 24th November.
James, Oliver (2010). *How Not to F*** Them Up: The First Three Years*. London: Vermilion/Ebury Publishing/Random House Group.
Jones, Ernest (1910). The Oedipus-Complex as an Explanation of Hamlet's Mystery: A Study in Motive. *American Journal of Psychology, 21*, 72–113.
Jones, Ernest (1920). Preface. In Barbara Low. *Psycho-Analysis: A Brief Account of the Freudian Theory*, pp. 5–8. London: George Allen and Unwin.
Jones, Ernest (1924). The Relation Between Psycho-Analysis and Sociology. In Ernest Jones, James Glover, John C. Flügel, Montague David Eder, Barbara Low, and Ella Sharpe. *Social Aspects of Psycho-Analysis: Lectures Delivered Under the Auspices of the Sociological Society*. Ernest Jones (Ed.), pp. 8–41. London: Williams and Norgate.
Jones, Ernest (1933). The Unconscious Mind. In Cyril Burt, Ernest Jones, Emanuel Miller, and William Moodie. *How the Mind Works*. Cyril Burt (Ed.), pp. 61–103. London: George Allen and Unwin.

Jones, Ernest (1934). Draft Letter to *The Times*. 18th December. Unpublished Letter. G13/BD/009. Ernest Jones Collection. Archives of the British Psychoanalytical Society, British Psychoanalytical Society, Byron House, Maida Vale, London. Cited in Richard Overy (2009). *The Morbid Age: Britain Between the Wars*, p. 421, n. 101. London: Allen Lane/Penguin Books, Penguin Group.

Jones, Ernest (1936). M.D. Eder: 1866–1936. *International Journal of Psycho-Analysis*, *17*, 143–146.

Jones, Ernest (1944). Letter to Donald W. Winnicott. 26th January. PP/DWW/B/A/16. Donald Woods Winnicott Collection. Archives and Manuscripts, Rare Materials Room, Wellcome Library, Wellcome Collection, The Wellcome Building, London.

Jones, Ernest (1947). Introduction: The Problem of Hamlet and the Oedipus-Complex. In William Shakespeare. *Hamlet*, pp. 7–42. London: Vision Press.

Jones, Ernest (1949). *Hamlet and Oedipus*. London: Victor Gollancz.

Jones, Ernest (1955). *The Life and Work of Sigmund Freud: Volume 2. Years of Maturity. 1901–1919*. New York: Basic Books.

Jones, Ernest (1957). *The Life and Work of Sigmund Freud: Volume 3. The Last Phase. 1919–1939*. New York: Basic Books.

Jones, Mervyn, and Ferris, Paul (1959). *Dr. Ernest Jones: Portrait Assembled from Reminiscences of People Who Knew Him*. Radio Broadcast. 15th March. Tape T30130. B.B.C. Home Service. B.B.C. Sound Archives, National Sound Archives, London.

Joyce, Angela (Ed.). (2018). *Donald W. Winnicott and the History of the Present: Understanding the Man and His Work*. London: Karnac Books.

Kahr, Brett (1984). Interview with John Bowlby. 20th February.

Kahr, Brett (1991). The Sexual Molestation of Children: Historical Perspectives. *Journal of Psychohistory*, *19*, 191–214.

Kahr, Brett (1993). Ancient Infanticide and Modern Schizophrenia: The Clinical Uses of Psychohistorical Research. *Journal of Psychohistory*, *20*, 267–273.

Kahr, Brett (1994a). The Historical Foundations of Ritual Abuse: An Excavation of Ancient Infanticide. In Valerie Sinason (Ed.). *Treating Survivors of Satanist Abuse*, pp. 45–56. London: Routledge.

Kahr, Brett (1994b). A.P.P. Conference on Satanist Abuse: Psychodynamic Perspectives. 4th December 1993. *Bulletin of the Association of Child Psychotherapists*, *34*, 13–15.

Kahr, Brett (1994c). Child Abuse Has an Ancient History. *The Independent*. 2nd May, p. 19.

Kahr, Brett (1994d). Telephone Interview with Frances Tustin. 22nd February.

Kahr, Brett (1994e). Telephone Interview with Mary Boston. 28th September.

Kahr, Brett (1994f). Interview with Joyce Coles. 18th December.

Kahr, Brett (1996a). *D.W. Winnicott: A Biographical Portrait*. London: H. Karnac (Books).

Kahr, Brett (1996b). Donald Winnicott and the Foundations of Child Psychotherapy. *Journal of Child Psychotherapy*, *22*, 327–342.

Kahr, Brett (1996c). Foetal Trauma and National Disaster: A British Perspective. *Journal of Psychohistory*, *23*, 406–409.

Kahr, Brett (1996d). Book Review of Valerie Sinason (Ed.). *Treating Survivors of Satanist Abuse*. *Tavistock and Portman Gazette*, Autumn, pp. 69–70.

Kahr, Brett (1997). Book Review of Valerie Sinason (Ed.). *Treating Survivors of Satanist Abuse. Journal of Psychohistory, 24*, 417–421.

Kahr, Brett (1998). Listen and Lerner.... *The Stage.* 10th September, p. 11.

Kahr, Brett (1999a). The Adventures of a Psychotherapist: How to Write a Musical for Prince Charles in Six Months or Less. *Psychotherapy Review, 1*, 95–97.

Kahr, Brett (1999b). The Adventures of a Psychotherapist: Lucy Freeman and Her Fight Against Fear. *Psychotherapy Review, 1*, 199.

Kahr, Brett (1999c). The Adventures of a Psychotherapist: Lucy Freeman's Pioneering Contributions to the Study of Mental Health Journalism. *Psychotherapy Review, 1*, 244–248.

Kahr, Brett (2000). Psychoanalysis on Stage: Moss Hart's *Lady in the Dark. Psychoanalytic Review, 87*, 377–383.

Kahr, Brett (2001a). *Exhibitionism.* Duxford, Cambridge: Icon Books.

Kahr, Brett (Ed.). (2001b). *Forensic Psychotherapy and Psychopathology: Winnicottian Perspectives.* London: H. Karnac (Books), and New York: Other Press.

Kahr, Brett (2001c). Winnicott's Contribution to the Study of Dangerousness. In Brett Kahr (Ed.). *Forensic Psychotherapy and Psychopathology: Winnicottian Perspectives*, pp. 1–10. London: H. Karnac (Books), and New York: Other Press.

Kahr, Brett (2001d). The Legacy of Infanticide. *Journal of Psychohistory, 29*, 40–44.

Kahr, Brett (Ed.). (2002a). *The Legacy of Winnicott: Essays on Infant and Child Mental Health.* London: H. Karnac (Books), and New York: Other Press.

Kahr, Brett (2002b). Donald Woods Winnicott: The Cartographer of Infancy. In Brett Kahr (Ed.). *The Legacy of Winnicott: Essays on Infant and Child Mental Health*, pp. 1–10. London: H. Karnac (Books), and New York: Other Press.

Kahr, Brett (2002c). Multiple Personality Disorder and Schizophrenia: An Interview with Professor Flora Rheta Schreiber. In Valerie Sinason (Ed.). *Attachment, Trauma and Multiplicity: Working with Dissociative Identity Disorder*, pp. 240–264. London: Brunner-Routledge.

Kahr, Brett (2002d). Family Romance. In Edward Erwin (Ed.). *The Freud Encyclopedia: Theory, Therapy, and Culture*, pp. 187–188. New York: Routledge.

Kahr, Brett (2002e). Interview with Brendan MacCarthy. 24th July.

Kahr, Brett (2005a). On Practicing Therapy at 1:45 A.M. *American Imago, 62*, 125–131.

Kahr, Brett (2005b). On Practicing Therapy at 1.45 A.M. All About Psychotherapy: The Online Resource for Psychotherapy. [http://www.allaboutpsychotherapy.com].

Kahr, Brett (2005c). How to Make a Forty-Seven-Minute Television Program in Only Three Years. *American Imago, 62*, 483–491.

Kahr, Brett (2005d). Why Freud Turned Down $25,000: Mental Health Professionals in the Witness Box. *American Imago, 62*, 365–371.

Kahr, Brett (2005e). Lecture on "Why Freud Turned Down an Enormous Fee as an Expert Witness in a Sensational Murder Trial: Heroism and Anxiety in the Pioneers of Forensic Psychotherapy". Pre-Conference Address. Reception, Fourteenth Annual Conference, International Association for Forensic Psychotherapy, at the Davenport Hotel, Dublin, Ireland. 19th May.

Kahr, Brett (2006a). Filming Sexual Fantasies. *American Imago, 63*, 227–233.

Kahr, Brett (2006b). How to Make 120,000 People Happy in Just Ten Weeks. *American Imago*, *63*, 485–495.
Kahr, Brett (2007a). *Sex and the Psyche*. London: Allen Lane/Penguin Books, Penguin Group.
Kahr, Brett (2007b). Why Freud Turned Down $25,000. In Jane Ryan (Ed.). *Tales of Psychotherapy*, pp. 5–9. London: Karnac Books.
Kahr, Brett (2007c). The Infanticidal Attachment. *Attachment: New Directions in Psychotherapy and Relational Psychoanalysis*, *1*, 117–132.
Kahr, Brett (2007d). The Infanticidal Attachment in Schizophrenia and Dissociative Identity Disorder. *Attachment: New Directions in Psychotherapy and Relational Psychoanalysis*, *1*, 305–309.
Kahr, Brett (2007e). A Night at the Opera: The Freudians at Covent Garden. *American Imago*, *64*, 261–272.
Kahr, Brett (2007f). Lecture on "Can One Practice Therapy at 1.45 A.M. with 5,000,000 People Listening In?: Donald Winnicott and the Origins of Media Psychology". Public Lecture Programme 2006–2007. The Squiggle Foundation, Centre for Winnicottian Studies, London, at the Primrose Hill Community Centre, Primrose Hill, London. 12th May.
Kahr, Brett (2008a). *Who's Been Sleeping in Your Head?: The Secret World of Sexual Fantasies*. New York: Basic Books/Perseus Books Group.
Kahr, Brett (2008b). *Sex and the Psyche: The Truth About Our Most Secret Fantasies*. London: Penguin Press.
Kahr, Brett (2009). Psychoanalysis and Sexpertise. In Christopher Clulow (Ed.). *Sex, Attachment, and Couple Psychotherapy: Psychoanalytic Perspectives*, pp. 1–23. London: Karnac Books.
Kahr, Brett (2010). Telephone Interview with Timothy Bentley. 5th August.
Kahr, Brett (2011a). Dr Paul Weston and the Bloodstained Couch. *International Journal of Psychoanalysis*, *92*, 1051–1058.
Kahr, Brett (2011b). Winnicott's *"Anni Horribiles"*: The Biographical Roots of "Hate in the Counter-Transference". *American Imago*, *68*, 173–211.
Kahr, Brett (2011c). John Carl Flügel: The Forgotten Pioneer of Couple and Family Psychoanalysis. *Couple and Family Psychoanalysis*, *1*, 167–173.
Kahr, Brett (2012a). The Infanticidal Origins of Psychosis: The Role of Trauma in Schizophrenia. In Judy Yellin and Kate White (Eds.). *Shattered States: Disorganised Attachment and its Repair. The John Bowlby Memorial Conference Monograph 2007*, pp. 7–126. London: Karnac Books.
Kahr, Brett (2012b). Le Divan taché de sang du Dr Paul Weston. Marcel Hudon (Transl.). In Louis Brunet, Jean-Michel Quinodoz, Pierre Dajez, Danielle Goldstein, François Gross, Florence Guignard, Céline Gür, Marcel Hudon, Luc Magnenat, Diana Messina Pizzuti, André Renaud, Michel Sanchez-Cardenas, and Patricia Waltz (Eds.). *L'Année psychanalytique internationale: 2012. Traduction en langue française d'un choix de textes publiés en 2011 dans* The International Journal of Psychoanalysis, pp. 199–210. Paris: Éditions In Press.
Kahr, Brett (Ed.). (2012c). Reminiscences by John Bowlby: Portraits of Colleagues, 1935–1945. (Previously Unpublished). *Attachment: New Directions in Psychotherapy and Relational Psychoanalysis*, *6*, 27–49.

Kahr, Brett (2013). Media Monasticism and Media Whoredom: The Uncomfortable Marriage Between Psychoanalysis and Public Exposure. Unpublished Typescript.

Kahr, Brett (2014). Television as Rorschach: The Unconscious Use of the Cathode Nipple. In Caroline Bainbridge, Ivan Ward, and Candida Yates (Eds.). *Television and Psychoanalysis: Psycho-Cultural Perspectives*, pp. 31–46. London: Karnac Books.

Kahr, Brett (2018a). The Public Psychoanalyst: Donald Winnicott as Broadcaster. In Angela Joyce (Ed.). *Donald W. Winnicott and the History of the Present: Understanding the Man and His Work*, pp. 111–121. London: Karnac Books.

Kahr, Brett (2018b). Lecture on "Castration Anxiety in Men Who Murder". Panel on "Criminal Minds". Seminar Series on "Spotlight on the Archive: Film and Psychoanalysis in Focus". *The International Journal of Psychoanalysis*, London, and Media and the Inner World, School of Arts, University of Roehampton, London, and Faculty of Media and Communication, Bournemouth University, Ferne Barrow, Poole, Dorset, at the Sigmund Freud Room, Institute of Psychoanalysis, Byron House, Maida Vale, London. 11th December.

Kahr, Brett (2019a). Penile Trauma and Genital Exhibitionism: From Castration Anxiety to Verbal Potency. *International Journal of Forensic Psychotherapy*, *1*, 93–108.

Kahr, Brett (2019b). The First Mrs Winnicott and the Second Mrs Winnicott: Does Psychoanalysis Facilitate Healthy Marital Choice? *Couple and Family Psychoanalysis*, *9*, 105–131.

Kahr, Brett (2019c). On Winnicott's Marriages: A Response. *Couple and Family Psychoanalysis*, *9*, 151–153.

Kahr, Brett (2020a). *Celebrity Mad: Why Otherwise Intelligent People Worship Fame*. London: Routledge/Taylor and Francis Group, and Abingdon, Oxfordshire: Routledge/Taylor and Francis Group.

Kahr, Brett (2020b). *On Practising Therapy at 1.45 A.M.: Adventures of a Clinician*. London: Routledge/Taylor and Francis Group, and Abingdon, Oxfordshire: Routledge/Taylor and Francis Group.

Kahr, Brett (2020c). The Woman Who Could Not Sing "Happy Birthday": Couple Psychoanalysis at the Baby Grand Piano. *Couple and Family Psychoanalysis*, *10*, 93–98.

Kahr, Brett (2020d). The Tavistock Institute of Medical Psychology, 1920–2020. *Couple and Family Psychoanalysis*, *10*, 173–178.

Kahr, Brett (2020e). Lecture on "How Freud Would Have Handled the Coronavirus: Lessons from a Beacon of Survival". Live-Streamed Talk/Online Webinar. Freud Museum London, Swiss Cottage, London. 19th June. [Via Zoom].

Kahr, Brett (2020f). Lecture on "How Donald Winnicott Survived the COVID of His Time". Anna Freud Centre Academic Faculty for Psychoanalytic Research, Anna Freud National Centre for Children and Families, The Kantor Centre of Excellence, King's Cross, London, and University College London, University of London, London. 30th June. [Via Zoom].

Kahr, Brett (2021a). *Freud's Pandemics: Surviving Global War, Spanish Flu, and the Nazis*. London: Karnac/Karnac Books, Confer.

Kahr, Brett (2021b). The Tavistock Institute of Medical Psychology, 1920–2020. In Margot Waddell and Sebastian Kraemer (Eds.). *The Tavistock Century: 2020 Vision*, pp. 61–66. Bicester, Oxfordshire: Phoenix Publishing House.

Kahr, Brett (2021c). "The Piggle Papers": An Archival Investigation, 1961–1977. In Corinne Masur (Ed.). *Finding the Piggle: Reconsidering D.W. Winnicott's Most Famous Child Case*, pp. 41–100. Bicester, Oxfordshire: Phoenix Publishing House.

Kahr, Brett (2021d). 'Zoom Psychoanalysis' in Old Vienna: How Freud Transformed His Career in 1919. Freud Museum London. [https://www.freud.org.uk/2021/05/06/zoom-psychoanalysis-in-old-vienna-how-freud-transformed-his-career-in-1919/].

Kahr, Brett (2021e). Lecture on "Donald Winnicott's Pandemics: Surviving the Spanish Flu of 1918 and the Hong Kong Flu of 1968". Evening Meeting Programme 2021. Wessex Psychotherapy Society, Horizon Centre Western Community Hospital Site, Southampton, Hampshire. 17th March. [Via Zoom].

Kahr, Brett (2021f). Lecture on "Winnicott's Pandemics: Surviving the Spanish Flu of 1918 and the Hong Kong Flu of 1968". Parallel Session, Breakout Room 1, Online Conference 2021. Conference on "Winnicott: A Present for the Future". The Winnicott Trust, London, in association with the Squiggle Foundation, Harrow, London, The Independent Psychoanalysis Trust, London, and the British Psychoanalytic Association, London. 25th September. [Via Zoom].

Kahr, Brett (2021g). Lecture on "Donald Winnicott's Pandemics: Surviving the Spanish Flu of 1918 and the Hong Kong Flu of 1968". Fall 2021. The Richardson History of Psychiatry Research Seminar. DeWitt Wallace Institute of Psychiatry: History, Policy, and the Arts, Department of Psychiatry, Joan and Sanford I. Weill Medical College, Cornell University, The New York Presbyterian Hospital, New York, New York, U.S.A. 17th November. [Via Zoom].

Kahr, Brett (2021–2022). 'Zoom Psychoanalysis' in Old Vienna: How Freud Transformed His Career in 1919. *Athene: Magazine 2021/2022*, pp. 10, 12–14.

Kanter, Joel (2004). Clare Winnicott: Her Life and Legacy. In Clare Winnicott. *Face to Face with Children: The Life and Work of Clare Winnicott*. Joel Kanter (Ed.), pp. 1–94. London: H. Karnac (Books).

Karpf, Anne (2014). Constructing and Addressing the 'Ordinary Devoted Mother'. *History Workshop Journal*, Number *78*, 82–106.

Kellum, Barbara A. (1974). Infanticide in England in the Later Middle Ages. *History of Childhood Quarterly*, *1*, 367–388.

Kernberg, Otto F. (1975). *Borderline Conditions and Pathological Narcissism*. New York: Jason Aronson.

King, F. Truby (1916). *The Expectant Mother, and Baby's First Month: Hints to Fathers and Mothers*. Wellington: Marcus F. Marks.

King, Greg (1990). *Empress Alexandra: (The Last Empress of Russia)*. New York: Atlantic International Publications.

King, Mary (1948). *Truby King: The Man*. London: George Allen and Unwin.

King, Pearl (1989). Activities of British Psychoanalysts During the Second World War and the Influence of Their Inter-Disciplinary Collaboration on the Development of Psychoanalysis in Great Britain. *International Review of Psycho-Analysis*, *16*, 15–33.

King, Pearl (2003). Introduction: The Rediscovery of John Rickman and His Work. In Pearl King (Ed.). *No Ordinary Psychoanalyst: The Exceptional Contributions of John Rickman*, pp. 1–68. London: H. Karnac (Books).

Kirsch, Thomas B. (2000). *The Jungians: A Comparative and Historical Perspective*. London: Routledge.

Klaus, Haagen D., and Shimada, Izumi (2016). Bodies and Blood: Middle Sicán Human Sacrifice in the Lambayeque Valley Complex (AD 900–1100). In Haagen D. Klaus and Marla J. Toyne (Eds.). *Ritual Violence in the Ancient Andes: Reconstructing Sacrifice on the North Coast of Peru*, pp. 120–149. Austin, Texas: University of Texas Press.

Klein, Melanie (1940). Mourning and its Relation to Manic-Depressive States. *International Journal of Psycho-Analysis, 21*, 125–153.

Klein, Melanie (1945). The Oedipus Complex in the Light of Early Anxieties. *International Journal of Psycho-Analysis, 26*, 11–33.

Klein, Melanie (1957). *Envy and Gratitude: A Study of Unconscious Sources.* London: Tavistock Publications.

Kohut, Heinz (1971). *The Analysis of the Self: A Systematic Approach to the Psychoanalytic Treatment of Narcissistic Personality Disorders.* New York: International Universities Press.

Kramer, Selma (1997). Work and its Inhibitions as Seen in Children and Adolescents. In Charles W. Socarides and Selma Kramer (Eds.). *Work and its Inhibitions: Psychoanalytic Essays*, pp. 159–179. Madison, Connecticut: International Universities Press.

Kris, Ernst; Speier, Hans; Axelrad, Sidney; Herma, Hans; Loeb, Janice; Paechter, Heinz, and White, Howard B. (1944). *German Radio Propaganda: Report on Home Broadcasting During the War.* New York: Oxford University Press.

Kubie, Lawrence S. (1962). Psychoanalysis and the American Scene. In Martin Wangh, Samuel Atkin, Edith L. Atkin, and David Kairys (Eds.). *Fruition of an Idea: Fifty Years of Psychoanalysis in New York*, pp. 62–76. New York: International Universities Press.

Kuhn, Philip (2002). "Romancing with a Wealth of Detail": Narratives of Ernest Jones's 1906 Trial for Indecent Assault. *Studies in Gender and Sexuality, 3*, 344–378.

Lacan, Jacques (1974). *Télévision.* Paris: Éditions du Seuil.

Laing, Ronald D. (1960). *The Divided Self: A Study of Sanity and Madness.* London: Tavistock Publications.

Laing, Ronald D. (1964). Is Schizophrenia a Disease? *International Journal of Social Psychiatry, 10*, 184–193.

Laing, Ronald D. (1968). Liberation by Orgasm. *New Society.* 28th March, pp. 464–465.

Laing, Ronald D. (1976). A Critique of Kallmann's and Slater's Genetic Theory of Schizophrenia. In Richard I. Evans. *Dialogue with R.D. Laing: The Man and His Ideas*, pp. 97–156. New York: E.P. Dutton and Company.

Laing, Ronald D. (1981). A Critique of Kallmann's and Slater's Genetic Theory of Schizophrenia. In Richard I. Evans. *Dialogue with R.D. Laing.* [Revised Edition], pp. 97–156. New York: Praeger Publishers/CBS Educational and Professional Publishing, Division of CBS.

Laing, Ronald D., and Esterson, Aaron (1964). *Sanity, Madness and the Family: Volume I. Families of Schizophrenics.* London: Tavistock Publications.

Langer, William L. (1974). Infanticide: A Historical Survey. *History of Childhood Quarterly, 1*, 353–365.

Laurents, Arthur (2000). *Original Story By: A Memoir of Broadway and Hollywood*. New York: Alfred A. Knopf.
Lawrie, Jean (1951). Letter to Donald W. Winnicott. 3rd May. PP/DWW/B/A/18. Donald Woods Winnicott Collection. Archives and Manuscripts, Rare Materials Room, Wellcome Library, Wellcome Collection, The Wellcome Building, London.
Layard, Richard (2005). *Happiness: Lessons from a New Science*. London: Allen Lane/Penguin Books, Penguin Group.
Layard, Richard, and Ward, George (2020). *Can We Be Happier?: Evidence and Ethics*. [London]: Pelican/Penguin Books/Pelican Books/Penguin Random House, Penguin Random House UK.
Le Rider, Jacques (1992). Une Interview retrouvée de Sigmund Freud (*Neue Freie Presse*, 14 août 1933). *Revue internationale d'histoire de la psychanalyse*, 5, 613–617.
Leader, Zachary (1991). *Writer's Block*. Baltimore, Maryland: Johns Hopkins University Press.
Lidz, Theodore (1973). *The Origin and Treatment of Schizophrenic Disorders*. New York: Basic Books.
Liebmann, Susanne (1977). Work. In Guy J. Manaster, Genevieve Painter, Danica Deutsch, and Betty Jane Overholt (Eds.). *Alfred Adler: As We Remember Him*, p. 65. n.p.: North American Society of Adlerian Psychology.
Linley, P. Alex; Joseph, Stephen; Harrington, Susan, and Wood, Alex M. (2006). Positive Psychology: Past, Present, and (Possible) Future. *Journal of Positive Psychology*, 1, 3–16.
Loughran, Cathy (2002). Life in the Flagship: Hitler's Bombs and Other Dramas Have Marked Eventful Times at Portman Place Where a New Broadcast Centre is Planned. *Ariel*. 30th April, p. 9.
Lumbroso, Daniela (2007). *Françoise Dolto: La Vie d'une femme libre*. Paris: Plon/Éditions Plon.
Lyman, Richard B., Jr. (1974). Barbarism and Religion: Late Roman and Early Medieval Childhood. In Lloyd deMause (Ed.). *The History of Childhood*, pp. 75–100. New York: Psychohistory Press.
MacCarthy, Brendan (2002). Personal Communication to the Author. 17th July.
MacCarthy, Brendan (2003). Personal Communication to the Author. 26th March.
MacCarthy, Brendan (2005). Personal Communication to the Author. 16th March.
MacCarthy, Fiona (2002). *Byron: Life and Legend*. London: John Murray/John Murray (Publishers).
Macfarlane, Aidan (1975). Olfaction in the Development of Social Preferences in the Human Neonate. In *Parent-Infant Interaction: Ciba Foundation Symposium 33 (New Series)*, pp. 103–113. Amsterdam: Elsevier/Excerpta Medica/North-Holland/Associated Scientific Publishers/American Elsevier.
MacGibbon, Jean (1997). *There's the Lighthouse: A Biography of Adrian Stephen*. London: James and James (Publishers).
Maddox, Brenda (2006). *Freud's Wizard: The Enigma of Ernest Jones*. London: John Murray (Publishers)/Hodder Headline.
Main, Agnes M. (1969). On Idealisation and Disillusion in Adolescence. In H. Sydney Klein (Ed.). *Sexuality and Aggression in Maturation: New Facets*, pp. 14–21. London: Baillière, Tindall and Cassell.

Makari, George (2008). *Revolution in Mind: The Creation of Psychoanalysis*. New York: Harper/HarperCollins Publishers.
Malcolm, Janet (1983). Annals of Scholarship: Trouble in the Archives – I. *The New Yorker*. 5th December, pp. 59–62, 65–66, 68, 73–74, 76, 79–80, 85–86, 89, 93–94, 98–101, 103–104, 106, 111–112, 114–132, 137–138, 141–142, 144, 149–152.
Malcolm, Janet (1984). *In the Freud Archives*. New York: Alfred A. Knopf.
Marx, Arthur (1976). *Goldwyn: A Biography of the Man Behind the Myth*. New York: W.W. Norton & Company.
Masson, Jeffrey Moussaieff (1984). *The Assault on Truth: Freud's Suppression of the Seduction Theory*. New York: Farrar, Straus and Giroux.
Mawson, Andrew (2008). *The Social Entrepreneur: Making Communities Work*. London: Atlantic Books/Grove/Atlantic, Grove Atlantic.
mcclung, bruce d. (2007). *Lady in the Dark: Biography of a Musical*. New York: Oxford University Press.
McCutcheon, Lynn E., Maltby, John; Houran, James, and Ashe, Diane D. (2004). *Celebrity Worshippers: Inside the Minds of Stargazers*. Baltimore, Maryland: PublishAmerica.
McLaughlin, Mary Martin (1974). Survivors and Surrogates: Children and Parents from the Ninth to the Thirteenth Centuries. In Lloyd deMause (Ed.). *The History of Childhood*, pp. 101–181. New York: Psychohistory Press.
McSheffrey, Shannon, and Tanner, Norman (Eds. and Transls.). (2003). *Lollards of Coventry: 1486–1522*. Cambridge: Cambridge University Press, and London: Royal Historical Society, University College London.
Menninger, Karl (1937). Letter to William C. Menninger, Charles F. Menninger, and John R. Stone. 27th February. In Karl Menninger (1988). *The Selected Correspondence of Karl A. Menninger, 1919–1945*. Howard J. Faulkner and Virginia D. Pruitt (Eds.), pp. 235–238. New Haven, Connecticut: Yale University Press.
Menninger, Karl (1973). *Sparks*. Lucy Freeman (Ed.). New York: Thomas Y. Crowell Company.
Menninger, Karl A. (1988). *The Selected Correspondence of Karl A. Menninger, 1919–1945*. Howard J. Faulkner and Virginia D. Pruitt (Eds.). New Haven, Connecticut: Yale University Press.
Miles, Richard (2010). *Carthage Must be Destroyed: The Rise and Fall of an Ancient Mediterranean Civilization*. London: Allen Lane/Penguin Books.
Miller, Alice (1988). *Der gemiedene Schlüssel*. Frankfurt am Main: Suhrkamp Verlag.
Miller, Emanuel (1933). How the Mind Works in the Child: Problems in the Development of the Child. In Cyril Burt, Ernest Jones, Emanuel Miller, and William Moodie. *How the Mind Works*. Cyril Burt (Ed.), pp. 107–156. London: George Allen and Unwin.
Miller, Hugh (2001). *More Secrets of the Dead*. London: Channel 4 Books/Macmillan Publishers.
Milner, Marion (1987). Personal Communication to the Author. 24th October.
Molnar, Michael (1992). 1934. In Sigmund Freud. *The Diary of Sigmund Freud: 1929–1939. A Record of the Final Decade*. Michael Molnar (Ed. and Transl.), pp. 165–177. New York: Charles Scribner's Sons, and Toronto: Maxwell Macmillan Canada, and New York: Maxwell Macmillan International, and New York:

Charles Scribner's Sons/Macmillan Publishing Company, Maxwell Communication Group of Companies, and Don Mills, Ontario: Maxwell Macmillan Canada.

Moore, Thomas (1833). *Letters and Journals of Lord Byron: With Notices of His Life. Vol. I.* Paris: Baudry's European Library.

Moore, Thomas (1838). *Life, Letters, and Journals of Lord Byron: Complete in One Volume. With Notes.* London: John Murray.

Morse, Arthur H. (1925). *Radio: Beam and Broadcast. Its Story and Patents.* London: Ernest Benn.

Mullen, Paul E., James, David V., Meloy, J. Reid; Pathé, Michele T., Farnham, Frank R., Preston, Lulu; Darnley, Brian, and Berman, Jeremy (2009). The Fixated and the Pursuit of Public Figures. *Journal of Forensic Psychiatry and Psychology, 20,* 33–47.

Norman, Philip (2008). *John Lennon: The Life.* Hammersmith, London: HarperCollins Publishers.

Olinick, Stanley L. (1997). On Writer's Block: For Whom Does One Write or Not Write? In Charles W. Socarides and Selma Kramer (Eds.). *Work and its Inhibitions: Psychoanalytic Essays,* pp. 183–190. Madison, Connecticut: International Universities Press.

Olivier, Laurence (1982). *Confessions of an Actor.* London: George Weidenfeld and Nicolson.

Orbach, Susie (2016). *In Therapy: How Conversations with Psychotherapists Really Work.* London: Profile Books.

Orbach, Susie (2018). *In Therapy: The Unfolding Story.* London: Profile Books/Wellcome Collection.

Ostwald, Peter (1985). *Schumann: The Inner Voices of a Musical Genius.* Boston, Massachusetts: Northeastern University Press.

Overy, Richard (2009). *The Morbid Age: Britain Between the Wars.* London: Allen Lane/Penguin Books, Penguin Group.

Pais, Abraham (1994). *Einstein Lived Here.* Oxford: Clarendon Press, and New York: Oxford University Press.

Palmer, Vicki (1967). Letter to Joyce Coles. 20th September. Box 6. File 14. Donald W. Winnicott Papers. Archives of Psychiatry, The Oskar Diethelm Library, The DeWitt Wallace Institute of Psychiatry: History, Policy, and the Arts, Department of Psychiatry, Joan and Sanford I. Weill Medical College, Cornell University, The New York Presbyterian Hospital, New York, New York, U.S.A.

Parker, Derek (1977). *Radio: The Great Years.* Newton Abbot, Devon: David and Charles (Publishers).

Peck, Martin W. (1940). A Brief Visit with Freud. *Psychoanalytic Quarterly, 9,* 205–206.

Pegg, Mark (1983). *Broadcasting and Society: 1918–1939.* London, and Beckenham, Kent: Croom Helm.

Peters, Uwe Henrik (1979). *Anna Freud: Ein Leben für das Kind.* Munich: Kindler Verlag.

Pflaum, Rosalind (1989). *Grand Obsession: Madame Curie and Her World.* New York: Doubleday/Bantam Doubleday Dell Publishing Group.

Pizzitola, Louis (2002). *Hearst Over Hollywood: Power, Passion, and Propaganda in the Movies.* New York: Columbia University Press.

Plunkett, John (2003). *Queen Victoria: First Media Monarch*. Oxford: Oxford University Press.
Postle, Denis (1977). Letter to Michael Fordham and Frieda Fordham. 31st November [*sic*]. PP/FOR/F.2/5. Michael Fordham Collection. Archives and Manuscripts, Rare Materials Room, Wellcome Library, Wellcome Collection, The Wellcome Building, London.
Prochnik, George (2006). *Putnam Camp: Sigmund Freud, James Jackson Putnam, and the Purpose of American Psychology*. New York: Other Press.
Pryce-Jones, Jessica (2010). *Happiness at Work: Maximizing Your Psychological Capital for Success*. Chichester, West Sussex: Wiley-Blackwell/John Wiley and Sons.
Pudney, John (1978). *John Wesley and His World*. London: Thames and Hudson.
Quennell, Peter (1935). *Byron: The Years of Fame*. London: Faber and Faber.
Quigley, Janet (1944). Letter to Donald W. Winnicott. 10th January. PP/DWW/B/B/5/1. Donald Woods Winnicott Collection. Archives and Manuscripts, Rare Materials Room, Wellcome Library, Wellcome Collection, The Wellcome Building, London.
Quinn, Susan (1987). *A Mind of Her Own: The Life of Karen Horney*. New York: Summit Books/Simon & Schuster.
Rank, Otto (1909). *Der Mythus von der Geburt des Helden: Versuch einer psychologischen Mythendeutung*. Vienna: Franz Deuticke.
Rapp, Dean (1988). The Reception of Freud by the British Press: General Interest and Literary Magazines, 1920–1925. *Journal of the History of the Behavioral Sciences*, 24, 191–201.
Rapp, Dean (1990). The Early Discovery of Freud by the British General Educated Public, 1912–1919. *Social History of Medicine*, 3, 217–243.
Reeves, Richard (2007). *John Stuart Mill: Victorian Firebrand*. London: Atlantic Books/Grove Atlantic.
Report of the Care of Children Committee: Presented by the Secretary of State for the Home Department, the Minister of Health, and the Minister of Education, to Parliament by Command of His Majesty: September, 1946 (1946). London: His Majesty's Stationery Office.
Rex, Richard (1993). *Henry VIII and the English Reformation*. Houndmills, Basingstoke, Hampshire: Macmillan Press.
Rich, Anne (1948). Letter to Donald W. Winnicott. 21st January. PP/DWW/B/A/25. Donald Woods Winnicott Collection. Archives and Manuscripts, Rare Materials Room, Wellcome Library, Wellcome Collection, The Wellcome Building, London.
Richards, Arlene Kramer (1994). Introduction. In Arlene Kramer Richards and Arnold D. Richards (Eds.). *The Spectrum of Psychoanalysis: Essays in Honor of Martin S. Bergmann*, pp. 3–39. Madison, Connecticut: International Universities Press.
Rickman, John (1935). Letter to Roger Money-Kyrle. 26th June. PP/RMK/C.1. Roger Ernle Money-Kyrle (1898–1980), psychoanalyst Collection. Archives and Manuscripts, Rare Materials Room, Wellcome Library, Wellcome Collection, The Wellcome Building, London.
Rickman, John (1939). Sigmund Freud: A Personal Impression. *The Lancet*. 7th October, p. 813.

Ries, Paul (1995). Popularise and/or Be Damned: Psychoanalysis and Film at the Crossroads in 1925. *International Journal of Psycho-Analysis*, 76, 759–791.
Roazen, Paul (1969). *Brother Animal: The Story of Freud and Tausk*. New York: Alfred A. Knopf.
Roazen, Paul (1975). *Freud and His Followers*. New York: Alfred A. Knopf.
Roazen, Paul (1995a). *How Freud Worked: First-Hand Accounts of Patients*. Northvale, New Jersey: Jason Aronson.
Roazen, Paul (Ed.). (1995b). Oral History of Sandor Rado. In Paul Roazen and Bluma Swerdloff. *Heresy: Sandor Rado and the Psychoanalytic Movement*, pp. 19–174. Northvale, New Jersey: Jason Aronson.
Roazen, Paul (1995c). Footnote 17. In Sigmund Freud. Letter to Sándor Radó. 14th September. In Paul Roazen (Ed.). (1995). Freud's Letters to Rado. Tom Taylor (Transl.), p. 161. In Paul Roazen and Bluma Swerdloff. *Heresy: Sandor Rado and the Psychoanalytic Movement*, pp. 151–173. Northvale, New Jersey: Jason Aronson.
Roazen, Paul (2000a). *Oedipus in Britain: Edward Glover and the Struggle Over Klein*. New York: Other Press.
Roazen, Paul (2000b). The Correspondence of Edward Glover and Lawrence S. Kubie. *Psychoanalysis and History*, 2, 162–188.
Rodman, F. Robert (2003). *Winnicott: Life and Work*. New York: Perseus Publishing/Perseus Books Group.
Romm, Sharon (1983). *The Unwelcome Intruder: Freud's Struggle with Cancer*. New York: Praeger Publishers/CBS Educational and Professional Publishing, Division of CBS/Praeger Special Studies/Praeger Scientific.
Ross, Thomas A. (1932). *An Introduction to Analytical Psychotherapy*. London: Edward Arnold and Company.
Ross, Thomas A. (1937). The Psychological Approach. In Eleanor Joyce Partridge, Hugh Crichton-Miller, Thomas A. Ross, and Francis G. Crookshank. *The Management of Early Infancy. Puberty and Adolescence. The Psychological Approach. The Neurotic Character*, pp. 33–48. London: C.W. Daniel Company.
Ross, Thomas A. (1938). The Mental Factors in Medicine. *British Medical Journal*. 30th July, pp. 209–211.
Roudinesco, Élisabeth (1993). *Jacques Lacan: Esquisse d'une vie, histoire d'un système de pensée*. Paris: Éditions Fayard.
Roudinesco, Élisabeth (1994). *Généalogies*. Paris: Librairie Arthème Fayard.
Rugg-Gunn, Andrew (1939). Freud and Sex. *The Lancet*. 14th October, p. 854.
Rupp, Gordon (1957). *Six Makers of English Religion: 1500–1700*. London: Hodder and Stoughton.
Sachs, Hanns (1944). *Freud: Master and Friend*. Cambridge, Massachusetts: Harvard University Press.
Scannell, Paddy, and Cardiff, David (1991). *A Social History of British Broadcasting: Volume One 1922–1939. Serving the Nation*. Oxford: Basil Blackwell.
Schmideberg, Melitta (1981). A Contribution to the History of the Psycho-Analytic Movement in Britain. *British Journal of Psychiatry*, 118, 61–68.
Schoenl, William (2009). BBC Broadcasters' Unpublished Views on Jung: Priestley and Freeman. *International Journal of Jungian Studies*, 1, 158–162.
Schur, Max (1972). *Freud: Living and Dying*. New York: International Universities Press.

Schwartz, Joseph (1999). *Cassandra's Daughter: A History of Psychoanalysis in Europe and America*. London: Allen Lane/Penguin Press, Penguin Group, Penguin Books.
Seldes, George (1953). *Tell the Truth and Run*. New York: Greenberg: Publisher.
Selznick, Irene Mayer (1983). *A Private View*. New York: Alfred A. Knopf.
Shaffer, Peter (1980). *Amadeus*. London: André Deutsch.
Shamdasani, Sonu (2005). *Jung Stripped Bare by His Biographers, Even*. London: H. Karnac (Books).
Shamdasani, Sonu (2012). Psychotherapy, 1909: Notes on a Vintage. In John Burnham (Ed.). *After Freud Left: A Century of Psychoanalysis in America*, pp. 31–47. Chicago, Illinois: University of Chicago Press.
Shengold, Leonard (1971). Freud and Joseph. In Mark Kanzer (Ed.). *The Unconscious Today: Essays in Honor of Max Schur*, pp. 473–494. New York: International Universities Press.
Shorter, Edward (1997). *A History of Psychiatry: From the Era of the Asylum to the Age of Prozac*. New York: John Wiley and Sons.
Sievers, W. David (1955). *Freud on Broadway: A History of Psychoanalysis and the American Drama*. New York: Hermitage House.
Simon, John S. (1925). *John Wesley and the Advance of Methodism*. London: Epworth Press/J. Alfred Sharp.
Sinason, Valerie (2001). Children Who Kill Their Teddy Bears. In Brett Kahr (Ed.). *Forensic Psychotherapy and Psychopathology: Winnicottian Perspectives*, pp. 43–49. London: H. Karnac (Books), and New York: Other Press.
Sinason, Valerie (2020). *The Truth About Trauma and Dissociation: Everything You Didn't Want to Know and Were Afraid to Ask*. London: Confer Books.
Skues, Richard (2012). Clark Revisited: Reappraising Freud in America. In John Burnham (Ed.). *After Freud Left: A Century of Psychoanalysis in America*, pp. 49–84. Chicago, Illinois: University of Chicago Press.
Smith, Anthony (Ed.). (1974). *British Broadcasting*. Newton Abbot, Devon: David and Charles (Holdings).
Snagge, John, and Barsley, Michael (1972). *Those Vintage Years of Radio*. London: Pitman Publishing/Sir Isaac Pitman and Sons.
Solomon, Maynard (1995). *Mozart: A Life*. New York: HarperCollins Publishers.
Stager, Lawrence E., and Wolff, Samuel R. (1984). Child Sacrifice at Carthage: Religious Rite or Population Control? Archaeological Evidence Provides Basis for a New Analysis. *Biblical Archaeology Review*, 10, Number 1, 31–51.
Stekel, Wilhelm (1949). Autobiography (VIII). *American Journal of Psychotherapy*, 3, 46–73.
Stekel, Wilhelm (1950). *The Autobiography of Wilhelm Stekel: The Life Story of a Pioneer Psychoanalyst*. Emil A. Gutheil (Ed.). New York: Liveright Publishing Corporation.
Stenn, David (1988). *Clara Bow: Runnin' Wild*. New York: Doubleday/Bantam Doubleday Dell Publishing Group.
Stephen, Adrian (1944). Letter to Vanessa Bell. 6th August. In Jean MacGibbon (1997). *There's the Lighthouse: A Biography of Adrian Stephen*, p. 161. London: James and James (Publishers).
Sterba, Richard F. (1982). *Reminiscences of a Viennese Psychoanalyst*. Detroit, Michigan: Wayne State University Press.

Sterne, Laurence (1760). Letter to Dr. ******. 30th January. In Laurence Sterne (1788). *The Works of Laurence Sterne: In Ten Volumes Complete. Containing, I. The Life and Opinions of Tristram Shandy, Gent. II. A Sentimental Journey Through France and Italy. III. Sermons – IV. Letters. With a Life of the Author, Written by Himself. Volume the Ninth*, pp. 16–24. London: J. Rivington and Sons/J. Dodsley/G. Kearsley/J. Johnson/G.G.J. and J. Robinson/T. Cadell/J. Murray/T. Becket/R. Baldwin/A. Strahan/W. Lowndes/G. and T. Wilkie/W. Bent/D. Ogilvie.
Stevens, Richard (1983a). *Freud and Psychoanalysis: An Exposition and Appraisal*. Stony Stratford, Milton Keynes, Buckinghamshire: Open University Press/Open University Educational Enterprises.
Stevens, Richard (1983b). *Erik Erikson: An Introduction*. Stony Stratford, Milton Keynes, Buckinghamshire: Open University Press/Open University Educational Enterprises.
Stevens, Richard (2005). Questionnaire Results for Making Slough Happy: Final Report. Unpublished Typescript.
Stoddart, William H.B. (1940). Sigmund Freud. *Journal of Mental Science*, *86*, 190–192.
Stoller, Robert J. (1975). *Perversion: The Erotic Form of Hatred*. New York: Pantheon Books.
Stoller, Robert J. (1979a). *Sexual Excitement: Dynamics of Erotic Life*. New York: Pantheon Books.
Stoller, Robert J. (1979b). Centerfold: An Essay on Excitement. *Archives of General Psychiatry*, *36*, 1019–1024.
Stoller, Robert J. (1985). *Observing the Erotic Imagination*. New Haven, Connecticut: Yale University Press.
Stone, Ronald H. (2001). *John Wesley's Life & Ethics*. Nashville, Tennessee: Abingdon Press.
Storr, Anthony (1968). On Aggression. *New Society*. 28th March, p. 466.
Street, Seán (2002). *A Concise History of British Radio: 1922–2002*. Tiverton, Devon: Kelly Publications.
Street, Seán (2006). *Historical Dictionary of British Radio*. Lanham, Maryland: Scarecrow Press/Rowman and Littlefield Publishing Group.
Strozier, Charles B. (2001). *Heinz Kohut: The Making of a Psychoanalyst*. New York: Farrar, Straus and Giroux.
Sturmey, S.G. (1958). *The Economic Development of Radio*. London: Gerald Duckworth and Company.
Summers, Julie (2011). *When the Children Came Home: Stories of Wartime Evacuees*. London: Simon & Schuster, Simon & Schuster UK/CBS Company.
Sutherland, John D. (Ed.). (1958). *Psycho-Analysis and Contemporary Thought*. London: Hogarth Press and the Institute of Psycho-Analysis.
Szasz, Thomas S. (1961). *The Myth of Mental Illness: Foundations of a Theory of Personal Conduct*. New York: Paul B. Hoeber/Medical Division, Harper and Brothers.
Tartakoff, Helen H. (1966). The Normal Personality in Our Culture and the Nobel Prize Complex. In Rudolph M. Loewenstein, Lottie M. Newman, Max Schur, and Albert J. Solnit (Eds.). *Psychoanalysis – A General Psychology: Essays in Honor of Heinz Hartmann*, pp. 222–252. New York: International Universities Press.
Taylor, David (Ed.). (1999). *Talking Cure: Mind and Method of The Tavistock Clinic*. London: Gerald Duckworth and Company.

Taylor, John Cranes (1956). Letter to Donald W. Winnicott. 30th October. PP/DWW/B/D/7. Donald Woods Winnicott Collection. Archives and Manuscripts, Rare Materials Room, Wellcome Library, Wellcome Collection, The Wellcome Building, London.

Taylor, John C. (1996). Letter to the Author. 16th March.

The Institute of Psycho-Analysis (The London Clinic of Psycho-Analysis) (1934). *Report for the Year Ending 30th June, 1934.* London: Institute of Psycho-Analysis.

The Medical Who's Who: Seventh Edition. 1925 (1925). London: Grafton Publishing Company.

Thomson, David G. (1917). Psycho-Analysis. *British Medical Journal.* 6th January, pp. 32–33.

Thomson, Mathew (2011). 'The Solution to His Own Enigma': Connecting the Life of Montague David Eder (1865–1936), Socialist, Psychoanalyst, Zionist and Modern Saint. *Medical History*, 55, 61–84.

Tichy, Marina, and Zwettler-Otte, Sylvia (1999). *Freud in der Presse: Rezeption Sigmund Freuds und der Psychoanalyse in Österreich 1895–1938.* Vienna: Sonderzahl Verlagsgesellschaft.

Torrie, Margaret (1987). *My Years with Cruse.* Richmond, Surrey: Cruse House.

Trevelyan, Helen (1944). Letter to Donald W. Winnicott. 16th December. PP/DWW/B/A/29. Donald Woods Winnicott Collection. Archives and Manuscripts, Rare Materials Room, Wellcome Library, Wellcome Collection, The Wellcome Building, London.

Trevelyan, Helen (1945). Letter to Donald W. Winnicott. 4th March. PP/DWW/B/A/29. Donald Woods Winnicott Collection. Archives and Manuscripts, Rare Materials Room, Wellcome Library, Wellcome Collection, The Wellcome Building, London.

Tritton, Paul (1991). *The Lost Voice of Queen Victoria: The Search for the First Royal Recording.* London: Academy Books.

Tritton, Paul (1993). *The Godfather of Rolls-Royce: The Life and Times of Henry Edmunds, M.I.C.E., M.I.E.E., Science and Technology's Forgotten Pioneer.* London: Academy Books.

Tye, Larry (1998). *The Father of Spin: Edward L. Bernays and the Birth of Public Relations.* New York: Crown Publishers/Crown Publishing Group.

Uceda, Santiago (2008). The Priests of the Bicephalus Arc: Tombs and Effigies Found in Huaca de la Luna and Their Relation to Moche Rituals. In Steve Bourget and Kimberly L. Jones (Eds.). *The Art and Archaeology of the Moche: An Ancient Andean Society of the Peruvian North Coast*, pp. 153–178. Austin, Texas: University of Texas Press.

Verano, John W. (2008). Communality and Diversity in Moche Human Sacrifice. In Steve Bourget and Kimberly L. Jones (Eds.). *The Art and Archaeology of the Moche: An Ancient Andean Society of the Peruvian North Coast*, pp. 195–213. Austin, Texas: University of Texas Press.

Volkov, Peggy (1944). Letter to Donald W. Winnicott. 25th May. PP/DWW/B/B/5/4. Donald Woods Winnicott Collection. Archives and Manuscripts, Rare Materials Room, Wellcome Library, Wellcome Collection, The Wellcome Building, London.

Volkov, Peggy (1945a). Letter to Donald W. Winnicott. 13th February. PP/DWW/ B/B/5/4. Donald Woods Winnicott Collection. Archives and Manuscripts, Rare Materials Room, Wellcome Library, Wellcome Collection, The Wellcome Building, London.

Volkov, Peggy (1945b). Letter to Donald W. Winnicott. 21St February. PP/DWW/ B/B/5/4. Donald Woods Winnicott Collection. Archives and Manuscripts, Rare Materials Room, Wellcome Library, Wellcome Collection, The Wellcome Building, London.

Volkov, Peggy (1945c). Letter to Donald W. Winnicott. 16th March. PP/DWW/ B/B/5/4. Donald Woods Winnicott Collection. Archives and Manuscripts, Rare Materials Room, Wellcome Library, Wellcome Collection, The Wellcome Building, London.

Von Eckardt, Wolf; Gilman, Sander L., and Chamberlin, J. Edward (1987). *Oscar Wilde's London: A Scrapbook of Vices and Virtues. 1880–1900.* Garden City, New York: Anchor Press/Doubleday and Company.

Walker, Andrew (1992). *A Skyful of Freedom: 60 Years of the BBC World Service.* London: Broadside Books.

Wall, Oisín (2018). *The British Anti-Psychiatrists: From Institutional Psychiatry to the Counter-Culture, 1960–1971.* New York: Routledge/Taylor and Francis Group, and Abingdon, Oxfordshire: Routledge/Taylor and Francis Group.

Wallace, Amy (1986). *The Prodigy.* New York: E.P. Dutton.

Weber, Jacqueline (1966). Letter to Donald W. Winnicott. 6th December. Box 6. File 7. Donald W. Winnicott Papers. Archives of Psychiatry, The Oskar Diethelm Library, The DeWitt Wallace Institute of Psychiatry: History, Policy, and the Arts, Department of Psychiatry, Joan and Sanford I. Weill Medical College, Cornell University, The New York Presbyterian Hospital, New York, New York, U.S.A.

Weiss, Edoardo (1970). My Recollections of Sigmund Freud. In Edoardo Weiss. *Sigmund Freud as a Consultant: Recollections of a Pioneer in Psychoanalysis,* pp. 1–22. New York: Intercontinental Medical Book Corporation.

Welshman, John (2010). *Churchill's Children: The Evacuee Experience in Wartime Britain.* Oxford: Oxford University Press.

Willig, Wanda (1991). My Reminiscences About Karen Horney as a Teacher and as a Person. *American Journal of Psychoanalysis, 51,* 249–253.

Willoughby, Roger (2005). *Masud Khan: The Myth and the Reality.* London: Free Association Books.

Winnicott, Clare (1978). D.W.W.: A Reflection. In Simon A. Grolnick, Leonard Barkin, and Werner Muensterberger (Eds.). *Between Reality and Fantasy: Transitional Objects and Phenomena,* pp. 17–33. New York: Jason Aronson.

Winnicott, Donald W. (1928). The Only Child. In Eva Isaacs, Viscountess Erleigh (Ed.). *The Mind of the Growing Child: A Series of Lectures,* pp. 47–64. London: Scientific Press/Faber and Gwyer.

Winnicott, Donald W. (1931). *Clinical Notes on Disorders of Childhood.* London: William Heinemann (Medical Books).

Winnicott, Donald W. (1935). The Manic Defence. In Donald W. Winnicott (1958). *Collected Papers: Through Paediatrics to Psycho-Analysis,* pp. 129–144. London: Tavistock Publications.

Winnicott, Donald W. (1940a). The Deprived Mother. In John Rickman (Ed.). *Children in War-Time: The Uprooted Child, the Problem of the Young Child, the Deprived Mother, Foster-Parents, Visiting, the Teacher's Problems, Homes for Difficult Children*, pp. 31–43. London: New Education Fellowship.
Winnicott, Donald W. (1940b). Book Review of Sylvia Anthony. *The Child's Discovery of Death. New Era in Home and School, 21*, 263.
Winnicott, Donald W. (1941a). The Observation of Infants in a Set Situation. *International Journal of Psycho-Analysis, 22*, 229–249.
Winnicott, Donald W. (1941b). On Influencing and Being Influenced. *New Era in Home and School, 22*, 118–120.
Winnicott, Donald W. (1941c). Book Review of John C. Flügel. *The Moral Paradox of Peace and War. New Era in Home and School, 22*, 183.
Winnicott, Donald W. (1941d). Book Review of Georgina Bathurst, Sibyl Clement Brown, John Bowlby, G.A. Bullen, Nancy Fairbairn, Susan Isaacs, N.S. Mercer, Madeline Rooff, and Robert H. Thouless. *The Cambridge Evacuation Survey: A Wartime Study in Social Welfare and Education*. Susan Isaacs, Sibyl Clement Brown, and Robert H. Thouless (Eds.). *New Era in Home and School, 22*, 256–257.
Winnicott, Donald W. (1942a). Child Department Consultations. *International Journal of Psycho-Analysis, 23*, 139–146.
Winnicott, Donald W. (1942b). Why Children Play. *New Era in Home and School, 23*, 12–14.
Winnicott, Donald W. (1943a). Prefrontal Leucotomy. *The Lancet*. 10th April, p. 475.
Winnicott, Donald W. (1943b). Shock Treatment of Mental Disorder. *British Medical Journal*. 25th December, pp. 829–830.
Winnicott, Donald W. (1943c). Delinquency Research. *New Era in Home and School, 24*, 65–67.
Winnicott, Donald W. (1943d). Treatment of Mental Disease by Induction of Fits. In Donald W. Winnicott (1989). *Psycho-Analytic Explorations*. Clare Winnicott, Ray Shepherd, and Madeleine Davis (Eds.), pp. 516–521. London: H. Karnac (Books).
Winnicott, Donald W. (1943–1945). *Log Book of The South Oxon Hostels Scheme from Jan 1st 1943*. PP/DWW/L.1/2. Donald Woods Winnicott Collection. Archives and Manuscripts, Rare Materials Room, Wellcome Library, Wellcome Collection, The Wellcome Building, London.
Winnicott, Donald W. (1944a). General Discussion. *Transactions of the Ophthalmological Society of the United Kingdom, 64*, 46–52.
Winnicott, Donald W. (1944b). Shock Therapy. *British Medical Journal*. 12th February, pp. 234–235.
Winnicott, Donald W. (1944c). Introduction to a Symposium on the Psycho-Analytic Contribution to the Theory of Shock Therapy. In Donald W. Winnicott (1989). *Psycho-Analytic Explorations*. Clare Winnicott, Ray Shepherd, and Madeleine Davis (Eds.), pp. 525–528. London: H. Karnac (Books).
Winnicott, Donald W. (1944d). Kinds of Psychological Effect of Shock Therapy. In Donald W. Winnicott (1989). *Psycho-Analytic Explorations*. Clare Winnicott, Ray Shepherd, and Madeleine Davis (Eds.), pp. 529–533. London: H. Karnac (Books).
Winnicott, Donald W. (1944e). Letter to Roger North. *New Era in Home and School, 25*, 7–8.

Winnicott, Donald W. (1945a). *Getting to Know Your Baby*. London: William Heinemann (Medical Books).
Winnicott, Donald W. (1945b). Primitive Emotional Development. *International Journal of Psycho-Analysis, 26*, 137–143.
Winnicott, Donald W. (1945c). Getting to Know Your Baby. *New Era in Home and School, 26*, 1–3.
Winnicott, Donald W. (1945d). Why Do Babies Cry? *New Era in Home and School, 26*, 3, 5–7.
Winnicott, Donald W. (1945e). Infant Feeding. *New Era in Home and School, 26*, 9–10.
Winnicott, Donald W. (1945f). What About Father? *New Era in Home and School, 26*, 11–13.
Winnicott, Donald W. (1945g). Their Standards and Yours. *New Era in Home and School, 26*, 13–15.
Winnicott, Donald W. (1945h). Postscript. *New Era in Home and School, 26*, 16–17.
Winnicott, Donald W. (1945i). Talking About Psychology ... *New Era in Home and School, 26*, 179–182.
Winnicott, Donald W. (1945j). The Only Child. In Donald W. Winnicott (1957). *The Child and the Family: First Relationships*. Janet Hardenberg (Ed.), pp. 107–111. London: Tavistock Publications.
Winnicott, Donald W. (1945k). Twins. In Donald W. Winnicott (1957). *The Child and the Family: First Relationships*. Janet Hardenberg (Ed.), pp. 112–116. London: Tavistock Publications.
Winnicott, Donald W. (1945l). The Evacuated Child. In Donald W. Winnicott (1957). *The Child and the Outside World: Studies in Developing Relationships*. Janet Hardenberg (Ed.), pp. 83–87. London: Tavistock Publications.
Winnicott, Donald W. (1945m). The Return of the Evacuated Child. In Donald W. Winnicott (1957). *The Child and the Outside World: Studies in Developing Relationships*. Janet Hardenberg (Ed.), pp. 88–92. London: Tavistock Publications.
Winnicott, Donald W. (1945n). Home Again. In Donald W. Winnicott (1957). *The Child and the Outside World: Studies in Developing Relationships*. Janet Hardenberg (Ed.), pp. 93–97. London: Tavistock Publications.
Winnicott, Donald W. (1947a). Physical Therapy of Mental Disorder. *British Medical Journal*. 17th May, pp. 688–689.
Winnicott, Donald W. (1947b). Battle Neurosis Treated with Leucotomy. *British Medical Journal*. 13th December, p. 974.
Winnicott, Donald W. (1949a). *The Ordinary Devoted Mother and Her Baby: Nine Broadcast Talks. (Autumn 1949)*. London: C.A. Brock and Company.
Winnicott, Donald W. (1949b). Hate in the Counter-Transference. *International Journal of Psycho-Analysis, 30*, 69–74.
Winnicott, Donald W. (1949c). Leucotomy. *British Medical Students' Journal, 3*, Number *2*, 35–38.
Winnicott, Donald W. (1949d). Letter to Isa D. Benzie. 24th January. PP/DWW/B/B/5/1. Donald Woods Winnicott Collection. Archives and Manuscripts, Rare Materials Room, Wellcome Library, Wellcome Collection, The Wellcome Building, London.

Winnicott, Donald W. (1949e). Letter to Isa D. Benzie. 26th January. PP/DWW/B/B/5/1. Donald Woods Winnicott Collection. Archives and Manuscripts, Rare Materials Room, Wellcome Library, Wellcome Collection, The Wellcome Building, London.

Winnicott, Donald W. (1949f). Letter to Dorothy E.M. Gardner. 24th November. PP/DWW/B/A/10. Donald Woods Winnicott Collection. Archives and Manuscripts, Rare Materials Room, Wellcome Library, Wellcome Collection, The Wellcome Building, London.

Winnicott, Donald W. (1949g). Letter to Isa D. Benzie. 7th December. PP/DWW/B/B/5/1. Donald Woods Winnicott Collection. Archives and Manuscripts, Rare Materials Room, Wellcome Library, Wellcome Collection, The Wellcome Building, London.

Winnicott, Donald W. (1950a). Knowing and Learning. In Donald W. Winnicott (1957). *The Child and the Family: First Relationships*. Janet Hardenberg (Ed.), pp. 69–73. London: Tavistock Publications.

Winnicott, Donald W. (1950b). Instincts and Normal Difficulties. In Donald W. Winnicott (1957). *The Child and the Family: First Relationships*. Janet Hardenberg (Ed.), pp. 74–79. London: Tavistock Publications.

Winnicott, Donald W. (1950c). Neglected Children. *The Times*. 31st January, p. 5.

Winnicott, Donald W. (1950d). Letter to Brenda Brennan. 19th January. PP/DWW/B/D/21. Donald Woods Winnicott Collection. Archives and Manuscripts, Rare Materials Room, Wellcome Library, Wellcome Collection, The Wellcome Building, London.

Winnicott, Donald W. (1951a). Leucotomy in Psychosomatic Disorders. *The Lancet*. 18th August, pp. 314–315.

Winnicott, Donald W. (1951b). Ethics of Prefrontal Leucotomy. *British Medical Journal*. 25th August, pp. 496–497.

Winnicott, Donald W. (1951c). Visiting Children in Hospital. In Donald W. Winnicott (1957). *The Child and the Family: First Relationships*. Janet Hardenberg (Ed.), pp. 121–126. London: Tavistock Publications.

Winnicott, Donald W. (1951d). Notes on the General Implications of Leucotomy. In Donald W. Winnicott (1989). *Psycho-Analytic Explorations*. Clare Winnicott, Ray Shepherd, and Madeleine Davis (Eds.), pp. 548–552. London: H. Karnac (Books).

Winnicott, Donald W. (1951e). Letter to Hilda Abraham. 6th December. Joyce Coles Papers. Ealing, London.

Winnicott, Donald W. (1952). Letter to Lalit C. Bhandari. 18th June. PP/DWW/B/A/2. Donald Woods Winnicott Collection. Archives and Manuscripts, Rare Materials Room, Wellcome Library, Wellcome Collection, The Wellcome Building, London.

Winnicott, Donald W. (1953a). Book Review of John Bowlby. *Maternal Care and Mental Health. British Journal of Medical Psychology*, 26, 76–78.

Winnicott, Donald W. (1953b). Letter to Esther Bick. 11th June. In Donald W. Winnicott (1987). *The Spontaneous Gesture: Selected Letters of D.W. Winnicott*. F. Robert Rodman (Ed.), pp. 50–52. Cambridge, Massachusetts: Harvard University Press.

Winnicott, Donald W. (1953c). Letter to The Editor, Tavistock Publications. 7th December. PP/DWW/B/B/5/5. Donald Woods Winnicott Collection. Archives and

Manuscripts, Rare Materials Room, Wellcome Library, Wellcome Collection, The Wellcome Building, London.

Winnicott, Donald W. (1954a). A Psychiatrist's Choice. *The Spectator.* 12th February, p. 175.

Winnicott, Donald W. (1954b). Letters to the Editor of the *Spectator.* In *Physical Treatments of the Mind and Spiritual Healing: Articles and Correspondence Reprinted from the Spectator,* p. 12. London: The Spectator.

Winnicott, Donald W. (1955a). On Adoption. In Donald W. Winnicott (1957). *The Child and the Family: First Relationships.* Janet Hardenberg (Ed.), pp. 127–130. London: Tavistock Publications.

Winnicott, Donald W. (1955b). For Stepparents. In Donald W. Winnicott (1993). *Talking to Parents.* Clare Winnicott, Christopher Bollas, Madeleine Davis, and Ray Shepherd (Eds.), pp. 7–13. Reading, Massachusetts: Addison-Wesley Publishing Company.

Winnicott, Donald W. (1955c). Letter to Nancy Russ. 9th September. PP/DWW/B/A/34. Donald Woods Winnicott Collection. Archives and Manuscripts, Rare Materials Room, Wellcome Library, Wellcome Collection, The Wellcome Building, London.

Winnicott, Donald W. (1956a). Prefrontal Leucotomy. *British Medical Journal.* 28th January, pp. 229–230.

Winnicott, Donald W. (1956b). What Do We Know About Babies as Cloth Suckers? In Donald W. Winnicott (1993). *Talking to Parents.* Clare Winnicott, Christopher Bollas, Madeleine Davis, and Ray Shepherd (Eds.), pp. 15–20. Reading, Massachusetts: Addison-Wesley Publishing Company.

Winnicott, Donald W. (1957a). *The Child and the Family: First Relationships.* Janet Hardenberg (Ed.). London: Tavistock Publications.

Winnicott, Donald W. (1957b). *The Child and the Outside World: Studies in Developing Relationships.* Janet Hardenberg (Ed.). London: Tavistock Publications.

Winnicott, Donald W. (1960a). On Security. In Donald W. Winnicott (1965). *The Family and Individual Development,* pp. 30–33. London: Tavistock Publications.

Winnicott, Donald W. (1960b). Saying "No". In Donald W. Winnicott (1993). *Talking to Parents.* Clare Winnicott, Christopher Bollas, Madeleine Davis, and Ray Shepherd (Eds.), pp. 21–39. Reading, Massachusetts: Addison-Wesley Publishing Company.

Winnicott, Donald W. (1960c). Jealousy. In Donald W. Winnicott (1993). *Talking to Parents.* Clare Winnicott, Christopher Bollas, Madeleine Davis, and Ray Shepherd (Eds.), pp. 41–64. Reading, Massachusetts: Addison-Wesley Publishing Company.

Winnicott, Donald W. (1960d). What Irks? In Donald W. Winnicott (1993). *Talking to Parents.* Clare Winnicott, Christopher Bollas, Madeleine Davis, and Ray Shepherd (Eds.), pp. 65–86. Reading, Massachusetts: Addison-Wesley Publishing Company.

Winnicott, Donald W. (1960e). Security. In Donald W. Winnicott (1993). *Talking to Parents.* Clare Winnicott, Christopher Bollas, Madeleine Davis, and Ray Shepherd (Eds.), pp. 87–93. Reading, Massachusetts: Addison-Wesley Publishing Company.

Winnicott, Donald W. (1961a). Loving. *New Statesman.* 5th May, pp. 722–723.

Winnicott, Donald W. (1961b). Feeling Guilty. In Donald W. Winnicott (1993). *Talking to Parents*. Clare Winnicott, Christopher Bollas, Madeleine Davis, and Ray Shepherd (Eds.), pp. 95–103. Reading, Massachusetts: Addison-Wesley Publishing Company.

Winnicott, Donald W. (1961c). Letter to Joyce Coles. 1st January. PP/DWW/B/C/1. Donald Woods Winnicott Collection. Archives and Manuscripts, Rare Materials Room, Wellcome Library, Wellcome Collection, The Wellcome Building, London.

Winnicott, Donald W. (1962a). The Development of a Child's Sense of Right and Wrong. In Donald W. Winnicott (1993). *Talking to Parents*. Clare Winnicott, Christopher Bollas, Madeleine Davis, and Ray Shepherd (Eds.), pp. 105–110. Reading, Massachusetts: Addison-Wesley Publishing Company.

Winnicott, Donald W. (1962b). Now They Are Five. In Donald W. Winnicott (1993). *Talking to Parents*. Clare Winnicott, Christopher Bollas, Madeleine Davis, and Ray Shepherd (Eds.), pp. 111–120. Reading, Massachusetts: Addison-Wesley Publishing Company.

Winnicott, Donald W. (1962c). Introduction. In Robert W. Shields. *A Cure of Delinquents: The Treatment of Maladjustment*, pp. 9–10. London: Heinemann Educational Books.

Winnicott, Donald W. (1963a). Communicating and Not Communicating Leading to a Study of Certain Opposites. In Donald W. Winnicott (1965). *The Maturational Processes and the Facilitating Environment: Studies in the Theory of Emotional Development*, pp. 179–192. London: Hogarth Press and the Institute of Psycho-Analysis.

Winnicott, Donald W. (1963b). Struggling Through the Doldrums. *New Society*. 25th April, pp. 8–11.

Winnicott, Donald W. (1964a). *The Child, the Family, and the Outside World*. Harmondsworth, Middlesex: Penguin Books.

Winnicott, Donald W. (1964b). Children in a Muddled World. *New Society*. 30th January, p. 27.

Winnicott, Donald W. (1964c). Love or Skill? *New Society*. 2nd April, p. 33.

Winnicott, Donald W. (1964d). Youth Will Not Sleep. *New Society*. 28th May, p. 6.

Winnicott, Donald W. (1965a). *The Family and Individual Development*. London: Tavistock Publications.

Winnicott, Donald W. (1965b). *The Maturational Processes and the Facilitating Environment: Studies in the Theory of Emotional Development*. London: Hogarth Press and the Institute of Psycho-Analysis.

Winnicott, Donald W. (1965c). Acknowledge the Difference. *New Society*. 9th September, p. 29.

Winnicott, Donald W. (1965d). The Child Behind Society. *New Society*. 30th September, p. 35.

Winnicott, Donald W. (1966a). The Ordinary Devoted Mother. In Donald W. Winnicott (1987). *Babies and Their Mothers*. Clare Winnicott, Ray Shepherd, and Madeleine Davis (Eds.), pp. 3–14. Reading, Massachusetts: Addison-Wesley Publishing Company.

Winnicott, Donald W. (1966b). Unwillingly to School. *New Society*. 29th September, pp. 507–508.

Winnicott, Donald W. (1966c). Not Illnesses, But Ill People. *New Society*. 17th November, p. 771.

Winnicott, Donald W. (1966d). Choosing a Family. *New Society*. 24th November, pp. 806–807.
Winnicott, Donald W. (1967a). Steps to Good Parenthood. *New Society*. 13th April, pp. 545–546.
Winnicott, Donald W. (1967b). The Persecution That Wasn't. *New Society*. 25th May, pp. 772–773.
Winnicott, Donald W. (1967c). A Problem for Mothers. *New Society*. 26th October, p. 601.
Winnicott, Donald W. (1967d). Small Things, for Small People. *New Society*. 7th December, p. 835.
Winnicott, Donald W. (1967e). Letter to Robin Hughes. 9th January. Box 6. File 1. Donald W. Winnicott Papers. Archives of Psychiatry, The Oskar Diethelm Library, The DeWitt Wallace Institute of Psychiatry: History, Policy, and the Arts, Department of Psychiatry, Joan and Sanford I. Weill Medical College, Cornell University, The New York Presbyterian Hospital, New York, New York, U.S.A.
Winnicott, Donald W. (1968a). Delinquency as a Sign of Hope. *Prison Service Journal*, 7, Number 27, 2–7.
Winnicott, Donald W. (1968b). Childish Behaviour. *New Society*. 16th May, pp. 726–727.
Winnicott, Donald W. (1968c). Outlook Cloudy. *New Society*. 7th November, p. 688.
Winnicott, Donald W. (1969a). The Use of an Object. *International Journal of Psycho-Analysis*, 50, 711–716.
Winnicott, Donald W. (1969b). Children, War and Hampstead. *New Society*. 21st August, p. 297.
Winnicott, Donald W. (1969c). Letter to Ian Rodger. 28th May. Box 7. File 16. Donald W. Winnicott Papers. Archives of Psychiatry, The Oskar Diethelm Library, The DeWitt Wallace Institute of Psychiatry: History, Policy, and the Arts, Department of Psychiatry, Joan and Sanford I. Weill Medical College, Cornell University, The New York Presbyterian Hospital, New York, New York, U.S.A.
Winnicott, Donald W. (1970). The Place of the Monarchy. In Donald W. Winnicott (1986). *Home is Where We Start From: Essays by a Psychoanalyst*. Clare Winnicott, Ray Shepherd, and Madeleine Davis (Eds.), pp. 260–268. Harmondsworth, Middlesex: Penguin Books.
Winnicott, Donald W. (1971a). *Playing and Reality*. London: Tavistock Publications.
Winnicott, Donald W. (1971b). *Therapeutic Consultations in Child Psychiatry*. London: Hogarth Press and the Institute of Psycho-Analysis.
Winnicott, Donald W. (1977). *The Piggle: An Account of the Psychoanalytic Treatment of a Little Girl*. Ishak Ramzy (Ed.). New York: International Universities Press.
Winnicott, Donald W. (1984). *Deprivation and Delinquency*. Clare Winnicott, Ray Shepherd, and Madeleine Davis (Eds.). London: Tavistock Publications.
Winnicott, Donald W. (1987). *Babies and Their Mothers*. Clare Winnicott, Ray Shepherd, and Madeleine Davis (Eds.). Reading, Massachusetts: Addison-Wesley Publishing Company.
Winnicott, Donald W. (1993). *Talking to Parents*. Clare Winnicott, Christopher Bollas, Madeleine Davis, and Ray Shepherd (Eds.). Reading, Massachusetts: Addison-Wesley Publishing Company.
Winnicott, Donald W. (2021). *The Child, the Family and the Outside World*. [London]: Penguin Books/Penguin Random House, Penguin Random House UK.

Winnicott, Donald W. (n.d.). Letter to Joyce Coles. 4th August. PP/DWW/B/C/2. Donald Woods Winnicott Collection. Archives and Manuscripts, Rare Materials Room, Wellcome Library, Wellcome Collection, The Wellcome Building, London.

Winnicott, Donald W., and Britton, Clare (1944). The Problem of Homeless Children. *New Era in Home and School*, 25, 155–161.

Winnicott, Kathleen (1944). Letter to Donald W. Winnicott. 11th May. PP/DWW/B/D/2. Donald Woods Winnicott Collection. Archives and Manuscripts, Rare Materials Room, Wellcome Library, Wellcome Collection, The Wellcome Building, London.

Winnicott, Kathleen (1945). Letter to Donald W. Winnicott. 21st February. PP/DWW/B/D/2. Donald Woods Winnicott Collection. Archives and Manuscripts, Rare Materials Room, Wellcome Library, Wellcome Collection, The Wellcome Building, London.

Winnicott, Violet (n.d.). Letter to Donald W. Winnicott. n.d. PP/DWW/B/D/3. Donald Woods Winnicott Collection. Archives and Manuscripts, Rare Materials Room, Wellcome Library, Wellcome Collection, The Wellcome Building, London.

Woolf, Leonard (1939). Letter to John Lehmann. 4th September. In John Lehmann (1978). *Thrown to the Woolfs*, p. 81. London: Weidenfeld and Nicolson.

Yates, Candida (2007). *Masculine Jealousy and Contemporary Cinema*. Basingstoke, Hampshire: Palgrave Macmillan/St. Martin's Press.

Yates, Candida (2014). Psychoanalysis and Television: Notes Towards a Psycho-Cultural Approach. In Caroline Bainbridge, Ivan Ward, and Candida Yates (Eds.). *Television and Psychoanalysis: Psycho-Cultural Perspectives*, pp. 1–28. London: Karnac Books.

Yates, Sybille L. (1930). An Investigation of the Psychological Factors in Virginity and Ritual Defloration. *International Journal of Psycho-Analysis*, 11, 167–184.

Young-Bruehl, Elisabeth (1988). *Anna Freud: A Biography*. New York: Summit Books/Simon & Schuster.

Zavitzianos, George (1972). Homeovestism: Perverse Form of Behaviour Involving Wearing Clothes of the Same Sex. *International Journal of Psycho-Analysis*, 53, 471–477.

Zilboorg, Caroline (2022a). *The Life of Gregory Zilboorg, 1890–1940: Psyche, Psychiatry, and Psychoanalysis*. London: Routledge/Taylor and Francis Group, and Abingdon, Oxfordshire: Routledge/Taylor and Francis Group.

Zilboorg, Caroline (2022b). *The Life of Gregory Zilboorg, 1940–1959: Mind, Medicine, and Man*. London: Routledge/Taylor and Francis Group, and Abingdon, Oxfordshire: Routledge/Taylor and Francis Group.

Zilboorg, Gregory (1935). *The Medical Man and the Witch During the Renaissance*. Baltimore, Maryland: Johns Hopkins Press.

Zilboorg, Gregory (1943). *Mind, Medicine, and Man*. New York: Harcourt, Brace and Company.

Zilboorg, Gregory, and Henry, George W. (1941). *A History of Medical Psychology*. New York: W.W. Norton & Company.

Index

"A Talk with Dr. Freud, Psycho-Analyst" (Hans von Kaltenborn), 148
Aberfan, Wales, 187
Abraham, Hilda, 182, 206
Abraham, Karl, 146, 147, 153, 182, 206
Academy Awards, 50, 107, 109, 120, 137, 154
Adams, Victoria, 113
Addison, John, 70, 71, 72
Adler, Alfred, 45, 152–153, 158, 168, 175
Adler, Ben, 44, 47
Adoption, 172, 175, 183, 187
Aeneid (Homer), 110
Affectometer, 58
Al-Qaeda, 79
Albee, Edward, 69
"Albert Square", 120
Alcock, Theodora, 175
Alcoholism, 84, 131, 132
Aldgate, London, 79
Aldwych, London, 30
"Alexander Brooks", 81, 100
Alexander the Great, 110
Alexandra, 121
"Alfredo", 69
Allen, Malcolm, 161
Allen, Woody, 157, 160
Allen Lane, Penguin Books, London, 38
Amadeus (Peter Shaffer), 141
Amazon Prime, 90
America's Got Talent, 107
America's Next Top Model, 108
American Film Institute, Los Angeles, California, U.S.A., 94
American Idol, 107, 117, 124
American Idol: Idol Gives Back, 107
American Line, 189
American Magazine, 112

American Psychoanalytic Association, New York City, New York, U.S.A., 94, 96, 161
American Tobacco Company, 155
"An Old Fashioned Wedding" (*Annie Get Your Gun*), 71, 74
Analytical Psychology Club, London, 168
Anderson, Maxwell, 142
"Anna O", 2
Annie Get Your Gun (Irving Berlin, Dorothy Fields, and Herbert Fields), 71, 73–74
"Annie Oakley", 73, 74
Annunciation Day, 110
Anorexia nervosa, 9–10
Anschluß, 147, 192
Anti-psychiatry, 178, 201
Antichrist, 190
Antony, 146
Anxiety, 13, 15, 25, 49, 57, 72, 73, 83, 84, 86, 95, 99, 118, 120, 122, 145, 146, 148, 154, 163, 195, 208
"Anxiety Underlying Phobia of Sexual Intercourse in a Woman" (Esther Bick), 208
Any Dream Will Do, 108
"Anything You Can Do" (*Annie Get Your Gun*), 71, 74
"Apis", 123
Apollo Victoria Theatre, London, 71
Archives of the British Psychoanalytical Society, British Psychoanalytical Society, Maida Vale, London, 30
"Ariel", 166
Armstrong-Jones, Robert, 168, 190–191
Arundel, Thomas, 190

As You Like It (William Shakespeare), 111
Ashcroft, Peggy, 154, 192
Ashton, Frederick, 142
Asian Tsunami, 86
Association of Child Psychotherapists, London, 74
Athens, Greece, 123, 124
Attenborough, Richard, 85–86
Attlee, Clement, 177
Austen, Jane, 90
Australia, 159
Australian Broadcasting Corporation, 159
Ayrshire, Scotland, 11

B.A.F.T.A., *see* British Academy of Film and Television Arts, London
B.A.R.B., London, *see* Broadcasters' Audience Research Board, London
B.B.C., *see* British Broadcasting Corporation, London
B.B.C. Empire Service, 167
B.B.C. Interactive, British Broadcasting Corporation, London, 22
B.B.C. iPlayer, 90
B.B.C. Message Board, British Broadcasting Corporation, London, 22–23, 27, 29
B.B.C. Radio Berkshire, Reading, Berkshire, 51
B.B.C. Radio Oxford, British Broadcasting Corporation, Oxford, Oxfordshire, 2, 21
B.B.C. Radio 2, British Broadcasting Corporation, London, 3, 21–29
B.B.C. Radio 4, British Broadcasting Corporation, London, 11, 187
B.B.C. 2, British Broadcasting Corporation, London, 63
Bagenal, Hope, 171
Bainbridge, Caroline, 81, 93
Balderston, John L., 155
Baldwin, Stanley, 169
Balint, Michael, 175, 207
Balmoral, Aberdeenshire, Scotland, 166
"Banana O.", 45
Bantin, Florence, 157, 183
Barber, Dave, 22, 23
Barker, Paul, 201
Barrow, Clyde, 118–119
Barton, Elizabeth, 110

Basingstoke, Hampshire, 59
Bavaria, 141
Baxter, Warner, 112
Bay Ridge, Brooklyn, New York, U.S.A., 112
Be'Tipul, 94, 95
Beat the Clock, 45
Beatles, 9, 108, 109
Beatty, Warren, 119
Beaufort, Margaret, 110
Beckham, David, 113, 138, 139, 140
Beerbohm, Max, 169
Behind the Scenes at the Museum, 89
Bell, Alexander Graham, 165
Bentley, Timothy, 183
Benzie, Isa Donald, 156, 164, 177–179, 180, 181, 183, 184
Bereavement, 25–28, 54, 56, 68, 85, 88, 128–142, 170, 187, 199
Bereavement counselling, 26, 88, 128, 142, 199
Berggasse, Vienna, Austria, 148
Bergmann, Martin, 157
Berkeley, George, 127
Berkeley Square (John L. Balderston), 155
Berkshire, England, 47, 50, 51, 53, 58, 62
Berlin, Germany, 80, 146, 147, 149, 152, 198
Berlin, Irving, 71, 73, 74
Berlin Psycho-Analytical Society, Berlin, Germany, *see* Berliner Psychoanalytische Vereinigung, Berlin, Germany
Berliner Philharmoniker, Berlin, Germany, 71
Berliner Psychoanalytische Vereinigung, Berlin, Germany, 153
Bernays, Edward L., 155
Bernfeld, Siegfried, 153
Bernstein, Leonard, 71
Bettelheim, Bruno, 157
"Betty Draper", 83
"Betty Lou", 112
"Between the Thumb and the Teddy-Bear: The Psychology of Infancy" (Anonymous), 210
Bhandari, Lalit, 184
Bible, 190, 196
Bibring, Grete, 156
Bick, Esther, 174, 207–208
Big Brother, 117

"Billy Bigelow", 73
Binge-watching, 91
Bion, Wilfred, 197
Bishop Gore School, Swansea, Wales, 185
Black, Stephen, 152
Blair, David Hunter, 112
Blair, Tony, 75
Blithe Spirit (Noël Coward), 1
Bloomsbury, London, 65
Bloomsbury group, 169
Blount, William, Lord Mountjoy, 110, 204
Bollas, Christopher, 96
Bollingen Foundation, New York City, New York, U.S.A., 184
Bolshevism, 98
Bonaparte, Marie, 205
Boni and Liveright, New York City, New York, U.S.A., 146
Bonnie and Clyde, 118–119
Borderline personality disorder, 85, 106
"Bosco Albert (B.A.) Baracus", 79
Boston, Mary, 207–208
Boublil, Alain, 71
Bourget, Steve, 124
Bousfield, Paul, 168
Bow, Clara Gordon, 112
Bowlby, John, 158, 175, 184, 191
Boyle, Susan, 107
Bradshaw, Anthony, 171
Bragg, Melvyn, 14
Brains Trust, 156, 176, 182
Braudy, Leo, 110
Brennan, Brenda, 182
Breuer, Josef, 2
Brief psychotherapy, 163
Brill, Abraham Arden, 155
Bristol, England, 150
Britain's Got More Talent, 107
Britain's Got Talent, 107, 126
Britain's Sexual Fantasies, 30–43
British Academy of Film and Television Arts, London, 47, 85, 86
British Association for Counselling and Psychotherapy, Lutterworth, Leicestershire, 46
British Broadcasting Company, London, 166
British Broadcasting Corporation, London, 2–3, 9–11, 14, 15, 21–29, 36, 44–66, 81, 90, 108, 149, 155, 156–157, 159, 164, 166–167, 168, 169–175, 177–182, 185, 187, 194–195, 201
British Broadcasting Corporation Birmingham, Birmingham, West Midlands, 10
British Confederation of Psychotherapists, London, 46
British Isles, 21
British Medical Journal, 178
British Postgraduate Medical School, University of London, London, 191
British Psycho-Analytical Society, London, 114, 150, 153, 158, 165, 168, 172, 173, 182, 185, 188, 191, 192–193, 208
British Psychoanalytic Council, London, 46, 161
British Psychoanalytical Society, Maida Vale, London, 30, 74
British Psychological Society, Leicester, Leicestershire, 46
British Psychological Society, London, 178, 179
British Sexual Fantasy Research Project, 108–109
Britton, Clare, *see* Winnicott, Clare
Britton, Karl, 188
Broadbent, Jim, 50
Broadcasters' Audience Research Board, London, 90
Broadcasting House, British Broadcasting Corporation, London, 21, 23, 28, 166, 169, 170–171, 173, 174, 180
Broadway, New York City, New York, U.S.A., 52, 69, 71, 73, 81, 100, 155
Bromley-by-Bow, Tower Hamlets, London, 51, 58, 64
Brookings Institution, Washington, D.C., U.S.A., 64
Brooklyn, New York, U.S.A., 112, 148
Brooklyn Daily Eagle, Brooklyn, New York, U.S.A., 148
Brown, William, 168
Brunswick, Ruth Mack, 206
Brussels, Belgium, 196
"Brutus", 146
Buckingham Palace, London, 115
Bulimia nervosa, 9, 10–11, 12, 26
Bundeskanzler, 147
Burlingham, Dorothy, 175, 181, 206
Burt, Cyril, 153, 192, 194–195

Index

Bush Model DAC 90, 171
Bychowski, Gustav, 148
Bye Bye Birdie (Lee Adams, Michael Stewart, and Charles Strouse), 52
Byrne, Gabriel, 94, 101
"Byromania", 112
Byron, Lord, *see* Gordon, George, Lord Byron

C.A. Brock and Company, London, 181
Caird, John, 71
California, U.S.A., 82, 110, 129, 155, 165
Callas, Maria, 89
Cameron, David, 64
Cameron, James, 107
Campbell, Archibald, 176
Canada, 86, 158
Caplan, Gerald, 182
Cara, Irene, 120
Carnegie Hall, New York City, New York, U.S.A., 71
Carousel (Oscar Hammerstein II and Richard Rodgers), 71, 73
Casanova, 1, 98
Casella, Fred, 36–41
Castration anxiety, 86, 118–119, 122
"Cathode nipple", 90, 91, 107
Catholicism, 190
Cavalcade, 155
Caversham House, Caversham, Reading, Berkshire, 51
Celebdaq, 117
Celebrification, 113–116
Celebrity, 4, 86, 94, 103, 105–127, 142, 157–158, 161
Celebrity Alcatraz, 108
Celebrity Bedlam, 107
Celebrity Big Brother, 107
Celebrity Come Dine with Me, 108
Celebrity Deal or No Deal, 108
Celebrity Detox, 107
Celebrity Duets, 107
Celebrity Exposed, 108
Celebrity Fat Camp, 107
Celebrity First Dates, 108
Celebrity Fit Club, 107
Celebrity Four Weddings, 107
Celebrity Go Home, 108
Celebrity Juice, 107
Celebrity MasterChef, 108
Celebrity MasterChef Australia, 108
Celebrity Pressure Cooker, 108
Celebrity Wife Swap, 107
Celebrity Worship Syndrome, 107–109
Central Council for Health Education, 177
Central London, London, 14, 21, 38, 173, 180
Central Office of Information, 176
Central Tower, Broadcasting House, British Broadcasting Corporation, London, 170–171
Chambers, Dan, 32–33, 35
Chambers, Florence, 33
Channel Five Television, London, 33, 35, 36, 38, 42, 51
Channel Four Television, London, 36, 44
Channel 4 Television, London, *see* Channel Four Television, London
Chapman, Mark David, 122
Chapman, Philippa, 58, 59, 65
Charles, His Royal Highness The Prince of Wales, *see* Charles III
"Charles Foster Kane", 145
Charles III, 69
Chelmsford, Essex, 166
Chester, Cheshire, 174, 207
Chester Square, Belgravia, South West London, London, 209
Chicago, Illinois, U.S.A., 145, 146, 205
Chicago Daily Tribune, Chicago, Illinois, U.S.A., 145, 146
Chignell, Georgina, 33
Child, Julia, 44
Child and Family Department, Tavistock Clinic, Tavistock Centre, Tavistock and Portman NHS Trust, Belsize Park, London, 151
Child Department, Institute of Psycho-Analysis, London, 208
Child mental health, 30, 69
Child psychiatry, 33, 114, 126, 180, 182, 188, 196, 209
Child psychoanalysis, 119, 126, 164
Child psychology, 117, 157, 164, 176, 207
Child psychotherapy, 74, 163, 164, 207–208
Childe Harold's Pilgrimage (George Gordon, Lord Byron), 111–112
Chiswick, West London, London, 171
Christianity, 40, 113, 161
Churchill, Randolph, 66

Churchill, Winston, 66, 167, 173–174, 207
Citizen Kane, 145
City of London, London, 54
Civilization and its Discontents (Sigmund Freud), *see Das Unbehagen in der Kultur* (Sigmund Freud)
Claudius, 121
Clegg, Nick, 64
Cleisthenes, 124
Cleopatra, 146
Clinical Notes on Disorders of Childhood (Donald W. Winnicott), 174
Clulow, Christopher, 72
Coggan, Donald, 187
Coital fantasies, 31, 32, 38, 109
Cole, Cheryl, 124
Coles, Joyce, 181, 195, 207, 209
Combined parent-figure, 171
Combined parental figure, 171
Comic Relief Does Fame Academy, 108
Common Era, 124
Commonwealth, 167
Conciergerie, Paris, France, 111
Confessions of an Actor (Laurence Olivier), 154
Confidentiality, 15, 16, 24, 28, 34, 35, 52, 56, 57, 73, 83, 92, 95, 105, 106, 150, 159, 164, 183
Conscious, 32, 83, 87, 99, 164, 195
Contemporary Freudian Society, New York City, New York, U.S.A.
Cornwall, England, 11
Coronary thrombosis, 182
Coronation Street, 83
Coronavirus, 16, 90, 127, 137, 200, 202
Couch, 67, 81, 83, 89, 90, 92, 93, 96, 130, 137, 138, 151, 199
"Could I Leave You?" (*Follies*), 71
Counselling, 10, 12, 26, 27, 46, 67, 74, 88, 97, 128, 133, 142, 161, 199
Countertransference, 69, 92, 164, 177
Couple psychoanalysis, 31, 72
Couple psychoanalytic psychotherapy, *see* Couple psychotherapy
Couple psychotherapy, 31, 67, 68, 69, 70, 72, 73, 75, 84, 85, 92, 96, 99, 203
Couples Centre Stage, Society of Couple Psychoanalytic Psychotherapists, Tavistock Centre for Couple Relationships, Tavistock Institute of Medical Psychology, Tavistock Centre, Belsize Park, London, 75
"Couples in Counterpoint", 70, 72, 75
Court Circular, 114, 115
Covent Garden, London, 35, 38, 39, 70
Coventry, Warwickshire, 171
COVID-19, *see* Coronavirus
Coward, Noël, 1, 106, 108, 109
Creak, Mildred, 180
Creativity, 5, 12, 13, 15, 38, 44, 47, 51, 56, 57, 70, 75, 83, 89, 99, 101, 121, 128–142, 152, 173, 196
Creativity bereavement, 128–142
Crete, 123
Crewe, Cheshire, 59
Crimes and Misdemeanors, 157
Criminality, 82, 84, 107, 109, 150, 153, 155, 157
Criswell, Kim, 71, 73–74
Cruse, 142
Crystal Palace, London, 112
CSI: Crime Scene Investigation, 84
Curie, Marie, 126, 161
Curtis Report, 209

Daily Dispatch, 153
Daily Herald, 153
Daily Mail, 155
Dakota, The, New York City, New York, U.S.A., 122
Dann, Sophie, 181–182
Dante Alighieri, 123, 125
Das Unbehagen in der Kultur (Sigmund Freud), 148
David Freeman Programme, B.B.C. Radio Oxford, Oxford, Oxfordshire, 2, 21
Davidson, Audrey, 183
Davidson, Nicky, 22
de Palma, Brian, 95
Death anxiety, 120, 122
"Death pool", 120
Decline and Fall of the Freudian Empire (Hans J. Eysenck), 2
Delinquency, 163
Delusions of persecution, 81, 138
deMause, Lloyd, 123
Denmark, 108, 137, 142
Department of Experimental Psychology, University of Oxford, Oxford, Oxfordshire, 2
Depp, Johnny, 109

Depression (economic crisis), 112
Depression (psychological condition), 13, 27, 45, 47, 51, 56, 57, 58, 63, 64, 68, 72, 83, 84, 86, 91, 125, 128, 129, 132, 135, 138, 203–204
Deptford, South East London, London, 158
"Der Familienroman der Neurotiker" (Sigmund Freud), 114, 205
Derby, Derbyshire, 110
Desperate Housewives, 119
Devil, 141
Devon, England, 167, 172, 189
Diana, 86
Dickinson, Emily, 125
Diderot, Denis, 111
Die Frage der Laienanalyse: Unterredungen mit einem Unparteiischen (Sigmund Freud), 148
"Die Neue Sachlichkeit", 80
Dietrich, Marlene, 106
Difficult Children, 172
Disability, 119, 126, 128, 129, 135–136
"*Dispute sur la postérité*", 111
Dixon, Alesha, 124
Dockar-Drysdale, Barbara, 208
Doctors, 83
"Doctors and Dreams" (Montague David Eder), 153
Doing Psychoanalysis in Tehran (Gohar Homayounpour), 12
Dolto, Françoise, 156
Dom de Forest Wireless Telegraph Company, 167
"Don Draper", 83, 84
Donizetti, Gaetano, 70
"Dorothy", 125
Double Fantasy (John Lennon), 122
Douglas, Lesley, 21–22, 24
Downey, Robert, Jr., 120
"Dr. Craig Huffstodt", 93
"Dr. Frasier Crane", 93, 95, 160
"Dr. Jennifer Melfi", 93, 95, 101
"Dr. May Foster", 93
"Dr. Murchison", 95
"Dr. Paul Weston", 92–98, 99, 101
"Dr. Phil", *see* McGraw, Phil
"Dr. Robert Elliott", 95
Dressed to Kill, 95
Driver, Betty, 113
Drop the Celebrity, 107–108
Drug addiction, 93
Dublin, Ireland, 49, 113, 150

"Duke of Chicago", *see* McCormick, Robert Rutherford
Dyer, Simon, 37

E.R., 82
Early intervention, 163
East End, London, 58, 169
EastEnders, 40
Easter Sunday, 155
Eating disorders, 9, 10, 11
Eder, Montague David, 153, 192
Edison, Thomas Alva, 165, 167
Edmunds, Henry, 165–166, 167
Edward, Prince of Wales, 167, 191
Edward VII, 189, 191
Edward VIII, *see* Edward, Prince of Wales
Edward Street School, Deptford, South East London, London, 158
Ego, 119, 164
Eigen, Michael, 197
Einstein, Albert, 126, 161
Eissler, Kurt, 150
Electric shock, 178, 179
Elizabeth, the Queen Mother, 115
Elizabeth II, 58, 137, 191
Ellis, Havelock, 31
Elmhirst, Susanna Isaacs, 119
Elsted, West Sussex, 172
Emergency Medical Service, 191
Eminem, 120
En Thérapie, 94
England, United Kingdom, 12, 45, 49, 98, 110, 112, 130, 158, 190, 192, 196, 199, 207
Ensor, Beatrice, 175
Envy, 9, 15, 38, 74, 85, 121–122, 129, 138, 141, 157, 159, 198
"Éponine", 70
Erikson, Erik, 51
Europa, 123
Europe, 113, 145, 147, 148, 190
Evans, Richard I., 152
Evidences, 155
Exhibitionism, 106, 107, 109, 127, 159, 165, 193
Eye-witness, 153
Eysenck, Hans, 1–2, 3, 21

Face to Face, 152
Facilitating environment, 36, 164, 196
Fairbanks, Douglas, 112
Faith, Adam, 187

Falconet, Étienne Maurice, 111
False self, 164
Fame (concept), 4, 21, 105–127, 137, 141, 142, 170
Fame (film), 120
"Fame" (song), 120
Fame Academy, 108
Family romance, 114, 116–117, 122
"Family Romances" (Sigmund Freud), *see* "Der Familienroman der Neurotiker" (Sigmund Freud)
Family therapy, 163
Fantasy, 118
Ferenczi, Sándor, 153, 206
Ferris, Paul, 185
Fifth Avenue, New York City, New York, U.S.A., 155
Fight Against Fears (Lucy Freeman), 151
Film Programme, International Congress on Mental Health, London, 177
First Folio, 203, 204
Five, London, *see* Channel Five Television, London
Flügel, John Carl, 155, 177, 193
Follies (James Goldman and Stephen Sondheim), 71, 73
Foot's Kray, Kent, 171
Fordham, Frieda, 156
Fordham, Michael, 156
Forensic child and adolescent psychotherapy, 163
Forensic mental health, 49
Forensic psychotherapy, 98, 163
"Foreword" (Sándor Ferenczi), *see* "Vorwort" (Sándor Ferenczi)
Forrell, Lisa, 70, 71, 72
Forrell, Mildred, 70
Forster, Edward Morgan, 169
40 Most Shocking Celebrity Divorces, 108
40 Naughtiest Celebrity Scandals, 108
42nd Street, 112
France, 108, 111, 121, 124, 156, 161, 200
"Frank Butler", 73–74
Franklin, Marjorie, 175
Franks, Bobby, 145, 146
Fraser, Francis, 191
Frasier, 23, 93, 94, 95, 101, 160
Free association, 4, 28, 53, 85, 86, 91, 96, 98, 138, 199
Freeman, David, 2–3, 21
Freeman, John, 152

Freeman, Lucy, 151
Freud, Anna, 149, 152, 161, 175, 181, 206
Freud, Ernst L., 206
Freud, Julius, 146
Freud, Martin, 147
Freud, Sigmund, 1, 2, 3, 4, 5, 12, 14, 31, 39, 45, 46, 47, 51, 56, 80, 94, 96–97, 98, 105, 113–114, 116–117, 143, 145–149, 150, 151, 152, 153, 155, 157, 159, 160, 161, 163, 164, 165, 168, 181, 182, 185, 195, 198, 200, 205–206
Freud Museum, Swiss Cottage, London, 89, 90
Freud Museum London, Swiss Cottage, London, 200
Freud's Own Cookbook (James Hillman and Charles Boer), 45
Freudism, 168
Friday, Nancy, 31–32
Friday Morning Club, Hollywood, California, U.S.A., 155
Fromm, Erich, 156

G.C.H.Q., Caversham, Reading, Berkshire, *see* Government Communications Headquarters, Caversham, Reading, Berkshire
Gaius Plinius Secundus, *see* Pliny the Elder
Game of Thrones, 86–87
Gardner, Dorothy, 175
GEC Model BC 4941, 171
Geheimnisse einer Seele, 147, 153
"George", 69
George V, 167, 191
George VI, 182, 191
Gere, Richard, 122
Germany, 108, 182, 200
Gershwin, George, 100
Gershwin, Ira, 81, 100
"Gertrude", 192
Gervais, Ricky, 47
Gestalt psychology, 152
Getting to Know Your Baby (Donald W. Winnicott) (pamphlet), 174, 186
"Getting to Know Your Baby" (Donald W. Winnicott) (radio broadcast), 173, 174
Gilbert, Martin, 173–174, 207
Gilbert, William Schwenck, 112
Gilbert and Sullivan, *see* Gilbert, William Schwenck, and Sullivan Arthur

Gill, Eric, 166
Glasgow, Scotland, 177
Gloria Palast, Berlin, Germany, 80
Gloucestershire, England, 45
Glover, Edward, 153, 155, 192
Godwin, Richard, 79
Golden Globe Awards, 94
Goldwyn, Samuel, 80, 146–147, 161
Gone with the Wind, 130
Good-enough mother, 164
Google, 159–160
Gordon, George, Lord Byron, 111–112, 204
Goulstonian Lectures, Royal College of Physicians, London, 191
Government Communications Headquarters, Caversham, Reading, Berkshire, 51
Government Evacuation Scheme, 171, 173, 176
Gowers, Sarah, 49, 52, 61
Grable, Betty, 118
Grandiosity, 2, 15, 105, 106, 109, 129, 137, 138
Grant, Hugh, 109
Great Britain, 1, 2, 3, 98, 108, 113, 149, 150, 153, 156, 165, 166, 175, 178, 180, 181, 182, 187, 189, 192, 193, 194, 207, 208, 209
Greece, 110
Grief, 26, 112, 128, 131, 187, 189
Grief counselling, *see* Bereavement counselling
Griffiths, Lydia, 70, 71, 72
Grimsdale, Peter, 36
Group psychotherapy, 13, 52
Guernica (Pablo Picasso), 137, 142
"Guilt Feelings in Young Mothers", 185
Guntrip, Harry, 156
Guthrie, Tyrone ("Tony"), 154–155, 192
Gypsy (Arthur Laurents, Stephen Sondheim, and Jule Styne), 71

Habsburgs, 113
Hadfield, James, 168
Hagen, Jean, 125–126
Hale, Sonnie, 113
Hamlet (William Shakespeare), 137, 142, 154, 192, 206
"Hamlet", 154, 192, 206
Hammerstein, Oscar, II, 71
Hampstead, North West London, London, 11, 12, 47, 56

Hancock Park, Wilshire, Los Angeles, California, U.S.A., 155
Happiness at Work: Maximizing Your Psychological Capital for Success (Jessica Pryce-Jones), 65
Happiness Domains, 58
"Happy Birthday to You" (Mildred Hill and Patty Hill), 57
Happy Children (Donald W. Winnicott), 174, 176
Hardenberg, Herman, 186
Hardenberg, Janet, 186
Harley Street, London, 98
Hart, Moss, 81, 100
"Hate in the Counter-Transference" (Donald W. Winnicott), 177
Hate in the countertransference, 164, 177
Hearst, William Randolph, 145, 146
Hearst Press, New York City, New York, U.S.A., 145, 205
Hearst-Presse, *see* Hearst Press, New York City, New York, U.S.A.
Heat, 118
Heathrow Airport, London Borough of Hillingdon, West London, London, 49
Hébert, Jacques-René, 121
Helen Mayhew, B.B.C. Radio 2, British Broadcasting Corporation, London, 22–29
Hello, 114, 115
Hemmung, Symptom und Angst (Sigmund Freud), 148
Henry VII, 110
Henry VIII, 110
Hepburn, Katharine, 120
Herakles, 124
Herman, Jerry, 71, 73
Herodotus, 110
Hesiod, 110
Highgate, North London, London, 126
Hill, Mark, 22, 24
Hillman, James, 45
Hilton, John, 166
Hirschfeld, Magnus, 31
Hitchcock, Alfred, 95
Hitschmann, Eduard, 195
Hodson, Pauline, 68, 72, 73
Hogarth Press, London, 170
Hoggard, Liz, 63–64
Hohenzollerns, 113
Holding environment, 164
Holland, Jane, 86
Holland, Lucy, 86

Hollick, Clive, 75
Hollitscher, Mathilde Freud, 205, 206
Hollitscher, Robert, 206
Hollyoaks, 83
Hollywood, California, U.S.A., 80, 100, 105, 115, 117, 118, 119, 132, 146, 155
Holy Maid of Ipswich, 110
Holy Maid of Kent, *see* Barton, Elizabeth
Holy Maid of Leominster, 110
Homayounpour, Gohar, 12
"Home Again" (Donald W. Winnicott), 173
Home Box Office, 93
Homeovestism, 139
Homer, 110
Hong Kong flu, 188
Hope, Bob, 120
Horder, Thomas, 190–191
Horizon, 155
Horney, Karen, 156, 198
How Do You Solve a Problem Like Maria?, 108
"How Freud Would Have Handled the Coronavirus: Lessons from a Beacon of Survival" (Brett Kahr), 200
"How Much Do We Know About Babies as Cloth Suckers?" (Donald W. Winnicott), 184
How Not to F*** Them Up: The First Three Years (Oliver James), 89
How the Mind Works, 153
How to Be Famous, 108
How to Be Happy (Liz Hoggard), 63–64
Huff, 93
Hughes, Robin, 168
Hungary, 12, 108
Hurley, Elizabeth, 109
Huxley, Julian, 176
Hynes, Joe, 157
Hysteria, 2, 112, 127, 158, 191

"I Won't Send Roses" (*Mack and Mabel*), 71, 73
I'd Do Anything, 108
I'm a Celebrity ... Get Me Out of Here!, 108, 117
"Iago", 154
Id, 164
Iliad (Homer), 110
Illinois, U.S.A., 145
Impingement, 164
Impotence, 118–119, 122

In Bloom, 118
In Our Time, B.B.C. Radio 4, British Broadcasting Corporation, London, 14
In Treatment, 81, 92–99, 100, 101
Incommunicado, 32
India, 108, 184, 200
Individual psychotherapy, *see* Psychotherapy
"Infant Feeding" (Donald W. Winnicott), 173, 174
Infant observation, 163, 183
Infant psychology, 163
Infant psychopathology, 163
Infanticide, 122–125
Inferno (Dante Alighieri), 123
Infidelity, 93
Ingersoll, Ralph, 149
Inhibitions, Symptoms and Anxiety (Sigmund Freud), *see Hemmung, Symptom und Angst* (Sigmund Freud)
Inside the Nazi Mind, 155
"Instincts and Normal Difficulties" (Donald W. Winnicott), 182
Institute of Education, University of London, London, 175
Institute of Psycho-Analysis, London, 154
International Arts Centre, London, 142
International Association for Forensic Psychotherapy, 49
International Congress on Mental Health, London, 177
International Psycho-Analytical Association, 161
International Psycho-Analytical Press, Vienna, Austria, *see* Internationaler Psychoanalytischer Verlag, Vienna, Austria
Internationaler Psychoanalytischer Verlag, Vienna, Austria, 145
Interpretation, 28, 82, 96, 135, 138, 208
Inverness, Scotland, 172
iOpener Institute, Oxford, Oxfordshire, 58
Ioseph, Mighell, 110
Iran, 12, 200
Isaacs, Susan, 156, 175
Islam, 79
It, 112

Jackson, Michael, 142
"James", 25–28, 198–199

James, Martin, 171
James, Oliver, 89
"Jaques", 111
"Jealousy" (Donald W. Winnicott), 184
"Jealousy: I" (Donald W. Winnicott), 209
"Jealousy: II" (Donald W. Winnicott), 209
"Jealousy: III" (Donald W. Winnicott), 209
"Jealousy: IV" (Donald W. Winnicott), 209
Jeremy Vine, B.B.C. Radio 2, British Broadcasting Corporation, London, 22
Jerusalem, Israel, 182
Jesus Christ, 55
Jesus College, University of Cambridge, Cambridge, Cambridgeshire, 190
Joad, Cyril, 176
Johnnie Walker, B.B.C. Radio 2, British Broadcasting Corporation, London, 22
"Jon Snow", 87
Jones, Ernest, 147, 153–155, 158, 172, 185, 191–192, 193, 205, 206
Jones, Mervyn, 185
Joseph an Gof, Michael, *see* Ioseph, Mighell
"Julian Marsh", 112
"Juliet", 69
"Julius", 146
Jung, Carl Gustav, 45, 94, 152, 159–160, 168, 175

Karnac Books, London, 30
Karsten, Anitra, 152
KB Model BM20, 171
Keeler, Ruby, 112
Kemp, Ross, 40–41
Kershaw, Justine, 35, 36
Keynes, John Maynard, 169
Khan, Masud, 96, 208
Khan, Mohammad Sidique, 79
Khomeini, Ayatollah, 12
King, Truby, 183
Kinsey, Alfred, 31
Klein, Melanie, 30, 121, 159, 160
Knickerbocker, Laura, 156
Knossos, 123
"Knowing and Learning" (Donald W. Winnicott), 182
Knowles, Beyoncé, 118

Kohut, Heinz, 156
Krauss, Werner, 80
Kretzmer, Herbert, 71
Kris, Ernst, 156, 192
Kubie, Lawrence, 100, 156
Küsnacht, Switzerland, 152

L'Alliance Israélite universelle, Paris, France, 155
L'Elisir d'Amore (Gaetano Donizetti and Felice Romani), 70
L'Ordre, 155
La Divina Commedia (Dante Alighieri), 123
La Fenice, Venice, Italy, 71
La Traviata (Francesco Maria Piave and Giuseppe Verdi), 69
Labour Party, 75, 152
Lacan, Jacques, 156
Lady Gaga, 106
Lady in the Dark (Ira Gershwin, Moss Hart, and Kurt Weill), 81, 100, 203
Lady Margaret Hall, University of Oxford, Oxford, Oxfordshire, 177
Laing, Ronald D., 201
Langham Place, Central London, London, 21, 166, 173, 180
Laurence Olivier Awards, 73
Laurents, Arthur, 69
Lawrie, Jean, 181
Laye, Evelyn, 113
Le Matin, 155
Le Petit Parisien, 155
Leeds, Yorkshire, 70, 174, 207
Lehmann, John, 170
Lennon, John, 122
Leopold, Nathan Freudenthal, Jr., 80, 145, 146
Les Misérables (Alain Boublil, John Caird, Herbert Kretzmer, Jean-Marc Natel, Trevor Nunn, and Claude-Michel Schönberg), 70, 71, 73, 100
Les Nouvelles Littéraires, 155
Let's Be Famous, 113
Leucotomy, 178, 179
Leys School, Cambridge, Cambridgeshire, 189
"Liberation by Orgasm" (Ronald D. Laing), 201
Liebmann, Susanne, 152
"Life 2 Live", B.B.C. Radio 2, British Broadcasting Corporation, London, 3, 10, 22, 24, 27, 28

Lilley, Nigel, 70–71
"Lina Lamont", 125–126
Linbury Studio Theatre, Royal Opera House, Covent Garden, London, 70
Lindsay, Germaine Maurice, 79
Lineker, Gary, 138, 139
Liszt, Franz, 141
"Little Hansburgers", 45
Liverpool, Merseyside, 9, 108, 207
Liverpool Street, London, 79
Llewellyn, Patricia, 44–46, 47, 59
Lloyd Webber, Andrew, 61–62, 108
Lloyd's Weekly Newspaper, 158
Loeb, Richard Albert, 80, 145, 146
Loewenstein, Rudolph, 119
Lollardy, 190, 209
Lomax-Simpson, Josephine, 209
London, 4, 11, 14, 21, 26, 30, 31, 33, 35, 36, 37, 38, 39, 41, 42, 45, 47, 50, 51, 52, 53, 54, 55, 56, 58, 59, 61, 63, 64, 65, 67, 70, 71, 74, 75, 79, 82, 89, 98, 105, 112, 126, 149, 151, 152, 154, 157, 158, 159, 166, 168, 170, 171, 172, 173, 175, 177, 180, 181, 184, 186, 188, 191, 192, 193, 198, 200, 207, 208, 209
London Centre for Psychotherapy, Kentish Town, London, 74
London Evening Standard, 79
London School of Economics and Political Science, University of London, London, 41
Londres, see London
Long, Janice, 9–11
Los Angeles, California, U.S.A., 110
Louis Charles, 121
Loveday, Alexander, 169
Low, Barbara, 156, 158, 175, 191
Lucius Mestrius Plutarchus, see Plutarch
Ludwig II, 141
Luftwaffe, 173
Luttrellstown Castle, Dublin, Ireland, 113

"Mabel Normand", 73
MacCarthy, Brendan, 126, 150, 205
MacCarthy, Desmond, 169
MacCarthy, Fiona, 204–205
Macfarlane, Aidan, 118
MacGibbon, Jean, 1
Mack and Mabel (Jerry Herman and Michael Stewart), 71, 73
"Mack Sennett", 73

Mackintosh, Cameron, 70
Mad Men, 83, 84–85
Madonna, 106
Main, Agnes, 188
Main, Thomas, 188
Majors, Farah Fawcett, 118
Making Slough Happy, 44–66
Maltby, John, 109
Manchester, England, 207
Mandela, Nelson, 126
Manhattan, New York, U.S.A., see New York City, New York, U.S.A.
Maradona, Diego, 138, 139
Marconi Company, Chelmsford, Essex, 166
Maresfield Gardens, Swiss Cottage, London, 90
"Maria", 72
Marianne, 155
Marie Antoinette, 121
Marital psychotherapy, 31, 67, 73, 75, 84, 85, 92, 99
"Marius", 70
"Martha", 69
Martin, George R.R., 86
Martin, Jessica, 70, 71, 73
Martin, Steve, 109
Masochism, 93, 95, 97, 121
Masson, Jeffrey Moussaeiff, 150
Masturbatory fantasies, 31, 32, 37, 82, 109, 199
Matheson, Hilda, 169
Matthews, Jessie, 113
Mawson, Andrew, 58, 59, 61, 64
Mayhew, Helen, 23–28, 198
Maynard, Sam, 50–51
McCartney, Paul, 9, 106, 108
mcclung, bruce d., 203
McCormick, Robert Rutherford, 145, 146, 205
McGraw, Phil, 160
Me and My Girl (Stephen Fry, Douglas Furber, Noel Gay, and L. Arthur Rose), 70
Media monasticism, 145, 159
Media psychiatry, 4, 12
Media psychoanalysis, 4, 5, 7, 12, 16, 19, 81, 142, 152, 156, 162, 164, 165, 188, 198–202
Media psychology, 3, 4, 12, 13, 16, 28, 152, 153, 158, 163–197, 202
Media psychotherapy, 4, 12–13
Media whoredom, 145, 159

Medical Section, British Psychological Society, London, 178, 179
Medico-Psychological Association of Great Britain and Ireland, 1
Meeting Point, 187
Melba, Nellie, 166
Meloney, Marie ("Missy"), 161
Menlo Park, California, U.S.A., 165
Menninger, Karl, 115–116, 117–118, 156
Menninger Clinic, Topeka, Kansas, U.S.A., 156
Mental health, 3, 4, 5, 9, 10, 11, 12, 13, 14, 15, 16, 21, 22, 23, 25, 26, 27, 28, 29, 30, 32, 41, 44, 45, 46, 47, 48, 49, 52, 55, 67, 68, 69, 74, 75, 80, 91, 93, 96, 97, 99, 107, 121, 128, 136, 150, 151, 152, 155, 156, 157, 159, 160, 161, 163, 164, 165, 169, 173, 177, 180, 181, 195, 198, 199, 200, 201, 202, 204
Mental illness, 16, 136, 162
Merthyr Tydfil, Wales, 187
Messalina, 121
Messiah, 135
Meyer, George Val, 166
Middle Ages, 123
Middle East, 105, 123
Middleton, Cecil Henry, 166
Milan, Italy, 71
Mill, John Stuart, 64
Millennium Bridge, London, 36, 37, 40
Millennium New Year's Honours List, 58
Miller, Emanuel, 168
Milner, Marion, 175
"Mind and Medicine", 184
Minogue, Dannii, 124
Minos, 123
"Minotaur", 123, 124
Moche, 124
"Molech", *see* "Moloch"
"Moloch", 123
Monroe, Marilyn, 48, 118, 142
Montessori, Maria, 175
Moody, Nicola, 51, 56
Moore, Henry, 142
Moore, Thomas, 111
More, Thomas, 196
"More That Irks – and Why" (Donald W. Winnicott), 209
Morley, John Royston, 177
Morrison, Herbert, 169
Morse, Arthur Hyatt, 167

Morse, Sydney, 166
Morton, Andy, 70, 71, 73, 74
Mother fixation, 155
Mother Teresa, 107, 187
Motion Picture, 112
Motion Picture Classic, 112
Mountjoy, Lord, *see*, Blount, William, Lord Mountjoy
Mozart, Wolfgang Amadeus, 128, 129, 137, 141, 142
"Mr. T.", 79
Mulberry Bush, Standlake, Oxfordshire, 208
Murder, 67, 79, 80, 84, 115, 121–124, 125, 134, 138, 145, 146, 161, 203, 205
Murder She Wrote, 203
Musée Curie, Paris, France, 161
My Years with Cruse (Margaret Torrie), 142

Nafsiyat, London, 74
Narcissism, 2, 15, 106, 113, 127, 134, 136–137, 138, 139
Narcissistic personality disorder, 106, 113, 137, 139
Natel, Jean-Marc, 71
Nation, 153
National Celebrity Games, 107
National Health Service, 15, 52, 177
National Society for the Prevention of Cruelty to Children, 182
Naturalis Historiae (Pliny the Elder), 121
Nazism, 98, 147, 148, 149, 153, 155, 192, 200, 207
Neal Street, Covent Garden, London, 39
"Neglected Children" (Donald W. Winnicott), 182
Netanyahu, Benjamin, 105
Netflix, 90, 91, 94
Netherlands, The, 108
Neue Folge der Vorlesungen zur Einführung in die Psychoanalyse (Sigmund Freud), 148
Neue Freie Presse, Vienna, Austria, 148
New Age, 153
New Introductory Lectures on Psycho-Analysis (Sigmund Freud), *see Neue Folge der Vorlesungen zur Einführung in die Psychoanalyse* (Sigmund Freud)
New Judea, 153
New Society, 201
New Statesman, 185

New York, U.S.A., 145, 146, 159, 161, 184, 203
New York City, New York, U.S.A., 33, 71, 122, 155, 159, 161, 184, 198, 203
New York Freudian Society, New York City, New York, U.S.A., 70, 74, 203
New York Post, 155
New York Psychoanalytic Society, New York City, New York, U.S.A., 115
Nicolson, Harold, 169
Noack, Dunja, 33–35, 41
"Nobel Prize complex", 137, 138, 139
"Normal and Abnormal Personalities", 192
North America, 155
North London, London, 11, 54, 126
North West London, London, 31, 47, 56
Northern Peru, Peru, 124
Notting Hill, London, 105
"Now They Are Five" (Donald W. Winnicott), 185
Nunn, Trevor, 71

Obesity, 9
Object loss, 88, 117, 120, 122
Object use, 79, 115, 117–118, 121, 122, 125
Ofcom, London, *see* Office of Communications, London
Office of Communications, London, 91
Old Trafford, Trafford, Greater Manchester, 122
Old Vic, London, 154
Oliver, Jamie, 44, 89
Olivier, Laurence, 73, 137, 154–155, 192, 206
"On Aggression" (Anthony Storr), 201
"On Idealisation and Disillusion in Adolescence" (Agnes Main)
"On My Own" (*Les Misérables*), 71
"One Hand, One Heart" (*West Side Story*), 71, 72
Open University, Milton Keynes, Buckinghamshire, 58, 65
Opera North, Leeds, Yorkshire, 70
Optomen Television, London, 44, 45, 46, 47, 51, 53, 59
Orbach, Susie, 3
"Ordinary devoted mother", 156, 164, 180, 181, 184, 186, 208
"*Ostrakon*", 124
Ostwald, Peter, 129

Othello (William Shakespeare), 154, 192
Other People's Houses, 169
Over the Rainbow, 108
Oxford, Oxfordshire, 2
Oxford Psycho-Analytical Forum, University of Oxford, Oxford, Oxfordshire, 1–2
Oxford Psychotherapy Society, Oxford, Oxfordshire, 74
Oxford Street, London, 33, 41
Oxfordshire, England, 171, 176, 208

Pabst, Georg Wilhelm, 80, 147
Paddington, West London, London, 169, 188
Paddington Green Children's Hospital, West London, London, 119, 173, 175, 186
Paddington Station, West London, London, 48, 59, 62
Paediatric psychology, 163
Paediatrics, 114, 163, 174, 175, 178, 184
Paedophilia, 13
Paganini, Niccolò, 141
"*Pailleux*", 111
Pain, Nesta, 179
Pakistan, 200
Palace Theatre, London, 70
Pandemic, 13, 16, 90–91, 127, 160, 200
Panorama, 152
Paramount Pictures, Hollywood, California, U.S.A., 100
Paranoid schizophrenia, 81
Parent-infant psychotherapy, 13, 163
Parents and Children, 185
Paris, France, 71, 86, 111, 155
Paris Soir, 86
Parker, Bonnie, 118
Paterson, Jennifer, 44
Pavlov, Pavel, 80
Peck, Martin, 149
"Peggy Sawyer", 112
Pelican Books, Penguin Books, London, 186
Penguin Books, London, 2, 38, 186
Penn, Arthur, 119
"Peter Standish", 155
Philadelphia, 189
Phobia, 53, 55, 80, 115, 147
Physical violence, 68
Piave, Francesco Maria, 69
Piazza, Covent Garden, London, 38, 39

Picasso, Pablo, 128, 129, 137, 142
Pickford, Mary, 112
Play, 164, 193, 196, 208, 209
Playing and Reality (Donald W. Winnicott), 196, 209
Pliny the Elder, 121
Plunkett, John, 197
Plutarch, 110, 124–125
Plymouth, Devon, 30, 167, 189
Plymouth Mercantile Association, Plymouth, Devon, 189
PM, 149
Pointless Celebrities, 108
Pompeii, Italy, 187
Pop Idol, 107, 112
Pope, 190
Popstars, 107
Popular Talks on Psychoanalysis (Sándor Ferenczi), *see Populäre Vorträge über Psychoanalyse* (Sándor Ferenczi)
Populäre Vorträge über Psychoanalyse (Sándor Ferenczi), 153
Porchester Hall, Paddington, West London, London, 188
Pornography, 1, 98
Positive psychology, 64
Potts, Mrs., 187
Preconscious, 87, 164
"Preface" (Edward Glover), 155
Preventative psychiatry, 163
Price, Leontyne, 89
Pride and Prejudice: A Novel. In Three Volumes (Jane Austen), 90
Primal scene, 116, 117–118, 122
Prime Minister, 64, 66, 75, 137, 169, 174, 177
Primetime Emmy Awards, 94
Professional Standards Authority for Health and Social Care, London, 93
"Professor Louis S. Levy", 157
Projection, 74, 84, 96, 120
Projective identification, 73
Prostitution, 2, 121
Pryce-Jones, Jessica, 58, 59, 61, 62, 63, 65
Psychiatry, 1, 3, 4, 10, 12, 33, 39, 40, 46, 52, 56, 57, 81, 83, 93, 95, 101, 106, 114, 115, 118, 126, 129, 150, 156, 161, 163, 168, 171, 175, 178, 179, 180, 182, 188, 196, 201, 209
"Psycho-Analysis Dangers: Need for Protection Against Quacks Who Exploit Hysterical Women", 191

Psychoanalysis, 1, 2, 3, 4, 5, 10, 11, 12, 13, 14, 15, 16, 21, 28, 30, 31, 32, 33, 35, 37, 42, 45, 46, 51, 52, 56, 65, 67, 68, 69, 70, 72, 73, 74, 75, 80, 81, 83, 84, 85, 86, 87, 88, 91, 93, 94, 95, 96, 97, 98, 99, 100, 101, 105, 113, 114, 115, 116, 118, 119, 121, 123, 125, 126, 127, 130, 131, 133, 135, 137, 138, 139, 142, 145, 146, 147–148, 149, 150, 151, 152, 153, 154, 155, 156, 157, 158, 159, 160, 161, 162, 163, 164, 165, 167–168, 169, 171, 172, 173, 175, 176, 177, 178, 181, 182, 183, 184, 185, 186, 188, 190, 191–192, 193, 194, 195, 196, 197, 198–202, 206, 207, 208, 209
Psychology, 1, 2, 3, 4, 10, 12, 13, 14, 16, 21, 22, 26, 33, 35, 38, 42, 44, 45, 51, 56, 58, 64, 67, 80, 81, 82, 89, 97, 100, 106, 109, 113, 114, 117, 119, 120, 129, 131, 137, 152, 153, 154, 155, 156, 157, 158, 159, 163, 164, 165, 168, 175, 176, 177, 183, 184–188, 192, 193, 194, 195, 197, 198, 201, 202, 207, 210
"Psychoneurotic Institute for the Very, Very Nervous", 95
Psychopathology, 31, 94, 106, 107, 163
Psychosurgery, 178, 179
Psychotherapy, 3, 4, 10, 11, 12, 13, 14, 15, 16, 21, 22, 23, 24, 27, 28, 29, 30, 31, 32, 34, 35, 38, 42, 45, 46, 47, 48, 49, 50, 52, 53, 54, 56, 63, 64, 65, 67, 68–69, 70, 72, 73, 74, 75, 81, 82, 83, 84, 85, 86, 91, 92, 93, 94, 95, 96, 97, 98, 99, 101, 106, 121, 126, 127, 128, 129, 130, 133, 134, 136, 137, 142, 151, 153, 157, 159, 160, 161, 163, 164, 168, 194, 198, 199, 200, 201, 203, 204, 207, 208, 210
"Psychotherapy on the Couch: Exploring the Fantasies of *In Treatment*" (Caroline Bainbridge), 81
Public Relations Directorate, British Psycho-Analytical Society, London, 188
Publius Vergilius Maro, *see* Virgil
Puccini, Giacomo, 89
Purgatorio (Dante Alighieri), 125
"Put On a Happy Face" (*Bye Bye Birdie*), 52

Québec, Canada, 86
Queen Anne Street, London, 180, 181
Queen Mother, *see* Elizabeth, the Queen Mother

Quigley, Janet, 164, 174
Quintanilla-Pérez, Serena, *see* Serena
Quintus Septimius Florens Tertullianus, *see* Tertullius

R.O.H. 2, Royal Opera House, Covent Garden, London, *see* Linbury Studio Theatre, Royal Opera House, Covent Garden, London
Radio, 2–4, 9–15, 21–29, 42, 45, 48, 50, 51, 63, 68, 101, 107, 113, 118, 119, 127, 146, 147, 152, 153, 154, 155, 156–157, 162, 164, 165, 166, 167–187, 190, 191–192, 193, 194–195, 199, 200, 206, 207–208, 209
Radio Berlin, Berlin, Germany, 152
Radio Times, 107
Radó, Sándor, 12, 147, 149, 206
Ramzy, Ishak, 208
Rank, Otto, 114, 195
Rasputin, Grigori Efimovich, 121
Rathbone, Oliver, 30–31, 32, 41
Rattle, Candace, 75
Rattle, Simon, 75
Rayner, Claire, 185
Realist Film Unit, 176
Reality television, 109, 117, 124, 127
"Reason and Emotion", 192
Redgrave, Vanessa, 85–86
Reeves, Richard, 57, 59, 64
Regent's College, Inner Circle, Regent's Park, London, 74
Règne de la Terreur, 111
Reid, Whitelaw, 189
Reik, Theodor, 156
Reith, John, 166, 167
Relate, London, 74
Renaissance, 123
Requiem (Wolfgang Amadeus Mozart), 137
Retro 55, 44
Richards, Arlene Kramer, 157
Richardson, Natasha, 86
Richardson, Ralph, 154–155
Richmond, Surrey, 110
Rickman, John, 98, 156, 168–169, 172, 192–193
Rihanna, 118
Riviere, Joan, 175, 194
Robertson, James, 184
Rockville, Plymouth, Devon, 208
Rodgers, Richard, 71
Rodman, Robert, 164

Rogers, Ginger, 100
Romania, 108
Romanovs, 113
Rome, Italy, 93, 124
"Romeo", 69
Romm, May, 156
Rorschach, 89, 99, 175
Ross, Thomas, 168
Royal Albert Hall, London, 71
Royal Charter, 21, 166–167
Royal College of Physicians, London, 191
Royal College of Psychiatrists, London, 1
Royal College of Surgeons of England, London, 98
Royal Family, 114–115, 167
Royal Opera House, Covent Garden, London, 4, 67–76
Royal Society of Medicine, London, 184
Rugg-Gunn, Andrew, 98
Russ, Nancy, 184
Russia, 121
"Ruth Sherwood", 71

S.O.S., 169
Sachs, Hanns, 147, 153
Sacrifice, 123–125
Sadomasochism, 31
Saïd Business School, University of Oxford, Oxford, Oxfordshire, 63
Saint George's Hotel, London, 21
Saldívar, Yolanda, 122
Salem, Massachusetts, U.S.A., 124
Salieri, Antonio, 141
San Francisco, California, U.S.A., 129
Sandilands, Cynthia, 172
Sandringham House, Norfolk, 182
Savoy Hill, London, 166
"Saying No" (Donald W. Winnicott), 184
"Saying No: I" (Donald W. Winnicott), 209
"Saying No: II" (Donald W. Winnicott), 209
"Saying No: III" (Donald W. Winnicott), 209
Scandinavia, 58
Scherzinger, Nicole, 124
Schindler's List, 105
Schizophrenia, 30, 81, 148, 155
Schmideberg, Melitta, 159, 175

School of Psychotherapy and Counselling, Regent's College, Inner Circle, Regent's Park, London, 74
Schulberg, Adeline Jaffe, 155
Schulberg, Benjamin Percival ("B.J."), 155
Schumann, Robert, 129
"Science and Broadcasting" (Edward Glover), 201
Scotland, United Kingdom, 172, 177
Scott, Clifford, 208
Scott, Peggy, 112
Second Boer War, 166
Second World War, *see* World War II
Secrets of a Soul, *see Geheimnisse einer Seele*
Section of Paediatrics, Royal Society of Medicine, London, 184
"Security" (Donald W. Winnicott), 184, 209
Seldes, George, 145, 146, 205–206
Selena, 122
7/7 Inquest, 79
Sex, 2, 30–43, 51, 68, 74, 81, 82, 84, 87, 91, 93, 98, 106, 108–109, 115, 116, 119, 121, 134, 137, 139, 146, 163, 168, 187, 188, 195, 196, 203, 208
Sex and the Psyche (Brett Kahr), 35
Sexual abuse, 10, 27, 41
Sexual anaesthesia, 31
Sexual fantasies, 30–43, 108–109, 115, 137
"Sexuality and Aggression in Maturation: New Facets", British Psychoanalytical Society, London, 188
Shadowland, 112
Shaffer, Peter, 141
Shakespeare, Hamnet, 142
Shakespeare, William, 38, 69, 105, 111, 128, 129, 137, 141, 142, 154, 203, 206
Sharpe, Ella Freeman, 155, 175, 193
Shaw, George Bernard, 169
"Shedu", 123
Siepmann, Charles, 169
Sigmund Freud Archives, New York City, New York, U.S.A., 150
Silberstein, Eduard, 148
Simmel, Ernst, 147
Singin' in the Rain, 125–126
Slough, Berkshire, 47, 48, 49, 50, 51, 52, 53, 54, 55, 56, 57, 58, 59, 61, 62, 63, 64, 65

Slough Choir, Slough, Berkshire, 52, 56–57, 59, 61–62
Slough 50, Slough, Berkshire, 51–52, 53, 56, 57, 58, 62
Slough Questionnaire, 58
Smith, Chris, 75
Smith, Delia, 44
Smith, John Gladstone, 61–62
Social Action, B.B.C. Radio 2, British Broadcasting Corporation, London, 23, 28
Social work, 97, 128, 163, 170, 171, 176, 179
Society of Couple Psychoanalytic Psychotherapists, Tavistock Centre for Couple Relationships, Tavistock Institute of Medical Psychology, London, Tavistock Centre, Belsize Park, London, 67, 68, 72, 75
Society of Psychoanalytical Marital Psychotherapists, London, 72
Sociological Society, London, 154
Soho Square, London, 33, 41
"Soliloquy" (*Carousel*), 71, 73
"Some Aspects of Love and Hate" (Donald W. Winnicott), 188
"Some Reasons for Personal Prejudice Against the So-Called Physical Therapy of Mental Disorder" (Donald W. Winnicott), 178
Sommers, Paul, 33
Sondheim, Stephen, 69, 71
South Bank Centre, London, 75
South East London, London, 158
South London, London, 44
South Parks Road, Oxford, Oxfordshire, 2
Spanish flu, 200
Spears, Britney, 118
Spellbound, 95
Spender, Stephen, 142
"Spice Girl", *see* Adams, Victoria
Spielberg, Stephen, 105
Splitting, 73, 98
Squiggle, 164
Squiggle Foundation, London, 198–199
St. Bartholomew's Hospital Medical School, University of London, London, 168, 190–191
St. Martin's School of Art, London, 142
St. Paul's Cathedral, London, 36
Star Academy, 107

Star Academy Arab World, 107
Star F.M., Slough, Berkshire, 48
Star Search, 107
Starbucks, 38
Stars in Their Eyes, 107
Stekel, Wilhelm, 153
Stephen, Adrian, 1, 156, 192
Stephen, Karin, 156, 158
Stepparents, 184
"Steps to Good Parenthood" (Donald W. Winnicott), 201
Sterne, Laurence, 111
Steve Wright, B.B.C. Radio 2, British Broadcasting Corporation, London, 22
Stevens, Richard, 51, 58, 59, 62, 64–65
Stoke Newington, North London, London, 54–55
Stoller, Robert, 33
Storr, Anthony, 3, 201
Strachey, James, 194
Strand, The, London, 166
"Struggling Through the Doldrums" (Donald W. Winnicott), 201
Stuart, Gloria, 107
Styne, Jule, 71
Subconscious, 154
Sublimation, 116
Suicide, 79, 87, 88, 92, 96, 125, 141
Sullivan, Arthur, 112, 193
Sunset Boulevard, Hollywood, California, U.S.A., 115
Superego, 99, 164
"Support for Normal Parents" (Donald W. Winnicott), 173, 207
Sutherland, Joan, 89
Swansea, City and County of Swansea, Wales, 185
Sweden, 108
Sweeney, Terry, 22
Swift, Taylor, 118
Swindon, Wiltshire, 45, 46, 47, 48, 59
Switzerland, 152, 207
Sydmonton, Hampshire, 108

"Talking cure", 46, 94, 97, 157
Talks Department, British Broadcasting Corporation, London, 155, 166, 169, 178, 179, 184
Talks on Child Care, 186
Tarsh, Helen, 72

Tartakoff, Helen, 137
Tavistock Centre for Couple Relationships, Tavistock Institute of Medical Psychology, Tavistock Centre, Belsize Park, London, 67, 72, 75
Tavistock Clinic, Tavistock Centre, Tavistock and Portman NHS Trust, Belsize Park, London, 25, 52, 57, 151, 157, 158, 186, 207, 208
Tavistock Clinic Choir, Tavistock Centre, Tavistock and Portman NHS Trust, Belsize Park, London, 52, 56, 74
Tavistock Institute of Medical Psychology, Tavistock Centre, Belsize Lane, London, 67
Tavistock Marital Studies Institute, Tavistock Institute of Medical Psychology, Belsize Park, London, 31, 42, 67, 72
Tavistock Publications, London, 186
Tavistock Relationships, Tavistock Institute of Medical Psychology, Belsize Park, London, 67
Tavistock Society of Psychotherapists, Tavistock Clinic, Tavistock Centre, Tavistock and Portman NHS Trust, Belsize Park, London, 74
Tavistock Square Clinic for Functional Nervous Disorders, London, 168
Taylor, James, 187
Taylor, John Cranes, 187
Teatro alla Scala, Milan, Italy, 71
Television, 3, 4, 9, 11, 13, 14, 15, 21–22, 30–43, 44–66, 69, 70, 75, 77, 79–91, 92–101, 107–108, 113, 117, 119, 122, 124, 126, 127, 131, 138, 140, 141, 152, 156, 159, 160, 162, 165, 177, 186–187, 193, 194, 199, 200, 203–204
Tell Me You Love Me, 93
10 Cutest Celebrity Babies, 108
Tertullian, 124–125
Texas, U.S.A., 122, 124
The A-Team, 79
The Archers, 119
The Brains Trust, 156, 176, 182
The Celebrity Apprentice, 107
The Child, the Family, and the Outside World (Donald W. Winnicott), 186
The Child and the Family: First Relationships (Donald W. Winnicott), 186

The Child and the Outside World: Studies in Developing Relationships (Donald W. Winnicott), 186
"The Child Behind Society" (Donald W. Winnicott), 201
The Dangers of Being Human (Edward Glover), 155
The Delineator, 161
"The Deprived Mother" (Donald W. Winnicott), 170, 173
"The Development of a Child's Sense of Right and Wrong" (Donald W. Winnicott), 185
"The Divorce Song" (Brett Kahr), 74
"The Evacuated Child" (Donald W. Winnicott), 173
The Family and Individual Development (Donald W. Winnicott), 195–196
The First Five Years, 185
"The Girl That I Marry" (*Annie Get Your Gun*), 71, 74
The Guardian, 57
The Human Mind, 194
The International Journal of Psycho-Analysis, 201
The Jewish Chronicle, 153
The Lancet, 64, 98
The Legacy of Winnicott: Essays on Infant and Child Mental Health (Brett Kahr), 30
The Life and Opinions of Tristram Shandy, Gentleman (Laurence Sterne), 111
The Listener, 153
"The Manic Defence" (Donald W. Winnicott), 114–115
The Maturational Processes and the Facilitating Environment: Studies in the Theory of Emotional Development (Donald W. Winnicott), 196
"The Naked Chef", *see* Oliver, Jamie
The New Era in Home and School, 174, 175–176
"The New Reality", *see* "Die Neue Sachlichkeit"
The New York Times, 150, 151, 155, 156, 192
The Office, 47
"The Only Child" (Donald W. Winnicott), 172, 173
The Ordinary Devoted Mother, 180
The Ordinary Devoted Mother and Her Baby: Nine Broadcast Talks. (Autumn 1949) (Donald W. Winnicott), 181, 186
"The Problem of Homeless Children" (Donald W. Winnicott), 176
The Question of Lay Analysis: Conversations with an Impartial Person (Sigmund Freud), *see Die Frage der Laienanalyse: Unterredungen mit einem Unparteiischen* (Sigmund Freud)
"The Return of the Evacuated Child" (Donald W. Winnicott), 172, 173
The Rising Generation, 181
"The Rovers", 120
The Shortlist, 108
The Social Entrepreneur: Making Communities Work (Andrew Mawson), 64
The Sopranos, 87–88, 89, 91, 93, 94, 95, 101, 194, 204
The Spectator, 155
The Talking Cure, 157
The Tempest (Arthur Sullivan), 112
The Times, 114, 150, 154, 155, 182, 189, 192, 209
The Times Literary Supplement, 186, 196
The Tragedie of Hamlet, Prince of Denmarke (William Shakespeare), *see Hamlet* (William Shakespeare)
The Tragedie of Romeo and Ivliet (William Shakespeare), 69
"The Use of an Object" (Donald W. Winnicott), 115
The World at One, 187
The X Factor, 107
The Wizard of Oz, 125
Théâtre du Châtelet, Paris, France, 71
"Their Standards and Yours" (Donald W. Winnicott), 173, 174
Therapeutic consultation, 53, 56, 95, 99, 157, 163, 194, 196, 209
Therapeutic Consultations in Child Psychiatry (Donald W. Winnicott), 196, 209
"Therapy without Mystery" (Anonymous), 210
Theseus, 123
"They Say It's Wonderful" (*Annie Get Your Gun*), 71, 74
Thomson, David G., 1
Thomson, Donald, 159
Thorndike, Sybil, 142

Tiger Aspect Productions, London, 33–34
Titanic, 107
Today, 178
"Together" (*Gypsy*), 71
"Tony", 69, 72
"Tony Soprano", 87, 88, 194, 204
Top of the Pops, 9
Topeka, Kansas, U.S.A., 115
Tophet, 124
Torrie, Margaret, 142
Tower Hamlets, London, 58
Towse, Ernest Beachcroft Beckwith, 166
Transference, 69, 82, 87, 90, 96, 164, 208
Transitional object, 88, 164
Transvestism, 95, 139
Trevelyan, Catriona, 175
Trevelyan, Charles, 172
Trevelyan, George, 172
Trevelyan, Helen, 172, 175
True self, 164
Twitter, 3, 110
"Two Fat Ladies", *see* Wright, Clarissa Dickson, and Paterson, Jennifer
"Twins" (Donald W. Winnicott), 173
Tyndale, William, 196, 197
"Tyrion Lannister", 86–87

U.F.A., *see* Universum Film Aktiengesellschaft
Unconscious, 4, 28, 32, 39, 69, 73, 79, 80, 83, 84, 87, 91, 99, 105, 107, 115, 120, 123, 125, 129, 130, 132, 146, 154, 164, 168, 188, 189, 192, 195, 199
United Arab Emirates, 200
United Kingdom, 14, 21, 23, 34, 42, 44, 45, 59, 64, 65, 67, 68, 70, 75, 91, 108, 137, 142, 168, 177, 186, 200, 201
United Kingdom Council for Psychotherapy, London, 46
United States of America, 75, 100, 108, 120, 145, 146, 149, 161, 186
United Wireless Telegraph Company, 167
University College Dublin, Dublin, Ireland, 150
University of Leicester, Leicester, Leicestershire, 109
University of London, London, 65, 175
University of Oxford, Oxford, Oxfordshire, 1, 36, 57, 63, 112, 177

University of Southern California, Los Angeles, California, U.S.A., 110
Universum Film Aktiengesellschaft, 147
Upper East Side, New York City, New York, U.S.A., 12
Upper West Side, New York City, New York, U.S.A., 122
"Urszene", *see* Primal scene
"Ushi-oni", 123

Valentino, Rudolf, 112
Vaughan, Mr., 185
Vendôme, Hollywood, California, U.S.A., 115, 117
Venice, Italy, 71
Verdi, Giuseppe, 69, 89
Victoria, 165–166, 189, 197
Vienna, Austria, 146, 147, 149, 181, 195, 198, 206
Vienna Psycho-Analytical Society, Vienna, Austro-Hungarian empire, *see* Wiener Psychoanalytische Vereinigung, Vienna, Austro-Hungarian empire
Viking, 2
Vine, Jeremy, 22
"Violetta", 69
Virgil, 110
"Visiting Children in Hospital" (Donald W. Winnicott), 182, 209
Volkov, Peggy, 174, 175, 208
von Kaltenborn, Hans, 148
von Schuschnigg, Kurt, 147
"Vorwort" (Sándor Ferenczi), 153, 206

Wagner, Richard, 141
Walder, 209
Walker, Angie, 48
Wallerstein, Robert, 161
Walling, John, 189
Walters, Barbara, 122
Warner Brothers Pictures, 112
Washington, D.C., U.S.A., 64
Waterloo, South London, London, 44
"We're Gonna Change the World" (Brett Kahr), 60–61, 62
Weber, Jacqueline, 186
Weeds, 203
Weill, Kurt, 81, 100
Wellcome Library, Wellcome Collection, London, 30
Welles, Orson, 145

Wells, Herbert George, 169
Wembley Arena, Wembley, London, 122
Wembley Empire Exhibition, Wembley, London, 167
Wesley, John, 189
Wesleyan Methodism, 189, 190
Wessex Psychotherapy Society, Department of Psychotherapy, Psychological Therapies Service, Department of Psychiatry, Royal South Hants Hospital, Southampton, Hampshire, 74
West End, London, 59, 61, 62, 70, 71, 73, 108, 152
West London, London, 171, 188
West Midlands, England, 9
West Side Story (Leonard Bernstein, Arthur Laurents, and Stephen Sondheim), 69, 71, 72, 73
Western Ophthalmic Hospital, London, 98
Western world, 112, 113
Westminster Gazette, 153
"What About Father?" (Donald W. Winnicott), 170, 173, 174
"What Irks" (Donald W. Winnicott), 184
"What Irks: I" (Donald W. Winnicott), 209
"What Irks: III" (Donald W. Winnicott), 209
When Will I Be Famous?, 107
Whitehouse, Mary, 187
Who's Afraid of Virginia Woolf (Edward Albee), 69
Who's Been Sleeping in Your Head?: The Secret World of Sexual Fantasies (Brett Kahr), 35
"Why Do Babies Cry?" (Donald W. Winnicott), 173
Wicked (Winnie Holzman and Stephen Schwartz), 71
Wiener Psychoanalytische Vereinigung, Vienna, Austro-Hungarian empire, 149, 195
Wiest, Dianne, 94
Wigmore Hall, London, 71
Wilde, Oscar, 112
William Ellis School, Highgate, North London, London, 126
William Heinemann (Medical Books), London, 174, 175
William of Wales, 86
Wilson, Woodrow, 112
Winfrey, Oprah, 160
Winger, Debra, 94
Winnicott, Alice, 173, 174, 176, 182, 187
Winnicott, Clare, 170, 171, 176, 182, 197, 209
Winnicott, Donald W., 3, 5, 30, 32, 114–115, 117, 119, 121, 150, 156–157, 160, 163–197, 198, 201, 207–210
Winnicott, Frederick, 30, 31, 172, 189, 190
Winnicott, Kathleen, 172, 207, 208
Winnicott, Richard, 189, 190
Winnicott, Violet, 172, 208
Witchcraft, 1
Witherspoon, Reese, 118
Wittelsbachs, 113
Wogan, Terry, 21–22
Woman's Hour, 182
Wonderful Town (Leonard Bernstein, Jerome Chodorov, Betty Comden, Joseph Fields, and Adolph Green), 71
Woods, Tiger, 109
Woolf, Leonard, 169, 170
Woolf, Virginia, 1, 69, 192
World War II, 1, 51, 98, 100, 142, 149, 155, 156, 167, 168, 169–170, 172, 173, 176, 177, 178, 188, 191, 194, 198, 207
Wright, Clarissa Dickson, 44
Writers Guild of America, New York City, New York, U.S.A., and Los Angeles, California, U.S.A., 94
Wycliffe, John, 190, 209

Xenophon, 110

Yates, Sybille, 175
Yeats, William Butler, 169
Yorkshire, England, 58, 88, 165
"You Can't Get a Man with a Gun" (*Annie Get Your Gun*), 71, 74
YouGov, London, 35, 36, 161
Your Child's Sleep, 176–177
YouTube, 201

Zelig, 157
"Zeus", 123
Zilboorg, Gregory, 198
Zoom, 91, 200
Zoom psychoanalysis, 91
Zoom psychotherapy, 91

For Product Safety Concerns and Information please contact our EU representative GPSR@taylorandfrancis.com
Taylor & Francis Verlag GmbH, Kaufingerstraße 24, 80331 München, Germany

www.ingramcontent.com/pod-product-compliance
Lightning Source LLC
Chambersburg PA
CBHW050529300426
44113CB00012B/2017